Central Banking Functions
Of the United States
Treasury, 1789-1941

Central Banking Functions Of the United States Treasury, 1789-1941

By ESTHER ROGOFF TAUS

New York : Morningside Heights

COLUMBIA UNIVERSITY PRESS

1943

This Book Is Dedicated to

MY MOTHER AND MY FATHER

Acknowledgments

I WISH to express my deep indebtedness to Professor B. Haggott Beckhart, of Columbia University, for the original stimulus to write on this subject and for the many helpful suggestions and criticisms which materially affected the style, scope, and arrangement of this book.

Professors Angell and Saulnier, of Columbia University, contributed many valuable criticisms, for which I am deeply grateful.

It is a pleasure to acknowledge here my indebtedness to Professor R. K. Michels, of Hunter College, who as teacher and colleague has given me constructive counsel, sustained interest, and encouragement.

Also, my sincere gratitude goes to my husband, H. Harold Taus, M.D., for his constant interest and encouragement, which substantially hastened the publication of this book.

ESTHER ROGOFF TAUS

Hunter College
New York
September 1, 1943

Contents

Tables

Central Banking Functions
Of the United States
Treasury, 1789-1941

CHAPTER I

Introduction

THE BEGINNINGS of economic institutions are difficult to trace and frequently unperceived. But as these institutions become generally accepted, they are recognized for their effectiveness both by the public and by the writers in the field of economics. The development of the United States Treasury as the "policy making agency" in the field of central banking has conformed to this customary trend in economic institutions.

The present overshadowing position and dominating influence of the Treasury on the banking system could hardly be denied and does not require elaborate proof. Students of economics do not seem to be aware, however, of the fact that the United States Treasury has always performed some central banking functions and that its activities show a continuous trend toward the assumption of additional central banking functions as the need for them gradually increased.

The term "central banking" is often used loosely, and the functions ascribed to a central bank at any one time are based largely upon the tasks performed by contemporary institutions. Among the early central banks was the Bank of England. Consequently, the historical development and the resultant traditions of the Bank of England may fairly be said to have formed the starting point for the principles and doctrines associated with central banking. As the economic order progressed from relatively simple agrarianism to more complex industrialization, there was a parallel expansion in the functions of a central bank, in theory as well as practice. In general this expansion has been toward greater control of the money and banking system.

A summary of the duties of a central bank as conceived in 1926 is given by the testimony of the Governor of the Bank of England before the Royal Commission on Indian Currency and Finance. He said:

It should have the sole right of note issue; it should be the channel, and the sole channel, for the output and intake of legal tender currency. It should be the holder of all government balances; the holder of all the reserves of the other banks and branches of banks in the country. It should be the agent, so to speak, through which the financial operations at home and abroad of the government would be performed. It would further be the duty of a central bank to effect, as far as it could, suitable contraction and suitable expansion in addition to aiming generally at stability, and to maintain stability within as well as without. When necessary it would be the ultimate source from which emergency credit might be obtained in the form of rediscounting of approved bills, or advances on approved short securities, or government paper.[1]

This statement of the functions of a central bank was made after a long period in which these functions were debated vigorously. It is typical of the statements of many careful students of banking who sought from time to time to arrive at a final judgment concerning the proper scope and aims of central banks.[2] It is unlikely that this statement of 1926 or any other which might have been quoted could present an exhaustive account of all the operations of central banks at that time; it is equally unlikely that a perfect forecast of future interpretations of all the proper functions of any central bank can be made today. However, from a study of the emerging of various central banking functions two conclusions can be drawn with fair assurance. First, that the essential role of a central bank is the coördination of the money and banking system with other economic activities so that economic stability is promoted. Second, that all the other duties performed by a central bank or that are likely to be assigned to it are merely operations designed to carry out its essential role.

There are many ways of achieving stability through the coördination of banking and other economic institutions. The traditional method of linking economic activities (such as production, trade, and the employment of labor), to the monetary system is through the central bank, which may influence the reserves of commercial banks. Adequate reserves are necessary to support currency and credit in use and to permit the extension of further loans when needed. When reserves expand, banks acquire additional lending power. The agency which can provide additional reserves and distribute them to banks generally may be able in time of monetary stringency to facilitate business recovery and expansion. Such an agency has been tradition-

---

[1] Quoted by Kisch and Elkin, *Central Banks*, p. 100.
[2] Willis, *The Theory and Practice of Central Banking*, pp. 7–9.

ally called a "central bank." It can exercise this power of expanding reserves by devices such as the increasing of the type of paper eligible for rediscount, the buying of Government securities, or the lowering of the percentage of reserves required against liabilities.

If reserves contract substantially, business may be compelled to retrench, inasmuch as banks may find their reserves inadequate for their existing deposits and be forced to reduce their loans and investments. The devices at the disposal of a central bank for reducing reserves of commercial banks are the decreasing of types of paper eligible for rediscount, the selling of Government obligations, or the raising of the percentage of reserves required against liabilities.

Most of these devices of a central bank have not been at the disposal of any agency in the United States until fairly recently. In the United States general recognition of the need for central banking developed slowly, and no official acknowledgment of the need was made by Congress until after the beginning of the twentieth century. However, there was no time in American banking history when some substitute organization or system did not exist which provided at least a slight possibility for the attainment of the major objectives of central banking. It is the intent of this study to show that an agency which always performed at least some of the duties associated with a central bank, from the earliest days of the Republic, was the United States Treasury. By the nature of its fiscal operations it was the only branch of the Government in a position to render such services to the Nation. The growth and effectiveness of the Treasury's central banking activities will be set forth in this study.

For our purposes the term "Treasury central banking" connotes those powers and activities of the United States Treasury which do or may influence the reserves of commercial banks. It is obvious that the Treasury, as the largest disburser and receiver of public funds, may through its transactions affect the reserves of commercial banks. The means the Treasury has used to increase commercial bank reserves were mainly the issuing of paper money, the depositing of Government cash funds in commercial banks, and the prepaying of the interest and principal on its outstanding obligations from idle Treasury cash balances. These ways differ from those available to a nongovernmental central bank which tries to increase bank reserves. In a similar way, steps by which the Treasury contracted reserves also differ from those available to an ordinary central bank. Treasury transactions having that effect were the withdrawing of Treasury deposits from commercial banks and the holding of idle funds in Treasury vaults.

The trend shows a continuous increase in Treasury central banking functions, but there were some slight deviations from the general rising trend. These deviations were largely caused by the establishment of other separate Federal institutions, such as the first and second banks of the United States, which temporarily performed certain central banking functions without being fully aware of it themselves. The Federal Reserve System assumed many central banking duties formerly performed by the United States Treasury. Other deviations from the trend are due to the personalities of various secretaries of the Treasury. Some of them held unusually strong and pronounced views concerning the proper functions of a "mere fiscal agent" of the Government. They felt that the Treasury should occupy a modest place in our economic life, namely, that of a purely fiscal agent, not that of a "policy making agency" in the money and banking system. Under their leadership Treasury central banking activities were temporarily much reduced.

The proof of a thesis claiming a more-or-less-consistent trend toward steadily increasing central banking activities of the Treasury can be established only by presenting in historical order sufficient factual data to prove the point. The best proof of the thesis would be an exhaustive description of all activities of the United States Treasury since its beginning, but that would be a monumental task and unnecessarily complex. It seemed quite sufficient for purposes of proving the trend asserted in this monograph to limit the factual material to four major fields or aspects: (1) the monetary and banking legislation which from time to time increased or decreased the central banking activities of the Treasury; (2) the prevailing central banking theories which influenced the actions of the various secretaries of the Treasury; (3) the intentional and unintentional effects which Treasury activities had upon the reserves of commercial banks during special periods in United States history, as in wars and depressions; (4) the effects which strictly fiscal operations of the Treasury had upon the reserves of commercial banks.

Since the beginnings of the trend are more difficult to trace than its more recent developments, an attempt will be made to present for the earlier periods of the Republic a rather exhaustive picture of the more important actions of the Treasury affecting central banking. The beginnings of the trend occurred during the years from 1789 to 1845, when the central banking activities were performed by the Treasury. Especially important is the delegation of central banking powers to the first and second banks of the United States. The War of 1812, the chaotic eras of state banking, the specie circular, the distribution of the Treasury surplus, and the Panic of 1837 also deserve analysis from the point of view of increasing Treasury participation in the banking field. Central banking activities substantially increased during the period from 1846 to 1865, when the Independent Treasury System and the National Banking System were developed. The highly important role of the Treasury during the Mexican War, during the Crisis of 1856 and during the Civil War foreshadows later developments. Subsequent attempts which the Treasury made to bring about improved business conditions during the periods when the Treasury felt they were needed (1873 and 1884) show new methods. The effects of specie resumption and the silver purchase legislation greatly enhanced the Treasury influence in the money market. The period between 1890 and 1913 yields abundant material for the study of central banking activities of the Treasury, now reaching a stage of full development. Additions to central banking theory and practice were brought about by the monetary stringency of 1890, the Crisis of 1893, the Spanish American War, the terms of office of secretaries Gage, Shaw, and Cortelyou, the Gold Standard Act of 1900, the Panic of 1907, and the Aldrich Vreeland Act of 1908.

As our analysis proceeds to the establishment of the Federal Reserve System, two factors dictate a more rigid limitation on the evidence presented: first, the trend of Treasury activity and influence is more clearly established and requires less proof; secondly, Treasury central banking activities and influence have multiplied to such an extent that a complete description of all its numerous recent ramifications is outside the scope of this treatise. The increasing complexity of the banking structure, the various types and degrees of interrelationship between commercial banks, the Federal Reserve System, and the United States Treasury, and finally Treasury intervention in connection with World War I and postwar financial problems make it imperative to confine the discussion to the more important character-istic and essential activities of the United States Treasury in its role as a central banking agency. Accordingly, the theory behind the Federal Reserve Act and the changes which, theoretically, the legislation would have had upon the central banking influence of the Treasury are worthy of notice. In the great effort made toward the winning of World War I, the United States Government had to take full command of economic activity, and the Treasury emerged as the "policy-making agency" in the monetary field, despite the presence of the Federal Reserve System. The Treasury continued in its role as an important central banking agency during the period of the nineteen twenties, when the powers of the Treasury were directed to combating the agricultural depression of 1920 and to the refunding of our World War debt.

During the period of the nineteen thirties, in an attempt to bring about business recovery, the concentration of economic power with the Federal Government became so pronounced and the ramifications of Treasury influence on our entire financial system so numerous and involved that only the most momentous activities need be treated in this book. The activities demonstrating the greatest increase in Treasury central banking are the gold policies, including the creation of the gold stabilization fund, and the gold sterilization program. The Treasury silver policies, including the silver purchase program are also important.

Since December 7, 1941, the nation has been occupied in a great war program calculated to help its allies, Great Britain, Russia, and China, win World War II. All economic activities are subordinated to this national policy, and the Treasury, as the representative of the Government in the financial sphere, assumes the role of regulator of the money and banking fields in order that the national will be executed. This situation means that the Treasury is more powerful in the central banking field than ever before.

Due to the sudden realization of the predominant influence of the Treasury, the question was raised how radically this situation deviated from traditional policies. Chapter XI indicates that although some of the recent developments may have exceeded what might have been expected under the old trend of Treasury power in the monetary sphere, there is no reason in sight why this established and continuous trend should stop or be reversed. This thesis shows that the Treasury as a central bank is not a mere depression or emergency phenomenon, nor is it a symbol of the totalitarian tendency which exerts a powerful influence at the present time. It is extremely difficult to visualize any major retreat of the Treasury from its present eminence in the predictable future.

CHAPTER II

Treasury Central Banking before 1846

T HE FIFTY-SEVEN YEARS from 1789 to 1846 mark an epoch in
Treasury history characterized by experimentation and vacilla-
tion. The Treasury performed vital central banking functions even
when state banks were serving as Federal depositories or when the
banks of the United States were guarding the Nation's revenue and
currency. The period 1789 to 1846 can be divided into seven parts:

(1) 1789–1791, the establishment of the Treasury and its influence
on the early commercial banks; (2) 1791–1810, the Treasury as rival
of the first Bank of the United States; (3) 1811–1816, Treasury central banking during the interval between the first and second Bank
of the United States; (4) 1817–1833, the Treasury rivaling the second Bank of the United States as a central banking institution; (5)
1834–1840, Treasury central banking during the second era of state
banks as government depositories; (6) 1840–1841, the Treasury independent of the banks and the first Independent Treasury System;
(7) 1841–1845, Treasury central banking during the third era of state
banking.

1789–1791

THE ESTABLISHMENT OF THE TREASURY AND ITS
INFLUENCE ON THE EARLY COMMERCIAL BANKS

James Madison, Jr., is credited with making the motion in the
House of Representatives on May 19, 1789, which established a
Treasury Department. The motion brought forth considerable oppo-
sition, since it advocated a "single head" system.[1]

By a "single head" system was meant vesting control of the Treasury Department in the hands of one man. Americans have always
been opposed to granting sweeping powers to one officer. It was foreseen that the Treasury would be the largest receiver and disburser

[1] U.S., Congress, *Annals of Congress, the Debates and Proceedings in the Congress
of the United States*, Vol. I, p. 385.

of funds [2] and would have an unusual influence in the money market, and it did not appear wise to some legislators to entrust this influence to a single individual. The opposition preferred that the powers of the Secretary of the Treasury be distributed among a board of three commissioners. But the bungling of the Continental and Confederation Treasury commissions was not easily forgotten,[3] and the objection was overcome. Even though it was recognized that the tremendous responsibilities of the Treasury Department and the unrestrained grant of financial power would be entrusted to one man—probably the stanch federalist, Alexander Hamilton—such a system was finally adopted on September 2, 1789.

It is evident, therefore, that as early as 1789 the potential importance of the Treasury Department in influencing the destiny of the new country was realized.

Section 2 of the Act of September 2, 1789, states that the Secretary of the Treasury is "to digest and prepare plans for the improvement of the revenue and for the support of public credit; to prepare and report estimates of the public revenue and the public expenditures; to superintend the collection of revenue . . ." Section 4 of the act also indicates that the Treasurer is "to receive and keep the monies of the United States and to disburse the same upon warrants drawn by the Secretary of the Treasury.[4]

Debt—Funding Operations and the Effect on Banks

The Treasury's influence on the commercial banks was marked even at this early stage in the field of the public debt. On January 9, 1790, Alexander Hamilton, Secretary of the Treasury, submitted his "Report on Public Credit" to Congress, wherein he discussed a plan for disposing of the $79,000,000 public indebtedness.[5] Hamilton was very anxious to restore the credit position of the country by repaying its debts. By funding the public debt, the Treasury tried to provide an adequate supply of a circulating medium for the business needs of the country. This is not a fiscal but a central banking function.

[2] Beckhart, ed., *The New York Money Market*, Vol. I, p. 152.
[3] Chapman, *Fiscal Functions of the Federal Reserve Banks*, p. 3.
[4] U.S., Congress, *Annals of Congress, the Debates and Proceedings in the Congress of the United States*, Vol. I, pp. 615–631; I Stat. 65.
[5] Hamilton, "Report on Public Credit," January 9, 1790, in U.S., Treasury Dept., *Reports of the Secretary*, Vol. I, p. 15.

Briefly, the refunding plan provided that the Federal Government assume the Continental and Confederation domestic and foreign debts and the Revolutionary state indebtedness. The Federal Government would issue its own bonds or stocks for the various elements of the earlier debts. It would make provision for the payment of interest on the Federal debt and for its eventual retirement.

This tremendous debt for a Nation so small in numbers and so recently established did not dismay Hamilton. He viewed Federal bonds as a sort of circulating capital for the people. He explained:

It is a well-known fact, that in the countries in which the national debt is properly funded, and an object of established confidence, it answers most of the purposes of money. Transfers of stock, or public debt, are then equivalent to payments in specie; or, in other words, stock, in the principal transactions of business, passes current as species. The same thing would, in all probability, happen here, under the like circumstances.[6]

Funding of the public debt would serve three purposes, according to Hamilton. It would gain popular support for the Federal Government; it would give the future credit of the Government a sound base; it would solve the problem of currency shortage, at least for large-scale business transactions.

By the Funding Act of August 12, 1790, Federal bonds were issued to cover all the exchanges of the old debt.[7] To Hamilton the bonds represented circulating wealth available for the promotion of trade and industry.[8] Thus, we see that this first Secretary of the Treasury thought it was the duty of the Treasury Department to supply the Nation with an adequate circulating medium.

The key motive of Hamilton's public debt policy, to establish firmly the national credit, was in accordance with the aims of the act establishing the Treasury Department. The bonds issued under the Act of August 12, 1790, were to be sustained at a premium; a board was to buy up in the open market any Federal debt issues that fell below par.[9] Here we have under the Purchase Fund (later Sinking Fund) arrangement of the Act of 1790, a fiscal device for supporting the prices of bonds by means of Government purchases. Central banks may purchase Government bonds to increase the reserve funds of

[6] *Ibid.*, p. 5.

[7] Love, Federal Financing, Appendix, Item No. 21; 1 Stat. 186.

[8] Hamilton, "Report on Public Credit," January 9, 1790, in U.S., Treasury Dept., *Reports of the Secretary*, Vol. I, p. 5.

[9] I Stat. 186; Dunbar, *Laws of the United States Relating to Currency, Finance and Banking*, p. 20.

commercial banks. In 1790 the aim of open market purchases was to sustain Government credit and retire the public debt, but not to influence commercial bank reserves. Some banks held large quantities of Government obligations, and if the Treasury purchased the bonds, the cash position of the banks which sold the bonds would be strengthened. Other banks extended considerable cash loans to the Government, which were used in the purchase of Treasury obligations. Temporarily, the cash position of these banks would be weakened.[10] Thus, unintentionally the Treasury purchases must have affected the reserves of the few existing commercial banks which held quantities of Government obligations. Government securities were a more important part of the whole investment field in the early history of the United States than today because of the relatively small supply of corporate securities in those early years.[11]

According to Hamilton's plans the Government intended to purchase its obligations in the market if their price fell below par. But the expenditures of the new Government proved larger than Hamilton's expectations, its revenues lower,[12] and the plan had to be abandoned. The Government had to resort to bond sales and borrowed heavily from the banks, notably the Bank of New York and the Bank of North America, to pay the expenses of the Army and Navy. Government expenditures for Army and Navy during this period did not help the banks to pursue a sound policy. Government expenditures meant that the banks had to part with Government deposits. If the banks paid out specie for the Government, their reserves and lending ability decreased.[13]

[10] Lewis, *Bank of North America,* pp. 41, 47, 88. In 1796 the President of the Bank of the United States instructed the manager of its New York branch to present a draft for payment of money due from the Bank of New York. This greatly alarmed the Bank of New York and forced it to contract, which occasioned considerable trouble in New York. Thereupon, Hamilton wrote to Wolcott, his successor in office, asking him to request a modification of his policy from the Bank of the United States because any weakness of the Bank of New York was due to its loans to the Government. To Hamilton's request Wolcott gave his assurance, "I will thank you to inform the president of the New York Bank, or any other confidential person, that they may rest assured of as full and cordial assistance in any pressure of their affairs as shall be in my power . . . I think, however, that they must rely principally on sale of stock, and in my opinion, any sacrifice ought to be preferred to a continuance of temporary expedience." Hoggson, *Epochs in American Banking,* pp. 83–84.

[11] Beckhart, ed., *The New York Money Market,* Vol. I, p. 152.

[12] Hamilton, "Report on a National Bank," December 13, 1790, in U.S., Treasury Dept., *Reports of the Secretary,* Vol. I, p. 54; see Appendix III, below.

[13] Sound banking practice demands the maintenance of adequate reserves, although many banks then failed to observe the principle. Not until the 1830's was state legis-

Major Treasury disbursements affect the reserves of the commercial banks. This is unfortunate, because the alteration of reserves should be at the discretion of a banking authority such as the head of a central bank. Such a man specializes in the study of money and banking conditions and is not influenced in his outlook by the fiscal needs of the Government as the Secretary of the Treasury must be. If the Treasury must affect banking reserves, its influence may at least be minimized by attempts to balance income and outgo at any one time.

Government Deposits in Banks

Revenue receipts form a major part of the fiscal activities of the Treasury, and they also affect, perhaps only temporarily, the reserves of banks and thereby their credit facilities. By depositing revenue receipts in banks, the Treasury increases reserves [14] as well as the deposits of commercial banks. The banks which first benefited from the Treasury deposits were selected by Alexander Hamilton as Secretary of the Treasury. They were the Bank of North America, the Bank of Massachusetts, and the Bank of New York. Most of their business was governmental. The third figure of Table I includes the Bank of Maryland, which was made a Federal depository in 1791.

TABLE I

UNITED STATES TREASURY BALANCES IN DEPOSITORY BANKS, 1789–1791[a]

Date	Treasury Deposits
December 31, 1789	$ 28,239.61
December 31, 1790	570,023.80
September 30, 1791	679,579.99

[a] Chapman, *Fiscal Functions of the Federal Reserve Banks*, p. 5; see also Appendix II, below.

---

lation enacted setting up legal standards for the maintenance of reserves. By "adequate reserve" is meant holding by a bank of sufficient money on hand to answer the demands of customers who prefer to have some of their monetary funds in the form of currency in their own possession rather than on deposit in the banks. U.S., Board of Governors of the Federal Reserve System, *Federal Reserve System; Its Purposes and Functions*, p. 4.

[14] Since no national legal requirements existed before 1863 for the maintenance of reserves, the banks could lend without restrictions. "History of Reserve Requirements for Banks in the United States," *Federal Reserve Bulletin*, November, 1938, p. 954.

Interest Payment by Banks for the Government

Also, the Act of August 12, 1790 (1 Stat. 186), earmarked certain items of Federal revenue for interest payment on the new Federal debt. This clause was designed to help maintain national credit, but it temporarily and unintentionally affected bank reserves. Interest payments by the Government involved transfers on the books of the banks from the deposit account of the Government to those of the bondholders.

Not until 1864 were cash reserves against Government deposits required.[15] But prudent banking policy always demanded a stipulated reserve percentage against ordinary deposits. Thus the adequacy of a given reserve decreased as the account balance of the government (no reserve requirement) [16] decreased, and the bondholders' deposit accounts (reserve required) increased.

Currency

In addition Hamilton's "Report on a National Bank," December 13, 1790, and "Report on Public Credit," January 9, 1790, indicated that he also believed a shortage of currency existed and should be remedied. He felt that business was being retarded, interest rates were high, and usurers were flourishing because of the lack of currency. He thought that capital is created in the process of increasing the circulating medium.[17] If capital were expanded, business enterprise would flourish and the "improvement of the revenue" be guaranteed. As revenue expanded, bank reserves would increase through greater deposits. Hamilton's fiscal program [18] thus affected bank reserves, and the Treasury was performing a central banking function, although the primary motive was the establishment of Government credit.

The Secretary of the Treasury knew that Congress has the "power to coin money, regulate the value thereof, and of foreign coin," [19] and

---

[15] National Banking Act, June 3, 1864 (13 Stat. 113); see also p. 105, below.

[16] Kinley, *Independent Treasury*, p. 15; U.S., Treasury Dept., *Annual Report of the Secretary, 1907*, pp. 144–146.

[17] Hamilton, "Report on a National Bank," December 13, 1790, in U.S., Treasury Dept., *Reports of the Secretary*, Vol. I, p. 57.

[18] Refunding Plan; see above, p. 12.

[19] U.S., Constitution, Article I, Section 8, Paragraph 5.

he also knew that the function of the Treasury was to "support public credit" and "keep the monies of the United States." It is not improbable, considering his broad interpretation of the Constitution, that he felt it the duty of the Treasury to help supply the country with additional currency. This broad view of his duties is understandable, since neither a central bank nor any other national coinage facilities existed. The United States Mint was not established until April 2, 1792 (1 Stat. 246), and Hamilton was convinced that a scanty currency brought evil. He felt that the fiscal powers entrusted to the Secretary of the Treasury gave him the chance to meet the currency problem, which was apparent to him because of his excellent knowledge of financial conditions. It is difficult to see how he could have acted otherwise, but his intervention in the monetary sphere did set a precedent for other secretaries of the Treasury.

The experience of the first few years of the United States Treasury may be summarized in the statement that as early as 1789 the Treasury began to be influential in the money market and to affect the reserves of banks through its handling of the public funds and public debt.

1791–1810

THE TREASURY AS RIVAL OF THE FIRST BANK OF THE UNITED STATES

The position and influence of the Treasury was altered after the establishment of the first Bank of the United States—from 1791 to 1810. Whatever organization acts as the fiscal agent of the Government wields an important influence in the money market because of the huge Government receipts and disbursements. But it in turn is greatly affected by Treasury policies which may extend beyond fiscal considerations and include the financial leadership associated with a central bank.

Hamilton, the first Secretary of the Treasury, considered establishing the first Bank of the United States in 1791 as a larger-than-usual commercial bank and also as an essential and vital part of the general scheme for the support of public credit.[20] He showed in his December 13, 1790, report that in enlightened commercial nations

---

[20] Holdsworth, *First Bank of the United States*, p. 9; Hamilton, "Report on Public Credit," January 9, 1790, in U.S., Treasury Dept., *Reports of the Secretary*, Vol. I, p. 28.

of the world public banks render invaluable service to the Government and to trade, and he recommended the creation of a national commercial bank. The first advantage which Hamilton claimed for such a bank was "the augmentation of the active or productive capital of the country through the credit values created by the Bank's operation." [21] He meant not only the creation of additional capital but also more effective utilization of capital. Scattered and otherwise idle amounts were to be concentrated and made to serve the uses of business. The Treasury could not perform the function of keeping scattered and idle funds where they might be used. It was not authorized to keep any moneys but its own. Furthermore, it was not empowered to discount commercial paper, a task necessary for the full utilization of capital and considered as belonging within the province of a bank.

Hamilton recognized that bank deposits are currency,[22] but he did mistake currency for capital.[23] If Treasury funds remained in its own vaults rather than in a bank, he felt that business would not benefit from them. On the contrary, these idle funds of the Treasury would retard business and diminish the public revenue. As Secretary of the Treasury he was responsible for the improvement of the revenue.

Hamilton also laid great stress upon the advantage of a bank in making loans to the Government, especially in sudden emergencies and in facilitating the payment of taxes. But these considerations were to him of secondary importance. A national bank was not a mere matter of private property, but a political machine of the greatest importance to the state.[24]

Hamilton also argued strongly in favor of bank currency issues payable in coin and against the issue of paper by the Government. There was a scarcity of currency in the country, and Hamilton's favorite notion was that the proposed bank be used to remedy the shortage of media of payment.[25] Possibilities of overissue and overextension of loans were considered small and no real counterargument, since a report of the condition of the bank was to be furnished to the Secretary of the Treasury at his command and he was to have the

[21] Hamilton, "Report on a National Bank," December 13, 1790, in U.S., Treasury Dept., *Reports of the Secretary*, Vol. I, p. 55.

[22] *Ibid.*, p. 56.

[23] Miller, *Banking Theories in the United States before 1860*, p. 36.

[24] Hamilton, "Report on a National Bank," December 13, 1790, in U.S., Treasury Dept., *Reports of the Secretary*, Vol. I, p. 56.

[25] *Ibid.*, p. 62.

right to inspect the books.[26] The proposed national bank was to be under private management, but the Secretary of the Treasury reserved the right of supervision—supervision of private commercial banks is, not a fiscal, but a central banking function.[27]

Hamilton urged public control of the first Bank of the United States, but thought it was undesirable that the bank be managed wholly by the Government.[28] A bank managed by the Government would have to be founded upon the credit of the Government and its revenues. To Hamilton this meant that the Government would embark on a business enterprise and would enter the field of lending money to its citizens. In 1790 the Treasury had too meager a revenue to permit lending money.[29] It frequently had to resort to borrowing, and Hamilton intended to look to the new bank for assistance. He hoped "the monied aristocracy" would be interested in the bank adventure [30] and supply funds and management.

Hamilton argued against those who quoted the proceedings of the Constitutional Convention to show that a Federal chartered bank was a violation of the constitutional compact. To him the Constitution should be interpreted liberally especially when it threatened to hamper the Secretary of the Treasury in carrying out a program fostering commerce and industry. Hamilton's ideas of the functions of the proposed national bank coincide with the objectives of the present Federal Reserve System as given by the Board of Governors.[31] Truly Hamilton was a man far ahead of his times in his concepts of money and banking.

Hamilton's arguments prevailed. The bill to establish the bank was introduced in the Senate on January 3, 1791, and finally passed on February 25, 1791.[32] The act chartering the bank made no special

[26] *Ibid.*, pp. 20, 74.

[27] The Treasury Department still exercised the right of supervision of banks under the National Banking Act of June 3, 1864, Section 54; 13 Stat. 99; and under the Federal Reserve Act of December 23, 1913; 38 Stat. 265.

[28] Hamilton, "Report on a National Bank," December 13, 1790, in U.S., Treasury Dept., *Reports of the Secretary*, Vol. I, pp. 71–72.

[29] See Appendix III, below.

[30] Holdsworth, *First Bank of the United States*, p. 23.

[31] U.S., Board of Governors of the Federal Reserve System, *Federal Reserve System; Its Purposes and Functions*, p. 115.

[32] Chapman, *Fiscal Functions of the Federal Reserve Banks*, p. 6; Lewis, *Bank of North America*, p. 80; 1 Stat. 191; Dunbar, *Laws of the United States Relating to Currency, Finance and Banking*, pp. 22–29.

provision regarding the keeping and transferring of Government deposits, but Hamilton felt that the bank should be the fiscal agent of the Government and that the terms of the transactions should be settled by the Secretary of the Treasury and the bank officials.[33] Consequently the bank was employed as a depository of Federal funds, following the precedent established at the Bank of North America and the Bank of New York. The first Bank of the United States transferred funds for the Government free of charge, and in return the Government did not collect interest on its deposits.[34]

The Government deposits were relatively small, as is indicated by Table II.

TABLE II

UNITED STATES TREASURY BALANCES IN
DEPOSITORY BANKS, 1793–1810[a]

Year	Number of Depository Banks	Total Treasury Balances in All Banks	Deposits in Bank of United States
Dec. 31, 1793	8	$ 753,661.69	$ 624,431
Dec. 31, 1807	15	9,643,850.07	5,500,000 (peak year)
Dec. 31, 1810	15	2,672,296.57	2,000,000

[a] Holdsworth, *First Bank of the United States*, pp. 59–60; see also Appendix II, below.

Even when Treasury deposits were large the bank found the Government business unprofitable because of the great expense involved in transferring Government funds from one section of the country to another. Also, the Government account fluctuated continually, and the first Bank of the United States had to be prepared at all times to transfer Government funds. This diminished seriously the possibility of gainfully employing the Government deposits. The fiscal activities of the Treasury affected the reserve position of the bank and consequently its lending policy. These fluctuations in the deposits involved care and expense in transferring them from place to place. The Government account added little profit to the income of

---

[33] Holdsworth, *First Bank of the United States*, p. 58; Hamilton, "Report on a National Bank," December 13, 1790, in U.S., Treasury Dept., *Reports of the Secretary*, Vol. I, p. 72.

[34] Gallatin, "Report on Bank of the United States," January 23, 1811, in U.S., Congress, *American State Papers, Finance*, Vol. II, pp. 469–470; Holdsworth, *First Bank of the United States*, p. 61.

the first Bank of the United States.[35] However, the Treasury was well satisfied, and Secretary Gallatin stated that the bank was very efficient.[36] On January 23, 1811, just before the expiration of its charter, the bank's total resources were $24,200,000, $4,807,000 representing loans to the Government. Of the total liabilities of $13,673,-000, Government deposits aggregated $1,930,000.[37]

By the Act of February 25, 1791, the Bank of the United States was not permitted to purchase any securities representing the National debt, but it could advance loans to the Treasury directly.[38] Loans could be effected by creating Government deposits, that is, book credit, or by issuing notes to the Government which were not legal tender but passed freely in general circulation because they were receivable for dues at the Federal Treasury. During the first year of the bank's operation the loans to the Government rose to more than $2,500,000; by January 31, 1795, the amount had advanced to $4,700,000, and by December 31, 1795, to $6,200,000.[39]

Such extension of credit, even to the Government, was a serious matter for a bank of this size. The loans to the Treasury had diminished the bank's reserves and hampered its lending policy, because the deposit account which the first Bank of the United States created for the Treasury was subject to the call of the Treasury and of the Treasury's creditors. The bank had to maintain reserves sufficient to meet these demands. As the extension of credit to the Government increased the ratio of reserves to deposit liabilities decreased. Therefore the first Bank of the United States found that it had either to curtail its loans to private customers or diminish its loans to the Government. Accordingly, the first Bank of the United States asked the Government to settle its indebtedness. This Gallatin, the Secretary of the Treasury, did in 1802 by selling the Treasury's interest in the bank.[40]

Since the first Bank of the United States was the largest commercial bank of that day, its lending facilities touched upon the lives of

[35] *Ibid.*, p. 62.

[36] Letter of Gallatin to Jefferson regarding Bank of the United States, December 13, 1803, in Gallatin, *Writings,* Vol. I, p. 171.

[37] Gallatin, "Report on Bank of the United States," January 23, 1811, in U.S., Congress, *American State Papers, Finance,* Vol. II, pp. 469–470.

[38] Sections 11–12, 1 Stat. 191; Dunbar, *Laws of the United States Relating to Currency, Finance and Banking,* p. 26.

[39] Holdsworth, *First Bank of the United States,* pp. 44–45.

[40] "Report on the Finances, 1802," in U.S., Treasury Dept., *Reports of the Secretary,* Vol. I, p. 254; Holdsworth, *First Bank of the United States,* p. 49.

many men and affected the credit conditions of the other banks. But the bank itself was always subject to strong Treasury influence, which in fact prevailed in the entire money market. While created as a sort of central bank, the first Bank of the United States had to share this position throughout its career with the United States Treasury. A discussion of the foreign-exchange situation and of assistance to commercial banks will confirm this evaluation.

The Treasury and Foreign Exchange, 1791–1810

During the existence of the first Bank of the United States the financing of foreign trade business was small,[41] but most of it was handled by the first Bank of the United States and its branches. Previously state banks had financed the business. The Government was strongly interested in foreign trade because customs duties supplied a major source of revenue which was used partly for the repayment of interest and principal on the public debt.[42] The bank sent Government remittances to meet foreign debt maturities and helped importers pay custom duties on imported goods by advancing funds.[43] This assistance to importers was not only sound banking business but also was induced by the wishes and needs of the United States Treasury. The bank aided the Treasury in collecting its revenue. A bank may choose preferred customers, which is the category into which the directors of the first Bank of the United States placed the importers, but the Treasury should not influence the directors' choice. At that time and until the establishment of the Federal income tax under the terms of the Revenue Act of September 8, 1916 (39 Stat. 756), revenue from foreign trade was a very important source of income to the Treasury.[44] Naturally, the Treasury Department continued to encourage importing.[45] It is permissible for a commercial bank to extend preferential credit facilities to one group if it deems that the wisest use of its funds. But a commercial bank is not in full control of its lending policy if the Treasury can influence it in determining its pre-

---

[41] *Ibid.*, p. 54.

[42] Hamilton, "Report on Public Credit," January 21, 1795, in U.S., Treasury Dept., *Reports of the Secretary*, Vol. I, p. 157; "Report on the Finances, 1811," in *Reports of the Secretary*, Vol. I, pp. 447–448.

[43] Holdsworth, *First Bank of the United States*, p. 54.

[44] *Ibid.*, p. 175; see also Appendixes III–IV, below.

[45] Later examples of assistance given to importers appear in the reports of secretaries of the Treasury Boutwell and Shaw. See pp. 81, 104.

ferred customers or if the bank extends aid to one group of business-men at the expense of another, because public funds constitute the bulk of the bank's deposits. Theoretically the bank was free to determine its own lending policy. Actually the lending policy of the first Bank of the United States was dictated largely by Treasury practices.

The Treasury and Panic Insurance, 1781–1810

The Treasury gave assistance to the commercial banks in several crises. The maintenance of an institution to render aid to a bank whose assets are not liquid is often termed "panic insurance." [46] This is the most popular idea of the function of a central bank. In the early history of our country there was a dearth of currency and specie. It was difficult for a bank to have cash on hand, especially when most of the specie was used to pay for imports. In March, 1792, when heavy duty payments were maturing in the Philadelphia district, the Treasury informed the president of the first Bank of the United States that post dated notes of the commercial banks, if not issued for a period longer than thirty days, would be acceptable by the collector [47] in payment of customs duties. By this action the demand for specie was diminished and the reserve position of the banks was not reduced. This decision illustrates the concern of Hamilton, Secretary of the Treasury, for the banks and emphasizes the central banking aspects of the Treasury even at the expense of fiscal considerations. In order to avoid embarrassment for the commercial banks, he permitted the central bank, the first Bank of the United States, to accept for the Government account short-term commercial paper in place of the specie to which the Treasury was entitled. Another illustration of Hamilton's concern for the commercial banks of the country was his intention to leave the Bank of New York, a Government depository, in undisturbed possession of whatever funds it might have until the commercial crisis impending in 1792 should subside. He wrote to William Seton, cashier of the Bank of New York on January 24, 1792, "I consider the public interest as materially involved in aiding a valuable institution like yours to withstand the attacks of a confederated

[46] Willis, *The Theory and Practice of Central Banking*, p. 5.
[47] Holdsworth, *First Bank of the United States*, p. 63; Crawford, W., "Loans of Money from the Treasury to Individuals or Banking Institutions since March 3, 1789" (February 28, 1823), in U.S., Congress, *American State Papers, Finance*, Vol. IV, p. 265.

host of frantic and, I fear, in too many instances, unprincipled gamblers." [48]

Again in 1801, Gallatin, the Secretary of the Treasury, ordered $50,000 of Government money to be placed in the Bank of Columbia, in Washington, D.C., in order to protect the bank against a run.[49] In 1802 the Bank of Pennsylvania ran in debt to the Bank of the United States because of the Government deposits in the latter. The cashier of the Bank of Pennsylvania went to Washington to apply for relief. Gallatin, writing to Jefferson, says: "It is evident that they have extended their discounts too far. They say they can not at once curtail without ruining their customers, chiefly retail shopkeepers. Those for whom the Bank of the United States discounts are generally importers." Gallatin suggests possible lines of relief: (1) to write to the United States Bank to spare them; (2) to deposit $300,000 with them or to direct the collector at Philadelphia to deposit part of his public money with them.[50] He resorted to both methods. Such action directly increased the reserves of the bank and set a precedent for future secretaries of the Treasury. A central bank is expected to assist in an emergency. However, the Treasury extended aid to the commercial banks, whereas the legally constituted central bank, the first Bank of the United States, did not. The Treasury, perhaps off the record, was assuming the duties of a leader in the money market.

The Bank of the United States was not rechartered, partly because it was envied by the state banks and the now powerful Republican party wanted to dispense with Federalist projects. Yet the bank had performed satisfactorily the following central banking functions:[51] (1) safekeeping of public money; (2) assisting in the collection of the revenues; (3) transferring Government funds; (4) extending aid to importers; (5) advancing loans to the Government; (6) providing a sound bank-note currency. These functions, with the exception of the fifth, were later assumed by the Treasury.

[48] Hamilton, *Works,* Vol. V, p. 492.

[49] Beckhart, ed., *The New York Money Market,* Vol. I, p. 153; Crawford, "Loans of Money from the Treasury to Individuals or Banking Institutions since March 3, 1789," (February 28, 1823) in U.S., Congress, *American State Papers, Finance,* Vol. IV, p. 266.

[50] Letter of Gallatin to Jefferson regarding Bank of the United States, June 18, 1802, in Gallatin, *Writings,* Vol. I, p. 80; Holdsworth, *First Bank of the United States,* p. 67.

[51] Dewey, *Financial History of the United States,* pp. 126–127.

1811–1816

TREASURY CENTRAL BANKING DURING THE INTERVAL
BETWEEN THE FIRST BANK AND THE SECOND
BANK OF THE UNITED STATES

The period 1811–1816 includes the years between the end of the
first Bank of the United States and the beginning of the second Bank
of the United States. During this time no national bank existed which
could perform central banking functions; no central bank coördi-
nated the reserves of various banks, was responsible for a sound note
currency, advanced loans to a bank whose liquid position was threatened or to the Government in time of emergency, kept safe Government funds, and transferred Treasury revenue. The various state
banks which were serving as Government depositories tried to fulfill
these duties for the Treasury, but their attempts were unsuccessful.
The first Bank of the United States, in addition to serving as a fiscal
agent, had tended to restrain the state banks from an overissue of
currency. After the dissolution of the first Bank of the United States
sound note currency was scarce. Furthermore, the dubious credit
condition of the Treasury made it unlikely that it could finance the
War with England without aid from the banks. Moreover, the Treasury, because of its heavy expenses and insufficient revenue, that is,
lack of surplus funds, was unable to increase its deposits in banks, but
was instead dependent on bank support.[52] Apparently the Treasury
could more readily dominate the banks and the money market in
times of a Government surplus.[53] Without a strong leader, whether
the Treasury or a central bank, chaotic conditions occur in the monetary field in the time of a national emergency, as in the War of 1812.

No immediate shortage of banking facilities or bank note circulation was felt as a result of the closing of the first United States bank,
in 1811. In fact, the growth in state bank-note circulation ($17,000,-
000 between 1811 and 1820) more than compensated for the loss of
the $5,000,000 outstanding notes of the first Bank of the United
States.[54] The Treasury increased the number of state banks used as
depositories. In 1811, fifteen state banks were used as Government

52 See Appendix III, below.
53 Willis, *The Theory and Practice of Central Banking*, p. 63.
54 Holdsworth, *First Bank of the United States*, p. 15; U.S., Comptroller of the
Currency, *Annual Report, 1916*, Vol. II, p. 45.

depositories; by 1816 the number had increased to ninety-four.[55] The number of state banks increased by about 120 during the four-year period from 1811 to 1814.[56] These banks were established in localities where they were not needed, and every effort was made to circulate their notes at a sufficient distance from home to prevent their early return. Specie disappeared from circulation; its place "was usurped" by the "excessive issue of bank paper." [57] A large number of banks failed during and following the War of 1812, bringing ruin to many depositors.[58] The main cause of failure was a tendency among state banks to finance speculation, especially in foreign trade, and to inflate bank-note issues. As a result many of them were unable to meet successfully the burden thrust upon them by the Government during the War of 1812.[59] The banks could not finance the heavy import trade and the war. The war was unpopular, and Treasury revenue was low.[60]

The Government failed to adopt an effective fiscal policy at the outbreak of the war with England. It had no national banking institution to advance necessary funds. Instead it depended largely upon the tax levies of peace time and upon Government loans, which were difficult to arrange, since the banks of New England were opposed to the war.[61] During the year 1812 the Treasury could borrow only about $10,000,000 on long-term bonds and approximately $3,000,000 by selling Treasury notes.[62] The financial position of the Government was critical, and the banking situation was not much better.

In August and September, 1814, more than one hundred banks outside of New York, which held Government deposits amounting to $9,000,000, suspended specie payments, thereby placing a very difficult burden on Secretary Campbell of the Treasury Department.[63] In

[55] Kinley, *Independent Treasury*, p. 13; see also Appendix II.

[56] Chapman, *Fiscal Functions of the Federal Reserve Banks*, p. 12; see also Appendix VI, below.

[57] "Report on the Finances, 1815," in U.S., Treasury Dept., *Reports of the Secretary*, Vol. II, p. 42.

[58] Dewey, *Financial History of the United States*, pp. 144–145; see also Appendix VI, below.

[59] Gouge, *The Curse of Paper Money and Banking*, pp. 16–17.

[60] See Appendix III, below.

[61] Kinley, *Independent Treasury*, p. 17.

[62] "Report on the Finances, 1812," in U.S., Treasury Dept., *Reports of the Secretary*, Vol. I, p. 469.

[63] Kinley, *Independent Treasury*, p. 16; "Report on the Finances, 1814" in U.S., Treasury Dept., *Reports of the Secretary*, Vol. I, p. 529.

November, 1814, Secretary Dallas informed the security holders of Massachusetts that the Treasury Department could not pay interest on the national debt.[64]

If the Government was one of the chief sufferers because of the financial difficulties of the country, it also contributed to them. The Government borrowed heavily during 1813–1815 and paid by "manufactured" credit.[65] The inflationary policy of the Treasury affected the banking system by increasing the bank-note circulation. The country was on a paper money basis, and bank notes of state banks were not acceptable in other parts of the country except at a heavy discount. The unequal rates of domestic exchange injured both the Federal Government and the business public.[66] The depreciated bank notes were paid to the Treasury at par for Government securities and cost the Treasury at least 10 percent of the proceeds of the sales.[67] The credit position of the Federal Government was seriously injured by the bank suspensions of specie payments, by the increase in note issues, and by the continuous drain of specie for payments of imports.[68]

The return of peace with improved revenues and diminished expenditures finally helped the Treasury regain its prestige.[69] Furthermore, the postwar years had taught the opponents of the United States Bank that, whatever demerits characterized the old system, the state banks were by no means able to render the public service required.[70] It was the intention of Secretary Dallas to restore an orderly currency by generally resuming specie payments.[71] At a special session of Congress and in his annual report for 1815 he recommended the establishment of a national bank as "the only efficient remedy for the disordered condition of our circulating medium." [72] At first the plan was opposed,

[64] "Report on the Finances, 1815," in U.S., Treasury Dept., *Reports of the Secretary,* Vol. II, p. 14.

[65] Beckhart, ed., *The New York Money Market,* Vol. I, p. 157; Crawford, W., "Report on Currency," February 24, 1820, in U.S., Treasury Dept., *Reports of the Secretary,* Vol. II, p. 484.

[66] Chapman, *Fiscal Functions of the Federal Reserve Banks,* p. 15.

[67] Beckhart, ed., *The New York Money Market,* Vol. I, p. 156.

[68] "Report on the Finances, 1815," in U.S., Treasury Dept., *Reports of the Secretary,* Vol. II, p. 41.

[69] "Report on the Finances, 1817," in U.S., Treasury Dept., *Reports of the Secretary,* Vol. II, p. 93.

[70] Kinley, *Independent Treasury,* p. 17.

[71] "Report on the Finances, 1815," in U.S., Treasury Dept., *Reports of the Secretary,* Vol. II, p. 43.

[72] *Ibid.,* p. 44.

but finally, on April 10, 1816, the bill was passed establishing the second Bank of the United States.[73]

Although the absence of a central bank during the years from 1811–1816 might have been expected to increase the scope and effectiveness of Treasury central banking activities, such was not the result. Treasury deficits and poor credit standing undermined its effectiveness as a central bank, although the secretaries of the Treasury continued to consider themselves responsible for the general currency and banking conditions.

1817–1833

THE TREASURY AS RIVAL OF THE SECOND BANK OF THE UNITED STATES

Central Banking under the Second Bank of the United States

During the years 1817–1833, which mark the active service to the Treasury of the second Bank of the United States, the leadership in the money market was held, not by the National or central bank, but by the United States Treasury. One reason for the Treasury leadership may have been the lack of recognition of the possible usefulness of a central bank. It was not yet recognized that in order to be effective as a central bank the Bank of the United States should have held reserve funds upon which the commercial banks could rely in times of necessity. But the void created by the absence of a central reserve reservoir was filled by the Treasury. After five chaotic years, 1811–1816, "of uncontrolled State banking, with suspension of specie payment and with deep confusion in both public and private finance and credit," [74] it was inevitable that there should be agitation for a return to the system of entrusting the Nation's finances to a single strong institution. The duties of the second Bank of the United States were to be based upon the functions of the first Bank of the United States, many of which are now considered central banking activities. The sponsors of the act were not conscious that the duties of the new bank were those of a central bank, but considered them merely those of a great commercial bank.[75]

[73] Gallatin, *Consideration of the Currency and Banking System,* pp. 45, 49, 53; 3 Stat. 266; Dunbar, *Laws of the United States Relating to Currency, Finance and Banking,* p. 94.
[74] Willis, *The Theory and Practice of Central Banking,* p. 60.
[75] *Ibid.,* p. 61.

The function of the second Bank of the United States was to hold public deposits which were to be instantly convertible into cash on demand [76] so that the Treasury might not incur the risk of becoming a creditor of an insolvent state bank. The second Bank of the United States, furthermore, was to make short-term loans to the Government. It also assumed the duty of regulating and maintaining the notes issued by state banks on a convertible basis. This meant maintenance of stability and regularity in exchange costs between different sections of the country, which in turn implied a currency of uniform value free of local depreciation. It was this last function which finally contributed to the bank's downfall. The local commercial banks were jealous of its influence.[77]

The Treasury and the second Bank of the United States proceeded with laudable circumspection to transfer Treasury deposits from state banks to the Federal bank. Forced action would have driven state banks into collapse. Transfers were made at the convenience of state banks, in order to protect their reserve position, although in many cases the service of the state banks was inadequate to meet the needs of the Treasury. The machinery for the transfer of Government funds between state banks was especially poor. For example, in January, 1817, the Treasury needed $500,000 to pay the interest on Government bonds in Boston. Although the Treasury had a balance of $22,000,000 in various state banks,[78] the required $500,000 could not be transferred, as the banks were in danger of suspending specie payments. The funds had to be borrowed from the second Bank of the United States.[79] It is not surprising that the period (1817–1833) showed a decline in the use of state banks as depositories.

Through the efforts of Secretary Dallas, the second Bank of the United States entered into agreements with the banks of New York, Philadelphia, Baltimore, and Richmond to refuse to handle after February 20, 1817, notes of banks which were not paying specie.[80]

[76] Catterall, *The Second Bank of the United States*, p. 475; Chapman, *Fiscal Functions of the Federal Reserve Banks*, p. 19.

[77] Dewey, *The Second Bank of the United States*, pp. 159, 192.

[78] See Appendix II, below.

[79] Gouge, *The Curse of Paper Money and Banking*, p. 47; Dewey, *The Second Bank of the United States*, p. 188.

[80] Hoggson, *Epochs in American Banking*, p. 107; Dewey, *The Second Bank of the United States*, p. 158; "Agreement for Resumption of Specie Payments," February 1, 1817, in U.S., Congress, *American State Papers, Finance*, Vol. IV, p. 769.

According to Secretary Crawford, his successor, the most obvious task of the second bank, the agency of the Treasury, was to induce the state banks to resume specie payments.[81] The favorable trade balance in the winter of 1816–1817 probably helped banks to accumulate specie. Finally, the second Bank of the United States negotiated an agreement with state banks to resume specie redemption on February 20, 1817. A contraction of the state banks' note issue could easily have resulted in the parity of state bank notes with specie. But the banks disregarded the agreement and the second Bank of the United States under the William Jones administration was exceedingly lax in enforcing it and preventing an overexpansion of loans and notes.[82] Particularly the state banks of the South and the West increased their note circulation, and in 1818 the credit structure of the country collapsed. The volume of specie was not adequate to support the credit created, and what specie there was in the country rapidly drifted to New England, where prices were low and transactions were upon a metallic basis.[83] The second Bank of the United States was in no position to help Southern and Western state banks. The bank had to keep large amounts of specie on hand to meet calls by the Treasury.[84] But the Treasury, under Secretary Crawford, stepped in and lent assistance to the southern banks by means of specie deposits, fearing that a run on one institution would produce a general run.[85] As a result the Bank of Alexandria, Virginia, the Union and Central Banks of Georgetown, the Patriotic Bank, and the Bank of Washington improved their reserve position.[86] Also, banks did not hesitate to call upon the Treasury to support their credit. On August 23, 1819, the Franklin Bank, in Alexandria, asked Secretary Crawford for a Government deposit, as it was in danger of suspending specie payments.[87] These illustrations of Treasury assistance in times of crisis show not

[81] Kinley, *Independent Treasury*, p. 17; Dewey, *The Second Bank of the United States*, p. 158; Crawford, W., "Report on Currency," February 24, 1820, in U.S., Treasury Dept., *Reports of the Secretary*, Vol. II, p. 511.

[82] Dewey, *The Second Bank of the United States*, p. 156.

[83] Conant, *History of Modern Banks of Issue*, p. 618.

[84] Dewey, *The Second Bank of the United States*, p. 160; Catterall, *The Second Bank of the United States*, pp. 25–26.

[85] See Appendix II, below.

[86] Crawford, "Loans of Money from the Treasury to Individuals or Banking Institutions since March 3, 1789," in U.S., Congress, Senate 17th Congress, 2d Session, Senate Paper 40, pp. 4, 170, 177.

[87] Dewey, *The Second Bank of the United States*, p. 186.

only what the Treasury considers its functions to be but also the need for a central bank with reserve power to aid commercial banks whose position is temporarily not liquid. If the second Bank of the United States had been a true central bank, it might have been able to force the commercial banks to maintain adequate specie reserves against their notes and have helped to prevent the inflationary bubble of 1818. Furthermore, even later, when the expansion was beyond its control, it still could have helped the Virginia banks without leaving this task to the Treasury.

The beginning of the eighteen twenties witnessed a general economic recovery.[88] Again it was the Treasury that insisted on bringing bank notes back to a specie redemption basis.[89] All bank notes received at the Treasury's fiscal agent, the second Bank of the United States, were presented for specie redemption and notes were refused which could not be so redeemed.[90] The insistence of the Treasury upon payments in "specie backed notes" helped to establish a stable and uniform currency throughout the country. This central banking function had been entrusted to the second Bank of the United States, which was merely the agent of the Treasury.

The second Bank of the United States and the Treasury coöperated. The Government deposits were larger than "other deposits," and the bank rendered many services to the Treasury free of charge. In return the Treasury received no interest on its deposits.[91] The bank transferred the Treasury funds wherever the Treasury wanted them and even established branches to take care of the Treasury needs, since the profits derived from the Treasury account were great.[92] On the whole, the transfer system worked well and the second Bank of the United States always honored Treasury drafts at sight as the fiscal agent of the Government.[93]

The notes of the Bank of the United States increased in volume, acceptability, and stability as had been expected, and an effort was made to force state banks to maintain their notes at the same high standard. The volume of state bank notes declined, and in 1824 a

[88] Kinley, *Independent Treasury*, p. 20.
[89] Dewey, *The Second Bank of the United States*, p. 161.
[90] "Report on the Finances, 1820," in U.S., Treasury Dept., *Reports of the Secretary*, Vol. II, p. 178; Dewey, *The Second Bank of the United States*, p. 189.
[91] *Ibid.*, p. 215.
[92] Catteral, *The Second Bank of the United States*, p. 175.
[93] *Ibid.*, p. 468.

minor crisis occurred due to money stringency. Secretary of the Treasury Crawford then aided the banks by obtaining permission from Congress to pay off immediately part of the public debt, which did not mature until January 1, 1825, out of surplus funds on hand.[94] In this way funds were released to the money market and the shortage was relieved.[95] This action set the precedent for future secretaries of the Treasury who used Treasury surplus revenue to prepay the Government debt in times of monetary stringency. Instead of keeping the Government funds until the date of maturity of the bonds, the banks were authorized to use the funds for the purchase of the bonds. In this way the Treasury saved the interest payment and put funds into circulation. Relieving a stringency is properly within the sphere of activity of a central bank. The second Bank of the United States was the nominal central bank, but the Treasury considered relief of the money market its own task and performed it. At other times of monetary stringency the Treasury went so far as to pay a premium when Government securities were purchased.[96] This procedure may not have been sound fiscal policy, but it did help to eliminate the monetary stringency. Once again, it is to be noted that the Treasury can render assistance to banks when it has surplus specie funds at its disposal.

Although it had been the expressed intention to create a great commercial bank to serve the needs of the Government, the second Bank of the United States performed many duties which are today considered central banking functions. But it was not until the second Bank of the United States had gone out of existence and the severe panic of 1837 had resulted in a serious destruction of credit that the idea of a central bank which would have ultimate reserves or surplus lending power became definitely and consciously expressed.[97] Even in 1837 political fears and anxieties prevented the idea from making much headway. The establishment of a central banking system with all central banking powers did not occur until December 23, 1913 (38 Stat. 265), or seventy-six years later. In the meantime some central banking functions were performed by the Treasury. The nation needed

[94] See Appendix V, below.

[95] "Report on the Finances, 1824," in U.S., Treasury Dept., *Reports of the Secretary,* Vol. II, p. 278.

[96] Dewey, *Financial History of the United States,* p. 171; see below, p. 52.

[97] Willis, *The Theory and Practice of Central Banking,* p. 61; Miller, *Banking Theories in the United States before 1860,* p. 165.

central banking service and yet did not wish to establish a central bank.

The Dissolution of the Second Bank

During the first five years of Biddle's administration as head of the second Bank of the United States, from 1823 to 1827, he followed a conservative policy, but in 1828 he decided to expand the loans and discounts of the Second Bank of the United States.[98] He did this to fill the void created by the decrease in state bank-note circulation which would occur if their issue were forced down to a point where consistent specie redemption would be practical and depreciation would end.[99] He reasoned that the contraction of state bank-note currency that would result would be offset by an expansion of note issues of the second Bank of the United States. The bank was quite able to support such expansion. Between 1825 and 1831 the rapid retirement of the Federal debt had drawn out about $10,000,000 of the investments of the second Bank of the United States and had made this amount available in specie for additional credit operations.[100] Accordingly, the second Bank of the United States increased its operations in the South and the West, where long-term financing was preferred for agricultural purposes.[101] But such financing tended to reduce the liquidity of the bank, and in the fall of 1831 Biddle tried to call a halt to the bank's agricultural long-term credit expansion in the South and the West.[102] The West and the South were incensed at the thought of decreased credit facilities and retaliated by cries of "financial strangulation" and "the Monster." [103] The second Bank of the United States should never have extended long-term loans in the agricultural area. In those days a commercial bank should have confined itself to self-liquidating, short-term commercial paper. The banks in the South and the West might have extended some long-term credit to their customers, if their liquid position permitted it. At any rate, the second Bank of the United States, as the large Federal bank, should not have competed with the smaller, commercial banks, especially not in loans of doubtful desirability. Jackson subscribed to the popular western concept of the bank as "the Monster." He was sure it was

---

[98] Dewey, *The Second Bank of the United States*, p. 243.
[99] *Ibid.*, pp. 227, 235, 236.   [100] *Ibid.*, p. 211.   [101] *Ibid.*, pp. 243, 244.
[102] *Ibid.*, p. 245.   [103] *Ibid.*, p. 252.

an unconstitutional financial monopoly.[104] Also Jackson asserted the bank was corrupt and had failed to establish a uniform and sound currency.[105] Catterall, who made a most thorough study of the bank, pronounced it sound.[106] Secretary of the Treasury McLane considered the second Bank of the United States a help to the Government and business, and asserted that its notes gave the Nation a standard currency, more uniform even than the specie then in circulation.[107] After Jackson's election, in 1832, the bank charter still had four years to run; but President Jackson feared that Biddle might use this period to cripple the finances of the country. He immediately ordered Secretary McLane to remove the Government deposits and distribute them among the state banks.[108] In May, 1833, McLane was promoted to the office of Secretary of State, and William J. Duane came to the Treasury post. Duane was forced, in September, 1833, to yield his position to Mr. Taney, who carried out Jackson's order on October 1, 1833.[109] Jackson's original orders were to remove deposits from the second Bank of the United States, but later they were modified to permit old deposits to remain. All new deposits were to be made in state banks. This action forced the second Bank of the United States to curtail its credit extension. Loans of the second Bank of the United States were called in, and its note circulation was reduced.[110] Within a few months a scarcity of currency resulted, discount rates rose, and by May, 1834, severe financial distress was widespread. The credit deflation caused by the decrease in loans and notes of the second Bank of the United States terrified many and appeared to give substance to charges of the Jackson clique of "financial strangulation." [111]

The Treasury might have rendered assistance to the bank during

---

[104] *Ibid.*

[105] First Annual Message to Congress, December 8, 1829, in U.S., Congress, *Register of Debates and Proceedings in the Congress of the United States,* 21st Congress, 1st Session, Vol. VI, Part II, Appendix, p. 18.

[106] Catterall, *The Second Bank of the United States,* p. 245.

[107] "Report on the Finances, 1831," in U.S., Treasury Dept., *Reports of the Secretary,* Vol. III, pp. 224–225.

[108] Dewey, *The Second Bank of the United States,* p. 265.

[109] Chapman, *Fiscal Functions of the Federal Reserve Banks,* p. 21; Taney, "Removal of Public Deposits," December 3, 1833, in U.S., Treasury Dept., *Reports of the Secretary,* Vol. III, p. 339; "Report on the Finances, 1834," in U.S., Treasury Dept., *Reports of the Secretary,* Vol. III, p. 559.

[110] Kinley, *Independent Treasury,* p. 26.

[111] Woodbury, *On the Public Money,* December 12, 1834, in U.S., Treasury Dept., *Reports of the Secretary,* Vol. III, pp. 581–582.

the deflation of 1833, but the Secretary of the Treasury was Mr. Taney, who is better known for taking orders than for giving them.[112] Because of adverse public opinion a recharter of the bank was now impossible, and it continued to be gradually liquidated until March, 1836, when the State of Pennsylvania chartered it as a state bank.[113]

During the entire period from 1791 to 1833 the outstanding position in the money market was held by the Treasury. The two national banks served in some respects as a central bank, since they facilitated fiscal operations of the Government, collected the revenues, and tried to equalize the domestic exchanges. However, it was the Treasury that actually performed the more important central banking functions. It insisted upon payment in specie-backed notes, which induced the resumption of specie payment on state bank notes and resulted in equalized domestic exchanges. Furthermore, the Treasury aided the banks in time of stress by accepting thirty-day commercial paper instead of currency, by increasing Government deposits, and by prepaying the national debt. The Treasury felt responsible for the general banking and currency situation and acted accordingly.

1834–1840

TREASURY CENTRAL BANKING DURING THE SECOND ERA OF STATE BANKS AS GOVERNMENT DEPOSITORIES

The years 1833 and 1845 mark, respectively, the beginning of the dissolution of the second Bank of the United States and the beginning of the final independent Treasury system. The period between 1833 and 1846 is characterized by a brief experiment with an independent Treasury system and otherwise by the handling of Government funds by state banks. Treasury measures, such as the "Specie Circular" and the "Surplus Distribution," had an important influence on the banks and the business communities. During the years 1833–1845 the position of the Treasury as the most influential factor in the money market was uncontested, and it assumed several new duties of a central bank.

The use of state banks as depositories began again on a large scale in October, 1833. The Secretary of the Treasury selected the banks to be entrusted with the public deposits. At first the standards of se-

[112] Beard, *Rise of American Civilization*, Vol. I, p. 571.
[113] Dewey, *The Second Bank of the United States*, p. 265.

lection were high. The Bank of the Manhattan Company, the Mechanics Bank, and the Bank of America were among those chosen.[114] Only banks whose note circulation was on a specie paying basis were considered. Depository banks rendered weekly reports and had to submit to examination by the Treasury Department. The first examination privilege had been granted to the Treasury Department in the Act of February 25, 1791 (1 Stat. 191), which established the first Bank of the United States.[115] As deposits of Federal funds increased during 1835 and 1836, the standards of selecting qualified depositories were relaxed.[116] Especially in the West, many new banks were created whose only initial cash resources were the Federal deposits.[117] This reflected gross negligence on the part of the Secretary of the Treasury in safeguarding the funds entrusted to his care.[118]

From 1829 to 1840 the number of state banks increased by 572 (from 329 to 901).[119] One of the causes for the increase can be found in the circular letter of the Treasury Department to the depository banks, dated September 26, 1833, stating that "the deposits of public money will enable you to afford increased facilities to commerce and to extend your accommodations to individuals." The implication was clear; Government funds were being supplied for commercial banking purposes. The hint was not disregarded; new banks came daily into existence.[120] They were assured that the Government would not draw on its balances. The circular letter also recommended "merchants engaged in foreign trade" as the most deserving recipients of extended credit.

The intentions of the Secretary of the Treasury were good. He wished the banks to extend credit to importers. A large part of the

[114] Beckhart, ed., *The New York Money Market*, p. 160; "Report on the Finances, 1833," in U.S., Treasury Dept., *Reports of the Secretary*, Vol. III, p. 357.

[115] Hamilton, "Report on a National Bank," December 13, 1790, in U.S., Treasury Dept., *Reports of the Secretary*, Vol. I, p. 72; Holdsworth, *First Bank of the United States*, p. 20; Dewey, *The Second Bank of the United States*, p. 172.

[116] "Report on the Finances, 1836," in U.S., Treasury Dept., *Reports of the Secretary*, Vol. III, p. 693; see also Appendix II, below.

[117] Shannon, *America's Economic Growth*, p. 291.

[118] However, an attempt was made to remedy the condition. The Act of June 23, 1836, reaffirmed the former high standards of selection for government depositories. The Banks had to be on a specie paying basis; had to render weekly reports to the Treasury; had to submit to examination; etc. See "Report on the Finances, 1836," in U.S., Treasury Dept., *Reports of the Secretary*, Vol. III, p. 691; 5 Stat. 52; Dunbar, *Laws of the United States Relating to Currency, Finance and Banking*, pp. 110–116.

[119] Dewey, *The Second Bank of the United States*, p. 274; see also Appendix VI.

[120] "Report on the Finances, 1833," in U.S., Treasury Dept., *Reports of the Secretary*, Vol. III, p. 369; Sumner, *History of American Currency*, p. 123.

Government revenue came from this group of businessmen and the Treasury funds could be increased by aiding them. However, the Government deposits were used only partly to assist foreign trade, but mostly for long-term investment purposes.[121] Thus, indirectly the Treasury was furthering the excessive speculation leading to the Panic of 1837.

The Treasury and the Panic of 1837

The early eighteen thirties had been exceptionally prosperous years for the United States. Agriculture, manufacturing, commerce, transportation, and so forth were experiencing unusual growth. The minor depression which followed the contraction of credit by the second Bank of the United States in 1834 was soon forgotten. Imports had risen, customs receipts were large, and the income from the sales of public land was substantial.[122] The heavy imports indicated a rising domestic price level of which foreign manufacturers were taking advantage. It was believed that the upward trend in prices came from inflation of the currency due to excessive issues of bank notes.[123] In January, 1835, as a result of the unusually large revenue, the Government was enabled to pay off its debt, thus releasing other millions of dollars for deposit in banks which were used for discounts to land speculators.[124] Clay and the Secretary of the Treasury suggested that the existing surplus revenue be distributed among the states for purposes of internal improvement.[125] Such distribution was to go into effect in January and April of 1837. Its purpose was sound, but it also led to an increase in note circulation and in bank deposits which became the basis of discounts to land speculators.[126]

In 1836 sharply rising prices and excessive speculation were the first signs of the coming storm; but they were heeded by few.[127] The credit structure became overextended and weak. Finally, in 1837, the inflation bubble burst.

[121] Kinley, *Independent Treasury*, p. 30.

[122] Dewey, *Financial History of the United States*, p. 222; "Report on the Finances, 1836," in U.S., Treasury Dept., *Reports of the Secretary*, Vol. III, p. 696.

[123] Miller, *Banking Theories in the United States before 1860*, p. 64; "Report on the Finances, 1836," in U.S., Treasury Dept., *Reports of the Secretary*, Vol. III, p. 697.

[124] Kinley, *Independent Treasury*, p. 30; see also Appendixes II–III, below.

[125] "Report on the Finances, 1836," in U.S., Treasury Dept., *Reports of the Secretary*, Vol. III, p. 686.

[126] Beckhart, ed., *The New York Money Market*, Vol. I, p. 170.

[127] "Report on the Finances, 1837," in U.S., Treasury Dept., *Reports of the Secretary*, Vol. IV, p. 30.

The Treasury and the Specie Circular

Another contributing cause to the Panic of 1837 was the so-called "Specie Circular" issued by the Treasury Department on July 11, 1836. It received severe condemnation at the time.[128] In retrospect the aim of the hard money advocates who brought about the issuance of the *Circular to Receivers of Public Money and to the Deposit Banks* has much to commend it. The object of the Treasury in issuing the circular was to prevent the absorption of the public lands by speculators and to check the accumulation in the Treasury of western bank notes received in payment, many of which would doubtless prove inconvertible. The circular required that payments for public lands be made in gold and silver and forbade any Government officer to accept "for land sold, any draft, certificate, or other evidence of money or deposit . . . unless signed by the Treasurer of the United States." [129] The Secretary of the Treasury calculated that the circular would force speculative land purchasers of the East to send or bring specie to the West. It was thought that since the western land offices would deposit the specie receipts, the specie reserves of the western deposit banks would be built up. It is doubtful whether the circular forced much specie to enter the West, but it did cast a shadow on the note issues of the western banks.[130] The banks were placed in a peculiar position, for their paper was now discredited by the Government—a dangerous phenomenon for any banking system.[131]

The western banks faced another problem caused by the Surplus Distribution Act, passed June 23, 1836 (5 Stat. 52). According to sections 13 and 14 of this act, in January, 1837, the Government would distribute its surplus to the various states largely on the basis of their respective population. The preparation for these payments required a shift of large parts of Government deposits from western banks to eastern institutions, since the populous eastern states received the larger share of the surplus revenue derived mainly from western land sales. The Government account on the books of the western bank was credited with specie, but more often than not the

[128] Miller, *Banking Theories in the United States before 1860*, p. 188; Dunbar, *Laws of the United States Relating to Currency, Finance and Banking*, p. 270.

[129] "Report on the Finances, 1836," in U.S., Treasury Dept., *Reports of the Secretary*, Vol. III, p. 764.

[130] "Report on the Finances, 1837," in U.S., Treasury Dept., *Reports of the Secretary*, Vol. IV, pp. 16, 18.

[131] *Ibid.*, p. 21.

western bank had received from the land office its own notes loaned
to a customer instead of specie. It was obvious that the western banks
could not shift the funds unless their specie reserves were built up.
This was unlikely unless the Treasury redeposited the coin which it
received in payment for the public land.[132] The Treasury refused to
do so. Its attitude toward banks seemed no longer friendly, but hostile.
The Act of June 23, 1836,[133] clearly indicated the same antagonism
by requiring

. . . that all warrants or orders for the purpose of transferring the public
funds from the banks in which they are now deposited, to other banks
whether of deposit or not, for the purpose of accommodating the banks to
which the transfers may be made or to sustain their credit, or for any other
purpose whatever, except it be to *facilitate the public disbursements* and
to comply with the provisions of this act, be and the same are hereby prohibited and declared to be illegal.[134]

This act is in sharp contrast to the circular letter of the Treasury Department issued September 26, 1833, which encouraged the use of
Treasury funds for credit accommodations.[135] Apparently Secretary
of the Treasury Woodbury felt the Treasury should confine itself to
fiscal duties only and leave banking to the bankers of the country.
But even he could not disregard the traditional central banking functions of the Treasury. Within one year of the Act of 1836, (5 Stat. 52)
he was actively supporting the money market.

The Treasury and the Distribution of the Surplus Revenue

The distribution of the Federal surplus by the Treasury during the
early months of 1837 attacked the country's inflationary prosperity
from another angle. Confident that Government funds were theirs to
hold for an indefinite period, the depository banks had in most cases
made extensive loans and discounts and issued large quantities of
notes on the basis of their Government deposits. Now that the Federal
deposits were withdrawn the banks had to contract their lines of
credit. If the extensions of credit had involved primarily short-term,

132 Beckhart, ed., *The New York Money Market*, Vol. I, p. 169.
133 Act to regulate the deposits of public money (5 Stat. 52).
134 Act of June 23, 1836. Section 12, quoted in Hepburn, *History of Coinage and
Currency in the United States and the Perennial Contest for Sound Money*, p. 484;
Dunbar, *Laws of the United States Relating to Currency, Finance and Banking*, p. 114.
135 "Report on the Finances, 1833," in U.S., Treasury Dept., *Reports of the Secretary*,
Vol. III, p. 369; see above, p. 35.

self-liquidating loans, the contraction would not have been very difficult or serious. But a large proportion of bank loans in the West were
for semipermanent advances on land. The calling in of the loans resulted in disaster.[136]

The amount involved in this surplus distribution was about $37,-
000,000, consisting of specie and specie backed bank notes. It was
to be paid in 1837 to the state treasuries on the basis of their representation in the Senate and the House in four equal installments. This
required a major operation in the money market. The first installment
of the surplus distribution was paid in January, according to schedule,
but the second, in April, found some banks unable to meet the payment, having lost much specie by the earlier installment. After the
dissolution of the second Bank of the United States the public deposits
had been distributed among the "pet banks," resulting in the arbitrary
placing of funds without regard for the legitimate needs of business.[137]
These pet banks were least able to make the necessary transfers.

In the spring of 1837 specie hoarding was again rampant, and bank
runs ensued. In spite of his recent emphasis on the fiscal activities of
the Treasury, Secretary Woodbury felt it his duty to support the
money market and the general business situation. To relieve the
money stringency Treasury notes receivable for all public dues were
issued resulting in the creation once more of a national debt.[138] These
notes were taken by hoarders and public creditors. Government deposits in banks increased.[139] The central banking action of the Treasury in helping the banks and the business community by issuing notes
followed within one year of the passage of the Act of June 23, 1836,
(5 Stat. 52) which had been sponsored by the Treasury and which
opposed Treasury assistance to the banks. Such inconsistency can
be condoned only on the grounds of business expediency. Conditions
in 1837 were not foreseen in 1836. It may be assumed that the Secretary of the Treasury did not anticipate that the "Specie Circular," of
July 11, 1836, would result in the discrediting of bank notes, in
hoarding of specie, and in monetary stringency. Also Secretary Wood-

[136] Schurz, *Henry Clay*, "American Statesmen Series," Vol. XX, p. 121; "Report on
the Finances, 1837," in U.S., Treasury Dept., *Reports of the Secretary*, Vol. IV, p. 6.
[137] Kinley, *Independent Treasury*, p. 33.
[138] See Appendix V, below.
[139] Dewey, *Financial History of the United States*, p. 234; "Report on the Finances,
1837," in U.S., Treasury Dept., *Reports of the Secretary*, Vol. IV, p. 9; see also
Appendix II, below.

bury did not foresee that the distribution of the surplus revenue would deprive the agricultural areas of much needed funds. Up to 1836 the secretary's motives seem to have been purely fiscal. The measures he sponsored were calculated to safeguard and dispose properly of the Treasury revenue. Unfortunately, too often the outlook of the Secretary of the Treasury must be wider than the confines of his fiscal duties. The fortunes of the Treasury Department are closely connected with those of the rest of the country. By 1837 Secretary Woodbury recognized this and acted accordingly.

The dilemma in which the Treasury found itself in 1837 is well illustrated by developments in New York. A double drain of specie, domestic and foreign, forced the New York City banks, on May 10, 1837, to suspend specie payments, and the Federal Government, caught in the midst of transferring its surplus millions to the states, was helpless. It was unlawful for the Treasury to deposit funds with non-specie-paying banks,[140] and the Treasury could not remove deposits, for it could not accept depreciated paper currency. The third installment of the surplus distribution already was met with a default, although of only $650,000, but the October payment involved a total default of $6,500,000.[141] Both the Government and the banks were enmeshed in the panic and in a year's depression, to which both had contributed. A short-lived business recovery began in the summer of 1838 and lasted until 1839. Then came a renewed and severe depression which continued until 1843, causing many more bank failures. The Treasury was in no position to help the banks, even if it had so desired.[142] Instead, the Treasury had to find a way to protect its funds. Since they were deposited in banks, they were subject to loss in times of crises. The lack of a strong central bank caused havoc in the financial life of the Nation. The Treasury's fiscal operations were so handicapped during this depression that a new method of handling Treasury

---

[140] Act of June 23, 1836, Section 5; 5 Stat. 52. Entire Act quoted in Hepburn, *History of Coinage and Currency in the United States and the Perennial Contest for Sound Money*, p. 482; Dunbar, *Laws of the United States Relating to Currency, Finance and Banking*, pp. 110-116.

[141] Beckhart, ed., *The New York Money Market*, Vol. I, p. 173; "Report on the Finances, 1837," in U.S., Treasury Dept., *Reports of the Secretary*, Vol. IV, pp. 90-91; the Act passed October 2, 1837 (5 Stat. 201), entitled "An Act to postpone the Fourth Instalment of Deposits with the States" until January 1, 1839, amended the Act of June 23, 1836 (5 Stat. 52).

[142] See Appendix III, below.

funds seemed urgently needed. The solution was the Independent Treasury System.

1840–1841

THE TREASURY INDEPENDENT OF THE BANKS

After the Panic of 1837 the financial problem of the United States took a new form. How could the Nation provide itself with central banking service without the establishment of an institution called a central bank? The banking funds of the Nation had increased in amount and its economic life in complexity. A large financial institution was needed which would at least manage the Government funds and which would devote itself primarily to the public interest. The state banks and the Federal depositories had treated the Government funds more or less as a gift and had not been too careful of their use.[143] Furthermore, many of them had been forced to suspend specie payments during the depression of 1837. The heavy losses which the Government had incurred during the panic brought to public attention the critical situation of the Nation's finances.[144] Many remembered the efficiency with which the national banks had transacted the Government business.[145] Some statesmen, including Clay, felt that the American banking system would constantly be threatened with panics and collapse unless a centralized Federal bank was created.[146] Yet the Jacksonian struggle with the national banks had given the public the wrong kind of impression with reference to central banking. No political party felt it could risk its chances of victory by violating the public prejudice against central banking. The result was, as so often happens in American politics, a compromise plan which could be used to attain substantially the same object that had been achieved under the national or quasi-central banking regime without admitting that what was being instituted was a form of central banking.[147] The plan eventually adopted was the Independent Treasury System. It was to be an institution, under direct Treasury control, which would hold the public money and make payments and disbursements upon

---

[143] Willis, *The Theory and Practice of Central Banking,* p. 62; "Report on the Finances, 1838," in U.S., Treasury Dept., *Reports of the Secretary,* Vol. IV, p. 197.
[144] *Ibid.*
[145] Beckhart, ed., *The New York Money Market,* Vol. I, p. 164.
[146] Schurz, Henry Clay, in "American Statesmen Series," Vol. XX, pp. 139–140.
[147] Willis, *Theory and Practice of Central Banking,* p. 63.

a specie basis.[148] It would not only guarantee safety of the public funds but also lay a foundation for the currency and banking system and as such would be performing several central banking functions.

The first concrete political approval of the idea of the Independent Treasury System, which was to separate public revenue from the risks of the banking system, came in the message of President Van Buren to the special session of the 25th Congress, on September 4, 1837, that the Government collect, keep, and disburse its own funds. Mr. Van Buren maintained that the fiscal receipts of the Government should not be kept in the banks. It was also recommended that all dues be collected in specie, and no exceptions were to be made even in the case of bank notes of specie paying banks.[149] Already on May 12, the Secretary of the Treasury, Mr. Woodbury, had ordered the collecting officials temporarily to retain all future Government receipts, instead of depositing them in banks.[150] To Mr. Van Buren the continuation of this policy seemed sound. He declared it was no part of the Government's business to regulate domestic exchange.[151] Mr. Van Buren felt that Government deposits in banks resulted in an unequal distribution of funds, more funds being available in the area where the Federal depositories were located than elsewhere. This unequal distribution in turn caused variations in the rate of domestic exchange. To offset these the Treasury felt obliged to try to equalize domestic exchange rates by new deposits.[152] Also, the notes of banks receiving Government specie deposits usually circulated at figures closer to par value than the notes of banks not enjoying the deposit privilege. But on the other hand, Van Buren was opposed to a national bank because the people had declared against it in two elections, and

[148] "Report on the Finances, 1837," in U.S., Treasury Dept., *Reports of the Secretary,* Vol. IV, p. 13.

[149] U.S., Congress, *Register of Debates and Proceedings in the Congress of the United States,* Vol. XIV, Part I, p. 78.

[150] "Report on the Finances, 1837," in U.S., Treasury Dept., *Reports of the Secretary,* Vol. IV, p. 59.

[151] Compare with the statement of Secretary Shaw in 1907. "The Treasury now holds (November 20) in its own vaults a working balance of $78,000,000, as much as can possibly be spared of which will be deposited if business conditions require it, though it become necessary to pay the current expenses of the government with checks on depositary banks. The money of the country belongs to the people, and Treasury operations must be made subordinate to the business interests of the country." U.S., Treasury Dept., *Annual Report of the Secretary, 1906,* p. 40.

[152] "Report on the Finances, 1837," in U.S., Treasury Dept., *Reports of the Secretary,* Vol. IV, pp. 29–30.

the heavy hand of Jackson lay over Van Buren.[153] The possibility of a revival of the Federal bank project was unlikely.

In 1837 Congress did not act upon the President's recommendation, but during the years 1837 to 1840 Van Buren kept the plan of the Independent Treasury constantly before Congress, hoping legislation to that end would be passed. The Government had been forced to discontinue the use of the state banks as depositories and to revert to the older method of leaving the money with the receivers and collectors on whom drafts were directly made.[154] As Government deposits could not be withdrawn immediately from the banks, the administration was much hampered; but Secretary Woodbury was indulgent. He was one of the few secretaries who by bitter experience learned of the close connection between Government finance and the banks and who came to recognize the necessity for adjusting Treasury operations to meet the exigencies of the money market.[155]

Secretary Woodbury learned from experience. During his early years of service with the Treasury he had seen the Surplus Distribution Act (5 Stat. 52) and the "Specie Circular," of July 11, 1836, seriously injure the banking structure. The adverse effects of those measures more than canceled out the fiscal improvements which they were planned to achieve. The Treasury can rarely benefit at the expense of the banking system. It was the same Secretary Woodbury who later in 1837 issued Treasury notes to alleviate the stringency and to support the banks.[156]

He also recognized that Government deposits would have to be withdrawn from the banks very gradually if the Independent Treasury System was to be installed without seriously injuring the credit structure of the business community. A vital source of credit would be cut off when Government funds became unavailable and were kept in the Treasury vaults instead of in the banks.[157] Still, he recognized that it was the problem of the banks, not the Treasury, to provide credit facilities for the business community. Finally, on July 4, 1840,

---

[153] Schurz, *Henry Clay,* "American Statesmen Series," Vol. XX, p. 134.

[154] "Report on the Finances, 1837," in U.S., Treasury Dept., *Reports of the Secretary,* Vol. IV, p. 11.

[155] "Report on the Finances, 1838," in U.S., Treasury Dept., *Reports of the Secretary,* Vol. IV, p. 184.

[156] See above, p. 42; "Report on the Finances, 1838," in U.S., Treasury Dept., *Reports of the Secretary,* Vol. IV, p. 182.

[157] *Ibid.,* p. 185.

toward the close of Van Buren's administration, the bill for an Independent Treasury was passed (5 Stat. 385).

Although Van Buren sponsored the bill, the idea did not originate with him. It has been said that the plan was suggested by Jefferson to Dallas. Later, Gouge advocated it.[158] Others maintain that Senator Gordon of Virginia supported such a measure in 1834, and in later debate Senator Silas Wright, of New York,[159] took an active part.

The arguments for and against the Independent Treasury were many and varied. The best case for it was made by William Gouge in his pamphlet *An Inquiry into the Expediency of Dispensing with Bank Agency and Bank Paper in the Fiscal Concerns of the United States,* published in 1837. Gouge was for thirty years connected with the Treasury Department and gave later secretaries of the Treasury the idea that business in general benefits from separation of the fiscal operations of the Government from the banks. He asserted that money lying in the Government's separate vaults was not being wasted in unproductive idleness. "In a country such as ours there ought to be somewhere a reserved fund of gold and silver, and no more appropriate place can be found for such a reservoir than the United States Treasury," urged Gouge. He elaborated further, "Nor should the banks complain, for they benefit by the system of keeping the public money in special vaults. If in their vaults, it would lead to new inflations; if in the public depositories, more or less of it will come to their aid in times of emergency." [160]

In favor of an Independent Treasury, it was also argued that public money would be more secure, that specie circulation would be promoted and currency made more uniform, and that the Government ought to be able to manage its own finances. Furthermore, without an Independent Treasury the failure of the banks might at any time deprive the Treasury of its deposits and jeopardize the credit of the country.[161] This last argument seemed particularly valid, since the

---

[158] Dewey, *Financial History of the United States,* p. 253.

[159] Kinley, *Independent Treasury,* p. 26; Chapman, *Fiscal Functions of the Federal Reserve Banks,* p. 28.

[160] Gouge quoted in the U.S., Treasury Dept., *Report of the Secretary, 1854,* p. 268; later secretaries, including Cobb, adopted Gouge's attitude that the Government should try to alleviate depressions. Cobb went further by stating that unemployment attending depressions could be relieved by increased Government expenditure on public works. This is certainly a modern view; U.S., Treasury Dept., *Report of the Secretary, 1857,* p. 21.

[161] Kinley, *Independent Treasury,* p. 37; "Report on the Finances, 1837," in U.S., Treasury Dept., *Reports of the Secretary,* Vol. IV, pp. 197–198.

state banks collapsed again in 1839. However, Government losses were minimized this time, because since 1837 collecting officers had held Government funds safe in their own possession.[162]

Opposition arguments against the Independent Treasury were best presented by Albert Gallatin. He opposed the Independent Treasury on two grounds: (1) The system was unfair to the specie-paying banks, because it deprived them of Treasury deposits; (2) The system led to the danger of an accumulation of specie in Treasury vaults, especially when income exceeded expenditure. The excess currency receipts could not be distributed to the country, since they could not be deposited in banks.[163] This latter point proved to be one of the most serious drawbacks of the system.

Webster characterized the bill as a backward step, from dependence on credit to bolts and bars.

The use of money is in the exchange. It is designed to circulate, not to be hoarded. All the Government should have to do with it is to receive it today, that it may pay it away tomorrow. It should not receive it before it needs it, and it should part with it as soon as it owes it. To keep it— that is, to detain it, to hold it back from general use, to hoard it, is a conception belonging to barbarous times and barbarous governments.[164]

This point of view reflects sound principles of public finance. The Treasury should arrange its fiscal operations in such fashion that its receipts and disbursements are balanced at any one time. If they are unequal, the funds should be deposited where they will advance the public welfare or do the least harm.

Most of the other arguments against the Independent Treasury were mainly political. For instance, Clary said: "Public funds would be unsafe in the hands of public officers . . . ."[165]

The act inaugurating the Independent Treasury System was finally passed on July 4, 1840 (5 Stat. 385), although as it turned out it was not to remain in force for very long (until August 13, 1841). During the months that the first Independent Treasury System was used the

[162] "Report on the Finances, 1838," in U.S., Treasury Dept., *Reports of the Secretary,* Vol. IV, p. 193.

[163] Gallatin, *Suggestions on the Banks and Currency of the Several United States,* p. 88.

[164] Speech on the Subtreasury delivered in the Senate, March 12, 1938 in Webster, *Writings and Speeches,* Vol. VIII, p. 193.

[165] Speeches on the Subtreasury Bill delivered in the Senate on September 25, 1837 in Clay, *Life and Speeches,* Vol. II, p. 293.

system worked smoothly. There seemed to have been little change in the operations of the Treasury. State banks were still employed as depositories, though to a limited extent.[166]

The first Independent Treasury had no satisfactory connections with the banking system. It inherited a few small accounts, remainders of the period between 1833 and 1837. Nevertheless, the specie receipts and disbursements of the Treasury affected the reserves of banks. Specie paid into the Treasury was no longer available for bank reserves. Specie disbursements by the Treasury speedily found their way into bank reserves. The accounts of individuals were changed by these transactions, as well as the reserve ratio of the banks. The first Independent Treasury was thus indirectly regulating the extension of credits and performing a central banking function. Not even a law can prevent Treasury fiscal operations from affecting the reserves of banks.

The first Independent Treasury held the public money and insisted at the same time upon actual specie payments and disbursements. The presence of a slowly increasing amount of specie in the Treasury vaults in 1840–1841 did not prevent depressed conditions from existing in the country.[167] To revive business, confidence was probably more needed than specie. However, the first Independent Treasury system did carry out successfully another function of a central banking institution—the safekeeping of Government funds.[168] The failure to produce a business recovery cannot be held against the Independent Treasury System. It was established primarily as a Government depository, not as an institution to maintain sound business conditions. Although its advocates, including Gouge, expected that the Independent Treasury would aid the business community in times of stress, the first Independent Treasury, because of its short life and small specie resources, was handicapped and could not fulfill what is today considered one of the primary functions of a central banking institution—to render assistance in the maintenance of economic stability.

The first use of the Independent Treasury system was short-lived. The act of July 4, 1840 (5 Stat. 385) was repealed August 13, 1841,

---

[166] Beckhart, ed., *The New York Money Market*, p. 180; "Report on the Finances, 1840," in U.S., Treasury Dept., *Reports of the Secretary*, Vol. IV, p. 368.

[167] *Ibid.*, p. 359; see also Appendix II, below.

[168] *Ibid.*, p. 366.

(5 Stat. 439) due to the fact that the Whigs dominated the 27th Congress, which met in session on May 31, 1841, and was pledged to establish a third Bank of the United States. Tyler thwarted the plan of organizing a new bank, maintaining that it was unconstitutional for the Federal Government to authorize branches in the states without their consent.[169]

1841–1845

TREASURY CENTRAL BANKING DURING THE THIRD ERA OF STATE BANKING

The repeal of the first Independent Treasury Act necessitated a complete return to the use of state banks as depositories until 1846, when the Independent Treasury was reëstablished and began its long career. In the meantime, from September, 1841 to August, 1846, bank notes were accepted in payment by the Treasury and deposits of the Government went to the state banks on terms similar to those under which the transfer from the second Bank of the United States to the state banks had been made in 1833.[170]

During the years 1841–1846 the fiscal operations of the Treasury, its receipts and disbursements, directly affected the Government balance on the books of the banks and therefore the reserves of the banks. The effect of Treasury transactions on the credit structure of the country during this period was more direct and continuous than it had been for many years. It is true that the effect was largely unintentional and therefore did not involve conscious central banking functions. But it was potent just the same because of the volume and size of the Treasury transactions. The Treasury, by affecting the reserves of banks, was unintentionally wielding power normally associated with a central bank.

SUMMARY

During the years from 1789 to 1846, inclusive, the Treasury established itself as the leader in the money market. Its leadership was twice reduced by the creation of national commercial banks, which

---

[169] Hepburn, *History of Coinage and Currency in the United States and the Perennial Contest for Sound Money,* p. 145; U.S., Congress, *Congressional Globe,* 27th Cong., 1st Sess., Vol. X, p. 7.

[170] Kinley, *Independent Treasury,* p. 43; see also Appendix II, below, and above, pp. 33–36.

performed vital central banking functions, such as, keeping the Government funds safe; disbursing and transferring Government "money"; and exercising care over the commercial banks by persuading them to redeem their notes and to keep their assets "liquid." The latter paternal influence was difficult to maintain, since the national banks were essentially large commercial banks and did not always have excess funds. The Treasury usually did have ultimate reserve power and could help them in times of difficulty by accepting thirty-day paper,[171] increasing Government deposits,[172] prepaying the public debt,[173] and issuing notes and bonds.[174]

Early in the history of the Treasury Department some secretaries of the Treasury seemed conscious of the fact that the Treasury Department because of its unique position as the largest disburser and receiver of funds would be able intentionally and unintentionally to affect the reserves of commercial banks. This power belongs in the hands of a central bank, and some officials realized that their Treasury duties would imply consideration of the monetary welfare of the Nation, as well as the fiscal problems of the Treasury Department.

After the chaos of state banking and the Panic of 1837, the need was felt for an agency which could keep the Government funds safe and the currency of the country sound. The Treasury assumed these duties under the Independent Treasury System; thus adding to the central banking functions which it was already performing.

[171] Secretary Hamilton in 1792.
[172] Secretary Dexter in Crisis of 1801; Secretary Crawford in Crisis of 1818.
[173] Secretary Crawford in the Stringency of 1824.
[174] Secretary Woodbury in the Crisis of 1837.

CHAPTER III

The Rise of the Independent Treasury as a Central Bank 1846–1865

THE YEARS from 1846 to 1865 saw a great extension in the central banking functions of the Treasury. The Independent Treasury System, first tried out in 1840, finally went into operation in 1846, and although it was legally designed as an institution calculated to serve only the fiscal needs of the Treasury, within a short time it developed into a powerful organization fulfilling vital central banking functions.

THE ACT OF 1846

In aims and contents the second Independent Treasury Act of 1846 (9 Stat. 59) followed practically the same lines as the first Independent Treasury Act of 1840 (5 Stat. 385). The second act, designed to provide for the better organization of the Treasury and for the collection, safe keeping, transfer, and disbursement of the public revenue, was unquestionably a victory for the hard-money Democrats. It provided in the first five sections for "places of deposit of the public money" in Washington, Philadelphia, New Orleans, New York, Boston, Charleston, and St. Louis.[1] The principal clause, section six, required all officers of the Government

. . . to keep safely, without loaning, using, depositing in banks or exchanging for other funds than as allowed by this act, all the public money collected by them or otherwise at any time placed in their possession and custody, until the same is ordered by the proper department or officers of the government, to be transferred or paid out.

Sections 18 and 19 contained the provisions around which debate had raged most fiercely. In these sections occur the famous specie clause,

---

[1] "Report on the Finances, 1846," in U.S., Treasury Dept., *Reports of the Secretary*, Vol. VI, pp. 41–42.

which requires the payment of public dues and disbursements in gold or silver coin or Treasury notes only.[2]

The Act of August 6, 1846, provided for the separation of the fiscal activities of the Treasury from the banks. It made the Government its own banker; and, taken in connection with the laws sanctioning the emission of Treasury notes,[3] the Sub-treasury, or Independent Treasury Act "virtually made the Treasury a bank of issue." [4] So far as the banks were concerned, the new system meant the loss of Government deposits, which in turn forced the banks to decrease their discounts; [5] and the Independent Treasury System also involved the withdrawal of the support of Government credit from the banks' notes. But the banks had no reason to complain. The Government is not responsible for bank notes which cannot be kept circulating at par without Treasury support. It is the duty of the bank itself to see that its notes are convertible at par without the aid of public credit.

The work which the second Independent Treasury System had to accomplish seemed simple enough, consisting merely of the receipt and payment of public money. Commercial banks could not be used as Government depositories and bank notes could not be accepted in payment by collectors of the revenue. Accordingly, these Government agents were compelled to handle huge amounts of specie. It has been said that the satisfactory operations of the second Independent Treasury System during the period from 1846 to the Civil War was due, not to the provisions of the law, but to the prosperity which the country enjoyed.[6] The unusually large grain exports of 1847 brought in more

---

[2] 9 Stat. 59; Dunbar, *Laws of the United States Relating to Currency, Finance and Banking*, pp. 138–142.

[3] The first law sanctioning the emission of Treasury notes was passed on June 30, 1812 (2 Stat. 766). This was followed by further legislation along the same lines; the Acts of February 25, 1813 (2 Stat. 801); March 4, 1814 (3 Stat. 100); December 26, 1814 (3 Stat. 161); and February 24, 1815 (3 Stat. 213). On March 3, 1817, an act was passed terminating authority for loans and Treasury notes (3 Stat. 379). Some twenty years later, on October 12, 1837 (5 Stat. 201), an act was passed authorizing Treasury notes. Other similar laws which followed up to the time of the Independent Treasury Act were the Acts of March 2, 1839 (5 Stat. 370); February 15, 1841 (5 Stat. 411); July 4, 1840 (5 Stat. 370); February 15, 1841 (5 Stat. 411); July 4, 1840 (5 Stat. 385); January 31, 1842 (5 Stat. 469); August 31, 1842 (5 Stat. 581); and July 22, 1846 (9 Stat. 39). See Dunbar, *Laws of the United States Relating to Currency, Finance and Banking*, pp. 63, 68, 70, 75, 96, 118, 122, 124, 125, 130, 132, 135, 137.

[4] Kinley, *Independent Treasury*, p. 55.

[5] *Ibid.*, p. 58.

[6] Chapman, *Fiscal Functions of the Federal Reserve Banks*, p. 30.

than $37,000,000 of specie, and gold discoveries of California further helped the Treasury.[7]

SECRETARY WALKER AND THE MEXICAN WAR

The first crisis faced by the Independent Treasury was financing the Mexican War. Under the provisions of the Act of January 28, 1847, the Government issued $18,000,000 of Treasury notes of one to two years maturities and contracted a loan of $23,000,000, which was used in part to fund the notes.[8] But the Government did not encounter any difficulty in securing funds, as the war was popular and confidence in the country was widespread. The Government notes and bonds enjoyed a favorable market and were consistently selling at par or above because of the specie clause which provided for redemption in coin and because the "Constitutional Treasury" proved highly successful in preventing inflation and suspension.[9] The Treasury, by keeping the revenue in its own vaults rather than in the banks, checked an inflationary increase in bank notes and speculative excesses which normally follow. In this way, Secretary Walker asserted in his annual report, the country had been saved from the crisis of 1847 through which Great Britain was suffering.[10] During the Mexican War period the Independent Treasury, by maintaining specie payments, had protected the monetary standards of the country and helped stabilize prices of goods and securities. Secretary Walker further stated that if the specie had been deposited in banks, large quantities of additional bank notes might have been issued resulting in a ruinous paper inflation, rising prices, and finally exportation of specie.[11] However, the effect of Treasury action upon the banks was not wholly beneficial, as Walker asserted them to be; the accumulation of idle funds in the Treasury, although small, must have been a drawback to business activity, because the specie, if deposited in banks, might have formed the basis for loans and discounts necessary for legitimate business expansion.

[7] "Report on the Finances, 1847," in U.S., Treasury Dept., *Reports of the Secretary*, Vol. VI, pp. 129–130.

[8] *Ibid.*, p. 134; 9 Stat. 118; Dunbar, *Laws of the United States Relating to Currency, Finance and Banking*, p. 147.

[9] "Report on the Finances, 1847," in U.S., Treasury Dept., *Reports of the Secretary*, Vol. VI, p. 131.

[10] *Ibid.*   [11] *Ibid.*, p. 129.

SECRETARY GUTHRIE STARTS THE INDEPENDENT
TREASURY ON THE ROAD TO INTERVENTION
IN THE MONEY MARKET

The operation of the Independent Treasury Act exerted little influence upon the currency so long as the Federal revenues did not greatly exceed expenditures. Secretary Guthrie, in his report of December, 1856, said that the Sub-treasury or Independent Treasury might "exercise a fatal control over the currency, the banks, and the trade of the country and will do so whenever the revenue shall greatly exceed the expenditure." [12] In 1853 the Treasury Department faced the problem of dealing with surplus Government funds which were accumulating in the Treasury and being kept out of the channels of commerce.[13] Guthrie feared a panic, and in order to prevent a stringency in the money market the Secretary of the Treasury used part of the surplus funds to buy silver bullion for new coinage, thus returning the Government surplus to circulation and increasing the reserves of commercial banks.[14] But Guthrie found this method alone insufficient and soon used another method to restore funds to the banks by "forced debt payment" or redemption of the public debt before maturity.[15] By 1836 the public debt had been eliminated: but lowered revenues after 1837 and the Mexican War created a new debt which by 1850 amounted to about $63,000,000.[16] The repayment of such an amount would have been sufficient to absorb a large Treasury surplus, but the law required that redemption be made at par.[17] This seemed to preclude the possibility of redeeming bonds when they were selling at a premium. But when the market prices of Government bonds rose above par, the Secretary of the Treasury could not use the surplus, if such existed, to "redeem" bonds and thereby relieve a market stringency. However, Section 3 of the Civil and Diplomatic Appropriation Act of March 3, 1849, gave the Treasury the power to "buy" bonds at the market price.[18] Secretary Guthrie elected to purchase Government bonds under authority of the Act of March 3, 1849. Thereby, he took advantage of the possibility of prepaying the public debt, and even

[12] U.S., Treasury Dept., *Report of the Secretary, 1856*, p. 32.
[13] See Appendix II.   [14] U.S., Treasury Dept., *Report of the Secretary, 1853*, p. 6.
[15] *Ibid.*, pp. 6–7.   [16] See Appendix V.
[17] Act of March 3, 1795; 1 Stat. 433; Dunbar, *Laws of the United States Relating to Currency, Finance and Banking*, pp. 35–42.
[18] 9 Stat. 369; Dunbar, *Laws of the United States Relating to Currency, Finance and Banking*, p. 146.

when Government bonds were at a premium of 21 percent, in 1853, he purchased bonds in order to relieve the monetary stringency and avert a panic.[19] Throughout the remainder of his administration of the Treasury (1853–1857) Secretary Guthrie gave the subject of paper money in circulation much attention.

The history of the Sub-treasury system reveals periodic increases in Government revenue and repeated attempts by the Treasury to ease the stringency by use of the surplus in paying off the public debt.[20] The purchase of Government obligations by the Independent Treasury decreased its idle accumulations in the vaults and partly increased the money in circulation. Individual deposits and reserves of commercial banks may also have been increased by these purchases, thus enabling the banks to extend more credit to their customers and relieve the stringency in the money market. This power of the Treasury of increasing reserves of commercial banks through open market operations is usually reserved for a central bank. It is true, in giving the Treasury the power to buy and sell Government obligations the legislators were not aware of its central banking implications. At that time Congress was merely concerned with fiscal activities of the Treasury. But several secretaries of the Treasury realized the influence which Treasury fiscal activities have on the reserves of commercial banks and considered in their actions the banking problems of the country, as well as the fiscal necessities of the Treasury. Other secretaries took a more narrow view and let fiscal considerations predominate. But even these secretaries of the Treasury, because of the circumstances surrounding their fiscal duties, often unintentionally helped the banks and at times intentionally tried to fill the void created by the lack of a central banking institution.[21]

THE CRISIS OF 1856 AND TREASURY CENTRAL BANKING UNDER SECRETARY COBB

During the 1850's the banks had become heavily interested in railroad construction. As a result, the banks found it difficult in the

[19] U.S., Treasury Dept., *Report of the Secretary, 1853*, pp. 6, 41.

[20] See below, Crisis of 1884, Secretary Folger, p. 76; Stringency of 1887, Secretary Fairchild, p. 80; Stringency of 1890, Secretary Windom, p. 88.

[21] See above, Panic of 1837, Secretary Woodbury, p. 39; see below, Crisis of 1873, Secretary Richardson, p. 70; Treasury Surplus of 1888, Secretary Fairchild, p. 81, see pp. 101–104 on secretaries Shaw, Gage, and Cortelyou.

summer and fall of 1856 to satisfy their customers' demands for short-term commercial discounts.[22] Rates of interest rose steadily. During the years 1854 and 1855 the customs receipts were unusually heavy.[23] Large amounts of specie were allowed to accumulate in the Government vaults.[24] This policy contributed to the strain in the money market. In so far as the Treasury accumulations restrained further lending for speculative purposes, the Treasury influence, unintentional though it was, must have been to prevent the tide of speculation from rising as high as it otherwise would have done or to bring on the inevitable crash sooner.[25] Serious trouble concerning the liquidity of commercial bank assets began in August, and by October 13, 1856, eighteen New York City banks, the mainstays of the country's financial system, suspended specie payments.[26]

The symptoms of the coming panic had been felt early in the year, and to avert disaster Secretary Cobb began the purchase of bonds, his purpose being, in his own words, to afford "relief to the commercial and other interests of the country, which were then struggling to ward off the revulsion which finally came upon them." [27] He further justifies his intervention in the money market by stating,

A revulsion in the monetary affairs of the country always occasions more or less of distress among the people, the consequence is, that the public mind is directed to the government for relief, and particularly to that branch of it which has charge of its financial operations. There are many persons who seem to think that it is the duty of the government to provide relief in all cases of trouble and distress. . . . They see no other agency capable of affording relief, and their necessities force them to the conclusion that the government not only can, but ought to relieve them.[28]

Treasury intervention, exemplified by pumping funds into the market through payment for bonds repurchased, proved effective. Between the first of August and the seventh of December the banks gained specie from the proceeds of the purchases of bonds by the Government. The Secretary of the Treasury continued buying bonds and felt that it might be wise to spend the entire Treasury surplus

---

[22] Hepburn, *History of Coinage and Currency in the United States and the Perennial Contest for Sound Money,* p. 163.

[23] See Appendix IV.   [24] See Appendix II.

[25] Kinley, *Independent Treasury,* p. 223.

[26] U.S., Treasury Dept., *Report of the Secretary, 1856,* p. 16.

[27] U.S., Treasury Dept., *Report of the Secretary, 1857,* p. 11.

[28] *Ibid.*

revenues to aid the liquid position of the banks, even if Government expenses would have to be met later by new loans.[29] In fact, on December 23, 1857, the balance was so low that the Treasury felt obliged to borrow $20,000,000 on short-term notes.[30]

Whether the Treasury action in this crisis was wise is a matter of controversy. The early restraining influence on excessive speculation certainly was beneficial. But the restraining influence of the Treasury was discontinued too soon and replaced by a policy of feeding the money market through the repurchase of Government bonds. The Secretary offered help too far in advance of the real crisis and thus held out hope to speculators that they could rely on further aid.[31] It had been said that the accumulations in the Treasury vaults should have been permitted to increase until the speculation faltered and the crisis was at hand, for premature disbursements from the Treasury may intensify rather than mitigate financial distress. Whatever its effect on speculation, the specie outflow strengthened the banks and made resumption of specie payment of bank notes easier. The latter occurred about the middle of December, 1857.[32]

In retrospect it is, perhaps, easier to note wherein Treasury action to mitigate the crisis of 1856 might have been improved. We now can see the successive events of 1856 and 1857 in their true perspective, and we have learned much since that time about the causes and the nature of depressions.

Monetary theorists who believe that crises can be alleviated by Government disbursement of money might assert today that the Treasury in 1857 poured funds into the market too soon.[33] They seemingly overlook the fact that the Treasury used whatever knowledge and means it had at its disposal; the Treasury's only important weapons were its specie holdings. As for proper timing, too little was known of the causes of crises and their customary course to help Cobb in the timing of Treasury disbursements.

---

[29] U.S., Treasury Dept., *Report of the Secretary, 1857*, p. 12; Kinley, *Independent Treasury*, p. 222.

[30] 11 Stat. 257; Love, *Federal Financing*, Appendix, item 97; Dunbar, *Laws of the United States Relating to Currency, Finance and Banking*, p. 149; see also Appendix II, below.

[31] Chapman, *Fiscal Functions of the Federal Reserve Banks*, p. 30.

[32] Dewey, *Financial History of the United States*, p. 254.

[33] For a later depression, for example, 1873, they might maintain that the Treasury assistance came too late. See p. 70.

How was the Secretary of the Treasury to be able to apply exactly the correct remedy at precisely the correct moment when there was a general disagreement about the cause of the depression? Free traders, including Henry C. Carey, contended that high duties tend to produce crises,[34] while financiers, such as Samuel Hurd Walley, maintained that there would be little danger of crises if all business were conducted by barter or with hard money. According to Walley, it was to the introduction of the credit system that these troubles must be laid.[35] Edward Everett went further and said,

If I mistake not, the distress of 1857 was produced by an enemy more formidable than hostile armies; by a pestilence more deadly than fever or plague; by a visitation more destructive than the frost of Spring or the blights of Summer. I believe that it was caused by a mountain load of Debt.[36]

The remedy was to keep out of Debt. George Dutton in his exposition of the Crisis of 1857 stressed the psychology of businessmen and declared that "only a little confidence was needed" to restore prosperity.[37] Gouge held that the remedy was to do away with banks. By inflating the currency, he said, they raise prices above the level of other countries, inducing an unfavorable balance of trade and gold exports. As the notes are presented to the banks for specie to be shipped abroad, the banks are forced to call in their loans, contract the currency, and precipitate a fall in prices. The fall in prices checks imports and stimulates exports causing a reflux of specie into the country. The banks get renewed confidence, expand their loans and the cycle repeats itself.[38] Secretary Cobb had his own ideas; he felt that a stringency might be caused by the Treasury accumulations in its vaults, and accordingly he sought to relieve the situation by putting his idle funds into circulation by purchasing bonds.[39]

Qualitative theorists today might maintain that the difficulty was, not in the timing of the purchases of bonds by the Treasury, but in the type of investments which the banks had made. If they had extended loans for self-liquidating transactions instead of long-term

---

[34] Carey, *Financial Crises: Their Causes and Effects*, p. 8; Miller, *Banking Theories in the United States before 1860*, p. 188.

[35] Walley, *The Financial Revulsion of 1857*, p. 9.

[36] Everett, *Mount Vernon Papers*, p. 167.

[37] Dutton, *The Present Crisis or the Currency*, pp. 4–16.

[38] Gouge, *A Short History of Paper Money and Banking in the United States*, p. 25.

[39] U.S., Treasury Dept., *Report of the Secretary, 1857*, p. 12; see also Appendix V, below.

investments, the liquid position of the banks might not have been threatened at all. A fair judgment of Cobb's activities must admit that the Secretary of the Treasury did the very best that he could with the materials and knowledge at his disposal. In depleting the Treasury surplus to protect and strengthen the banking situation and general business, he subordinated fiscal considerations to the central banking activities of the Treasury.

A very desirable result of the existence of the Independent Treasury at that time was the maintenance of specie payments by the Government. Had the public money been deposited in the banks or had the receipt of bank notes for public dues been lawful, the Treasury would have been as seriously embarrassed as it was at the beginning of the Panic of 1837. At that time, the attempt of the Government to withdraw its deposits in order to meet its obligations weakened the banks and added to the general panic and pressure. Twenty years later, in 1857, the disbursement by the Government of its own funds which it had kept readily available in its own vaults, supplied the banks with specie, and strengthened their liquid position.[40]

By the summer of 1858 the bank crisis was over, but recovery had not set in when toward the end of 1859 the threat of secession of the southern states disturbed business again. The Treasury felt this long depression severely, for beginning with the summer of 1857 the customs receipts were steadily falling off.[41] From July, 1856, to June, 1861, the current needs of the Government could not be met by the revenues, and the accumulated deficit amounted to $65,000,000.[42] The Treasury borrowed, under the terms of the Act of June 14, 1858 (11 Stat. 365), $20,000,000 in fifteen-year, 5 percent bonds, and under the Act of June 22, 1860 (12 Stat. 79), another $21,000,000 in 5 percent bonds and $10,000,000 in 6 percent Treasury notes.[43]

THE INDEPENDENT TREASURY DURING THE CIVIL WAR

Borrowing from Banks

The lack of a surplus, insufficient revenue for the prosecution of the Civil War, and a system of taxation which could not easily be adjusted to the varying needs of the Government compelled the Treas-

[40] U.S., Treasury Dept., *Report of the Secretary, 1857*, p. 20.
[41] *Ibid.*, p. 6; see also Appendix IV, below.   [42] See Appendix III.
[43] Love, *Federal Financing*, Appendix, Items 98, 99, 100.

ury to borrow heavily in order to finance the Civil War. The Independent Treasury System was set up in time of peace and might have gone on functioning as originally planned, but for the intervention of the Civil War. This war created an emergency situation more grave than the Mexican War, and the general welfare was more directly and more seriously involved in all Treasury actions. During the Mexican War the Treasury did not have to depend upon the assistance of the banks, since the Mexican War lasted for only a brief period of time; the war was popular especially with the wealthy investors, and at the beginning of the war the Treasury held a large amount of specie which had come from heavy import revenues. The circumstances surrounding the Civil War were different. Treasury gold holdings were small; the country was divided in patriotic feelings; and the war dragged on for four years.

The Government attempted to maintain itself independent of the banks and on a specie basis, which formed the keystone of the Independent Treasury System. But large funds had to be raised quickly, and there seemed to be no alternative to borrowing. Under the Act of July 17, 1861, Secretary Chase applied to the banks for a loan of $50,000,000, payable in three years.[44] This solicitation of aid from the banks was a step away from the principle on which the Independent Treasury System had been built.[45] However, it was only a partial abandonment, since the Treasury still asked for gold and refused to receive bank notes. Also, the banks were not yet allowed to handle Government receipts or to have the custody of its money. The Act of July 17, 1861, was a necessity. The Government needed funds, and the only large accumulated stock of gold was in the banks. The banks were in a good financial position, since the recent decline of the southern and western business and the depression of 1860 had brought about a decrease in their loans and deposits and a corresponding relative increase in their specie reserves.[46] The banks welcomed the loans to the Government, since they filled their portfolios with quasi-short-term commercial paper. Government money expended in military operations eventually found its way back to the banks and enabled them to make further advances.

[44] U.S., Treasury Dept., *Report of the Secretary, 1861*, p. 8; 12 Stat. 259.
[45] Chapman, *Fiscal Functions of the Federal Reserve Banks*, p. 31.
[46] Beckhart, ed., *The New York Money Market*, Vol. I, p. 195.

While borrowing the gold of the banks to prosecute the war, Mr. Chase was also unintentionally driving bank notes from circulation by the issue of additional Treasury notes.[47] The increasing volume of Treasury notes in circulation led to a diminished demand for bank notes. The bank notes presented for redemption created a new drain on the gold reserves of the banks. The latter could furnish the Secretary of the Treasury with gold or they could sustain the redeemability of their notes, but they could not do both. They urged the Secretary of the Treasury to accept and to use bank notes and to cease the issue of additional Treasury notes. But Secretary Chase felt that the insistence on payment in specie was an important feature of the Independent Treasury Law. Also, the specie received provided backing for the Treasury notes. If he accepted bank notes, instead of specie, the Treasury notes might circulate at a discount. The Government credit had to be maintained at all cost. Thus the Secretary of the Treasury refused to accept bank notes, and in December, 1861, the banks suspended specie payment.[48]

If the Treasury had accepted bank notes, it would have been a departure from the Independent Treasury Law. But then possibly the banks might not have been compelled to suspend, and the Government could have kept the spirit of the specie clause of the law. It seems that the actions of the Treasury were not very wise. In avoiding Scylla, Secretary Chase was drawn into Charybdis. He had hoped to avoid both the acceptance of bank notes in payment of revenues to the Government, and the suspension of specie payments, but on January 6, 1862, the Government also dishonored its own promise and ceased paying coin.[49]

Thus another one of the important provisions of the Independent Treasury Act of August 6, 1846 (9 Stat. 59) became ineffective. It is to be remembered that among the important provisions of the second Independent Treasury Act were separation of the Treasury activities from the banks and the insistence that all payments to and by the Government be made in specie. With the advent of the Civil War the Treasury was compelled to turn to the banks for aid in financing the emergency. The Treasury and the banks resumed definite and direct

---

[47] Treasury Notes of 1861, about $22,500,000 issued under the Act of March 2, 1861, interest rate was 6 percent; two-year maturity; receivable for all dues (12 Stat. 178). See Love, *Federal Financing*, Appendix, Item 102.

[48] U.S., Treasury Dept., *Report of the Secretary, 1862*, p. 7.   [49] *Ibid.*

relationships. Furthermore, when the banks stopped advancing gold to the Treasury, the Treasury was compelled to pay with paper. From 1862 until the resumption of specie payments (1862–1879), the Subtreasury law was largely in abeyance.[50]

In earlier periods experience had proved that as long as the Treasury possessed surplus revenues it could assist the banks should a stringency arise.[51] Now, when the Treasury revenues were not sufficient for its expenditures, the Treasury became a burden rather than a help to the banks. It can at such times resort to increased taxation, issue fiat money, or borrow. If borrowing is used, the assets of the banks may change radically. The banks may become too heavily burdened with Government paper and be forced temporarily to restrict their loans to the business community. Usually Treasury fiscal policies affected the bank reserves and care had to be exercised that banking interests were not injured in supplying Government fiscal needs.[52]

Issue of Bonds

Secretary Chase thought that "the safest, surest, and most beneficial plan" of financing the war "would be to engage the banking institutions . . . to advance the amounts needed for disbursement."[53] First having borrowed from the banks directly, he later turned to the banks for assistance in selling bonds. This new departure from the tenets of the Independent Treasury System, that is, coöperation with the banks, was justified on the ground that the Treasury did not have machinery adequate for placing the loans required for the conduct of the war. The banks possessed the equipment necessary for selling bonds. Time and effort would be saved by using the existing machinery of the banks. The object of turning to the banks simply was to secure the much needed money and to secure it quickly. Secretary Chase wished the loans popularized so that people everywhere might subscribe for bonds. According to an early plan of Chase, in many places agents were employed who received their directions from the Treasury Department.[54] But funds came in too slowly. The plan had to be

[50] Kinley, *Independent Treasury*, p. 79.
[51] See above, p. 52, Secretary Guthrie in the Stringency of 1853.
[52] U.S., Treasury Dept., *Report of the Secretary, 1856*, p. 32.
[53] U.S., Treasury Dept., *Report of the Secretary, 1861*, p. 8.
[54] U.S., Treasury Dept., *Report of the Secretary, 1863*, p. 14.

abandoned and the entire work of selling bonds proved too difficult for the Treasury itself and was entrusted to an agent, the experienced banker, Jay Cooke.[55]

Greenbacks

In July, 1864, Secretary Fessenden, who succeeded Secretary Chase and refused to coöperate with the banks, found it necessary to raise more money. The Treasury again tried to procure funds through a direct sale of Government bonds. Fessenden advertised a loan but had to withdraw it because of an insufficient number of subscriptions. He was forced by this failure to turn to the banks, but was unwilling to meet their terms. He then issued "greenbacks" as a last resort,[56] under the authority of the three acts passed during Secretary Chase's term.[57] Three issues of greenbacks, totaling $450,000,000, were authorized by March 3, 1863, and by July, 1864, $431,000,000 were outstanding.[58] This fiat money (acceptable for all dues except customs), was a desperate method of financing a deficit and clearly constituted an addition to the circulating medium of the country.[59] It was a direct cause of inflation.[60] Specie had long been drained from the banks and hoarded, and the banks continued to suspend specie payments of their notes. The Treasury seemed to be at the end of its resources.

The National Banking System

The establishment of the National Banking System by the Act of June 3, 1864 (13 Stat. 113), was an open acknowledgment of the insufficiency of the Independent Treasury System for fiscal purposes in times of emergency. In fact, the primary purpose of creating the National Banking System was to provide a new market for Government bonds.[61] The law was an effort to force the banks to sustain

[55] Dewey, *Financial History of the United States*, p. 311.
[56] Kinley, *Independent Treasury*, p. 297.
[57] U.S., Treasury Dept., *Report of the Secretary, 1864*, p. 3; Act of February 25, 1862, amount authorized $150,000,000, 12 Stat. 345; Act of July 11, 1862, amount authorized $150,000,000, 12 Stat. 532; Act of March 3, 1863, amount authorized $150,-000,000, 12 Stat. 719; Love, *Federal Financing*, Appendix, Item 108.
[58] U.S., Treasury Dept., *Report of the Secretary, 1864*, p. 43.
[59] See Appendix VII, below.
[60] U.S., Treasury Dept., *Report of the Secretary, 1865*, pp. 8–15.
[61] U.S., Treasury Dept., *Report of the Secretary, 1862*, p. 8.

the public credit,[62] since under the system ownership of bonds of the Government would be required for certain banking purposes. This in turn would establish a steady market for the bonds and greatly facilitate their negotiation. Prices for the bonds would be maintained at a level higher than that of bonds of equally satisfactory quality, but not available as security for the circulation of national bank notes.[63]

During the Civil War funds were needed desperately, and the vaults of the banks were the only places where large amounts of money could be obtained in the early days of the war. The Secretary of the Treasury was compelled to turn to the banks as purchasers of bonds, and the terms had to be adjusted to suit the buyers. But the Treasury had been draining the banks of their specie, and the Treasury notes were replacing bank notes. New loans could be sold to the banks only if the Treasury permitted them to issue national bank notes against the newly acquired Government bonds. The result was a national bank note currency based on Federal Government bonds with the Government acting as guarantor of the bank notes. This relationship between the Government and the banks was entirely contrary to the aims and purposes of the Independent Treasury Law.

The Act of August 6, 1846 (9 Stat. 59), was virtually inoperative during the Civil War. The first step in the abandonment of the principle of separation of banks and Government was the use of banks to float loans. The second step was to make the banks the depositories of the public money which they received as subscriptions to Government loans.[64] Suspension of specie payments by the Treasury on January 6, 1862,[65] and the issuance of greenbacks under the Act of February 25, 1862 (12 Stat. 345),[66] cut away the last foundation of the Act of 1846.

The only important service of the Independent Treasury that continued throughout the war and afterward was keeping on hand the supply of gold received in payment of customs dues to pay the interest on the public debt in gold during the period of paper inflation.[67] If

---

[62] *Ibid.*, p. 16; Kinley, *Independent Treasury*, p. 299.

[63] U.S., Treasury Dept., *Report of the Secretary, 1862*, p. 18; Dewey, *Financial History of the United States*, p. 328.

[64] Section 45, Act of June 3, 1864; 13 Stat. 113; Dunbar, *Laws of the United States Relating to Currency, Finance and Banking*, p. 188.

[65] See above, p. 60.   [66] See above, p. 61.

[67] Kinley, *Independent Treasury*, p. 304.

the financial management of the war had been such as to render unnecessary the use of depreciated paper currency there would have been no special need for this service from the Independent Treasury.

Reserve Requirements and the Position of the Treasury under the National Banking Act

The keystone of the National Banking Act was the provision for a bank-note issue collateralized by bonds issued by the Federal Government. These notes were acceptable for all private transactions and were to provide the country with a sound and uniform currency. Another important section of the act provided for minimum cash reserve requirements against deposits and notes outstanding which revealed a sensible, progressive step in banking legislation conforming to the best banking practices. Reserve and central reserve cities were designated wherein the requirements were, respectively, 15 percent and 25 percent of deposits and note issues.[68] Note issues were no longer included in the computation of reserves after the Law of 1874.[69]

A declining reserve ratio had been considered a warning signal by prudent bankers long before 1863. But the reserve ratio had not then obtained full legal recognition as a controlling element in the banks' credit policies. Before 1863 the reserve ratio was a "slip·leash which loosely held together the cash reserve and the total of bank credit outstanding; from 1863 to 1913 it was a rope of limited length which jerked the banks up sharply if they ventured too far in the direction of expansion." [70]

At the time of the establishment of the National Banking System, the feeling still persisted that the first duty of a bank was to keep its notes redeemable. This attitude is reflected in the original requirement of the National Banking Act that a reserve in lawful money be held against national bank notes in addition to the bond collateral which more than covered them. But as the credit economy developed more fully, bank loans took the form of deposits rather than notes. Soon the deposit of actual cash diminished and deposit credits arising from the extension of bank credit rapidly rose in volume. Now it be-

[68] Section 31, Act of June 3, 1864; 13 Stat. 108; Dunbar, *Laws of the United States Relating to Currency, Finance and Banking*, p. 184.

[69] Section 2 of the Act of June 20, 1874; 18 Stat. 123; Dunbar, *Laws of the United States Relating to Currency, Finance and Banking*, p. 210.

[70] Beckhart, ed., *The New York Money Market*, Vol. I, p. 234.

came of equal or greater importance to protect the depositor rather than the note holder. The banks' responsibility for these deposits was emphasized by a provision of the National Banking Act requiring a definite reserve to be held against them. Out of this first requirement grew the idea that the reserves against deposits must be kept safe and adequate. Also, in the National Banking Act the view was accepted that a definite supervision is needed over banking conditions for the purpose of enforcing the banking law and protecting depositors.[71]

Supervision of the reserve position of the national banks under the Federal charters was delegated to the United States Treasury. Within the Treasury the office of Comptroller of the Currency was created. This branch of the Treasury Department has been performing the task of inspecting the books and records of national banks ever since, thus assuming one more function usually entrusted to a central bank.[72]

SUMMARY

The relationship between the Treasury and the commercial banks during the period of 1846 to 1866 consisted primarily of efforts on the part of the Treasury to exercise certain financial powers usually entrusted to central banks, such as guarding the money market during national emergencies, periods of war,[73] periods of stringencies,[74] and of depressions.[75] Paradoxically enough, the Treasury tried to achieve its aims through the manipulation of machinery designed primarily to divorce the Treasury from participation in the affairs of the money market.[76] Instead, the Treasury fulfilled its fiscal functions and central banking functions through active coöperation with the banks and unquestioned leadership in the monetary sphere.

[71] Section 54, Act of June 3, 1864; 13 Stat. 116; Dunbar, *Laws of the United States Relating to Currency, Finance and Banking*, p. 189.

[72] U.S., Federal Reserve System, Board of Governors, *Federal Reserve System; Its Purposes and Functions*, p. 33.

[73] On Mexican War see Secretary Walker, p. 51; on Civil War, secretaries Chase and Fessenden, pp. 57–61.

[74] On Stringency of 1853 see Secretary Guthrie, p. 52.

[75] On Crisis of 1856 see Secretary Cobb, p. 53–54.

[76] Brown, "The Government and the Money Market," in Beckhart, ed., *The New York Money Market*, Vol. IV, p. 185.

CHAPTER IV

Treasury Central Banking after the Civil War and under the National Banking System
1866–1889

WITH THE RETURN of peace the problems and aims of the Treasury changed. Instead of the subordination of every activity to the main goal of winning the war by adequate financing, the restoration and maintenance of a sound system of money and credit became the primary aim.

TREASURY SALES OF SURPLUS GOLD IN 1866 AND THEIR EFFECTS ON CURRENCY AND BANKING

After 1862, under the Independent Treasury system, gold, not legal tender currency,[1] was received for custom duties and paid out mostly for interest on the Government debt. The amount of gold coin received for customs dues far exceeded that paid out for interest on the public debt.[2] But gold was not used in ordinary commercial transactions, since it was more valuable than the depreciated currency— the national bank notes and the greenbacks which circulated widely. The suspension of specie payments on January 6, 1862, also had produced speculation in gold.[3] The violent speculations in the value of the metal reacted on all prices.[4] The Secretary of the Treasury, McCullough (March 3, 1865–March 9, 1869), deplored these effects and

[1] Greenbacks were not acceptable as payment for custom dues under the Act of February 25, 1862 (12 Stat. 345). The reason for excluding them was the desire on the part of the Treasury to accumulate gold. For the same reason the Treasury did not permit custom payments to be deposited in national banks. With the resumption of specie payments, greenbacks were accepted at the customs offices. U.S., Treasury Dept., *Annual Report of the Secretary, 1879*, p. 11. Custom dues could not be deposited in national banks until the passage of the Act of March 4, 1907 (34 Stat. 1290) ; see also below p. 72, footnote 38.

[2] See Appendixes IV and V.

[3] U.S., Treasury Dept., *Report of the Secretary, 1862*, p. 13; U.S., Treasury Dept., *Report of the Secretary, 1866*, p. 9.

[4] *Ibid.*, p. 12; see also Appendix VIII, below.

felt that some stability in the general price level might be produced if the Treasury gold holdings were sold and the price fluctuations of gold reduced.[5] In 1866, therefore, the Secretary of the Treasury sold surplus gold and took in payment other currency.

Gold transactions between the Treasury and the banks established another contact, frowned upon by the original Independent Treasury Act of August 6, 1846 (9 Stat. 59). Sales of gold gave the Treasury a method of changing the composition of the reserves of banks. By selling gold just as by selling bonds, the Government received legal tender in payment and the legal tender reserves of the banks were decreased, while the gold reserves of the banks increased. McCullough hoped that the sale of Treasury gold might encourage the use of gold as currency, that the price of gold might decrease, and that other commodity prices might change accordingly. However, the Secretary of the Treasury did not carry the idea of stabilizing prices to its logical conclusion; although willing to sell surplus gold, he refused to permit gold which came in payment of custom duties to be deposited in the banks. Secretary McCullough, in his report for 1866, explained that the purpose of holding gold in Treasury vaults was to form a reserve against the irredeemable currency, greenbacks. The function he assigned to the gold in the Treasury was precisely the same as a bank's reserve against its issues. He claimed also that the sale of gold reduced its premium and thereby limited the depreciation of United States Treasury notes.[6]

Secretary McCullough was interested in keeping prices and the currency stable.[7] He thought that by changing the supply of gold available in the market he could help achieve his aim. Thus his interests reached well beyond the confines of the fiscal activities of the Treasury. Through gold sales he could exert an influence upon prices and banking which is normally associated only with central banks. Secretary McCullough was not blind to his powers, and he tried to exercise them for the public benefit.

[5] U.S., Treasury Dept., *Report of the Secretary, 1866,* p. 9. "The Secretary of the Treasury permitted gold to accumulate when the use or the sale of it was not necessary for paying government obligations, or to prevent commercial panics, or successful combinations against the national credit; and he has sold whenever sales were necessary to supply the Treasury with currency, to ward off financial crises, and to save the paper circulation of the country, as far as practicable, from unnecessary and damaging depreciation." U.S., Treasury Dept., *Report of the Secretary, 1866,* p. 10

[6] *Ibid.,* p. 10.   [7] *Ibid.,* p. 9; Dewey, *Financial History of the United States,* p. 368.

After 1866 sales of gold by the Treasury brought into its vaults such a volume of paper currency that the Secretary of the Treasury had to resort finally to the purchase of bonds in order to put this currency back into circulation.[8] Sales of gold by the Treasury took so much money out of the market that Secretary of the Treasury Boutwell (March 12, 1869–March 16, 1873) finally decided that the proceeds should be kept on deposit with the banks, to be withdrawn gradually to avoid a sudden credit contraction.[9] Other deposits of Government funds in the national banks were very small during this period, because only the proceeds from sales of bonds and collections of internal revenue could be kept outside the Treasury.[10] The latter could be put into banks only at the time of their collection, while custom receipts of gold were placed directly into the vaults of the Sub-treasury.[11] These regulations proved very burdensome and were disregarded later on.[12]

To observe the letter of the Independent Treasury law regarding specie holdings was difficult for a Secretary of the Treasury who was conscious of the great responsibilities of his office and of the market's needs. Secretary McCullough had sold gold and taken legal tender in payment because he thought putting gold on the market would stop speculation in the metal and bring about price stability.[13] Secretary Boutwell felt called upon to deal with the money stringency in the market in the autumn of 1872.[14] He, too, had to reconsider the tenet of the Independent Treasury Law. The sale of gold by the Treasury had resulted in the Treasury's keeping the legal tender currency and the banks the gold which did not enter into circulation. For the relief of both importers and bankers Secretary of the Treasury Boutwell decided to sell gold in large amounts, but he also agreed to name banks as depositories for the proceeds of these gold sales. Similar action had been taken by the Treasury in connection with land sales

---

[8] U.S., Treasury Dept., *Annual Report of the Secretary, 1872*, p. xxi; U.S., Treasury Dept., *Annual Report of the Secretary, 1873*, pp. xi–xii.

[9] *Ibid.*, p. xx.   [10] Appendix II, below.

[11] Beckhart, ed., *The New York Money Market*, Vol. I, p. 355; see also above, p. 62.

[12] See below, p. 103, section on Secretary Shaw.

[13] U.S., Treasury Dept., *Report of the Secretary, 1866*, p. 9.

[14] U.S., Treasury Dept., *Annual Report of the Secretary, 1872*, p. xxi. "The problem is to find a way of increasing the currency for moving the crops and diminishing it at once when that work is done. This is a necessary work, and, inasmuch as it cannot be confided to the banks, where, but in the Treasury Department, can the power be reposed."

during the Civil War. Again, the reserves of the banks rose immediately. Not only was this action of Secretary Boutwell commendable
but it also clearly revealed his motives. It is evident that the secretaries of the Treasury were interpreting their duties to include not
only the fiscal activities of the Treasury but also the safeguarding of
general business conditions. The leadership and guardianship which
these men assumed properly belong to the head of a central bank.

In spite of gold sales and the legal-tender deposits in the banks by
the Treasury, the stringency of 1872 continued, and the Treasury
adopted the most direct way of increasing the currency supply known
to finance—the issue of fiat money. The total supply of United States
notes was increased by about $2,295,000 to meet the need for cur-
rency, especially in moving the crops.[15] Secretary Richardson (March
17, 1873–March 3, 1874) the successor to Secretary Boutwell, went
still further in 1873.[16] He also used the "reserve" of retired and un-
issued greenbacks when he found that the refunding of bonds was
inadequate.[17]

This particular means, manipulation of the public debt, for increasing the supply of currency and strengthening the reserves of
banks was not resorted to on a large scale, but the ingenuity of the
Treasury was adequate to find other means of increasing the currency supply.[18] In 1873 the Treasury again bought Government bonds
to increase the currency in circulation, and it strengthened bank reserves by transferring gold and legal tender from the vaults of the
Independent Treasury to the banks.

TREASURY ACTIONS INTENDED TO MITIGATE THE PANIC OF 1873

The Panic of 1873 brought still further development of the Treasury as a central banking mechanism. The forerunner of the disaster

[15] Dewey, *Financial History of the United States*, p. 360; Patton, "Secretary Shaw
and Precedents as to Treasury Control over the Money Market," *Journal of Political
Economy*, Vol. XV (February, 1907), pp. 80–81; U.S., Treasury Dept., *Annual Report
of the Secretary, 1872*, contains no reference to the reissue of greenbacks; see Appendix
VII, below.

[16] Between March 7, 1873, and January 15, 1874, he issued about $23,000,000 in
greenbacks. U.S., Treasury Dept., *Annual Report of the Secretary, 1874*, p. 20; U.S.,
Treasury Dept., *Annual Report of the Secretary, 1879*, p. 374; see Appendix VII, below.

[17] Patton, "Secretary Shaw and Precedents as to Treasury Control over the Money
Market," *Journal of Political Economy*, Vol. XV (February, 1907), pp. 74–75.

[18] Brown, "The Government and the Money Market," in Beckhart, ed., *The New
York Money Market*, Vol. IV, p. 193.

was the money stringency in the fall of 1872 to which the gold sales of the Treasury had contributed. Secretary Boutwell had lessened the money afloat by selling gold to a greater extent than he had bought bonds. As the gold could not circulate, the net result had been a loss of currency to business. So far as this process had not occurred in the spring and fall, the seasons at which the interior demand for money was most active, it was not very objectionable. The years 1871, 1872, and 1873 were years of great speculation, and the absorption of currency through gold sales by the Treasury had restricted the ability of the banks to loan, and so had somewhat retarded speculation.[19]

The banks had become accustomed to looking to the Secretary of the Treasury for help in an emergency.[20] The Secretary of the Treasury had been called upon to relieve the stringency in the fall of 1872. The autumnal demand for funds was always great, and the Secretary of the Treasury had tried to help the market. He had sold gold and deposited the proceeds in designated banks. Also, he had bought bonds. Reserves had risen immediately, and the banks had enlarged their discounts.[21] But the stringency persisted. The Secretary of the Treasury then went further. He issued fiat money. But even that measure was not sufficient. In fact, during December, a month when money is in demand, the banks lost heavily to the Treasury, despite the remonstrances of the mercantile community.[22] Heavy payments due to the Treasury from customs dues should have been left on deposit with the banks, but even that measure might not have helped. Treasury indecision and half measures also characterized the year 1873. No definite, consistent, and continuous policy was adopted for guiding the relations of the Treasury to the business community. The stringency degenerated into a panic.

On the eighteenth of September, 1873, Jay Cooke and Company,

[19] U.S., Treasury Dept., *Annual Report of the Secretary, 1874,* p. 17; see Appendix II, below.

[20] U.S., Treasury Dept., *Annual Report of the Secretary, 1857,* pp. 11–13 (quoted on p. 54, above); U.S., Treasury Dept., *Annual Report of the Secretary, 1873,* p. xv. "It should be stated that there were many persons who insisted with great earnestness that it was the duty of the executive to disregard any and all laws which stood in the way of affording the relief suggested by them—a proposition which indicates the state of feeling and the excitement under which applications were made to the Secretary of the Treasury to use the public money." *Commercial and Financial Chronicle, December 6, 1890,* Vol. LI, p. 754 (quoted on p. 88, below).

[21] U.S., Treasury Dept., *Annual Report of the Secretary, 1873,* pp. xi–xii.

[22] Dewey, *Financial History of the United States,* p. 372.

a leading firm of New York bankers, was suspended.[23] During the first nine months of the year Secretary Richardson had taken no action to ease the situation. Now, on the nineteenth of September, he ordered the purchase of bonds and continued buying until the twenty-fifth.[24] The panic was not stopped, because most of the money disbursed by the Government seems to have been hoarded.[25] Some of it went into savings banks, but this did not help the general situation.[26]

Economists who adhere to the quantity theory of money would claim that the Treasury did not accomplish its purpose of checking the panic because it did not take steps early enough. They would say that the proper time for the purchase of bonds was before the suspension by Jay Cooke and Company. After the failure of that firm, suspicion and distrust were too strong to be stopped by the limited aid which the Government could give. Quantitative theorists have maintained that in almost every crisis the fault lay in the timing or in the amount of funds disbursed.

Secretary Richardson summarized the situation thus: "The panic ran its course and the reason is obvious: what was needed was a reëstablishment of confidence in the enterprise which had been the primary source of distrust. But no amount of money disbursed by the Government could produce this result." [27] The summation of Secretary Richardson was wise, and he seemed to understand one of the causes for the lack of confidence: the faulty investment policies of the banks. Credit conditions were strained.[28] The commercial banks had invested funds in long-term capital enterprises, especially in railroads. The funds, now frozen, should have been invested in short-term self-liquidating commercial ventures. The banks would probably not have been pressed for funds if their investments had been liquid. The Treasury tried to inject liquidity into the banking structure, but it did not have the discount power. It could not convert sound assets into cash. The Treasury recognized its duties and used whatever methods it had at its disposal; the sale of gold, the purchase of bonds, the issuance of fiat money, the use of the "reserve" of retired greenbacks,

[23] U.S., Treasury Dept., *Annual Report of the Secretary, 1873*, p. xii.
[24] *Ibid.*, p. xv.
[25] U.S., Comptroller of the Currency, *Annual Report, 1876*, pp. 177, 251.
[26] U.S., Treasury Dept., *Annual Report of the Secretary, 1873*, p. xv; Sprague, *History of Crises under the National Banking System*, p. 69.
[27] U.S., Treasury Dept., *Annual Report of the Secretary, 1873*, pp. xv–xvi.
[28] *Ibid.*, p. xvi.

and so forth. If the results were unsatisfactory, the intentions of both Secretary Boutwell and Secretary Richardson were not at fault.

THE TREASURY AND THE RESUMPTION OF SPECIE PAYMENTS

Benjamin H. Bristow (June 4, 1874–June 20, 1876) followed Richardson as Secretary of the Treasury, in June, 1874, and was a vigorous champion of sound finance. He regarded the Government's failure to provide for resumption of specie payment a breach of the Nation's pledges. In his opinion the United States notes were merely a temporary expedient, warranted only by the exigency of the war. Redemption was essential to the honor of the Government and the general welfare.[29] To accomplish this, contraction was necessary. Accordingly, he recommended legislation which would fix a day in the near future when the United States notes would cease to be legal tender as to contracts thereafter made.[30] He advocated also the conversion of the United States notes into bonds or their redemption in coin, for the acquisition of which sales of bonds should be authorized.[31]

In the spring of 1874 Senator Sherman, later Secretary of the Treasury, had already prepared a bill which contained, among other clauses, provisions for the retirement of greenbacks to the extent of 80 percent of new national bank note issues, until the amount of the former was reduced to $300,000,000; the redemption of greenbacks in coin on and after January 1, 1879; authorization of the use of the surplus coin in the Treasury for this purpose and the sale of bonds without limit to provide such further coin as might be needed. This bill became law January 14, 1875,[32] and gave greater powers to the Secretary of the Treasury than the Act of April 12, 1866,[33] which had merely aimed at a contraction of unsecured paper currency and promotion of specie payments.

There was a good deal of opposition to resumption of specie payments and retirement of the greenbacks in the areas south of the Potomac and west of the Alleghanies. This great and growing agri-

---

[29] U.S., Treasury Dept., *Annual Report of the Secretary, 1874*, p. xiv.
[30] *Ibid.*   [31] *Ibid.*, p. xv.
[32] Dunbar, *Laws of the United States Relating to Currency, Finance and Banking*, p. 215; 18 Stat., 296.
[33] Dunbar, *Laws of the United States Relating to Currency, Finance and Banking*, p. 199; 14 Stat., 31.

cultural section needed capital and favored rising prices. It advocated "more paper money" and accordingly centered its efforts on further issues of greenbacks, the type of currency which could most easily be immediately increased. The inflationists won a mild victory in the Act of May 31, 1878,[34] which forbade the further retirement of United States legal-tender notes. The volume of greenbacks was pegged at the circulation figure of that day—$346,681,016.

As the date for resumption of specie payments drew near, the Secretary of the Treasury began to accumulate gold against the resumption of its notes.[35] Under the Refunding Act of July 14, 1870,[36] the Secretary of the Treasury had been authorized to save future annual surpluses and to sell bonds in order to accumulate a gold fund to redeem in specie all greenbacks presented. By the day of resumption the total Treasury reserve was more than $133,000,000.[37]

The Act of July 14, 1870 (16 Stat. 274) had placed a heavy responsibility on the Secretary of the Treasury because too great an accumulation of gold would result in a gold premuim and render resumption impossible. Inadequate accumulations would also doom the plan. But fortune favored Secretary Sherman. European investments had brought much gold into the country. Treasury acquisitions did not produce a shortage. In addition Secretary of the Treasury Sherman could readily sell bonds to acquire the necessary gold for resumption. At the close of the first day of resumption the Treasury had paid out more greenbacks for gold than gold for greenbacks. So great was the Treasury's gold reserve that in September, 1879, eight months after resumption, Secretary Sherman ordered that gold need not be accumulated any longer and should be paid out for Government obligations along with notes and silver whenever convenient to do so.[38]

[34] Dunbar, *Laws of the United States Relating to Currency, Finance and Banking*, p. 217; 20 Stat., 87.

[35] U.S., Treasury Dept., *Annual Report of the Secretary, 1879*, p. xi.

[36] Dunbar, *Laws of the United States Relating to Currency, Finance and Banking*, p. 205; 16 Stat., 274.

[37] U.S., Treasury Dept., *Annual Report of the Secretary, 1879*, p. ix.

[38] *Ibid.* With the resumption of specie payments, greenbacks would be acceptable for payment of custom dues. The reason for excluding custom dues in the Act of June 3, 1864 (13 Stat., 99) from deposit in national banks was that they were paid in gold which the government wanted to accumulate, while the banks carried on their transactions in discounted paper money. The exception remained on the statute books until March 4, 1907 (34 Stat., 1290), although the occasion for its existence ceased with the resumption of specie payments. Andrew, "The Treasury and the Banks under Secretary Shaw," *Quarterly Journal of Economics*, Vol. XXI (August, 1907), p. 523.

Readiness on the part of the Treasury to redeem greenbacks in coin was sufficient to give the United States notes the solid backing which other currency, such as gold certificates, enjoyed. In this way the greenbacks ceased to be the cheaper money and a step had been taken toward securing a safe and stable currency of uniform value. The latter is an objective of a central bank. If an authority such as a central bank had existed in 1879, it might have gone much further along the lines of creating a uniform, safe, and stable currency by advocating the retirement of the United States notes, which in reality were a war debt and should have been canceled. But Secretary Sherman was interested in politics and would not jeopardize his chances of a presidential nomination by advocating the unpopular retirement of the greenbacks. There were too many people interested in increasing the quantity of money and in inflation. Under the circumstances resumption was as far as Secretary Sherman dared go. Soon afterward the inflationists found that to coin silver was an easier way to increase the stock of money.

SILVER POLICIES OF THE UNITED STATES TREASURY

In the Coinage Act of February 12, 1873, there was no provision for the coinage of standard silver dollars.[39] The bill had been before Congress nearly three years, and yet the inflationists were unaware of the omission and of its implications until after the bill was passed. If the "sound money" men knew, they did not confide in the inflationists.[40] When the latter learned of the omission of the coinage provisions for the standard silver dollar they declared the act "a crime" and maintained that the existing economic troubles in the entire commercial world were due to a diminishing money supply. To overcome the money shortage they urged free coinage of silver. The "silverites" won a partial victory in the Bland Allison Act of February 28, 1878, which provided for the purchase and coinage of not less than $2,000,000 and not more than $4,000,000 worth of silver per month.[41] Due to

[39] Dunbar, *Laws of the United States Relating to Currency, Finance and Banking*, p. 241; 17 Stat., 424.

[40] Hepburn, *History of Coinage and Currency in the United States and the Perennial Contest for Sound Money*, p. 279.

[41] Dunbar, *Laws of the United States Relating to Currency, Finance and Banking*, pp. 245–248; 20 Stat., 25.

this additional coinage of silver the volume of circulating currency increased, but the effect was partly offset by the decreasing volume of national bank notes.[42] Resumption of specie payments had improved the credit of the Nation, and as a result Federal Government bonds sold at a premium. At the prevailing high prices the banks found it more profitable to sell their holdings of Federal bonds than to deposit them with the Comptroller as backing for their national bank notes.

None of the secretaries of the Treasury who held office from 1880 to 1890 were silver advocates.[43] They were not carried away by the inflationist movement and thought that existing legislation made sufficient provisions for the monetary needs of the Nation. They were mindful of their duty to help maintain a stable currency. They knew that the overissue of silver might lead to a decline in the value of silver and that it would force the readjustment of other commodity prices.[44] Therefore each secretary kept the Treasury purchases of silver down to the minimum prescribed by the Bland Allison Law. Such action was commendable and worthy of an impartial authority dedicated to the public welfare.

Under the act new silver dollars were made legal tender and acceptable at the Treasury for customs along with gold.[45] One of the results of this provision was that silver dollars poured into the Treasury and remained there.[46] The policy of the secretaries of the Treasury

TABLE III

SILVER DOLLARS, 1878–1879[a]

	December, 1878	December, 1879
Silver dollars coined	$18,282,000	$45,206,000
Silver dollars in circulation	4,922,000	13,002,000
Silver dollars in treasury	13,360,000	32,204,000

[a] U.S., Treasury Dept., *Annual Report of the Secretary, 1883*, p. xxix.

[42] U.S., Treasury Dept., *Annual Report of the Secretary, 1879*, p. 353; see also Appendix VII, below.

[43] U.S., Treasury Dept., *Annual Report of the Secretary, 1884*, p. xxviii; U.S., Treasury Dept., *Annual Report of the Secretary, 1885*, Vol. I, p. xvii.

[44] U.S., Treasury Dept., *Annual Report of the Secretary, 1879*, p. xiv.

[45] Act of February 28, 1878, Section 3; Dunbar, *Laws of the United States Relating to Currency, Finance and Banking*, p. 248; 20 Stat., 25.

[46] See Table III and U.S., Treasury Dept., *Annual Report of the Secretary, 1879*, pp. 334, 346.

throughout the decade was to keep silver in circulation, but the people preferred any form of money to silver. The unpopular large silver coins returned to the Treasury, whereas gold and greenbacks remained in circulation. The Treasury was anxious to have an adequate gold reserve and decided to force silver dollar circulation on a reluctant country. Silver certificates in denominations of $1, $2, and $5 were issued against silver bullion in the Treasury vaults. The issue of greenbacks in these lower denominations was stopped.[47] By this action, the Treasury was diminishing one form of paper money in circulation and replacing it by silver certificates, without disturbing the total quantity of money in circulation. However, the easy money policy involved the silver purchase program and contributed toward the speculative excesses preceding the Panic of 1884.

TREASURY POLICIES DURING THE PANIC OF MAY, 1884

The panic was confined to the New York security market and its banking aspects were simple and definite. The difficulties of 1884 were the culmination of the period of prosperity which had marked the recovery from the Panic of 1873. There had been a decline in security prices for three years.[48] Apparently banks were in a very strong cash position. This was partly due to an artificial cause, the monthly addition of $2,000,000 of silver under the provisions of the Bland Allison Act, of February 28, 1878 (20 Stat. 25). Silver purchases by the Treasury had the effect of permitting unwanted coins eventually to accumulate with banks which could use them as reserves.

As the market in securities became depressed, orders to sell and remit funds were received. But the outflow of gold caused by orders to sell was offset by the steady additions of silver. Total reserves were not reduced. No general money stringency resulted. The interest rate on loans did not advance.[49] The failure of certain banks, the Marine Bank of New York, the Metropolitan Bank,[50] and brokers helped bring on the panic. Cash was withdrawn into the interior of the country, but this did not result in suspension of specie payments by the

[47] U.S., Treasury Dept., *Annual Report of the Secretary, 1884*, pp. xxxiv, 403.
[48] Kinley, *Independent Treasury*, p. 236.
[49] Sprague, *History of Crises under the National Banking System*, p. 108.
[50] Conant, *History of Modern Banks of Issue*, pp. 661–662.

New York banks. The Secretary of the Treasury, Folger (November 14, 1881–September 4, 1884), lent his assistance through the usual devices, especially the prepayment of the debt which was soon to mature.[51]

If the emergency had been more serious or more widespread, the problem of pyramided reserves might have received immediate attention by the banking communities. Under the prevailing system the interior banks had kept their surplus reserves on deposit with the New York banks. After the Panic of 1884 some thought was given to the safety of these reserves in New York. The banking communities of Chicago and St. Louis felt their reserves might be safer at home and sponsored legislation to that end.

AMENDMENT TO THE RESERVE CLAUSES OF THE NATIONAL BANKING ACT

The first change in the system of reserves provided for in the National Banking Act was made in the Act of March 3, 1887.[52] Cities with minimum population of 50,000 might on application of three-fourths of the national banks in those cities become reserve cities, and cities with minimum population of 200,000 might become central reserve cities. Chicago and St. Louis became central reserve cities, with the responsibility of maintaining cash reserves of 25 percent and the attendant privilege of holding reserve balances for reserve city and country banks. Banks in reserve cities and in country areas were to maintain reserves against demand liabilities of 18 percent and 15 percent, respectively.

Little attention had so far been paid to reserves in banking legislation. In the period following the Panic of 1873 popular demand centered upon an increase in the amount of money in circulation rather than upon changing reserve requirements, which is a more refined technique of increasing the amount of currency and credit available. It is true that the Act of June 20, 1874,[53] altered the reserve provision of national banks by requiring reserve percentage to be com-

---

[51] Chapman, *Fiscal Functions of the Federal Reserve Banks,* p. 35; Kinley, *Independent Treasury,* p. 236; see also Appendix V, below.

[52] 24 Stat., 559; Dunbar, *Laws of the United States Relating to Currency, Finance and Banking,* p. 224.

[53] 18 Stat., 123; Dunbar, *Laws of the United States Relating to Currency, Finance and Banking,* p. 210.

puted thereafter only against deposits. Notes, which were anyhow secured by Government bonds, were no longer included in the computation of required legal tender reserves. This released about $20,-351,000 of greenbacks which had been in vaults as reserve against notes.[54] The effect of this change was to provide banks with additional reserves and to appease the inflationists by increasing the quantity of money.

The use of actual cash in the American banking system was steadily diminishing. A larger volume of credit was being built upon a smaller base of specie and legal tenders. This economy in the use of metals and currency was made possible by the substitution of deposit credit for cash payment in ordinary transactions so that banks were able to meet daily requirements with relatively less till money than before.[55]

In general, the highly industrial sections of the country which were equipped with more adequate banking facilities tended to keep as large a share of their reserves in the form of bank balances as the law permitted and a small proportion in cash, while the agricultural sections followed the reverse policy. The highest proportion of reserves in the form of cash was to be found in the western states. This showing was a reflection of the preference for coin money which still prevails in the West.

The increased use of deposit credit in place of cash and the increased practice of keeping reserves in the form of bank balances meant greater risks to the banks and greater interdependence. With greater interdependence an urgent need developed for a central reserve authority to supervise and safeguard the central reserve funds. Otherwise it was likely that these funds might be tied up in frozen assets or moved hither and thither according to the speculative propensities of the bankers to whom they had been entrusted. If the cash position of the banks in the central reserve cities became impaired, repercussions certainly would be felt in the interior. The lack of elasticity in reserves was another drawback. A central agency was clearly needed with legal authority and adequate funds to convert sound assets of hard-pressed banks into immediate cash. The Treasury did not possess the rediscount privilege, but it tried with the

[54] U.S., Treasury Dept., *Annual Report of the Secretary, 1874*, p. xx.
[55] Beckhart, ed., *The New York Money Market*, Vol. I, p. 239.

devices at its command to supply hard-pressed banks with cash. Various secretaries of the Treasury considered themselves charged with the central banking function of supervising credit conditions.[56] The secretaries could be of great assistance to the banks when the Treasury coffers were filled.[57] In the eighteen eighties high protective tariffs helped fill the Treasury vaults.

TREASURY POLICIES DURING THE PERIOD OF THE SURPLUS, THE EIGHTIES

The principal source of Treasury revenue was the Morrill Tariff, Act of March 2, 1861 (12 Stat. 178), which was permitted to remain highly protective and at wartime level long after the Civil War. During the eighties the Treasury coffers were filled. But advocates of cheap money, greenback partisans, and silverites regarded the revenue in the Treasury vaults as a hoard of currency unavailable for circulation and as an unmitigated evil.[58]

They maintained that if the Government would pay off its bonded indebtedness so as to avoid having an idle surplus, there would be no evil effects from alternate contraction and expansion of currency by the Independent Treasury.[59] Their opinion, however, was an oversimplification of the true state of affairs, since it overlooks certain features of the system. Custom receipts of the Government flow into its vaults in a steady stream, while interest, amortization and salary payments are paid periodically. The Treasury must therefore gather beforehand a sufficient amount of cash to meet its periodic payments. For example, to meet the interest on bonds money may have to be

[56] U.S., Treasury Dept., *Annual Report of the Secretary, 1857*, p. 13; U.S., Treasury Dept., *Annual Report of the Secretary, 1866*, p. 10; U.S., Treasury Dept., *Annual Report of the Secretary, 1873*, p. xv.

[57] "But the continuing depression, universal in varying degrees over the world obliges us all now to consider and undertake some reforms which our surplus revenues make feasible." U.S., Treasury Dept., *Annual Report of the Secretary, 1885*, p. xiv.

[58] "If we take into the Treasury large amounts of these circulating media in excess of what we pay out, there will soon not be money enough in the hands of the people for the purpose of business; serious derangement and disaster must follow." U.S., Treasury Dept., *Annual Report of the Secretary, 1887*, p. xxvi; Beckhart, ed., *The New York Money Market*, Vol. I, p. 366.

[59] The only authority possessed by the Treasury whereby it can restore to business the surplus money thus accumulated, is that given to the Secretary by the Act of March 3, 1881, by which he may at any time apply the surplus money in the Treasury not otherwise appropriated, to the purchase or redemption of United States bonds. U.S., Treasury Dept., *Annual Report of the Secretary, 1883*, p. XLV; 21 Stat. 457.

withdrawn from circulation for three months; and at the end of the quarter it will be released and find its way back into the banks. This irregularity of Treasury disbursements and receipts seriously interfered with the stability of the money market.[60]

It is true that payments made by the Government every three months amounted to a small sum compared with the total volume of the circulating medium. But even a slight contraction in the amount of money available for reserves may have an important effect on the money market, especially if reserves are near the legal minimum. Contraction (though apparently insignificant in amount) may contribute to or even produce a money stringency. This in turn may result in a violent reaction in the general level of price, a disturbance in interbank settlements and disorder in almost every part of business activity.[61]

In addition to the disturbing influences of the seasonal irregularity of receipts and disbursements of the Independent Treasury, the accumulating surplus revenue not needed for periodic payments presented further problems. This surplus was held in the Treasury. By that policy a large amount of money collected in excess of the expenses of Government was withdrawn from actual circulation. To acquire a surplus was not the intention of the Treasury, but to hold a possible surplus in its own vaults was definitely a policy of the Independent Treasury System. The result of holding surplus revenues in the Treasury was pressure for funds in the money market, especially in the autumn, when money was needed for harvesting. The shortage of funds was felt more severely in agricultural areas, and the western banks had to call in their loans or restrict the advances to their town customers. If the Treasury surplus had been kept in the commercial banks, subject to the call of the Government, the evils of hoarding might have been avoided. But the Treasury was not permitted by law to keep customs receipts, the largest form of revenue, in the banks.[62] As a way out of this dilemma the Treasury adopted a policy of spending its surplus funds on the repurchase of Government bonds. When the surplus revenue became too large the Secretary of the Treas-

[60] U.S., Treasury Dept., *Annual Report of the Secretary, 1882*, p. xxviii.
[61] Grosvenor, *American Securities*, pp. 216 ff.; Turner, *Member Bank Borrowing*, p. 13.
[62] See Appendices III–IV.

ury resorted to buying bonds, if necessary, even at a premium. This seemed to be a wise way to spend the surplus hoard.[63]

In the fall and winter of 1887, for instance, a stringency occurred which was closely related to the accumulation of surplus revenues in the Treasury.[64] The idle hoard had been a serious danger for several years, and Secretary Fairchild (April 1, 1887–March 6, 1889) thought he ought to help check impending financial pressure by restoring money to trade. Accordingly, he purchased bonds in the open market.[65] But by 1888 the entire short-term debt had been retired.[66] No other issues were due or callable. Secretary Fairchild then went into the open market and bought Federal bonds, although he had to pay a premium—sometimes even as high as 29 percent.[67] These purchases in turn caused a further rise in the price of the bonds, making this method of distributing the surplus more and more expensive.[68]

This method of reducing the surplus had been used by Secretary Guthrie (1853–1856) and Secretary Cobb (1857–1859),[69] but Fairchild resorted to prepaying the debt on an even larger scale.[70] The implications of retiring the public debt on our monetary system were far-reaching. The Federal debt was the foundation of an important element of the country's currency. The national bank notes had to be backed by a 100 percent reserve consisting of Federal Government bonds. With a redemption of these bonds, the volume of national bank notes decreased just when an expansion of currency was needed. The amount of Federal bonds outstanding constituted the ceiling beyond which national bank notes could not be issued.

In 1887–1888 the Treasury surplus was so large [71] that bond pur-

---

[63] U.S., Treasury Dept., *Annual Report of the Secretary, 1883*, p. xxx.

[64] Conant, *History of Modern Banks of Issue*, p. 666.

[65] U.S., Treasury Dept., *Annual Report of the Secretary, 1887*, p. xxvii; see also Appendix V, below.

[66] *Ibid.*, p. xxviii.

[67] Public opinion was opposed to such purchases, since under the Act of March 3, 1881 (21 Stat., 457), no reference had been made to bond purchases above par. Resolutions were adopted by both houses of Congress on April 17, 1888, to the effect that it was lawful and proper to invest the government surplus in bonds at the premium necessary to obtain them. U.S., Treasury Dept., *Annual Report of the Secretary, 1888*, pp. xxvi–xxvii.

[68] U.S., Treasury Dept., *Annual Report of the Secretary, 1887*, p. xxvii.

[69] See pp. 67–71.

[70] Andrew, "Partial Responsibility of Secretaries Gage and Shaw for the Crisis of 1907," *Bankers Magazine*, Vol. LXXVI (April, 1908), p. 493.

[71] See Appendix III, below.

chases alone were not sufficient to disburse it.[72] Fairchild decided to increase Government deposits in national banks. That public money (except customs dues) might be deposited in national banks was a part of the National Banking System.[73] However, it was regarded as an exceptional method, to be used only in emergencies.[74] In the course of the Civil War the banks which helped place loans were allowed to retain the funds from bond sales (sometimes $30,000,000 to $40,-000,000) until they were used. Throughout the seventies public deposits rarely reached $10,000,000, except during the refunding operations of 1879, when the proceeds of new bond sales were temporarily left in the banks pending the retirement of old bonds. During the early eighties the amount of public funds deposited in national banks were somewhat higher, but they did not at any time rise above $10,000,000.[75]

Fairchild's new policy of depositing public funds in the national banks made Government deposits jump to $54,000,000 by 1888. Depository banks had to give the Treasury satisfactory collateral in the form of "United States bonds and otherwise." [76] The amount of deposits banks could receive had been limited to 90 percent of the par value of the bonds pledged as collateral. This rule was now changed to allow maximum deposits fully equaling the par value of the 4½ percent bonds and even as high as 110 percent of the 4 percent bonds.[77] In justification of his new rulings Fairchild pointed out that the interpretation of the clause "satisfactory collateral in the form of the United States bonds and/or otherwise" had been left to the discretion of the Secretary of the Treasury. Secretary Fairchild wished to place much of the surplus revenue into the hands of the banks so that pressure for funds might be mitigated.[78] Consequently he interpreted satisfactory collateral to mean, not collateral exceeding the deposits, but deposits equaling or exceeding the collateral. In this fashion he could increase Treasury deposits. Secretary Fairchild always con-

[72] U.S., Treasury Dept., *Annual Report of the Secretary, 1887*, p. xxvii.
[73] See below, p. 80.
[74] U.S., Treasury Dept., *Annual Report of the Secretary, 1887*, p. xxviii.
[75] See Appendix II, below.
[76] The phrase was later interpreted by Secretary Shaw to read, "United States bonds or otherwise." This interpretation helped him to meet the central banking problem of a Treasury surplus. See p. 104.
[77] *Commercial and Financial Chronicle,* Vol. XLV (October 15, 1887), p. 488.
[78] Andrew, "The Treasury and the Banks under Secretary Shaw," *Quarterly Journal of Economics,* Vol. XXI (August, 1907), p. 525.

sidered the needs of the banks, and his guardianship over the general banking situation shows that he acted like the head of a central bank.

However, the effects of the changed ruling concerning Government deposits were not entirely satisfactory. As a result of the increase in Government deposits, bonds needed to secure national bank notes were used as collateral for Government deposits in the national banks and the volume of national bank notes outstanding fell.[79] Further Government deposits were, therefore, stopped by Secretary Fairchild in 1888 in an attempt to halt the decline of national bank note circulation.

TABLE IV

NATIONAL BANK NOTES, 1884–1889 [a]

Date	Issued	Retired	Decrease
July 30, 1884	$2,778,960	$ 7,883,997	$ 5,105,037
1885	2,160,110	5,731,673	3,571,563
1886	1,469,325	8,425,486	6,956,161
1887	2,936,670	11,307,718	8,371,048
1888	6,188,531	15,115,185	8,926,654
1889	1,376,200	11,791,639	10,415,438

[a] Andrew, "The Treasury and the Banks under Secretary Shaw," *Quarterly Journal of Economics,* Vol. XXI (August, 1907), p. 527.

Secretary Windom, who took office in 1889 (March 7, 1889–January 29, 1891), was a strict observer of the letter of the Law of 1846. He believed that the policy of depositing public money in banks was wholly unjustifiable. Accordingly, he gradually reduced Government deposits.[80] These frequent reversals of Treasury policy concerning deposits in national banks clearly show that the money market was at the mercy of the man who happened to be Secretary of the Treasury. Bank reserves increased or decreased depending upon the views of the secretaries and their actions. Government deposits readily lent themselves to favoritism; and the withdrawal of deposits disturbed business. Both gave the Secretary of the Treasury the power, according to Mr. Windom, to "expand or contract the currency at will." [81]

[79] See Table IV; see also U.S., Treasury Dept., *Annual Report of the Secretary, 1893,* p. 389.

[80] See Appendix II, below.

[81] Secretary Windom thought the Treasury's power to change the amount of currency was dangerous. U.S., Treasury Dept., *Annual Report of the Secretary, 1889,* p. lxxxviii; Secretary Boutwell said that the power to change the volume of paper in circulation should remain in the Treasury Department. U.S., Treasury Dept., *Annual Report of the Secretary, 1872,* p. xx.

The surplus disappeared during Secretary Carlyle's term (March 7, 1893–March 5, 1897), and it did not reappear until 1900, under Secretary Gage (March 6, 1897–January 31, 1902).[82] Decreasing revenues were partly responsible for the disappearance of the surplus. The enormous Treasury surplus had been attacked in the Presidential campaign. Both candidates promised reduction of taxation. This was carried out. The McKinley Tariff Act of October 1, 1890 (26 Stat. 567) lowered the duties on sugar and other large revenue yielding commodities not produced to any considerable extent in the United States. All revenue receipts declined during the business depression of the early eighteen nineties.[83]

A Treasury surplus began to reappear with the business recovery of 1900. The Dingley Tariff Act of July 24, 1897 (30 Stat. 151) and new higher taxes further added to the Treasury funds. In 1900 the Treasury balance had passed the $200,000,000 figure.[84] Secretary Gage (March 6, 1897–January 31, 1902) met the situation in the same manner as had Fairchild (April 1, 1887–March 6, 1889). He also increased Treasury deposits in national banks to almost double the figures of Fairchild. His policy was assailed bitterly, but deposits in July, 1901, increased to $93,442,683.[85] Treasury activities in the nineties, however, were not primarily attempts to deal with a surplus. The Crisis of 1893 and the financing of the Spanish-American War presented a challenge to the wisdom and efficiency of the Treasury. How these problems were met will be shown at some length in the next chapter.

SUMMARY

The relationship of the Independent Treasury to the commercial banks of the country was in some respects similar to that of a central banking institution. While the Independent Treasury Act had been designed to sever the connections which the Treasury had with the banks, no such separation could actually be accomplished. It is true that the Treasury became its own depository, keeping and disbursing its funds. But these activities gave the Treasury an opportunity to influence the reserves of banks to a much greater extent than before 1846.

[82] See Appendix III, below.

[83] Andrew, "The Treasury and the Banks under Secretary Shaw," *Quarterly Journal of Economics,* Vol. XXI (August, 1907), p. 528; see also Appendix IV, below.

[84] See Appendix II, below.   [85] *Ibid.*

During the years 1866–1890 the Treasury was faced with many problems; periods of Treasury surplus revenues and several periods of depression. The secretaries of the Treasury consistently went well beyond the confines of a mere fiscal department. They devised methods of meeting the monetary problems which a central bank would normally have faced. The techniques employed varied and revealed the legal limitations imposed upon the Treasury and the ingenuity of the secretaries. These men were making the Treasury, in some instances unintentionally, function as a central banking organization.

Most of the men who managed the affairs of the Treasury, including Guthrie, Cobb, Boutwell, Richardson, Sherman, Folger, Fairchild, and others were conscious of the wide influence which the fiscal activities of the Treasury had upon the reserves of the commercial banks throughout the country. Activities which influence bank reserves properly belong in the hands of a central bank. A central bank is under obligation to see that its activities safeguard the commercial banking structure. Since no central bank existed in the United States, some of the secretaries of the Treasury, perhaps unintentionally, filled the void. But most of the men knew that the influence of their activities paralleled those of a central bank, and they tried to change or interpret the laws under which the Treasury functioned to protect and support also the banks and the business community. Others, including Windom, felt the Secretary of the Treasury should be guided mainly by the needs of the Treasury Department. This view may be sound in times of prosperity relatively free from disturbances, but in times of emergency intervention by the Treasury is not only desirable but necessary. The Treasury was often in a position to help the banks, and no other agency existed that could render assistance. The banks and the business community in turn were becoming accustomed to regard the Treasury as a superior financial authority which could and would render assistance in time of difficulty.

CHAPTER V

The Independent Treasury as the Real Central Bank 1890–1912

DURING THE PERIOD from 1890 to 1912 the problem associated with the surplus of the eighties disappeared and the Treasury's chief concern centered about the deficit. A slight decline in the ability of the Treasury to influence and help the banks will be noted during the period of the deficit. However, as the Treasury revenues again begin to increase, opportunities arose during times of money stringencies and panics which tested the wisdom of the secretaries of the Treasury, as well as the strength and weakness of the Independent Treasury as a central banking organization.

1890–1898
TREASURY DEFICITS AND SLIGHT DECLINE IN TREASURY CENTRAL BANKING

The Treasury Activities during the Money Stringency of 1890

In the summer of 1890 a money stringency occurred. In the panics of 1873 and 1884 the causes were primarily of domestic origin. In this crisis the United States was involved in a disturbance which had its origins elsewhere.[1] Excessive speculation developing in England had culminated in the Baring failure in November, 1889. English investment bankers then found themselves with more foreign securities than the English investment market could absorb. England not only stopped buying but also sold American railroad securities and withdrew the proceeds in the form of gold during July and August, 1890. There was an outflow of gold during those months. Loss of gold due to sales of American securities by London bankers was sufficiently large to affect bank reserves and to dimin-

[1] Sprague, *History of Crises under the National Banking System*, p. 124.

ish the currency available for early fall requirements.[2] A shortage of bank reserves produces effects more marked and more prompt (the curtailment of credit extension and the recalling of loans) than an excess of reserves which may remain unused. American importers who had increased their purchases in anticipation of the McKinley Tariff Act of October 1, 1890 (26 Stat. 567) discovered that they could not get the customary credit extensions when their bank loans fell due. In addition, the payment of higher duties under the new tariff threatened to sterilize for a time even more currency and potential bank reserves in idle Treasury holdings.

Furthermore, speculation had become rampant in anticipation of an inflation to be expected from new silver legislation. Mr. Windom (March 7, 1889–January 29, 1891), in his first report, in 1889, had come forth with a novel idea regarding silver.[3] He recommended the issue of Treasury notes against the deposit of silver bullion to the extent of the market price of the silver when deposited; the notes were to be redeemable in either gold or silver. Secretary Windom believed in a strict interpretation of the letter of the Independent Treasury Law. Accordingly he had set about decreasing the public deposits in national banks with its inevitable deflationary effects.[4] But the fear of a panic in 1890 disturbed the Secretary, and he was not entirely deaf to the political pleas of the inflationists. He thought he could evolve a scheme to win over the inflationists and still not appear to be changing his strict views on the Independent Treasury Law of 1846. Six new northwestern states had just been created, and their representation in the Senate added considerably to the strength of the advocates of free silver.

The scheme proposed by Secretary Windom led to the enactment of a bill, which was passed on July 14, 1890, known as the Sherman Silver Purchase Act. It authorized and instructed the Secretary of the Treasury to purchase 4,500,000 ounces of silver bullion each month and to issue in payment thereof Treasury notes of full legal tender.[5] This meant an increase in the currency at home, and American credit suffered abroad.[6] The new supply of currency backed by

---

[2] *Commercial and Financial Chronicle,* Vol. LI (August 2, 1890), p. 124.

[3] U.S., Treasury Dept., *Annual Report of the Secretary, 1889,* pp. lxxiv–lxxxiv.

[4] *Ibid.*, p. lxxxviii.   [5] 26 Stat. 289.

[6] Beckhart, ed., *The New York Money Market,* Vol. I, p. 376; see also Appendix VII, below.

silver had a temporary effect in easing the stringent money market. However, a greater supply of currency was not in itself sufficient for a restoration of confidence in the money market.[7] This would require the correction of the maladjustments in a faulty money and banking structure. But the Secretary's most pressing problem was that, not of long-range reform, but of immediate assistance to the money market. The disturbance in the money market during the summer and autumn months was partly caused by foreign withdrawals of gold, which in turn led to insufficient reserves in New York. The decrease in reserves in the early fall of 1890 was due not only to gold exports but also to the customary withdrawal of funds for crop-moving purposes. In the task of assisting the money market he was obliged to follow the methods of his predecessors.

Secretary Windom disbursed unusually large amounts of money ($99,000,000).[8] He started buying bonds as early as July 19, 1890, and continued until November 1. In addition, the Treasury's ordinary quarterly interest payments were made in September instead of October.[9] The assistance which he gave was effective; reserves of the New York banks rose, and the interest rate on call loans fell. Government disbursements succeeded in counteracting the disturbance of the summer and autumn months. This assistance rendered by the Treasury to the money market is usually that associated with a central bank, not that of a Government fiscal agency.

When the stringency recurred in November, 1890, it was caused primarily by a general lack of confidence in the general business outlook [10] and a precautionary marshaling of cash reserves by banks in the West, which had previously kept a large part of their reserves on deposit with New York banks. Again the Treasury responded to the appeals for help, and it aided the banks in regaining their cash position, although the ability of the Government to help had diminished.

By the early nineties the Treasury was regarded as the ultimate

[7] *Commercial and Financial Chronicle*, Vol. LI (November 15, 1890), p. 655; Kinley, *Independent Treasury*, p. 238.

[8] U.S., Comptroller of the Currency, "Annual Report, 1891," in U.S., Treasury Dept., *Annual Report of the Secretary, 1891*, p. 326.

[9] U.S., Treasury Dept., *Annual Report of the Secretary, 1891*, p. xxvi.

[10] U.S., Comptroller of the Currency, "Annual Report, 1891," in the U.S., Treasury Dept., *Annual Report of the Secretary, 1891*, p. 326; Kinley, *Independent Treasury*, p. 240.

source of help in time of need. The banks turned to the Treasury to fulfill the function of a central bank. In tranquil times the banks were not willing to recognize the Treasury as a central bank, because that would have meant changes in their mode of operation and their individualistic attitude.[11] Instead they preferred to expect the Treasury to fulfill central banking functions only in times of stress. To such an extent did the banks depend on the Treasury that they no longer prepared even for the regular fall stringency. The *Commercial and Financial Chronicle* describes this situation as follows:

The time was when our banks provided beforehand for the fall trade and so trimmed their sails through the summer months to avert a storm by preparing themselves for the crop demand. Of late years they have looked to the Treasury wholly and have gone through the summer trenching on their reserves regardless of any increased drain sure to come later on.[12]

Whether the Treasury should aid the money market was much discussed by financial writers. Most agreed that it was proper for the Treasury to restore to general circulation money which had been recently withdrawn. Secretary Windom yielded to public opinion which was largely that of the inflationists and which stressed the fact that a Treasury surplus served no purpose if permitted to lie idle in the vaults.[13] On the other hand, it was argued that if used it would allay a stringency and safeguard the credit structure of the country. These arguments prevailed with Secretary Windom, and he followed a policy of his predecessor—spending the Treasury surplus by purchasing Government bonds. This action did increase the supply of money.[14] A Treasury surplus is too unreliable a foundation for a national credit structure, because its existence depends upon an excess of revenues over expenditures and it cannot be expected that there will always be an excess. In addition, funds for the

---

[11] "Admirable in many respects, experience shows that our banking system is devised for fair weather, not for storms. This can be clearly shown. The individual banks stand isolated and apart, separated units, with no tie of mutuality between them. There is no obligation of duty from the strong to the weak or exposed, nor any method of legal association for common protection or defense in periods of adversity and depression." U.S., Treasury Dept., *Annual Report of the Secretary, 1901*, pp. 79–80.

[12] *Commercial and Financial Chronicle*, Vol. LI (December 6, 1890), p. 754.

[13] See above, p. 82, the quotation from the statement of Secretary Fairchild, Windom's predecessor, U.S., Treasury Dept., *Annual Report of the Secretary, 1887*, p. xxvi.

[14] See Appendixes V and VII, below.

money market and for crop-moving purposes should be provided by the banks, not by the Treasury.

The Treasury in the Crisis of 1893

In the panics of 1873, 1884, and 1890 the Treasury had given aid to the money market. In the Panic of 1893 the situation was reversed. The Treasury needed the aid of the banks and had to issue bonds during this crisis for the purpose of meeting a deficit.[15]

The Treasury was faced with a deficit as the decline of trade caused customs duties to shrink, in spite of the increased rate of the McKinley Tariff. Also, the Europeans doubted our ability to maintain the gold standard; orders to sell their holdings of American securities were increased, and gold had to be exported.[16] In addition, the Treasury's gold was at the mercy of the public, because a heavy demand for the redemption of notes in gold began in December, 1892, and continued throughout 1893. Notes presented for redemption included United States notes and Treasury notes of 1890. The Sherman Silver Purchase Act did not help the Treasury, for it required the purchase of 4,500,000 ounces of silver each month, to be paid for in legal tender notes. Nearly the entire increase in currency consisted of paper money based on silver,[17] resulting in an abundance of this cheap money.

The surplus revenue of the late eighties had been used in redeeming bonds, including even those selling at a premium.[18] Buying bonds had not only reduced the amount but also had raised the price of bonds available as a basis of national bank note circulation.[19] The circulation of notes of national banks had then begun to decrease. In 1892, however, the Treasury deficit forced the abandonment of bond purchases, thus checking the retirement of national bank notes.[20] At the same time silver legal tender issues

[15] Under Section 3 of the Specie Resumption Act, January 14, 1875 (18 Stat. 296), authority is given the Secretary of the Treasury to issue and sell United States bonds and to use such part of the proceeds as may be necessary to supply any deficiencies in the public revenue; U.S., Treasury Dept., *Annual Report of the Secretary, 1893*, p. lxx.

[16] U.S., Treasury Dept., *Annual Report of the Secretary, 1893*, p. lxxiv; Beckhart, ed., *The New York Money Market*, Vol. I, p. 397.

[17] U.S., Treasury Dept., *Annual Report of the Secretary, 1892*, p. xxx; U.S., Treasury Dept., *Annual Report of the Secretary, 1893*, p. 72; see also Appendix VII, below.

[18] U.S., Treasury Dept., *Annual Report of the Secretary, 1888*, p. xxvi.

[19] U.S., Treasury Dept., *Annual Report of the Secretary, 1887*, p. xxvii.

[20] See Table V.

TABLE V

NATIONAL BANK NOTES, 1888–1893[a]

Year Ending	Issued	Retired	Increase	Decrease
April 30, 1888	$7,755,416	$15,005,579	. . .	$ 7,250,163
April 30, 1889	1,179,165	11,789,161	. . .	10,609,996
April 30, 1890	3,469,345	8,496,305	. . .	5,026,960
April 30, 1891	1,397,135	6,578,579	. . .	5,181,444
April 30, 1892	3,217,945	3,934,429	. . .	716,484
April 30, 1893	4,735,660	2,267,346	2,468,314	. . .

[a] U.S., Treasury Dept., *Annual Report of the Secretary, 1893*, p. 389.

were rapidly increasing.[21] Both processes helped to produce inflation, and gold began to be exported. Prices in general were higher here than abroad, resulting in an unfavorable balance of trade and an adverse rate of exchange. Exports fell, and imports rose.[22] As early as May, 1892, the gold reserve fell to $114,000,000; it had been $133,000,000 in January, 1879.[23] The minimum was $100,-000,000, which Secretary Sherman had calculated was necessary to cover the paper currency in circulation in 1879.[24] The function of keeping the gold reserve of the country at an adequate figure was by implication assigned to the Treasury through the clause of the specie resumption law establishing the gold reserve.[25] This duty is usually delegated to a central bank.

TABLE VI

SILVER CERTIFICATES OUTSTANDING, 1888–1893[a]

Year Ending June 30	Silver Certificates Outstanding
1888	$229,491,772
1889	262,629,746
1890	301,539,751
1891	314,715,185
1892	331,614,304
1893	330,957,504

[a] U.S. Treasury Dept., *Annual Report of the Secretary, 1893*, p. 60.

[21] See Table VI.

[22] Sprague, *History of Crises under the National Banking System*, p. 157.

[23] U.S., Treasury Dept., *Annual Report of the Secretary, 1879*, p. 338.

[24] U.S., Treasury Dept., *Annual Report of the Secretary, 1893*, p. lxxxi.

[25] Not until the Act of March 14, 1900 (31 Stat. 45), was the Treasury's duty to keep the gold reserve of the country expressly established by law, and the amount was set at $150,000,000 in gold coin and bullion for the redemption of United States notes and notes issued under the Act of July 14, 1890. The Treasury may sell bonds to replenish the reserve (26 Stat. 289).

The gold receipts of the Treasury from customs payments diminished rapidly in 1892.[26] In addition, silver paper helped drive gold out of the country. More and more legal tender notes or greenbacks and silver certificates also appeared in bank reserves and in the general receipts of the Government. The composition of bank reserves changed. For many years the banks had supplied practically all the gold needed for export. Now their reserves consisted so largely of legal tender paper that the banks were compelled to turn paper currency into the Treasury for gold to meet the demands of their customers who needed the metal to send abroad. At the same time gold receipts of the Treasury were declining. By January, 1893, the Secretary of the Treasury had to ask the New York banks to supply gold in exchange for legal tender.[27] In April the Treasury gold reserve fell to the traditional minimum, and for the first time the issuance of gold certificates was stopped by the Treasury.[28] Public apprehension regarding the decrease in the gold reserve was becoming acute.

The Treasury was in the position of a bank which had issued more notes than it had reserves with which to redeem. This is a dangerous situation for the credit of the country which the Treasury is under obligation to protect.[29]

In addition to these complications the Treasury was faced with a deficit for ordinary expenses and was forced to draw on the gold reserve to meet them.[30] Thus there was a double drain upon the reserve to meet current expense and redeem legal tender notes. By February, 1893, the panic had come to the business world with the bankruptcy of the Philadelphia and Reading Railway Company, which occurred on the twenty-sixth of February. The failure of the National Cordage Company followed, in May. The public then began to hoard gold and the banks to lose their cash reserves. The severest panic came in midsummer. Reserves in the New York banks fell heavily, interest rates on call loans rose, and time loans could not be secured. Many banks refused to cash the checks even of their own depositors. About 578 banks failed, including 158 national banks.[31] Because of its own deficit, the Treasury was unable

---

[26] U.S., Treasury Dept., *Annual Report of the Secretary, 1892,* p. xxx; see also Appendix IV, below.

[27] U.S., Treasury Dept., *Annual Report of the Secretary, 1893,* p. lxxiii.

[28] *Ibid.*   [29] *Ibid.*

[30] *Ibid.,* p. lxx.   [31] *Ibid.,* p. 347.

to assist the banks and was not strong enough to maintain its own credit.

Clearly the Treasury was not fulfilling and could not fulfill the central banking function which it had formerly exercised, namely, that of helping the banks to increase their reserves. This period marked a temporary decline in the central banking activities of the Treasury.[32]

In August, 1893, a premium appeared not only on gold but also on paper currency. But a premium on currency had the effect of lowering the general price level in cash transactions. Lowered prices, in turn, induced foreigners to buy here. This change in the balance of trade again made the importation of gold possible. Furthermore, the premium on gold induced Americans to import gold to take advantage of its high value. As a result the tide finally began to turn.[33] Congress met in special session in August, and the President demanded the repeal of the Silver Purchase Act, which he argued was the sole reason for the financial crisis of 1893. In his opinion foreigners doubted the ability of the United States to maintain the gold standard and as a consequence were draining off our gold. The Sherman Silver Purchase Act of 1890 (26 Stat. 289) was repealed on November 1, 1893.[34]

Repeal of the act relieved the Treasury of its burdensome obligation to purchase a prescribed amount of silver, but it made no final provision for the retention or retirement of the $155,000,000 of Treasury notes issued under the Act of 1890 ($153,318,000 were outstanding on December 31, 1893).[35] On his own initiative Secretary Carlisle (March 7, 1893–March 5, 1897) who favored a gold standard adopted a policy of gradual retirement in accordance with the circumstances of the cash balance and by June 30, 1896, about $45,811,000 of the Sherman notes had been retired.[36] Final provision for their retirement was made in the Gold Standard Act of

[32] Years later, when a surplus appeared, the Treasury, under the leadership of Gage, Shaw, and Cortelyou, fully recovered from its temporary weakness and became the most important and dominating factor in the money market. It even assumed powers such as the head of a central bank would hesitate to assume.

[33] *Ibid.*, p. lxxiv.

[34] *Ibid.*; 28 Stat. 4; Dewey, *Financial History of the United States*, p. 445.

[35] U.S., Treasury Dept., *Annual Report of the Secretary, 1893*, p. lxxii.

[36] U.S., Treasury Dept., *Annual Report of the Secretary, 1896*, p. 113; see also Appendix VII, below.

1900 stipulating that the notes be withdrawn from circulation as rapidly as they returned to the Treasury.[37]

The repeal of the Sherman Silver Purchase Act and the importation of gold restored confidence in the monetary system. After the crisis of midsummer had passed hoarded currency returned to circulation, gold began to appear in Government receipts, and the gold reserve of the Government against notes outstanding temporarily rose to about $103,000,000. But by October, 1893, the reserve fell to about $81,000,000, due to the deficit in revenue,[38] and by June, 1894, it fell to about $65,000,000.[39]

Treasury Bond Sales, 1894-1898

In 1894 the Treasury found it necessary, in order to maintain its gold reserve, to sell a $50,000,000, 5 percent bond issue at 117.223. As the loan was not subscribed by the public, the Treasury asked the banks to take up the issue. The sale yielded $58,660,000 in gold, but the Treasury then had to redeem about $24,000,000 in greenbacks, with a corresponding loss of gold. In November another bond issue was sold, but the proceeds again did not for long replenish the gold supply of the Treasury, as most of the gold obtained was used to redeem greenbacks.[40] By 1895 the "endless chain" seriously threatened the gold reserves of the Treasury.

The "endless chain" worked somewhat in the following manner. Under the Specie Resumption Act of January 14, 1875, the Treasury was forced to redeem all greenbacks in gold that were presented for redemption.[41] But under the Act of May 31, 1878, the Treasury had to put greenbacks, once redeemed, back into circulation, since the total amount of greenbacks outstanding was to remain stationary.[42] This act had been passed in 1878 to satisfy the inflationist interests. The same greenbacks, first redeemed and then paid out, might again be presented for specie redemption.[43] If this re-

[37] 31 Stat. 47.
[38] U.S., Treasury Dept., *Annual Report of the Secretary, 1893,* p. lxxiii.
[39] U.S., Treasury Dept., *Annual Report of the Secretary, 1894,* p. lxviii; U.S., Treasury Dept., *Annual Report of the Secretary, 1928,* p. 550, Table 60.
[40] U.S., Treasury Dept., *Annual Report of the Secretary, 1894,* p. xix.
[41] 18 Stat. 296.   [42] 20 Stat. 87; see also above, p. 72.
[43] U.S., Treasury Dept., *Annual Report of the Secretary, 1893,* p. lxxv; Treasury notes issued under the silver purchasing act must be reissued when redeemed in gold, or, if canceled, standard silver dollars must be issued in their place; for if this were not done,

volving procedure were carried on quickly and frequently enough, a relatively small amount of greenbacks could take *all* the gold out of the Treasury. The Treasury was in the position of a central bank which found it almost impossible to maintain the value of its paper currency issues at par.

Late in 1894 the banks had given to the Treasury all the gold they could spare. An unfavorable balance of trade made the importation of gold extremely unlikely. In February, 1895, President Cleveland turned to a group of leading New York bankers for assistance. J. P. Morgan and H. P. Belmont took $50,000,000 of 4 percent thirty year bonds at 104½ and agreed not to withdraw gold from the Treasury and to induce others not to do so. In addition, the syndicate promised to deliver 300,000 ounces of gold each month for six months. The Government gold reserve rose to about $107,000,000.

At the same time a speculative boom broke out in England, embracing also American securities. Gold came into the United States in payment for American securities purchased by English investors.[44] Security prices rose rapidly also in New York, and soon foreign investors started selling some of their holdings and withdrawing the proceeds in the form of gold. Largely due to these gold exports, the Government gold reserve fell back to $61,000,000 in December, 1895.[45] The Treasury could not prevent the loss of gold and decided to strengthen its reserves by another bond sale. Accordingly, in January, 1896, the Treasury sold 4 percent bonds in gold for $100,000,000. This action on the part of the Treasury was based on Secretary Carlisle's (March 7, 1893–March 5, 1897) interpretation of the Specie Resumption Act of January 14, 1875, which directed the Treasury to accumulate a gold reserve fund or to sell bonds.[46] This loan was popular and oversubscribed. The Treas-

---

there would be a smaller amount of such notes outstanding than the cost of the silver bullion and the standard silver dollars coined therefrom and held in the Treasury, and this condition is expressly prohibited by the Act of July 14, 1890 (26 Stat. 289). Whether these notes are reissued or destroyed and standard silver dollars substituted for them, the practical result is the same; for in both cases the Secretary would be using notes redeemed in gold for the payment of the ordinary expenses of the Government or to procure coin to replenish the fund. U.S., Treasury Dept., *Annual Report of the Secretary, 1895*, p. lxvii.

[44] *Ibid.*, p. lxx.

[45] U.S., Treasury Dept., *Annual Report of the Secretary, 1896*, p. lxxi.

[46] 18 Stat. 296; see also pp. 71–72.

ury gold reserve rose to about $131,000,000 in February, 1896 [47] and from then on, the Treasury's difficulties were past. Its gold reserve steadily increased for the next two years. By 1898 the gold fund had reached $245,000,000.[48]

Treasury Activities during the 1890's

The Treasury difficulties during the nineties arose in part from the fact that the department was engaged in fiscal as well as banking operations. It had issued greenbacks in a national emergency and silver certificates to appease the inflationists. The Treasury was compelled by legislation to redeem them in gold. Inherent contradictions of the Specie Resumption Act of January 14, 1875, and the Act of May 31, 1878, caused the Treasury considerable trouble. On the one hand, the Treasury had to retire greenbacks which were presented for specie; while on the other hand, the Treasury was ordered to reissue the greenbacks once redeemed. The same greenbacks might come back for redemption several times. The Treasury notes of 1890 also presented a problem. If they were redeemed in gold, they must be reissued. If canceled, standard silver dollars must be issued in their place. Whether these notes were reissued or destroyed and standard silver dollars substituted for them, the Secretary would use the redeemed notes to pay for ordinary expenses or to buy more coin for the reserve fund.

To carry out these orders for any length of time the Treasury needed a huge gold supply. In addition, the Treasury paid ordinary expenses in gold when it was handicapped by a decline in the revenue. As a result, it had to borrow from banks to secure gold to pay its various obligations. The Treasury was drawing on the banks when they themselves needed funds. Consequently, bank reserves were decreased in order that the Treasury might maintain a currency convertible into gold. In fulfilling the latter central banking function, the Treasury had to humiliate itself by appealing to the banks to exchange its paper notes for gold. The Treasury, burdened by inconsistent laws, found itself unable to keep the gold reserve intact and place its own notes without the aid of brokers. The Treas-

---

[47] U.S., Treasury Dept., *Annual Report of the Secretary, 1896*, p. lxxii.
[48] U.S., Treasury Dept., *Annual Report of the Secretary, 1898*, p. xiii; Kinley, *Independent Treasury*, p. 253.

ury lost temporarily a good deal of its influence and power, but more important was the maintenance of the convertibility of the currency. This function the Treasury performed despite all handicaps.

The Treasury during the Spanish-American War

The Spanish-American War imposed new duties upon the Treasury, and they tended to relegate once more to the background whatever central banking functions the Treasury had tried to perform. In order to finance the Spanish-American War, Congress passed an act on June 13, 1898 (30 Stat. 466), providing for an issue of $400,000,000 in 3 percent bonds, of which $200,000,000 were offered at a uniform price of par. Some doubt was expressed whether bonds bearing so low a rate as 3 percent could be sold except at a discount. To avoid unnecessary risk, before the issue was released, the Secretary of the Treasury had arranged with New York underwriting syndicates—National City Bank, Vermilye and Company, Central Trust Company, and J. P. Morgan—to take up the bonds if the people did not subscribe to the issue in full. The syndicates were effective, not in taking up an unsold portion of the issue, for there was none, but in giving prestige to the loans. Secretary Gage said that it was the guaranty of the syndicates which "put spirit into the loan from the first moment." [49] It was a popular loan and was oversubscribed. Patriotism and the desire of the national banks to secure bonds for additional circulation made this flotation successful.[50] The Government was obliged, until it should spend the proceeds of the loan, to leave the money in the banks in order to prevent contraction of the currency.[51]

The bonds were sold at par, although there were reasons to believe that if competitive bidding had been permitted, the price would have been as high as 105.[52] That was the sacrifice made in order to allow a wide distribution of the bonds among the people at the uniform price of par.[53] Also the clerical costs of handling the

---

[49] Vanderlip, "Lessons of Our War Loan," *The Forum*, September, 1898, p. 29.

[50] U.S., Treasury Dept., *Annual Report of the Secretary, 1898*, p. lxxix.

[51] Vanderlip, "Lessons of Our War Loan," *The Forum*, Vol. XXVI (September, 1898), p. 27; see also Appendix II, below.

[52] Vanderlip, "Lessons of Our War Loan," *The Forum*, Vol. XXVI (September, 1898), p. 36.

[53] U.S., Treasury Dept., *Annual Report of the Secretary, 1898*, p. lxxxi.

loan directly through the Treasury Department were great.[54] Nevertheless, the Treasury felt that the expense of managing the loan and
the loss of a possible premium were overshadowed by the remarkable exhibition of faith in the Government's securities by people
of small means.[55]

During the Spanish-American War the Treasury confined itself
largely to the handling of Federal receipts and disbursements. It
sold bonds, received the customs duties which were collected, maintained an adequate gold reserve, and made the disbursements required during the war. It is true that the war was short and minor
in scope; nevertheless it is noteworthy that the Treasury did not
lean on the banks, and specie payments were not suspended. The
Treasury took no active part during this period in managing or influencing bank credit and the general banking situation. During
the Civil War financial conditions had been different. Specie payments were suspended, and the Independent Treasury accumulated
gold. The Government received gold in payment of duties. Most of
the gold remained in the vaults because the Treasury paid current
expenses with paper money.[56] No one wanted to pay his debts with
anything but depreciated currency. This state of affairs affected
prices and introduced an element of uncertainty into all business
transactions. Storing of gold caused speculation in gold itself, and
its price varied rapidly. These evils were avoided by the Treasury
during the Spanish-American War.

1899-1912

THE PERIOD OF REFORM AND MARKED INCREASE OF THE TREASURY CENTRAL BANKING ACTIVITIES

During the years 1896 to 1912, inclusive, the secretaries of the
Treasury assumed greater central banking powers than those enjoyed by the head of any established central bank of that time.
The Treasury was no longer beset with the difficulties resulting from
decreased revenue; its gold reserve was adequate for the conver-

[54] Vanderlip, "Lessons of Our War Loans," *The Forum,* Vol. XXVI (September, 1898), p. 35.

[55] *Ibid.*, p. 36.

[56] Kinley, *Independent Treasury,* p. 79; the Treasury kept on hand the supply of gold received in payment of custom dues to pay only the interest on the public debt; *ibid.*, p. 304.

sion of the Treasury paper currency. No war occurred which forced the Treasury to concentrate on fiscal matters to the exclusion of the banking and credit structure. The Treasury revenue increased so that the Treasury became an active and potent force in the money market. Finally, its powers frightened cautious businessmen and contributed to the establishment in 1913 of an organization which was intended to handle exclusively the central banking functions previously assumed by the Treasury. One of the measures which substantially increased the banking activities of the Treasury was the Gold Standard Act of 1900.

The Organization and Functions of the Treasury under the Act of 1900

Around the turn of the century the country was prosperous, and the usually implacable silverites allowed their inflationist sentiment to decline. On the other hand, the sound-money advocates felt safe in launching a gold currency campaign, which resulted in the Gold Standard Act of March 14, 1900.[57] Under Section I of this law all other forms of money were to be maintained "at parity" with gold. The foundation stone of the currency system was to be the Treasury gold reserve. Section II described in detail the banking functions of the Treasury, particularly regarding the management of the gold reserve.[58] Under Section IV the Treasury was divided into two departments: (1) the ordinary fiscal department, and (2) the department of issue and redemption.[59] The Treasury was instructed also to redeem in standard gold coin all United States notes and to retire the Treasury notes of 1890. For this purpose the Secretary of the Treasury was to set apart and maintain a reserve of $150,000,000 in gold coin or bullion. This fund succeeded the old $100,000,000 limit set by Secretary Sherman and kept by the Secretary of the Treasury under the implied authority of the Resumption Act.[60]

Whenever the Treasury paid out gold for United States notes, the Secretary of the Treasury after that time had to use the notes which came into his hands exclusively to purchase gold in order to

---

[57] Dewey, *Financial History of the United States,* p. 471.
[58] 31 Stat. 45.   [59] *Ibid.*
[60] U.S., Treasury Dept., *Annual Report of the Secretary, 1893,* p. lxxii; see above, p. 90.

restore and maintain the gold reserve. By using the redeemed notes only to purchase gold, he paved the way to end the "endless chain" started by the Act of May 31, 1878, which forced United States Notes once redeemed to be reissued and permitted them to be again redeemed in gold, and so forth, ad infinitum. Under the Act of 1900 if the reserve fell below $100,000,000 the Secretary of the Treasury was to sell bonds to restore the gold reserve to the maximum of $150,000,000. The gold coin received from sale of bonds went first to the General Fund of the Treasury and then was exchanged for notes that had been redeemed and were held in the Department of Issue and Redemption. Under Section IV of the Act these notes could then be used to redeem United States bonds or for any other lawful purpose except to meet deficiencies in current revenue.[61] Under the old arrangement, for instance in 1893, the fund was used to cover general Federal expenses.[62] Now redeemed notes must be held in the reserve fund until exchanged for gold, and neither they nor the gold may be used for any other purpose.

The division of Issue and Redemption of the Treasury Department maintained the trust funds of the Treasury—the gold coins held against gold certificates and the silver dollars represented by silver certificates. This Department of Issue and Redemption was in effect a bank of deposit and issue.[63] Under the law the Treasury received deposits of gold and issued warrants or certificates against them. It issued its own notes and held the specie reserve against them. It exchanged money of one kind for other kinds. It performed exchange operations by a transfer of currency.[64] These services represented a considerable expense to the Government. In other countries government treasuries do not usually perform banking functions. They do not hold specie and issue notes against it, nor do they exchange paper money for specie. In other countries central banks are obliged to perform these banking services, at their own expense.

---

[61] 31 Stat. 45.

[62] U.S., Treasury Dept., *Annual Report of the Secretary, 1893*, p. lxx; see also above, pp. 91–92.

[63] Kinley, *Independent Treasury*, p. 110.

[64] Deposits of gold were made in New York for the transfer of currency to other points. These deposits began early, and the Treasury supplied the kinds and amounts of paper currency desired, which were usually United States notes and silver certificates of small denominations. U.S., Treasury Dept., *Annual Report of the Secretary, 1902*, p. 14.

In the United States the Treasury assumed these burdens. All that was necessary to make the United States Treasury a bank of discount was to permit it to issue notes against some assets of the banks other than United States bonds. If the law permitted it to accept commercial paper from the banks and to give them additional circulation in exchange therefor during a crisis, it would be performing practically all the functions of a central bank and have all the functions and power necessary to "regulate the currency." [65]

Banking Activities of the Treasury after 1900

Secretary Carlisle (March 7, 1893–March 5, 1897) wrote as early as 1893 "under existing legislation the Treasury Department exercises to a larger extent than all the other financial institutions of the country combined the functions of a bank of issue." [66] He stated that the Sub-treasury had acted as a bank of deposit, issue, and redemption and as agents for the transfer of currency from one part of the country to another. Secretary Carlisle noted that the New York Sub-treasury was also a storage warehouse for gold and silver bullion used in international exchange to settle trade balances. These are functions normally performed by a great central bank. In Professor Kinley's remarkable study of the Treasury he gives a more complete list of the banking functions of the Treasury after 1900.[67] Professor Kinley does not indicate that the banking activities in which the Treasury was engaged were central banking functions, nor did Professor Kinley exhaust the banking activities of the Treasury. Nevertheless, his list bears repetition in that it confirms the fact that the Treasury did perform many more central banking functions after 1900 than it did before that time.

1. Issue and redemption of paper money—United States notes and United States Treasury notes of 1890
2. Preparation and supervision of the issue and redemption of national bank notes
3. Exchange of the various kinds of money for gold or for each other
4. Regional transfer of funds to move crops
5. Supervision of the division of the money into proper denominations so as to furnish the proper supplies of large and small notes as needed

[65] Kinley, *Independent Treasury*, p. 110.
[66] U.S., Treasury Dept., *Annual Report of the Secretary, 1893*, p. lxxiii.
[67] Kinley, *Independent Treasury*, p. 100.

6. Acting as an influence on the rate of discount by contracting and expanding the currency through a shifting of its funds between the commercial banks and its own vaults
7. Keeping the gold reserve of the country

United States notes were no longer newly issued; since the Act of May 31, 1878, a fixed amount was merely kept in circulation.[68] They were paid out by the Treasury, not on the basis of discounting transactions, but for ordinary expenses of the Government. Under the Act of March 14, 1900, if the notes had been redeemed in gold, they could be reissued only for the purchase of gold. If the Treasury had obtained them in payment of revenue or in any other way except for gold, the Treasury was free to use them for any Treasury purpose. If the Treasury had been a true central bank, it could have issued notes by discounting eligible assets. The volume of such bank notes issued would then have depended on the amount of paper presented for discount. No arrangement of this type existed in the United States until the Federal Reserve banks started to operate on November 16, 1914.[69]

Under the heading "Issue and Redemption of Paper Money" should also be included the transfer of money from one part of the country to another, since such transfers were used to substitute one type of currency for another. After the Bland-Allison Law of February 28, 1878 (20 Stat. 25), went into effect, it was found that silver dollars did not remain in circulation. They were exchanged for gold, and the silver dollars accumulated in the Treasury instead of passing permanently into circulation.[70] To overcome this difficulty the Secretary of the Treasury took advantage of the usual fall movement of currency to send silver rather than gold into the interior and thus conserve the Treasury reserve of gold.[71] Conservation of the gold stock of the country is a central banking function.[72]

The words "money for moving the crops" had come to be a familiar heading in the Treasury reports of the United States. The method of transfer was for the banks in interior cities to call on their New York creditors to remit funds by depositing gold at the

[68] 20 Stat. 87.
[69] U.S., Treasury Dept., *Annual Report of the Secretary, 1916*, p. 18.
[70] U.S., Treasury Dept., *Annual Report of the Secretary, 1879*, pp. 334, 346; see above, p. 74.
[71] U.S., Treasury Dept., *Annual Report of the Secretary, 1893*, p. lxxvi.
[72] Willis, *The Theory and Practice of Central Banking*, p. 7.

New York Sub-treasury, and in exchange the Secretary of the Treasury would order payment of the amount to the creditor bank in the kinds of money called for at the western bank.[73] An adequate supply of silver of small denominations is, of course, a matter of great importance. During the spring and fall the country districts need currency in small denominations suitable for wage payments. Unquestionably, it is the duty of a central bank to see that banks in all sections of the country are adequately supplied with the type of currency required for their purposes.[74] The Treasury ably performed this duty.[75] In addition, when the interior bank had no credit in New York from which it could draw, the Treasury advanced the funds based on Government bonds as collateral.[76]

The Treasury exercised its influence on rates of discount, listed above as one of its central banking functions, by alternately depositing and withdrawing public money in the national banks. These devices, along with others, including the sale and purchase of Government bonds, were used by the Treasury in its attempts to keep the money market steady and reasonably stable, which is a central banking function.[77] New methods for achieving the desired result were devised by various secretaries of the Treasury, including Gage (March 6, 1897–January 31, 1902), Shaw (February 1, 1902–March 3, 1907), and Cortelyou (March 4, 1907–March 7, 1909). Under the administrations of these men the Treasury was intentionally acting as the real central bank of the country.

The Treasury Extends Its Central Banking Activities under Secretaries Gage, Shaw, and Cortelyou

Some of the central banking problems of the period from 1900 to 1912 involved the proper management of a Treasury surplus. Fortune favored secretaries Gage, Shaw, and Cortelyou. Through-

---

[73] U.S., Treasury Dept., *Annual Report of the Secretary, 1916*, p. 277; see Section 16 of the Act of December 23, 1913 (38 Stat. 265).

[74] Willis, *The Theory and Practice of Central Banking*, p. 8.

[75] U.S., Treasury Dept., *Annual Report of the Secretary, 1893*, pp. lxxvi–lxxvii. There is express authority for the Secretary of the Treasury to substitute small silver certificates for larger ones and he also has the power to make such changes as he may deem proper in the denominations of the Treasury notes issued under the Act of July 14, 1890 (26 Stat. 289).

[76] U.S., Treasury Dept., *Annual Report of the Secretary, 1893*, pp. lxxvi–lxxvii; see below, pp. 104–110.

[77] Willis, *The Theory and Practice of Central Banking*, p. 8.

out the greater part of their terms of office a Treasury surplus existed, which gave them the funds necessary to influence the banking and business communities. "Secretaries Gage, Shaw, and Cortelyou considered themselves guardians of the money market as well as custodians of the Treasury. The Treasury became a sort of balance wheel which provided elasticity in the currency situation by alternately hoarding and releasing funds, giving assistance when panic threatened, and bringing in gold when the reserves of the banks grew low." [78] In 1897 Secretary Gage (March 6, 1897–January 31, 1902) stated that "for more than half a century it was the established policy of the government to endeavor to contribute toward the avoidance of commercial disaster." [79]

During his term the Treasury balance passed the $300,000,000 mark.[80] In discussing the period of the eighties I called attention to the problem of dealing with a Treasury surplus.[81] The same phenomenon occurred during Gage's term. The surplus revenue which was not needed for periodic payments was held in the Treasury vaults. This resulted in the withdrawal of huge amounts of money from circulation and from the banks.[82] Bank deposits and bank reserves declined, and the decline in bank reserves resulted in the contraction of loans by the banks.[83] Caution and hesitancy soon became widespread, and the volume of business started to recede.[84] Gage met the situation as had Fairchild, by prepaying the interest and principal of Government bonds and by increasing Treasury deposits with the national banks.[85] By prepaying the interest on bonds, the Treasury gave the banks an opportunity to

[78] Beckhart, ed., *The New York Money Market*, Vol. I, p. 382.

[79] U.S., Treasury Dept., *Transactions with Certain National Banks,* 56th Cong., 1st Sess., House Document 264, p. 5.

[80] U.S., Treasury Dept., *Annual Report of the Secretary, 1901,* p. 90; see Appendix II, below.

[81] See above, pp. 78–83.

[82] Fairchild's statement in the U.S., Treasury Dept., *Annual Report of the Secretary, 1887,* p. xxvi. See above, pp. 66–67. "Taking large sums of actual money out of the ordinary financial uses and locking them up as a dead mass in the vaults of the Treasury is a proceeding as unscientific and unreasoned as any other part of our unscientific and unreasoned banking and currency system." U.S., Treasury Dept., *Annual Report of the Secretary, 1912,* p. 3.

[83] "The diminishing ratio of cash reserves puts a strain on the expanding movement and impedes further development in that direction." U.S., Treasury Dept., *Annual Report of the Secretary, 1901,* p. 81.

[84] *Ibid.,* p. 82.

[85] *Ibid.,* pp. 20, 25–26; see also Appendixes II and V, below.

use funds for some time before the interest fell due. The banks received the funds from the Treasury in advance and could employ them for the extension of credits, but the banks were obliged to pay the bondholders only at the maturity date. As a result of Treasury intervention the Government deposits in national banks in July, 1901, reached $93,442,683.[86] When Secretary Shaw took office, in February, 1902, the Government was still collecting more than it was spending. He continued the policy of depositing Treasury funds with the banks.[87]

Secretary Shaw Relieves the Annual Autumnal Stringencies.—The cash reserve against deposits in the New York banks in the fall of 1902 fell below 25 percent.[88] This was the first time since 1893 that it had declined to such a low level. Secretary Shaw became concerned about the general banking situation and was firmly of the belief that one of the Treasury's functions was to serve the money market in time of difficulty.[89] Accordingly, he took drastic steps to strengthen the cash holdings of the banks. He anticipated payment of interest on outstanding bonds; he purchased bonds even if it required a premium as high as 35¾ percent—the highest premium any secretary ever paid, and he increased the number of depository banks as well as the amount of Government deposits.[90] Mr. Shaw was also determined to devise several new plans if necessary. Thus, on September 29, 1902, he offered to accept certain securities other than Government bonds for deposits of public money. First he included among the acceptable pledges the state and municipal bonds approved by New York State as legal investment for its savings banks. Finally, by October 23, 1902, all undefaulted bonds of any state or city were declared acceptable.[91] This procedure released Federal Government bonds which would now be used as a basis for

[86] See Appendix II, below.

[87] U.S., Treasury Dept., *Annual Report of the Secretary, 1902*, p. 19; see also Appendixes II and III, below.

[88] U.S., Treasury Dept., *Annual Report of the Secretary, 1902*, p. 23.

[89] U.S., Treasury Dept., *Annual Report of the Secretary, 1902*, p. 64; "During the summer of 1902 surplus bank reserves throughout the country ran relatively low. This is one of the surest indications of trouble in the fall. Preparatory for the crisis certain to ensue, the Secretary of the Treasury began special Treasury operations." U.S., Treasury Dept., *Annual Report of the Secretary, 1906*, p. 37.

[90] U.S., Treasury Dept., *Annual Report of the Secretary, 1902*, pp. 24, 64; see also Appendixes II and V, below.

[91] U.S., Treasury Dept., *Annual Report of the Secretary, 1902*, p. 14.

an increased circulation of national bank notes. During October and November, 1902, deposits by the Treasury increased by $15,000,-000, and the national bank note issues by $18,000,000.[92] In 1904 Shaw increased the range of securities eligible for collateral against Government deposits to include railroad bonds.[93]

Secretary Shaw interpreted the phrase requiring security for Government deposits in the form of "United States bonds and otherwise" as "United States bonds or otherwise." No official since 1864 had so interpreted the law.[94] Administrative leaders were conscious of the possible illegality of Shaw's policy and tried to secure adoption of an act of Congress which would clearly legalize the acceptance of other collateral.[95] However, no legal change was made until the last day of Shaw's term, March 4, 1907, when the so-called Aldrich Bill became law.[96] The Secretary of the Treasury, by permitting certain types of bonds other than Government bonds as adequate collateral for Government deposits in national banks helped to relieve a stringent money market. Government bonds which had formerly been used to back Government deposits could now be used by the national banks for further issues of national bank notes. However, the prices of all bonds required by the Treasury as adequate collateral were sure to rise, since a new demand had been created for them.[97] In this way the Treasury exerted an unintentional but definite influence on the bond market.

Government deposits with national banks, although secured by United States bonds and other securities pledged to the Government, are nevertheless deposits involving the liquidity of the banks. The deposits, against which cash reserves had to be kept, included Government deposits. Secretary Shaw recognized the burdensomeness of the double reserves required, one to protect the safety of Government funds (100 percent in Government bonds or approved collateral) and the other to assure the liquidity of the banks (in central reserve cities, 25 percent in legal tender money). To reduce

---

[92] *Ibid.*, p. 64.

[93] U.S., Treasury Dept., *Annual Report of the Secretary, 1904,* p. 117.

[94] Phillips, *Methods of Keeping the Public Money of the United States,* p. 131.

[95] U.S., Treasury Dept., *Annual Report of the Secretary, 1902,* p. 68.

[96] It provided that "the Secretary shall on or before the first of January of each year, make a public statement of the securities required during that year for such deposits." 34 Stat. 1290.

[97] U.S., Treasury Dept., *Annual Report of the Secretary, 1902,* p. 66.

the funds thus tied up in connection with Government deposits, Secretary Shaw, in 1902, informed the depository banks that they need no longer keep cash reserves against their holdings of public funds,[98] a measure which at once affected about $130,000,000 on deposit throughout the country. Thus he set free the base for a credit expansion of $130,000,000. This action had the same effect on bank reserves as a change in reserve requirements by a central bank would have had. Shaw's intention was to afford double relief to the stringent money market by increasing the reserves available for the commercial business of the banks and by making the banks eager recipients of Government deposits. He thought that Government deposits were amply protected by the bond collateral, but he seemed to have overlooked that public funds ought to be kept so readily available that their withdrawal, when desired, would not embarrass the liquidity of banks or disturb the general money market. A portion of the Government deposits should always be retained by the banks in ready cash to provide easy repayment in case of withdrawal. Secretary Shaw's authority for the "no reserve" ruling was even more open to question than was the "and/or other security" interpretation. From a central banking point of view a temporary lowering of reserve requirements might be permitted in cases of unusual stress, but the effect of this ruling was to make the banks depend on the Treasury rather than upon themselves whenever they encountered any difficulty.[99]

Secretary Shaw's next radical step was taken in the autumn of 1903. Previous secretaries had merely permitted internal revenues to accumulate in the commercial banks as they were paid in for the account of the Treasury. They thought it was illegal to deposit with banks money that had actually passed into the Treasury.[100] It was their belief that revenues once turned into the Treasury vaults could not be taken out and deposited elsewhere inasmuch as the

[98] *Ibid.*, p. 68. This radical change was embodied in Section 14 of the Act of May 30, 1908, which specifies that no reserve need be held against deposits of public money. 35 Stat. 546; see also pp. 161, 196, below.

[99] Andrew, "The Treasury and the Banks under Secretary Shaw," *Quarterly Journal of Economics,* Vol. XXI (August, 1907), p. 539.

[100] Secretary Shaw must have entertained a similar belief, for he says, "At present the purchase of outstanding government bonds for the credit of the Sinking Fund affords the only method of returning surplus revenues to the channels of trade after they have been once covered into the Treasury." U.S., Treasury Dept., *Annual Report of the Secretary, 1902,* p. 67.

Constitution explicitly enjoins that "no money shall be drawn from the Treasury but in consequence of appropriations made by law." [101] Secretaries Sherman (March 10, 1877–March 3, 1881), Fairchild (April 1, 1887–March 6, 1889), and Gage (March 6, 1897–January 31, 1902) allowed huge accumulations of deposits in the banks but did not transfer money from the Treasury to those institutions. They merely allowed bank holdings to accumulate out of the daily internal revenue receipts.[102] Mr. Shaw was not content to relieve the market to the extent of the $500,000 a day received from current internal revenue collections, and he set about discovering a means of escape.[103] If the Constitution said money could not be withdrawn from the Treasury except by vote of Congress, he concluded that the difficulty might be removed if one considered the banks which served as depositories as part of the Treasury. The funds could be moved from one "apartment" of the Treasury to "such other apartments as are provided as places of deposit of the public money." [104] This permitted the internal revenue collections which had already been put into the Treasury to be transferred from the Treasury to depository banks.

Throughout the summer of 1903 financial writers and banks debated whether the impending crop movements would cause the usual fall financial difficulties. In the fall the banks in New York usually had found themselves hard pressed for funds. The interior banks had been drawing on their balances in the east in order to provide their customers with funds for harvesting of the crops and payment of salaries to men who had worked since early spring. In the east the banks extended loans in the summer to some of their city customers engaged in producing articles for the fall trade. These loans were not repaid until the early winter. In addition, certain customers required special advances in the autumn. Consequently the fall had usually presented problems to the eastern bankers. They

[101] Constitution of the United States of America, Article I, Section IX, Paragraph 7.

[102] See above, pp. 70, 80, 103; see also Appendix II, below.

[103] "Having found it impracticable to relieve a monetary stringency with current internal revenue receipts, amounting only to about $500,000 per day, the Secretary early in 1903 ordered their segregation and the accumulation of a separate and distinct fund composed entirely of internal revenue, so as to be prepared in case of an emergency to grant prompt relief by large deposits." U.S., Treasury Dept., *Annual Report of the Secretary, 1906*, pp. 37–38.

[104] *Commercial and Financial Chronicle*, Vol. LXXVII (September 5, 1903), p. 471.

had to call in their loans or decrease their credit extensions. Obviously some central authority was needed which could discount eligible assets for the eastern banks or directly advance funds to sound banks.[105] Both methods are now used by the Federal Reserve System. However, prior to 1913, when no separate central bank existed, the secretaries helped "move the crops" by supplying the interior banks with appropriate kinds of money in exchange for gold received by the New York Sub-treasury from the New York creditors of the interior banks.[106]

In the fall of 1903 Mr. Shaw decided that the traditional assistance to the eastern banks was insufficient. He was willing not only to exchange gold for paper money or silver in proper denominations but also actually to advance the money, of course, based on adequate bond collateral. The Treasury was thus assuming the discount function and also conducting itself in this respect as a central bank.

Furthermore, the duty of a central bank is to foresee difficulties in the money market and, if possible, to ward them off. Secretary Shaw acted accordingly; already in his first year of office, in 1903, he reassured the banks that there would be no fall stringency. At the end of August he published his new ruling concerning the transfer of money from the Treasury. He indicated his willingness to place $40,000,000 of internal revenue and miscellaneous receipts in the general money market in case of stringency. The importance of this announcement was obvious to all concerned. The Secretary of the Treasury had stated in effect that the Treasury would relieve

---

[105] "By the concentration of unemployed reserves from sections where such reserves were not needed, it [a central bank] could redistribute them in part as loans where most needed, and thus bind together for a common strength and protection the loose unrelated units, in whose separation and isolation the greatest weakness of our banking system is now to be found." U.S., Treasury Dept., *Annual Report of the Secretary, 1901*, p. 83.

[106] See above, p. 97; U.S., Treasury Dept., *Annual Report of the Secretary, 1901*, p. 14; "The transfer of currency against deposits in New York attract year by year no little attention. They are in largest volume from July and especially from August to December, inclusive. They constitute the direct requirements upon the Treasury to cover what is popularly styled money to move the crops, and payment is made in most marked sums to New Orleans to help market cotton and sugar, and to Chicago for grain. Small denominations are wanted for local use in the producing districts and depositors offer gold certificates for the exchange. The Treasury gives out $10 United States notes and $5 silver certificates and receives gold certificates." U.S., Treasury Dept., *Annual Report of the Secretary, 1903*, p. 133.

the banks in case they were in temporary financial difficulties.[107]
He had also promised that the relief would not again be gradual,
but would be rendered promptly. The new policy implied that the
Secretary of the Treasury would lend if necessary, the entire Treasury balance at such times and to such banks as he chose in the interest of general business. Clearly Secretary Shaw felt that the
Treasury ought not to be administered as a mere fiscal institution
but also as the guardian and protector of the money market.[108]

During the years 1903 and 1904, Secretary Shaw still considered
himself the guardian of the money market, but his resourcefulness
for innovations was not put to any test. The Treasury operated with
a mild deficit due to the slackening of trade, diminishing receipts,
and heavy extraordinary expenditures (including $50,000,000 for
the Panama Canal).[109] Secretary Shaw had drawn about $100,000,-
000 from the banks to meet appropriations, and when a mild money
pressure was felt in October, 1905, he could not offer his customary
assistance.[110] However, in 1906, with abounding prosperity, Government receipts became more than adequate to meet expenditures.[111] Again the Secretary of the Treasury had ample funds and
opportunity to employ his ingenuity in devising new measures to
get money into trade channels and relieve any temporary market
setback that might occur.

Secretary Shaw and Gold Imports.—Probably the most important
new plan devised by Secretary Shaw in 1906 was the use of the
Government surplus to facilitate imports of gold. On April 14, 1906,
it was announced that the Secretary of the Treasury would allow
any depository national bank which engaged in importing gold to
anticipate the arrival of the gold by withdrawing a like amount in

[107] "Fortunately, the Treasury holds a surplus of $80,000,000 above a reasonable
working balance, available if unexpected conditions should arise. This surplus, in my
judgment, should not be encroached upon deliberately, for it will be found very convenient to offset the results of political or economic disturbances certain to arise in the
near or remote future." U.S., Treasury Dept., *Annual Report of the Secretary, 1905,*
p. 34.

[108] "Financiers generally now recognize, and some of the best known have publicly
announced, that but for what was then [1902] done a panic would have ensued rivaling
in severity any in our history, and which would possibly have continued until industrial
conditions were disastrously affected." U.S., Treasury Dept., *Annual Report of the Secretary, 1906,* p. 37.

[109] U.S., Treasury Dept., *Annual Report of the Secretary, 1905,* p. 7.

[110] U.S., Treasury Dept., *Annual Report of the Secretary, 1906,* p. 39.

[111] *Ibid.,* p. 7; see also Appendix III, below.

cash from the Treasury upon pledge of satisfactory collateral.[112] Securities approved for investments of savings banks were acceptable to the Treasury for these gold import transactions. The sum so withdrawn was considered a temporary loan to be returned to the Treasury when the gold arrived. The Treasury, by this arrangement, reduced the cost of importing gold by the amount of interest during transit. It also raised the "gold import point" by the amount of the interest and brought it nearer to par of exchange. In other words, he tried to make it profitable for the depository banks to import gold without waiting for sterling exchange to fall to the normal "gold import point."

This was a measure that had nothing to do with the fiscal interests of the Treasury. Gold imports were not a matter of direct Government concern; they were part of a banker's private business.[113] But Secretary Shaw felt that the importation of gold was a problem that concerned the Treasury in its central banking functions. He reasoned that the new gold would provide an adequate foundation for continuing business expansion.[114] If temporarily unused, the gold could also serve as an extra accumulation for times of emergency. Therefore he was determined to aid in the importation of gold. In the short time during which Secretary Shaw carried out this policy he eliminated for national banks their loss of interest as one item of expense in their foreign-exchange operations. This arrangement gave them an advantage over all other firms engaged in the same business. Private bankers naturally complained.[115] In addition, he was permitting certain banks to count as part of their reserves the importations of gold during the period when they were being transmitted to New York. The imported gold was accordingly a basis for loans from the moment of its purchase abroad.

Just why Mr. Shaw should have chosen to relieve the market by stimulating the import of gold rather than by placing additional deposits in national banks as in former years he never explained. He seemed to have believed that the natural movement of gold was toward this country, but that the gold was being directed to other

[112] U.S., Treasury Dept., *Annual Report of the Secretary,* 1906, p. 8.

[113] Andrew, "The Treasury and the Banks under Secretary Shaw," *Quarterly Journal of Economics,* Vol. XXI (August, 1907), p. 544.

[114] U.S., Treasury Dept., *Annual Report of the Secretary, 1906,* p. 40.

[115] *Commercial and Financial Chronicle,* Vol. LXXXII (May 12, 1906), p. 1069; Vol. LXXXIII (October 27, 1906), p. 1002.

markets by the higher interest rates of European banks. He hoped
to overcome what he thought was an artificial diversion of gold from
the United States by adopting Treasury measures similar to those
which were being employed by the French and the German central
banks. The foreign central banks had kept the volume of reserve
credit low in order that interest rates be high enough to attract gold.

For a while his measures helped to expedite the movement of gold
to this country, but in the long run Secretary Shaw's policy tended
to defeat itself. It caused a decline in rates of interest, and this in
turn reduced the volume of gold imports. In normal times gold
moves in the direction of the highest interest rates. Therefore his
policy could not for long possibly accomplish its purpose. On October 23, 1906, he abruptly terminated the practice, which had prevailed for only half a year.[116]

Secretary Shaw and the Problem of Inelasticity of the Credit.—The
problem of supplying the country with adequate credit facilities belongs to a central bank. Bank notes were always recognized as
representing one form of credit, and in order to control credit the
volume of the note issues also had to be controlled. During the
major part of the nineteenth century bank loans were usually made
by issuing bank notes to borrowers. The prevailing opinion was that
the volume of bank notes outstanding directly affected prices and
business. Mismanagement of the note issue (issuing too many or
too few bank notes for a given volume of business) brought about
business dislocations. Consequently the feeling quite generally prevailed that the issue of bank notes should be controlled by a central
bank. The Bank of England was the classic example of such an
arrangement.

Many banking theorists recognized that lending by crediting the
deposit accounts of the banks' customers might affect prices just as
lending by advancing bank notes to the borrowers affects prices. A
reasonable inference would have been that if the central bank was
to control the total volume of credit, it must be able to regulate also
the deposit function. Secretary Shaw was aware of the various theories of credit control,[117] and he paid equal attention to the effects

---

[116] U.S., Treasury Dept., *Annual Report of the Secretary, 1906*, p. 40.

[117] "Financial writers, doctrinaires, practical businessmen and impractical theorists,
men of experience and those wholly without, have discussed the question with much
learning and occasionally in much ignorance." See *ibid.*, p. 44.

of alterations in the volume of bank deposits and in bank notes.

The power of national banks to expand the amount of credit they could grant during an emergency and contract it in periods of diminished activity has been notoriously inadequate.[118] Country banks kept balances and also part of their reserves on deposit with New York City banks. New York banks paid interest on these accounts and tried to make a profit by lending the funds deposited; these loans were largely made to brokers on call. At harvest time country banks needed all their funds to move the crops, and they would start to withdraw their New York balances just when their funds were needed in New York. A money stringency usually resulted. It did not matter whether bank credit was extended in the form of deposit credit or of bank notes. The result was the same as long as the available amount of either form was rigidly limited under the National Banking System. The rigid requirement of a minimum cash reserve against all deposits had the effect of fixing an uncompromising limit to the extension of loans and discounts in the form of deposit credit. To counteract the limitation which an inadequate cash reserve against deposits imposed on credit extension a central bank with the note issuing and rediscounting privilege was needed. This institution should be able to advance additional funds to the banks, either directly or by discounting their eligible assets. However, Mr. Shaw considered himself the head of a central bank, and he decided to find means of extending bank credit facilities within the existing system of banking laws.[119]

Mr. Shaw believed that without further legislation the rigid limitations of American bank credit could be relieved through proper action of the Treasury. In his opinion all that was needed to infuse some elasticity into our currency and credit system was the further elaboration of expedients which he had invented and employed.

[118] U.S., Treasury Dept., *Annual Report of the Secretary, 1906,* p. 44.

[119] "The government quarantines against yellow fever; it spends millions to protect the people against unwholesome food; it inspects banks in the interest of depositors, and does a thousand other things to safeguard the people against disaster of various kinds. This policy of governmental supervision receives universal approbation. Believing it to be the duty of the government also to protect the people against financial panics, which, in this country, have caused more mental and more physical suffering than all the plagues known to man, and recognizing that under our system no possible cooperation can be secured among banks, each independent of the other . . . The Secretary of the Treasury undertook the task of making some provision for the inevitable." See U.S., Treasury Dept., *Annual Report of the Secretary, 1906,* p. 41.

On September 27, 1906, Shaw announced that the time had arrived for making the country's currency more elastic and that $26,000,000 of surplus revenues would temporarily be contributed to bank deposits and that the temporary deposits against engagements of gold would also be continued.[120] He intended that the funds should not foster speculation in the stock market, so when the $26,000,000 were distributed New York City banks received only $3,000,000.[121] But the funds came to New York anyway, because interior banks did not have or could not spare the collateral for such deposits, and because New York offered better investment opportunities. The Treasury had deposited the $26,000,000 on September 27, with the understanding that these funds would be recalled by February 1, 1907. The dates were fixed, not by fiscal considerations of the Treasury, but on the basis of probable changes in the currency demands of trade, based on the experience of former years. This action represented an effort of the Secretary of the Treasury to make the country's currency more elastic in meeting the increased seasonal demand.

Shaw's endeavors to introduce elasticity into our banking system were not confined to the increasing of deposit credit. He tried by executive decree to adjust the volume of national bank notes to the fluctuating needs of business. This elasticity he wished to accomplish by increasing or decreasing the amount of Government bonds available as a basis for national bank notes, and he could affect the volume of Government bonds by relaxing or tightening from time to time the Treasury regulations which defined the collateral acceptable against Government deposits. By releasing Government bonds previously pledged as collateral for Government deposits he made them available as reserve for new issues of national bank notes. These could then be used during the crop-moving season, and the normal reserve funds of the banks would not be depleted for these purposes. In less active months he tried to force a retirement of this emergency circulation by insisting on a resubstitution of the Government bonds for other securities as collateral for public deposits.

A good example of these policies may be found in the various steps taken during the fall and winter of 1902–1903. On September

[120] *Ibid.*, p. 42.   [121] *Ibid.*

29, 1902, Secretary Shaw permitted banks to use bonds other than Federal bonds for Government deposits; [122] on January 20, 1903, he rescinded the order and demanded withdrawal of the non-Government securities before the end of the following July. While he thus succeeded in 1902 in adding to the currency during the usual autumn drain of funds, efforts at currency contraction in 1903 were less successful. On August 1, 1903, there were no signs of contraction in the amount of national bank notes outstanding, and the note circulation on that date still was $30,000,000 above the level on January 1.[123] Shaw never acknowledged this as a failure, probably because he felt that business was much better in 1903 than in 1902 and the larger volume of trade required more currency.

Business did not remain on a high level during 1904 and 1905. There was a decrease in exports and in custom receipts,[124] and during this period Mr. Shaw primarily occupied himself with fiscal problems, the financing of the construction of the Panama Canal, and the mild Treasury deficit. He had not forgotten the guardianship of the money market he had previously assumed. The revival of business in 1906 gave Secretary Shaw an opportunity to attack again the problem of making the volume of currency elastic. On October 18, 1906, he said he would accept other securities against government deposits to the extent of $18,000,000, provided similar amounts of Government bonds were used to take out new national bank notes.[125] At the same time he planned for a future contraction of the circulation when the need should have passed, by stipulating that the notes so issued should be retired at the rate of $3,000,000 per month between March 15 and September 1 of the following year. He hoped thus to demonstrate that he could provide an elastic currency within the existing framework of the law.[126] Once more he succeeded in giving impetus to the expansion of notes, but his efforts for contraction were ineffectual, because the notes were needed to strengthen the cash reserves of the banks during the Panic of 1907.[127]

[122] *Ibid.*, p. 37.

[123] Date	National Bank Notes Outstanding
January 1, 1903	$753,607,562
August 1, 1903	783,238,991

U.S., Treasury Dept., *Annual Report of the Secretary, 1904*, p. 219.
[124] See Appendix IV, below.
[125] U.S., Treasury Dept., *Annual Report of the Secretary, 1906*, p. 43.
[126] *Ibid.*   [127] See below, pp. 120–128, for discussion of the Panic of 1907.

Mr. Shaw was not content with his "make-shift" control over currency and financial matters which he read into laws. Since his interpretation of the laws might very well be contrary to the original intentions of the lawmakers, he favored legislation that would clarify the position and functions of a Secretary of the Treasury. In his report of 1906 he asked that the Secretary of the Treasury be given legal recognition as head of the American banking system by express enactment so that he might have additional and virtually absolute control over the expansion and contraction of bank credit. Mr. Shaw recognized that the duty of a central bank included supervision and extension of credit. Since a central organization for the control of credit so far did not exist in the country, although it was definitely needed, he thought the Treasury could adequately fill the void. To this end he suggested that, "It would be wise to clothe the Secretary of the Treasury with discretion whether he will allow retirement of the circulation at any given time, and to place such limitation thereon as in his judgment will best conserve the business interests of the country." [128] Mr. Shaw thought that the Secretary of the Treasury ought to have the power "to require all banks at certain times fixed by him to slightly and gradually increase their reserves and hold the same within their own vaults, with corresponding authority to release the same from time to time as in his judgment will best serve the business interests of the country." [129] In other words, he wanted to regulate the ratio which bank reserves should bear to deposits. He was convinced that if he "were clothed with authority over reserves of the several banks, and with the power to contract the national bank circulation at pleasure" and if, in addition, he "were given $100,000,000 to be deposited with the banks or withdrawn as he might deem expedient" in his judgment, "no panic as distinguished from industrial stagnation could threaten either the United States or Europe that he could not avert." [130] Mr. Shaw seemed to think that no central or Government bank in the world could so readily influence financial conditions throughout the world as could the Secretary of the United States Treasury if he

---

[128] U.S., Treasury Dept., *Annual Report of the Secretary, 1906*, p. 46; Secretary Boutwell held ideas similar to those of Secretary Shaw. He said that the power to change the volume of paper in circulation should remain in the Treasury Department. U.S., Treasury Dept., *Annual Report of the Secretary, 1872*, p. xx.

[129] U.S., Treasury Dept., *Annual Report of the Secretary, 1906*, p. 48.

[130] *Ibid.*, p. 49.

were clothed with the proper authority over reserves, national bank notes, and Treasury funds.

In pursuing his policy and in proposing measures so alien to our traditions, especially to our system of checks and balances, Mr. Shaw was impressed with certain characteristics of American banking which differentiated it from the systems of most other countries. Nowhere else, he asserted, will one find such "equality of importance" among the banks and such absence of any predominant leadership.[131] In England and in most European countries the banks were arranged in a sort of hierarchy. Above them all stood the central bank exercising leadership. It regularly endeavored to influence the market rates of interest, to stimulate movements of gold in and out of the country, to check banking excesses in periods of speculative excitement, and to relieve banking distress in times of general difficulty. The central bank must be large, must have a sense of public responsibility, and must be uninfluenced by the profit motive. Such an institution did not exist in the United States. Mr. Shaw thought the Treasury should perform the functions of a central bank.[132] He tried to influence the market rates of interest, to stimulate gold movements, to check banking excesses, and to relieve banking distress.[133]

Many Americans before Secretary Shaw had admired the focalization of control and of responsibility in the money markets of Europe and had tried to devise methods of recasting our banking arrangements in one way or another on the European model. The usual plan contemplated the establishment of a relatively large and especially privileged bank. Twice in our history a national bank had been functioning. Both experiments were short-lived, largely

[131] U.S., Treasury Dept., *Annual Report of the Secretary, 1901*, p. 83; U.S., Treasury Dept., *Annual Report of the Secretary, 1906*, p. 47; Andrew, "The Treasury and the Banks under Secretary Shaw," *Quarterly Journal of Economics*, Vol. XXI (August, 1907), p. 557.

[132] "At first blush this [a central bank] seems desirable, but in practice I fear it would soon be found to work less satisfactorily than the present system. Such a bank would of necessity be governed by a board, the members of which would doubtless have outside interests. They would be responsible to no administration, to no political party, and each would shift the responsibility from himself to the board as an aggregation. It is doubtful whether such an institution could be managed less selfishly and more in the interest of the people generally than the Treasury department has been conducted even under the most unfortunate mismanagement to which it ever has been subjected." U.S., Treasury Dept., *Annual Report of the Secretary, 1906*, p. 47.

[133] See above, pp. 102–115.

because of the political intrigue surrounding the organization and operation of these banks.[134]

Mr. Shaw realized that central banking functions had to be performed. Our economy had developed to a high level of industrialization and economic interdependence, but our banking system, as evolved on our statute books, was suitable for an agricultural economy with a relatively large degree of local self-sufficiency. The economic development of the country and banking theory were far ahead of our legislation. Mr. Shaw showed a strong sense of public responsibility. He recognized that his position as head of the Treasury Department made it possible for him to render badly needed public services.[135] That he went further along the lines of intervention than previous secretaries may be due to the maturing of our industrial and credit economy and certainly also to personal factors, to his greater ingenuity, more intense craving for power, and wider interpretation of his duties as a public servant. Accordingly, Mr. Shaw proposed that the Government Treasury be given by specific legislation the powers exercised in Europe by central banks so that the Secretary of the Treasury would be intrusted with the guidance of banking policy and the general protection of the financial world.[136] The reasoning behind Mr. Shaw's proposal can readily be understood. To a large extent he was merely asking for the legal recognition of an existing practice. The Treasury had been regarded by both Treasury officials and the banks as the guardian of the money market.[137]

For example, for many years in periods of acute distress, when the accumulation of a surplus in the Treasury appeared alarming, secretaries of the Treasury had offered relief to business by prepaying the interest or principal on the bonds or by purchasing bonds in the open market or by increasing the Government deposits in the

---

[134] See above, pp. 16, 20, 27, 34.

[135] "It is never possible to measure the influence of Treasury transactions such as are here described, nor to state what our experience would have been had the Treasury failed to act in a given crisis." U.S., Treasury Dept., *Annual Report of the Secretary, 1906*, p. 43.

[136] *Ibid.*, p. 46.

[137] "Actual experience justifies the statement that the American people hold the Secretary of the Treasury quite largely responsible for financial conditions." *Ibid.*, p. 48; see above, p. 87 for quotation from *Commercial and Financial Chronicle*, December 6, 1890, p. 754; also see above p. 107 for quotation from U.S., Treasury Dept., *Annual Report of the Secretary, 1906*, p. 41.

national banks.[138] Sometimes during sudden emergencies secretaries had resorted to methods of doubtful legality, as when Secretary Boutwell allowed the reissue of retired greenbacks in October, 1872, and when Secretary Richardson did likewise in the autumn panic of 1873. Boutwell had also extended aid to American importers by selling Treasury gold to them because he feared that the distress of this small group might spread to other groups.[139]

Obviously it was no new thing for the Government to aid business in a crisis and to do what it could to check misfortune, but Secretary Shaw went further. According to his ideas it was the duty of the Treasury to concern itself with the general banking situation at all times, not only in times of panic,[140] and he attempted to include among the regular and ordinary duties of the American Government the paternalistic practices of the European central banks.[141] Most of Mr. Shaw's ideas on the position of the Treasury were well in advance of the prevailing opinions of his day and certainly well beyond the banking laws of his time. Eventually public opinion and banking legislation carried out some of Mr. Shaw's views. Being out of step with his time, of course, made Mr. Shaw unpopular; there was strong objection to him personally and to his ideas.[142] In addition, his plans would have tended to diminish the self-reliance of banks without replacing it by equally strong factors making for sound banking (such as much stricter supervision and better regulations).

Mr. Shaw's actions in periods of difficulty also tended to perpetuate maladjustments. For example, high call-money rates in Wall Street are not necessarily an evil for the country. These may be a much needed warning signal and may act as a brake on further unsound developments. If the high rates came from over-trading, a stringent market would discourage further borrowing and thereby

[138] See above, pp. 53–56, 81, 112.

[139] U.S., Treasury Dept., *Annual Report of the Secretary, 1874,* p. xx; see also above, p. 81.

[140] "The world throughout is enjoying an unprecedented period of prosperity, and no Government operations in this country must be permitted to interfere therewith either at home or abroad." U.S., Treasury Dept., *Annual Report of the Secretary, 1906,* p. 40. "The money of the country belongs to the people and Treasury operations must be made subordinate to the business interests of the country." *Ibid.*

[141] Sprague, *History of Crises under the National Banking Act,* p. 231.

[142] "The Treasury has always been the bloody angle of criticism of an administration." U.S., Treasury Dept., *Annual Report of the Secretary, 1906,* p. 47.

would induce a reduction of swollen bank liabilities. Furthermore, high interest rates tend to result in an inflow of gold. Intervention of the Government, by forcing down the call-money rate, may prevent these natural factors from working out their desirable results.

The system of Government assistance to banking, furthermore, is open to objections upon political grounds. It is likely to be abused for partisan purposes. At the close of Secretary Shaw's term of office some members of the American banking community and some students of the situation were seriously aroused over the possibility of arbitrary and dictatorial interference by a Secretary of the Treasury in the commercial banking field.[143] To counteract this possibility a law was suggested requiring the Secretary of the Treasury to deposit in banks daily all receipts in excess of a fixed balance, these deposits to be available to all national banks without discrimination. In this way the money market would be free from unpredictable and spasmodic superabundance or shortage of funds caused by the locking up and pouring out of Government money at the Secretary of the Treasury's personal decree. Thus, meddling on the part of the Secretary of the Treasury in the credit markets would be prevented. Also, arbitrary manipulation of bank reserves, of note circulation and of rates of foreign exchange would be avoided. Final legislation, however, was more nearly in line with Secretary Shaw's ideas.

Congress did recognize the need for a new attitude toward the Independent Treasury, and on March 4, 1907, they passed amendments to the law which expressly sanctioned certain actions of Mr. Shaw. The collateral required of depository banks was to be left to the discretion of the Secretary of the Treasury.[144] No longer was the Treasury forbidden to deposit customs receipts in national depositories.[145] Government funds could now be placed in properly qualified national banks. The obvious result of the law was greater

---

[143] "The abolition of the Independent Treasury would be, of course, involved in such a plan. Government money would be then regularly deposited in this central bank, from which disbursements would be made, and the government's supervision of and interference with the monetary operations and the financial conditions of the country would be effectually eliminated." U.S., Treasury Dept., *Annual Report of the Secretary, 1906*, p. 46.

[144] 34 Stat. 1290.

[145] U.S., Treasury Dept., *Annual Report of the Secretary, 1907*, p. 58; Act of March 4, 1907; see also above, pp. 80–81, 103.

leeway for the Treasury and an increase in possible Government deposits and in the number of depositories.[146] Another law which followed the ideas of Secretary Shaw was the Act of May 30, 1908, which stated that no reserve need be held against deposits of public money.[147]

Summary of Secretary Shaw's Activities and Opinions.—During the term of office of Secretary Shaw no major upheaval in the business world occurred. But Mr. Shaw felt that the position of a central bank was important not only during crises, that is, as a relief agency, but also in ordinary times. Especially in order to insure the smooth functioning of the economic system the central bank had to anticipate and counteract any disturbances which might arise in ordinary times. The fall stringency in the money market was an ordinary phenomenon which previous secretaries of the Treasury had tried to ameliorate only after it had arisen.[148] However, Mr. Shaw considered himself the permanent guardian of the money market and looked upon the Treasury as a central bank. Accordingly, he thought it was his duty to anticipate the fall stringencies and eliminate them. The devices which he used were numerous. They included prepayment of interest on bonds, purchasing Government bonds, even at a premium of 38 points,[149] increasing Government deposits in banks, permitting bonds other than Government bonds as collateral for Government deposits, allowing banks to hold no cash reserves against public deposits. Another radical measure which he undertook in anticipation of a regular fall stringency was to allow banks to import gold with funds advanced by the Treasury upon satisfactory collateral.

If a serious emergency had arisen during the years when Mr. Shaw served as Secretary of the Treasury, he might very well have undertaken many more extraordinary measures, and it is quite possible that he might even have prevailed upon the legislators to grant him greater powers. No extended period is entirely free from major political disturbances. When the next serious crisis occurred, the

---

[146] Beckhart, ed., *The New York Money Market,* Vol. I, p. 387; see also Appendix II, below.

[147] 35 Stat. 546.   [148] See above p. 86.

[149] In September, 1902, Secretary Shaw purchased for the Sinking Fund, United States 4 percent bonds of the loan of 1925 that were offered at 137¾ and interest to the date of purchase. See U.S., Treasury Dept., *Annual Report of the Secretary, 1906,* p. 37.

Secretary of the Treasury was Cortelyou (March 4, 1907–March 4, 1909), the successor to Mr. Shaw. His ideas about the position of the Treasury in the money market were very similar to those of his predecessor.

Secretary Cortelyou and the Panic of 1907

Various causes contributed to the Panic of 1907. There had been a slight disturbance of the money market in 1903, which after a year of relative quiet was followed in 1905–1906 by world-wide speculative excesses. In addition, from 1897 to 1907 a new element of weakness had been injected into the banking situation by the great development of trust companies, without provision for proper correlation to the National Banking System. These trust companies were subject only to state regulations, which in many instances did not require the keeping of reserves that could be considered adequate. Thus the deposit and credit operations of trust companies were capable of expanding to undue proportions without adequate reserves.[150] The entire credit structure was endangered by the inadequacy of the cash reserves. To this element of danger was added the fact that no central reservoir of credit resembling the central banks of Europe existed to which banks might look for help in time of stress.

Typical of the speculative conditions of 1907 was an organization of chain banks controlled, not by experienced commercial bankers, but by men interested in industrial and mining securities. Leading banks of this chain were the Mechanics' Bank, the Traders' Bank, and Knickerbocker Trust Company.[151] The vicious practice of using commercial banks and short-term deposits for the promotion of industrial enterprises undermined the confidence of the public in commercial banking.

George B. Cortelyou was Secretary of the Treasury in those days, and like Secretary Shaw he was convinced that the Treasury had to consider and protect the banking system as one of its Treasury

[150] "But they (trust companies) should be required to keep an appropriate, though relatively small, reserve within their own vaults, lest in times of financial distress their large deposits with national banks increase, rather than diminish, the evils of financial panics." U.S., Treasury Dept., *Annual Report of the Secretary, 1905*, p. 35; Conant, *History of Modern Banks of Issue*, p. 707.

[151] Sprague, *History of Crises under the National Banking System*, pp. 246–255.

functions. Fiscal and central banking functions combined, in his opinion, constitute the legitimate Treasury activities.[152] Beginning in March, 1907, when the crisis was only slowly developing, the Secretary was asked to relieve the market with Treasury reserves. He responded with weekly deposits in all parts of the country. But the crash was not avoided. Despite large gold imports and aid from the Government, the banks found it difficult to maintain adequate reserves.[153]

On October 21 the Knickerbocker Trust Company of New York closed its doors. Two weeks later the Lincoln Trust and the Trust Company of New York were in difficulty. On the twenty-fourth of October a panic broke out on the stock exchange, and the interest rate on demand loans rose to 125 percent per annum. The interior banks were calling for their balances, and the New York banks lost about $107,000,000 of their funds between October 27 and December 7. Treasury assistance was insufficient. Secretary Cortelyou could transfer to the national banks of New York City only about $36,000,000 in small bills to meet the demand of the interior banks for currency and to counteract the withdrawing of funds from the embattled banks of New York.[154] Hoarding set in, and about $291,-000,000 disappeared from circulation during the panic. So severe was the crisis that there was a demand from responsible quarters for a Government issue of fiat money.[155]

The money market had become accustomed to relying upon the Treasury. The money market and the Treasury were interdependent. Each could not pursue its own course without affecting the

[152] "This action [Treasury deposits in different sections of the country] is taken to meet the commercial and industrial needs of the country at this season [summer], and is believed to be preferable to waiting until a time of acute stringency when the only alternative would be a large general deposit." U.S., Treasury Dept., *Annual Report of the Secretary, 1907*, p. 59.

[153] U.S., Treasury Dept., *Annual Report of the Secretary, 1907*, p. 58; Sprague, *History of Crises under the National Banking System*, p. 241.

[154] U.S., Treasury Dept., *Annual Report of the Secretary, 1907*, p. 59.

[155] Similar requests were made before, for example, in the Panic of 1873. "It should be stated that there were many persons who insisted with great earnestness that it was the duty of the executive to disregard any and all laws which stood in the way of affording the relief suggested by them—a proposition which indicates the state of feeling and the excitement under which applications were made to the Secretary of the Treasury to use the public money." U.S., Treasury Dept., *Annual Report of the Secretary, 1873*, p. xv; Kinley, *Independent Treasury*, p. 258.

functions of the other. The money market had sacrificed its individual self-reliance for dependence upon the Treasury, upon which it relied for the maintenance of a smoothly functioning economic system and for direct financial help in times of difficulty. But neither task could be fully accomplished by the Treasury. The Treasury was not equipped to maintain economic stability.[156] A central planning board or central bank might have done better in this respect. By the middle of November the Treasury had deposited all the money it could spare, which was not very much, because revenue was declining. The money market was urgently in need of further help.

In order to relieve the situation Secretary Cortelyou, acting under authority of the Act of March 4, 1907 (34 Stat. 1290), notified the national banks that they might substitute "bonds suitable for savings banks' investment for government bonds which were held as securities against public deposits." [157] It was the same device which Secretary Shaw had used four years previously to increase the volume of United States bonds available for national bank notes. As a result national bank notes in circulation increased by about $83,-000,000 before December 31, 1907.[158] Even that amount was insufficient, and the long time involved in securing bonds suitable for note issues increased the circulation only after the need had passed away. Since Federal bonds outstanding were limited in quantity, attempts at further note issues led to competitive bidding for these bonds. The usual effect on bond prices followed. The increased demand drove the 2 percent bonds up to 110, and even at that price the amount available was too small for the needs of circulation.[159]

---

[156] "The laws under which he administers his office should be made to meet the daily needs of the people, and his duties, sufficiently onerous as they are, should not be made more burdensome by restrictions which leave him with the responsibility but with no adequate means at his disposal to meet it." . . . "In times of emergency his hands are virtually tied." U.S., Treasury Dept., *Annual Report of the Secretary, 1907,* p. 60.

[157] *Ibid.,* p. 59; U.S., Treasury Dept., *Annual Report of the Secretary, 1908,* p. 27.

[158] U.S., Treasury Dept., *Annual Report of the Secretary, 1909,* p. 202.

[158]

Month	Year	National Bank Notes in Circulation
October	1907	$595,123,866
November	1907	648,895,117
December	1907	679,034,664

U.S., Treasury Dept., *Annual Report of the Secretary, 1909,* p. 202.

[159] U.S., Treasury Dept., *Annual Report of the Secretary, 1908,* p. 27.

To relieve the shortage of Government bonds carrying the note-issuing privilege, the Secretary of the Treasury deemed it necessary, on November 17, to offer for sale an additional $50,000,000 Panama Canal bonds authorized under the Act of June 28, 1902 (32 Stat. 481), and $100,000,000 of 3 percent certificates of indebtedness authorized under the Act of June 27, 1898 (30 Stat. 494). National banks were the main purchasers of these securities. The general public took only $24,631,980 of the bonds and $15,436,500 of the loan certificates.[160] The Treasury probably had hoped to sell the bonds to those private persons who were hoarding money. But if banks or people who had not hoarded bought them, the circulation of money was reduced by taking their cash and thus the stringency was made worse. To avoid such an effect the Secretary of the Treasury transferred to national banks part of the purchase money which had been paid directly to the Treasury. Therefore, with one hand he was withdrawing money from circulation in accepting cash payment for the Treasury bonds and with the other was restoring the cash to circulation by depositing it in national banks. The banks which purchased these securities for themselves or their customers were allowed to retain as a deposit 90 percent of the purchase price of the Panama bonds and 75 percent of the purchase price of the certificates.[161]

In addition, the Comptroller of the Currency, whose superior officer is the Secretary of the Treasury, fearing that a revelation of the condition of the banks would add to the panic, postponed the call for a statement of the conditions of the banks which would normally have been issued in November. This period of grace aided the banks, which in the meantime put their finances in good order to meet the call. The delay made them cautious in making discounts and undertaking new commitments. Early in December, 1907, trade conditions began to improve. Soon the Secretary of the Treasury was able to ask the banks to return some of the deposited funds. The gold moving inward in payment for exports contributed to the

---

[160] All these obligations, except $91,820 in bonds, were used as basis for increasing circulation or securing Government deposits. See *ibid.*, p. 28; Professor Sprague claims that by December, 1907, there was an increase of $34,000,000 in new issues due to these securities. See Sprague, *History of Crises under the National Banking System*, p. 317.

[161] U.S., Treasury Dept., *Annual Report of the Secretary, 1908*, p. 28; Sprague, *History of Crises under the National Banking System*, p. 316.

mitigation of the stringency. By the middle of December more than $100,000,000 of the metal had arrived.[162]

In explanation of his action the Secretary of the Treasury said he wanted to convince the public, both at home and abroad, that the Government was alive to the stringent conditions and determined to give its aid to the money market in every legal and proper form.[163] The public and the banks, as well as Government officers, regarded the Treasury as a proper and necessary agent to step into the picture in times of monetary stringencies. In 1907 the Treasury could intervene because of a substantial surplus of revenue over expenditure, which it did not have in 1893. Theoretically the position of the Treasury had not changed and the same convictions and aims motivated the Secretary of the Treasury in both depressions. But in 1893 the Treasury, because of its own deficit, could not act as a central bank and come to the assistance of the money market. The Treasury actually had to appeal to the banks for help to save itself.

In aiding the money market during the stringency Secretary Cortelyou was criticized for issuing the Panama Canal bonds and Treasury certificates, much as Secretary Carlisle had been criticized fourteen years before.[164] In the Treasury there was cash on hand and deposited with national banks amounting to about $400,000,000,[165] and it was difficult to see why the Treasury should borrow on Treasury certificates, which by law (Act of June 13, 1898) can be issued only when necessary to meet Treasury expenses.[166] In 1907 Treasury borrowing could be considered necessary only if one were willing to admit that the Government funds on deposit with the na-

---

[162] U.S., Treasury Dept., *Annual Report of the Secretary, 1908*, p. 90; Sprague, *History of Crises under the National Banking System*, p. 317.

[163] "As the crisis approached the Department adopted the strongest measures at its command to give material assistance." U.S., Treasury Dept., *Annual Report of the Secretary, 1908*, p. 27.

[164] "The Secretary of the Treasury is given wide discretion in many matters wherein he is rarely called upon to exercise it, and little, if any, in others where it is needed daily, particularly as to certain of those having to do with the vitally important subject of our currency. In times of emergency his hands are virtually tied. If in such periods of stress, in an effort to avert calamity and serve the interests of all the people, he is obliged to resort to unusual measures, criticism is unfortunately in many instances directed not to the inadequacy of the system, but solely to the effort to give relief, even though it be successful in accomplishing that purpose." U.S., Treasury Dept., *Annual Report of the Secretary, 1907*, p. 60; see also above, pp. 91–93.

[165] See Appendix II, above.   [166] 30 Stat. 466.

tional banks were not readily available, that is, if it were admitted that the national banks were insolvent. The power of issuing certificates when the Treasury does not need the proceeds is a dangerous weapon in the hands of any person, particularly of a political appointee.

The new 2 percent issues were highly desired by national banks as collateral for new note issues. The bonds were allocated to national banks, and then individuals were permitted to buy them, but not in excess of $10,000 for any one person. By December 31 public funds amounting to about $156,000,000 were on deposit with national banks in various parts of the country in proportion to their respective capital and surplus. The Secretary of the Treasury had tried to place funds in areas in which he recognized that the particular trade movements created special demands for currency.

In this panic we find the first deliberate and general application of the section of the law of March 4, 1907, providing that the Secretary of the Treasury in depositing public funds in banks should make the distribution as equitable as possible.[167] But this term is very ambiguous, and the only real guides would be convenience and safety. In some instances it might be well to deposit all additional Treasury funds in a single place, the seat of the trouble. Money somehow gravitates to financial centers; time and expense could be saved by eliminating the spreading of deposits since funds will not stay scattered. Whichever way we look at the provision of the law, the Secretary of the Treasury is considered *the judge of the needs for additional money* in the different sections of the country as based upon their location, industrial condition, and the particular trade movements at the time. This is a tremendous responsibility for a fiscal officer and one that properly belongs to a central bank.

So keenly did Secretary Cortelyou feel the difficulties and the responsibilities of his office that in April, 1907, he appointed a commission to deal with the problem of allocating the public deposits. As a result of the commission's work, he found it necessary to send the funds to the points most seriously threatened, which happened to be the financial centers.[168]

[167] 34 Stat. 1290.
[168] "Every effort was made to distribute the funds that they would meet actual needs in sections where business activity was at the maximum and currency was most urgently required." U.S., Treasury Dept., *Annual Report of the Secretary, 1908*, p. 28.

By adding to the list of acceptable bonds some new bonds the Secretary of the Treasury, in aiding the money market, also tried to "broaden the basis on which public deposits might be made." First, state, railroad, and municipal bonds within the provisions of savings bank laws of Massachusetts and New York were declared acceptable as securities up to 90 percent of their market value. But these bonds also became scarce in October, 1907, and the Secretary of the Treasury then accepted bonds meeting the more lenient requirements of Connecticut and New Jersey for legal investments of savings banks. He also accepted bonds not in these top classes, but of good market value, up to 75 percent of their market value. If their market price was above par, they were accepted at 90 percent.[169]

It was easier to deposit money in the banks in times of stress without causing disturbance than it was to get it back again. The only method of recovering funds once deposited was by actual transfer to the Treasury, since the Treasury would not draw checks against its account with the national banks. The recall of public deposits in many instances meant payment out of the reserve funds of the banks involved. A reduction in reserves in turn diminished the capacity of the banks involved to lend to and to finance commerce and industry. Therefore the Secretary of the Treasury had to exercise caution when withdrawing funds from national banks, even though after a crisis money accumulates in banks, discount rates fall, and it is somewhat less difficult to recall deposits than at other times.

The Secretary of the Treasury seemed obliged to exercise guardianship over the money market, not only in crises, but also in more normal times. He felt obliged to relieve the seasonal fluctuations in the money market by depositing public money in the banks in the fall to meet the autumnal drain from the interior and by taking it out after the funds had returned to the central reserve city banks. In a report to the Senate, Secretary Cortelyou said,

The Secretary of the Treasury felt under our existing fiscal and monetary system to have regard not simply to the operations of the Treasury but to their effect on the financial condition of the country. The present head of

[169] U.S., Treasury Dept., *Annual Report of the Secretary, 1907*, p. 59; U.S., Treasury Dept., *Annual Report of the Secretary, 1908*, p. 28.

the department had not assumed this obligation willingly and would be glad to be relieved of it, at least in part, by suitable legislation, but under a fiscal and monetary system which results in large accumulations of actual currency in the Treasury at times when it may be most needed in the market and which affords inadequate means of adapting the circulation to the demands of business, it would in his opinion, be a narrow view of his function which should limit him to keeping his own balance sheet favorable, while ignoring the effects of Treasury operations on the conditions of the country. If recent events should lead to intelligent legislation, tending to adapt the movement of currency more nearly automatically to the requirements of business, it would be a source of gratification to the Secretary and would diminish the sense of responsibility which must weigh heavily upon any occupant of the office under conditions such as those of the recent crisis.[170]

In any event, the Panic of 1907 presented an additional illustration of the use of Government funds to meet emergencies. Indeed, surprise was expressed by the Treasury Department when it did not have to intervene in the affairs of the money market during normal times.[171] When later in 1913 a minor emergency occurred, no greater than the annual pressure of funds for "crop moving" purposes, special Government deposits were made to relieve the fall stringency.[172] In the same year the Treasury under Mr. MacVeagh (March 4, 1909–March 4, 1913) placed $2,000,000 of its funds in banks in Dayton, Ohio, to restore confidence following the flood.[173] The funds were secured by state, municipal, or other local bonds acceptable to the Secretary of the Treasury. Secretary MacVeagh assumed the role of guardian over the money market.[174]

[170] U.S., Treasury Dept., *Response of the Secretary of the Treasury Calling for Certain Information in Regard to Treasury Operations*, 60th Cong., 1st Sess., Senate Document 208, p. 32.

[171] "And it was at no time certain that the Treasury Department might not be fairly called upon to use its facilities to assist these ordinary business transactions [crop moving]. I should have been sorry to feel it necessary for the Treasury Department to intervene at such a normal period as this. But of course it would have assisted if it had become necessary; for the use of the surplus in the Treasury belongs of right to the business operations of the country whenever a real need for it arises. I think it fortunate that the financial world has been able to finance the enlarged business of the country this autumn without resort to the reserve which the Treasury Department has accumulated." U.S., Treasury Dept., *Annual Report of the Secretary, 1912*, p. 2.

[172] U.S., Treasury Dept., *Annual Report of the Secretary, 1913*, pp. 2–3.

[173] *Ibid.*, p. 1.

[174] "So long as the Government has the power to intervene in a beneficent and unselfish way, the danger of panics and of unjust practices will be largely, if not wholly, destroyed." *Ibid.*, p. 4. "It has been, and will continue to be, the policy of the Secretary to exercise all the powers of the Department for the protection of the public and

The Aldrich-Vreeland Act and the Treasury

As a result of the experiences of 1907 several bills were introduced in the spring of 1908 looking to the creation of a more flexible currency. As a compromise between various proposals the Aldrich-Vreeland Act was finally passed, May 30, 1908. It provided for a special bank note currency to be utilized in periods of financial stress. These notes could be issued on the deposit of state or municipal bonds or through "national currency associations" on the basis of commercial paper, up to 75 percent of the value of such paper. A 10 percent redemption fund had to be maintained in Washington. "Aldrich-Vreeland notes" were taxable to the issuing bank at the rate of 5 per cent for the first month and 1 percent each succeeding month until 10 percent was reached. Because of the high tax and redemption fund provisions, a bank could not profitably issue these notes.[175] Another important provision was that no reserve need be held against deposits of public money in national banks.[176]

The Aldrich-Vreeland Act was conclusive evidence that legislation was finally "catching up" with some of the central banking doctrines of the times. The provision for "national currency associations" showed the willingness of banks to coöperate and aid one another in times of difficulty. The clause allowing the issuance of emergency currency based on commercial paper showed that the legislators and the public were aware of the lack of elasticity of the national bank notes and its consequences. Also they knew that in times of stringency the Secretary of the Treasury, by various devices, had tried to inject some elasticity into the currency. But the Treasury had not always been strong enough to achieve its aim. The act indicated that one of the central banking functions which the Treasury had been performing—aiding the banks in times of difficulty—should largely be replaced by mutual assistance on the part of the banks themselves. The trend seemed to be in the direction of the creation of new institutions which would take over some of the central banking functions of the Treasury. The Treasury would then become predominantly a fiscal agent. The culmination

---

the legitimate business interests of the country." U.S., Treasury Dept., *Annual Report of the Secretary, 1913,* p. 4.

[175] 35 Stat. 546.   [176] See above, p. 120.

of this trend was the establishment of the Federal Reserve System which was to assume the central banking functions exercised by the Treasury Department.

The Federal Reserve System was supposed to be a privately owned central banking organization, free from politics and from domination by the Treasury and dedicated to the general welfare of the banking and business community. According to some writers the creation of this central banking system was the result of the findings of the National Monetary Commission, which was created under authority of the Aldrich-Vreeland Act to make extensive studies of banking conditions in the United States and abroad.[177] The commission reported in January, 1912, and Senator Aldrich introduced a bill, based on the report, which contemplated the creation of a central bank of rediscount and issue, the National Reserve Association, to be chartered for fifty years. The country did not favor the bill, because it was feared that the National Reserve Association would be dominated by the interests of Wall Street, whose misdeeds the Pujo Committee was currently exposing.[178] As a compromise the Federal Reserve System was finally created, consisting of twelve Reserve Banks instead of the usual single central bank found in other countries. The system was another illustration of the American antipathy to centralization and of the customary suspicion of any agency, public or private, that concentrates large powers in its hands.

CONCLUSION

In the last three chapters it has been shown that the Treasury exercised functions customarily attributed to a central bank. At times the Treasury's influence on the money market was incidental to its fiscal actions, but enough evidence has been introduced to show that as early as 1791 the Treasury deliberately intervened in the money market and that ever after it continued intentionally to exert an influence on the reserves of commercial banks. The steady and conscious interference of the Treasury Department reached its height under the leadership of Secretary Shaw who considered the Treasury not only a fiscal agent but also the central bank of our national banking system.

[177] 35 Stat. 546.   [178] Willis, *The Federal Reserve System*, p. 109.

Some of the means at the disposal of the Treasury Department were the following: deposits of funds, withdrawal of funds, prepayment of interest and principal on bonds, the buying and selling of bonds, the transfer of funds, the changing of collateral and reserves behind Government deposits, the issue of currency, gold and silver purchases.

All of these methods are associated with the quantity theory of central banking. Emphasis was centered on the amount of credit available or outstanding, not on the type of credit. Special efforts were made to discover what activities of a central bank increase or decrease bank deposits and reserves. Thus, the various secretaries of the Treasury developed the methods just enumerated and later others, such as devaluation, gold sterilization, and the establishment of the stabilization fund. They were also influenced by their conviction that the quantity of deposits and reserves has an ultimate effect on prices, interest rates, income, and employment. While there may well be disapproval of the quantity theory of money and credit which the Treasury followed, its motives as a central bank are in the interests of general welfare; namely, the avoidance of crises and the mitigation of depressions. Since no central bank existed and the secretaries of the Treasury felt that they alone possessed the means for assistance, they found it difficult to remain in the background. Furthermore, the size of ordinary Treasury transactions inevitably gave them a dominant position in the money market.[179]

In fighting the Panic of 1907 the Treasury had played an active part. While some agency must perform central banking functions, there was naturally considerable disagreement concerning the ideal agency. Some men thought the Treasury's role was too dominant and looked forward to a transfer of its powers over the market to a separate central bank.[180] A similar approach was taken by the National Monetary Commission established in 1908, and it found many followers among the legislators.[181] The Aldrich Bill or National Monetary Commission Bill proposed the creation of a permanent agency for the issuance of notes, the holding of public funds, and the regulation of relations between the banks and the money market.[182] With the termination of the National Monetary Commis-

---

[179] Ibid., p. 37.   [180] Ibid., p. 87.
[181] Willis, The Theory and Practice of Central Banking, p. 75.   [182] Ibid., p. 72.

sion (Act of August 22, 1911) [183] the ground had been cleared for the work of the Banking and Currency Committee of the House of Representatives, which formulated the Federal Reserve Act. This committee felt the methods which the Treasury had used (and which are now associated with the quantity theory) [184] were inappropriate for solutions of business fluctuation problems. Its members advocated a theory (that is now termed "qualitative") which holds that the extent of business fluctuations can be reduced and disturbing influences from the side of money and credit can be diminished through close supervision and control of the quality of bank assets.[185] Book credits should be created on the basis of discounts of short-term self-liquidating commercial paper.[186] Furthermore, the extension of commercial credit should be the only province of the individual bank.[187] Banks should not be used by the Government as instruments of national policy in the financing of Government deficits, in the lowering of interest rates, in attempts to stimulate business recovery, in overcoming rigidities in costs and prices, or in attempting to put into operation national economic planning.[188]

Both schools of thought believe in rediscounting as a method of credit control, but the qualitative school emphasizes, not the quantity of the assets that are turned into bank deposits, but the quality or type of business credits. Through rediscounting the central bank could select eligible paper—only self-liquidating assets—and so con-

[183] 37 Stat. 30; An act to require the National Monetary Commission to make final report on or before January 8, 1912, and to repeal the sections creating the Commission; namely, 17, 18, 19 of the Act entitled "An act to amend the National Banking Laws," approved May 30, 1908 (35 Stat. 546); the repeal to take effect March 31, 1912.

[184] "The post war years have witnessed the rapid popularization of a theory according to which the important thing to control is the quantity of the banks' liabilities. Whenever there appears a tendency toward the liquidation of bank credit and a consequent contraction of deposits and inflow of currency, or a tendency toward a slowing down of the rate of spending, the central bank should take steps to increase the volume of money." Hardy, *Control of Prices and Business by the Federal Reserve System*, p. 6.

[185] "In the planning of the Federal Reserve System the control of the quality of bank assets was undoubtedly the most important train of thought, next to the prevention of money panics." *Ibid.*, p. 7.

[186] "When the Reserve System started, the dominant idea was that Reserve Banks should be passive so far as the quantity of bank credit was concerned but exercise an important degree of control over the type of lending which the banks did by restricting eligibility for rediscount to notes and acceptances of an approved type." *Ibid.*, pp. 5–6.

[187] Beckhart, *Qualitative Credit Control*, p. 20.

[188] Willis, *The Theory and Practice of Central Banking*, p. 76.

trol the amount of credit. Self-liquidating paper helps to move goods to the consumer and does not retard the flow into consumption in the hope for speculative gains. Such paper will not increase in volume much beyond the needs of business even in times of overoptimism. Speculative excesses are thus prevented by permitting only short-term commercial paper to be discounted and turned into bank deposits or circulating medium. Thus the purchasing-power needs of the community are met. As the commercial paper matures, the notes formerly issued on the basis of this commercial paper are retired. Thus elasticity is injected into the currency, and both theories agreed that lack of elasticity was a major defect of the currency under the National Banking Act. The legislation finally enacted represented a compromise between the two theories.

CHAPTER VI

Treasury Activities from the Inception of the Federal Reserve System to the Beginning of the First World War
1913–1916

AN ANALYSIS OF THE FEDERAL RESERVE SYSTEM AS A COMPROMISE MEASURE

IN 1913 the Democrats came into power on a platform which contained the statement that, "We oppose the so-called Aldrich Bill or the establishment of a central bank." [1] Nevertheless, the pressure for some sort of banking reform was so strong that early in the first session of Congress Mr. Carter Glass, chairman of the Banking and Currency Committee, introduced a bill for a central banking system. After considerable wrangling, Congress finally passed the Glass Bill which was actively supported by President Wilson. [2]

This law of December 23, 1913, generally known as the Federal Reserve Act, made many changes in the position of the Treasury. The law emphasized decentralization rather than complete control by a single banking institution which should dominate the entire nation and concentrate all banking power in its hands. [3]

Basic to the act was the attitude of the Democratic Party, which traditionally was opposed to a single central bank. Accordingly the act provided for twelve reserve banks, each one a separate and distinct legal entity. As such, each had its own board of directors representing business or agriculture, member banks, and the Government. Centralization was limited to coördination among the reserve banks through the agency of the Federal Reserve Board, which included ex-officio membership for the Secretary of the Treasury and the Comptroller of the Currency. That more than mere coördination

[1] Willis, *The Federal Reserve System*, p. 103.   [2] *Ibid.*, p. ix.   [3] *Ibid.*, p. 85.

was intended appears from the sweeping powers vested in this board, which included all the powers customarily needed to perform central banking functions. In particular, this body was to determine and to harmonize discount rates, define eligible paper, and control the issue of notes.[4] The board was eventually to end the Sub-treasury System in order to bring about a satisfactory fiscal-agency relationship between the banks and the Treasury.[5]

In examining the actual operation of the Federal Reserve System we shall note continual intervention on the part of the Government in commercial banking affairs.[6] It is interesting that under the Independent Treasury Act no express provision was made for Government intervention in the monetary sphere, yet the Treasury clearly dominated the area. Treasury influence was expressly provided for in the Federal Reserve Act by giving seats on the Federal Reserve Board to the Secretary of the Treasury and the Comptroller of the Currency.[7] The Treasury Department can use its position on the board to further its needs and wishes.[8]

The straddle induced by political expediency was first apparent in the peculiar combination of decentralization in form and a high degree of centralization in operation; and again in presumably independent central banking and actual strong Government influence. The straddle is a result of the historical struggle in the United States between the recognized need for adequate central banking and the distrust of any agency upon which sufficient central banking powers might be conferred. In the last analysis the American electorate distrusts the Government less than Wall Street, or big

[4] Willis, *The Theory and Practice of Central Banking*, p. 76.

[5] U.S., Treasury Dept., *Annual Report of the Secretary, 1920*, p. 167. The Act of May 29, 1920 (41 Stat. 654) authorized the Secretary of the Treasury to discontinue the subtreasuries and to transfer all their duties to the Treasurer of the United States or to the mints or assay offices, or to the Federal Reserve Banks after July 1, 1921.

[6] "As time passed it [the Federal Reserve Board] gradually became more and more dependent upon Treasury dictations and less and less able to assert itself independent of the Treasury authorities. This was perhaps the most fundamental error in the process of organization, since it forever condemned the Board to a position of subordination and definitely established it as in fact, even if not in theory, a portion of the organization of the Treasury Department." Willis, *The Federal Reserve System*, p. 674.

[7] Section 10, Federal Reserve Act, quoted in U.S., Treasury Dept., *Annual Report of the Secretary, 1914*, p. 114.

[8] "Not only had the Treasury proven dictatorial, but the Board had found the relationship irksome and unpleasant in a variety of different ways." Willis, *The Federal Reserve System*, p. 835.

business, or the money powers.[9] Therefore central banking powers
and functions have for 150 years tended to gravitate toward the
Federal Government represented by the United States Treasury.

Other changes in our banking system affecting the Treasury's
central banking functions were involved in the creation of "Federal
Reserve notes." The lack of flexibility in the volume of notes outstanding had contributed to periodic stringencies and panics. One
of the main purposes of the Federal Reserve Act was the creation
of a note currency which would adjust itself in quantity outstanding to the "changing needs of business." [10] The framers of the act
accepted the concept of an "asset currency" as a flexible and adequately secured note currency. This implied currency based on
short-term self-liquidating paper rather than on gold. As in many
other respects, the act again straddles the issue: the reserve was
to be a maximum of 100 percent in the form of commercial paper
and a minimum of 40 percent in gold.[11] The entire 100 percent reserve could consist of gold.[12] Commercial paper, therefore, could
be replaced by gold as reserve for the new notes, whereas the oppo-
site was and is legally not permitted.[13] Such notes could be issued

[9] The new system should provide "for a central agency, to represent and act for
the organized and cooperative banks—this agency to be securely free from political or
trust control but with the government having adequate and intimate supervision of it."
U.S., Treasury Dept., *Annual Report of the Secretary, 1912,* p. 3.

[10] "Some writers who have reviewed the history of the Federal Reserve System have
been disposed to place great emphasis upon the problems of note issue, pointing out
that in the beginning the concept which was adhered to by the system was that of
providing a currency which should expand and contract as business needs expanded
and contracted." Willis, *The Federal Reserve System,* p. 1521.

[11] Section 16, Federal Reserve Act, quoted in U.S., Treasury Dept., *Annual Report
of the Secretary, 1914,* p. 120; Willis, *The Federal Reserve System,* p. 859.

[12] "Strictly and carefully framed, the original provisions of the Act were intended
to prevent the issue of notes save as the result of the discount of actual bona fide commercial paper. This provision was speedily qualified through the development of evasive
practices, prevailing throughout the system with the knowledge and consent of the
Federal Reserve Board, which soon made the original provision only a handicap and
led to its withdrawal. Its place was taken by an amended section, Act of June 21, 1917
(40 Stat. 232) which was intended to permit the issue of notes to take place practically
on a gold certificate basis." *Ibid.,* p. 1522.

[13] The late nineteen-thirties saw an almost complete elimination of commercial paper
as a backing for Federal Reserve notes, due to the diminishing volume of commercial
paper handled by the Federal Reserve banks and the heavy inflow of gold; *Federal
Reserve Bulletin,* April, 1940, p. 307. Collateral back of Federal Reserve notes has at different times consisted of different assets, including a larger or smaller volume of gold or
gold certificates, commercial paper, or United States Government securities. As required
by law, this collateral has been equal at all times to at least 100% of Federal Reserve

in any amount, restricted only by the reserve requirements and by the amount of gold and of self-liquidating paper in existence at any one time.

According to the act the Federal Reserve banks were to hold, supervise, and protect the Government's own funds. The Secretary of the Treasury was to transfer the funds from the sub-treasuries and from national banks serving as Government depositories to the Federal Reserve banks.[14] This transfer, if sudden and complete, would have entailed great hardships for some communities, where the funds and lending power of their national banks would have been seriously diminished. To prevent such difficulties and to encourage the purchase of government securities during the war, Treasury receipts from taxation and borrowing were left in the banks of those communities where they had originated.[15] Again the Federal Reserve Act in theory seemed to change the position of the Treasury more thoroughly than it proved to be changed under conditions of actual operation.

Since supervision and examination of commercial banks are considered central banking functions in most countries, with the exception of England, France, and Germany,[16] the Treasury's powers in that direction were again seemingly diminished by a clause in the Federal Reserve Act. The act gave the Federal Reserve banks the power of supervising the Federal Reserve member banks to insure law enforcement and protection of depositors.[17]

---

notes outstanding and the Reserve banks have maintained reserves of gold or gold certificates equal to at least 40% of Federal Reserve notes in circulation.

"As of June 30, 1940, Federal Reserve notes outstanding amounted to $5,163,284,000 Against these Federal Reserve notes the Federal Reserve banks had deposited $5,575,-500,000 in gold certificates with the Federal Reserve Agents." See U.S., Treasury Dept., *Annual Report of the Secretary, 1940*, pp. 778, 810.

[14] Section 15 of the Federal Reserve Act. Quoted in U.S., Treasury Dept., *Annual Report of the Secretary, 1914*, p. 119.

[15] Act of April 24, 1917 (40 Stat. 35); Act of September 24, 1917 (40 Stat. 288); U.S., Treasury Dept., *Annual Report of the Secretary, 1917*, p. 25; see below, pp. 176–177, for discussion of the discontinuance of the Sub-treasury System and the reduction in the number of national banks serving as Government depositaries.

[16] U.S., Board of Governors of the Federal Reserve System, *Federal Reserve System— Its Purposes and Functions*, p. 33.

[17] Section 21, Federal Reserve Act. Quoted in U.S., Treasury Dept., *Annual Report of the Secretary, 1914*, pp. 126–127. Another step in the direction of diminishing the direct control of the Treasury over banks was taken much later, when in 1935 the Federal Deposit Insurance Corporation was created, which by its very nature must supervise the insured banks and the risks they take. *However, neither act eliminated the exam-*

Despite the many central banking functions which the act transferred to the Federal Reserve Board, it was the Treasury which in practice continued to dominate the money market. This fact will become evident as the war and other major events of the next few years are discussed. In chronological order the first disturbance after 1913 to which a central banking institution had to give attention was the Crisis of 1914, which occurred several months before the Federal Reserve banks were organized.

THE CRISIS OF 1914 AND THE TREASURY

This crisis was primarily due to the war. By July 15 the signs that war was threatening caused a shortage of sterling exchange in New York, because London had discontinued the business of accepting and discounting foreign bills of exchange.[18] On the other hand, the demand for sterling exchange was unusually great. The New York Stock Exchange was flooded with selling orders originating with foreign investors who wished to liquidate their holdings of American securities and to repatriate their funds by converting the dollar proceeds of their securities in New York into pounds sterling for transmittal to England.

The result of these factors was keen bidding for sterling exchange in New York. By August 1, 1914, the rate for sterling cable transfers to London went as high as $7.20 per pound ($4.866 par of exchange). Security sales by foreigners had involved the United States in the need to move immediate cash payments to foreign countries which in the absence of a supply of sterling exchange could be met only by gold shipments. The banks were being drained of their reserves as gold moved abroad. To prevent further gold depletion, continued decline in the prices of securities, and complete disorganization, the Stock Exchange remained closed after July 31, 1914.

---

ination of national banks by the Comptroller of the Currency. To avoid duplication in auditing and supervision, the Federal Reserve banks and the Federal Deposit Insurance Corporation did not duplicate the Comptroller's audits *and the Treasury retained much of its former eminence.* U.S., Board of Governors of the Federal Reserve System, *Annual Report, 1938,* pp. 12-14.

[18] Sprague, "The Crisis of 1914 in the United States," *American Economic Review,* Vol. V (September, 1915), p. 504.

By the beginning of August the country was entering upon a crisis; [19] uncertainty spread, caution and timidity were evident, consumption declined, and many businessmen were failing to pay their contractual obligations.[20] Since their incomes and collections were diminished and their inventories were marketable only at substantial losses, business men requested additional loans from the commercial banks to tide them over the crisis. In this crisis the Secretary of the Treasury, Mr. McAdoo (March 6, 1913–December 15, 1918), as well as responsible bankers, knew that loan expansion would help restore confidence, reduce liquidation, and enable producers to carry their inventories until they could be absorbed. Although in major panics more drastic steps might be necessary, two factors were at work to mitigate the 1914 difficulties: the war stimulated production of war materials, and the domestic economic structure was basically sound. On the other hand, banks were not in a position to lend unusually large amounts, since excess reserves and unusual lending capacity normally occur only when business is stagnant, as after a severe crisis.

Thus it was left to the Secretary of the Treasury to help the banks. He recognized the need for Treasury interference in the general business situation,[21] and he made use of a varied list of effective measures. First, the Secretary of the Treasury, under the Aldrich-Vreeland Act, May 30, 1908 (35 Stat. 546) modified and extended until June 30, 1915, by Section 27 of the Federal Reserve Act, had discretionary power to issue emergency note currency to national banks upon their application and compliance with the provisions of the act.[22] The Secretary of the Treasury availed himself of this power and issued to national banks of New York City, from August 1 to October 31, 1914, emergency note currency in the amount of $141,228,000.[23]

The August 4, 1914, amendment to the Federal Reserve Act, supported by the Treasury, had reduced the tax on the use of emergency

---

[19] U.S., Treasury Dept., *Annual Report of the Secretary, 1914*, p. 2.

[20] Sprague, "The Crisis of 1914 in the United States," *American Economic Review*, Vol. V (September, 1915), p. 516.

[21] U.S., Treasury Dept., *Annual Report of the Secretary, 1914*, p. 2.

[22] 38 Stat. 265.

[23] U.S., Treasury Dept., *Annual Report of the Secretary, 1914*, p. 3.

notes from 5 percent to 3 percent for the first month, from 1 percent to ½ percent for each succeeding month, and the maximum tax from 10 percent to 6 percent.[24] The same amendment permitted bank notes to be issued up to 125 percent instead of 100 percent of the capital and surplus of the issuing national bank.[25] An increase in national bank notes in circulation resulted and contributed to the relief of the stringency. Little use was made of another provision of the August 4 amendment, which gave the Secretary of the Treasury discretionary powers to permit the issuance of emergency notes secured by bonds other than bonds of the United States Government deposited in the Treasury as security.[26]

The emergency notes enabled the banks to maintain payment on demand and to safeguard their reserves. The notes indirectly increased the reserve by releasing lawful money from circulation and allowing it to be withheld for reserve purposes. Gold, gold certificates, and other lawful money received by banks were retained, while banks paid out the new notes to their customers. These arrangements took care of one phase of the difficulties.

The Secretary of the Treasury also employed the time-tested method of depositing Treasury funds with the national banks to relieve a money stringency. Between August 1 and October 31, 1914, he deposited $3,400,000 in New York banks to help increase reserves, and during the same period he made special deposits of $19,-446,246 in the national banks of the cotton areas which were severely hit by the war.[27]

The steady flow of gold to Europe was another problem to be met. The Secretary of the Treasury was determined to help the country tide over the crisis, and he attempted another remedial measure. He met representatives of the clearing houses of New York, St. Louis, and Chicago on August 2 in a conference and decided to maintain an informal embargo on gold shipments abroad. Since the Stock Exchange was closed and orders to sell were not be-

[24] *Ibid.*, p. 131; 38 Stat. 682.

[25] U.S., Treasury Dept., *Annual Report of the Secretary, 1914*, p. 131; The Act of August 4, 1914, amending Section 27 of the Federal Reserve Act is quoted in U.S., Board of Governors of the Federal Reserve System, *Digest of Rulings of the Federal Reserve System*, p. 549.

[26] *Ibid.;* the provisions of this amendment are similar to those of Section 3 of the Act of May 30, 1908 (35 Stat. 546), which expired June 30, 1914.

[27] U.S., Treasury Dept., *Annual Report of the Secretary, 1914*, p. 31.

ing taken, the embargo was easy to maintain. While the agreement did not add to the bank reserves, it did not decrease them.

An informal embargo at best could be a mere temporary device. Thus on September 4 the Secretary of the Treasury again met New York bankers to discuss the gold situation. At the meeting he suggested a pool to provide gold for export.[28] The pool was formed, because all concerned recognized the necessity of promptly meeting the foreign obligations of banks, corporations, and individuals to Europe. This course of action could be expected to maintain the high credit of this country and demonstrate its ability to meet its obligations. The pool was expected to relieve the international exchange situation and to regulate the outflow of gold. The bankers agreed to the suggestion of the Treasury and contributed $150,-000,000 in gold.[29] A committee of bankers appointed by the Treasury and the New York Clearing House Association carried out the duties of handling the funds, fixing the price at which foreign exchange was to be bought and sold and supervising the general shipments and withdrawals of gold.

By the fifteenth of September the initial effect of the crisis in creating a demand for additional loans seems to have been over. Due to the maintenance of cash payments and a liberal loan policy by the banks, the crisis did not turn into a panic.

While the coöperative $150,000,000 gold pool helped to bring the high foreign exchange rates back to normal, the final result could not have been achieved without substantial commodity exports. Again, the Secretary of the Treasury recognized this fact and concluded it was his duty to stimulate exports. In doing so he certainly did not act as a fiscal agent of the Government. Commodity exports as a remedy for the foreign-exchange shortage were first advocated by Secretary of the Treasury McAdoo when he met the British Treasury officials in Washington regarding payment to English creditors. At that time it was emphasized that Secretary McAdoo met Sir George Paish and Mr. Basil Blackett, not as Secretary of the Treasury, but as chairman of the Federal Reserve Board.[30]

The various actions taken by the Secretary of the Treasury in

[28] *Ibid.*, p. 72. [29] *Ibid.*, p. 17.
[30] Brown, "The Government and the Money Market," in Beckhart, ed., *The New York Money Market*, Vol. IV, p. 208.

1914 to protect general business conditions in the country achieved their aim.[31] By November, 1914, the crisis was over, dealings in securities on the New York Stock Exchange were gradually resumed, and by April 1, 1915, all restrictions on security trading were removed.[32] The disturbance of 1914 was another indication that the Treasury's intervention can be effective. The Treasury was the leader in the money market, despite the existence of the Federal Reserve Board.

After the 1914 difficulties had passed, an orderly attempt could be made to put the Federal Reserve System into full and normal operation, as had been planned on December 23, 1913, when the Federal Reserve Act was passed. The Federal Reserve Board had been in existence since August 10, 1914, but the Federal Reserve banks did not begin to function until November 14, 1914.[33] Introduction of the system had been postponed because of the financial difficulties accompanying the outbreak of war in Europe. By 1915 financial conditions had quieted down sufficiently so that the Treasury could give the Federal Reserve System opportunity to assume its rightful position as leader in the money market.

TREASURY POWERS ASSUMED BY THE FEDERAL RESERVE SYSTEM

Originally it had been hoped that the relation existing between the national banks and the Treasury, because of Government deposits and withdrawals, would be severed. The Federal Reserve System would provide the banking services which the Treasury needed in the handling of its funds. Also, the Federal Reserve System had been created to relieve the Treasury of all responsibilities in money market crises, to keep politics from entering into the distribution of Government deposits, to cut the connection between the Government debt and the currency, to eliminate manipulation of the public debt in order to increase or decrease funds in the money market, and to prevent the receipt and disbursement of Govern-

---

[31] "Every power of the government was exerted to mitigate the situation and I believe that it is not inexact to say that but for the active agency of the government in protecting and conserving the business interests of the country during that critical period grave disaster would have resulted." U.S., Treasury Dept., *Annual Report of the Secretary, 1915*, p. 1.

[32] Sprague, "The Crisis of 1914 in the United States," *American Economic Review*, Vol. V (September, 1915), p. 532.

[33] U.S., Treasury Department, *Annual Report of the Secretary, 1914*, p. 18.

ment revenue from influencing bank reserves. In spite of the high hopes of the designers of the Federal Reserve System, the pressure of economic and political emergencies gradually converted the Federal Reserve System into an efficient tool for the consolidation of all banking under a single supreme authority—the Treasury.[34]

Transfer of Government Funds to be Handled by the Federal Reserve System

According to the first draft of the bill all Government money in the general fund was to be deposited in the Federal Reserve banks, and the amounts to be allocated to the various reserve banks were to be determined by the principle of equitable geographic distribution.[35] With this responsibility the Treasury retained the coincidental but important power of selecting its own depositories.[36] Repeatedly use was made of this authority. The Treasury continued to make deposits for crop-moving purposes.[37] The Secretary sent funds to meet special emergencies: for example, national banks in Dallas needed cash because of the drought in 1918.[38]

[34] "Perhaps it was not strange that the many trials and difficulties of the war and post-war periods gradually led up to a climax in which complete centralization was accomplished, with the government reasserting itself as the master of this centralization and the ultimate arbiter of all credit operations within American territory. It is intended to sketch the gradual evolution of this process of converting the Federal Reserve System originally designed as a framework for the development of local central banking in the United States, into an agency for the consolidation of all banking under a single supreme authority—the Federal Government." Willis, The Theory and Practice of Central Banking, pp. 89–90.

[35] Chapman, Fiscal Functions of the Federal Reserve Banks, p. 44; Willis, The Federal Reserve System, p. 144.

[36] Section 15 of the Federal Reserve Act, U.S., Treasury Dept., Annual Report of the Secretary, 1914, p. 119.

[37] "A critical situation was presented [respecting cotton, caused by the European war] it could be met only by prompt and decisive action. What the people of the cotton States needed more than any other thing at that particular moment was the assurance that every proper power of the Government would be exerted, as it was in 1914, for their protection and assistance. No other kind of assurance would have satisfied. The support of the Government alone would give confidence. I announced August 23, 1914, that I would, if necessary, deposit $30,000,000 in gold in the Federal Reserve banks at Atlanta, Dallas, and Richmond in order that these banks might have increased resources to rediscount loans made by national banks or member banks on cotton." U.S., Treasury Dept., Annual Report of the Secretary, 1915, pp. 4–5.

[38] "On March 13, 1918, the Secretary of the Treasury advised the chairman of the Federal Reserve Bank of Dallas, Texas, to the effect that, if he found that banks in the drought-stricken area were insufficiently supplied with loanable funds, deposits would be made in national bank depositories in drought stricken districts up to an aggregate of $50,000,000, having due regard to a fair distribution. Directions were given for the preparation of lists of applicants and specifying the securities to be taken. De-

Secretary McAdoo, on November 13, 1915, announced that he had appointed the Federal Reserve banks fiscal agents, effective as of January 1, 1916. Late in 1915 the bulk of the Treasury funds on deposit with national banks in cities where a Federal Reserve Bank was located were transferred to the Federal Reserve banks. Thus each Federal Reserve Bank secured some funds held by the national banks in its own city.[39] The accounts of the Treasury at the Federal Reserve banks were built up by tax receipts, customs, and other revenues. On the other hand, payments made by the Government to meet contracts and current expenses decreased the Treasury accounts and increased the reserve funds of the commercial banks. At some times and in some sections banks, through Government payments, were gaining funds that were then available for their reserves and credit expansion; while at other times and in other places banks lost funds to the Treasury account and had to retrench. The Treasury tried to avoid these disturbances and therefore continued its policy of transferring balances from one Federal Reserve district to another in order to offset inequalities.[40] The Federal Reserve System had to work out a technique whereby the increase or decrease of reserve funds of member banks due to Government payments and receipts would be offset by other expansions and contractions of reserve credit. Unless that were accomplished, the former payments to the Treasury in gold constituted no more of a drain upon bank reserves than did the new payments in form of transfers on the books of the Federal Reserve banks, inasmuch as deposits with the reserve banks constituted part of the required bank reserves of member banks.

The Treasury, Gold, and the Foreign Exchanges under the Federal Reserve System

Under the Independent Treasury System the Treasury did not have any direct relationship to the foreign exchange market. The Treasury affected foreign exchange rates only through its gold trans-

---

posits, after approval of application and approval of collateral, were made direct by the Treasurer of the United States." U.S., Treasury Dept., *Annual Report of the Secretary, 1918*, p. 105.

[39] U.S., Treasury Dept., *Annual Report of the Secretary, 1915*, p. 12.

[40] "I have announced my willingness to make deposits for like purposes [moving and marketing crops] in the Federal Reserve banks in other sections of the country if they should be in need of such funds." *Ibid.*, p. 9.

actions. After 1846 customs duties had to be paid to the Treasury in gold, although after the resumption of specie payments greenbacks were acceptable for customs dues under the Act of January 14, 1875 (18 Stat. 296). Nevertheless there was danger that the specie paid into the Treasury would deplete the gold reserves of the banks and thereby affect the general business situation; accordingly several secretaries of the Treasury had frequently resorted to devices to encourage gold imports on the part of the banks.[41] Moreover, even before the enactment of the Federal Reserve System, under the Act of March 4, 1907 (34 Stat. 1289), customs dues might be deposited in national banks, and under the Act of March 2, 1911, payment of custom dues could be made by certified bank checks, and new gold could also be deposited in the banks and paid for by checks drawn on the Treasury.[42] These provisions made it easier for the banks to maintain adequate gold reserves, and they also allowed new gold to pass into the reserves of banks.[43] The Treasury's anxiety with regard to the maintenance of adequate reserves for commercial banks was thus relieved. However, the Treasury always continued to have the final responsibility for maintaining the gold standard under the Act of March 14, 1900. It was required to keep sufficient gold in the Treasury to redeem all circulating media in gold when so demanded.[44]

Under the Federal Reserve System express powers to deal with foreign exchange problems were granted to the Federal Reserve Board. The board can supervise foreign branches of member banks, and far-reaching powers are granted to it to engage in open-market transactions involving gold, cable transfers, and foreign bills of exchange.[45] Beginning in 1914 it actively engaged in many of these

[41] On Secretary Boutwell, see p. 68; on Secretary Shaw, p. 104.

[42] 36 Stat. 965; "Why should an archaic regulation be permitted to continue that requires payment of revenue to be made in actual currency—and in only particular kinds of currency at that? There is no serious practical danger in taking a certified check. All of the similar business of the country is done by checks, many not even certified." U.S., Treasury Dept., *Annual Report of the Secretary, 1910*, p. 7; "In furtherance of the views expressed in the secretary's report of 1910, Congress passed the Act of March 2, 1911 making it lawful to receive certified checks in payment of duties on imports and internal taxes." U.S., Treasury Dept., *Annual Report of the Secretary, 1911*, p. 15.

[43] U.S., Treasury Dept., *Annual Report of the Secretary, 1913*, p. 230.

[44] 31 Stat. 45.

[45] Section 14 of the Federal Reserve Act quoted in U.S., Treasury Dept., *Annual Report of the Secretary, 1914*, pp. 118-119.

activities through the various Federal Reserve banks, and to that extent the role of the Treasury was reduced in importance.[46]

Currency and the Treasury under the Federal Reserve System

Under the Federal Reserve Act, national bank notes became of less importance and the country was released from the "strait jacket" of having to rely on an inflexible amount of National Bank notes. National Bank notes were now supplemented by Federal Reserve notes and deprived of their preëminent position among our various types of currency. The close connection between the size of the Federal debt and the amount of paper currency outstanding was broken. While an improvement in our monetary system, this change seemed to, but actually did not, deprive the Treasury of some of its effective means for intervening in the money market.[47]

The Federal Reserve Act in 1913 had made it possible that National Bank notes could eventually disappear from circulation.[48]

[46] However, as will be shown in later chapters, the financial consequences of World War I and of the Depression of 1929 could not be successfully overcome by any action of the Federal Reserve System and thus the Treasury again had to step into the foreign-exchange market and resume its place as the most active and influential central banking agency.

[47] See p. 148 for discussion on amendment to the Federal Reserve Act of September 7, 1916 (39 Stat. 752); Section 3 of the Glass-Steagell Act of February 27, 1932, provided that until March 3, 1933, should the Federal Reserve Board deem it in the public interest, it may, upon the affirmative vote of not less than a majority of its members, authorize the Federal Reserve banks to offer, and the Federal Reserve agents to accept, as such collateral security, direct obligations of the United States (47 Stat. 56). The Act of February 3, 1933, amends the Act of February 27, 1932, by striking out the date "March 3, 1933" wherever it appears and inserting in lieu thereof "March 3, 1934" (47 Stat. 795). The second paragraph of Section 16 of the Federal Reserve Act (38 Stat. 265) was amended by the Act of March 6, 1934. It provided that until March 3, 1935, or until the expiration of such additional period (not exceeding two years) as the President may prescribe, the Federal Reserve Board may, should it deem it in the public interest, upon the affirmative vote of not less than a majority of its members, authorize the Federal Reserve banks to offer and the Federal Reserve agents to accept as collateral security for Federal Reserve notes, direct obligations of the United States (48 Stat. 398). Text of proclamation of the President, dated February 14, 1935, extending for two years the provisions of the Act of March 6, 1934. See U.S., Treasury Dept., *Annual Report of the Secretary, 1935,* p. 265. The Act of March 1, 1937 (50 Stat. 23), further extended until June 30, 1939, the period during which direct obligations of the United States may be used as security for Federal Reserve notes. See U.S., Treasury Dept., *Annual Report of the Secretary, 1937,* p. 263. The Act of June 30, 1939 (53 Stat. 991), extended the period until June 30, 1941, on which date it was extended to June 30, 1943 (55 Stat. 395). See U.S., Treasury Dept., *Annual Report of the Secretary, 1941,* p. 356.

[48] On June 30, 1940, the amount of National Bank notes outstanding was $167,190,000. The notes long since have ceased to be the obligation of the banks, for the banks de-

The only Federal bonds outstanding after 1913 which carried the note circulation privilege were the 2 percent consols of 1930 and the 2 percent Panama Canal bonds of 1916–36 and 1918–38. The last bonds with the circulation privilege were called for redemption on July 1, and August 1, 1935 by order of the Secretary of the Treasury issued March 11, 1935.[49] National bank notes rapidly diminished in volume outstanding during the fiscal year 1935.[50]

Despite the introduction of Federal Reserve notes, the Treasury was not entirely eliminated from the currency picture. It continued to be the custodian of the $150,000,000 redemption fund against greenbacks and the Treasury notes of 1890, which had been established in 1900.[51] In this way the Treasury was still linked to the country's currency.

The Public Debt, the Treasury, and the Federal Reserve System

Under the new system the Treasury was able to change the size of the public debt without considering the effect of such action on the currency. The Federal debt was to become a mere fiscal matter, and it was deprived of its central banking implications. Even the handling of the details of such Treasury devices as the anticipation of interest payments, sale of special bond issues, and redemptions could be left to the Federal Reserve System as the fiscal agent of the Government if the Secretary of the Treasury should so desire. In other words, the work could be delegated to the Federal Reserve System, but the power of determining policies was retained by the Treasury. This is one of the earliest instances when it appeared that the Federal Reserve System might sink in importance to the status of a mere tool in the hands of the "central banking" Treasury.

---

posited with the Treasury cash to discharge their liability at the time the Treasury redeemed the bonds upon which the circulation was secured. U.S., Treasury Dept., *Annual Report of the Secretary, 1940*, p. 809.

[49] U.S., Board of Governors of the Federal Reserve System, *Digest of Rulings*, p. 186; see below, pp. 179, 193.

[50] U.S., Treasury Dept., *Annual Report of the Secretary, 1939*, p. 505.

On June 30, 1935, the amount of national bank
notes outstanding was $769,095,645
On June 30, 1936, the amount of national bank
notes outstanding was 371,721,815
Showing retirements during the year of $397,373,830

[51] Section 2 of the Act of March 14, 1900 (31 Stat. 45).

Under authority of Section 15 of the Federal Reserve Act the Secretary of the Treasury appointed the Federal Reserve banks fiscal agents, as of January 1, 1916. Thereupon they took care of many details concerning the public debt.[52] On September 7, 1916, the Federal Reserve Act was amended in such a way as to restore to the Federal bonds some of the importance which they seemed to have lost by the introduction of the Federal Reserve System.[53] Section 13 as amended reads:

Nothing in this Act contained shall be construed to prohibit such notes, drafts, and bills of exchange, secured by staple agricultural products, or other goods, wares, or merchandise from being eligible for such discount; but such definition does not include notes, drafts or bills covering merely investment or issued or drawn for the purpose of carrying or trading in stocks, bonds or other investment securities, *except bonds and notes of the Government of the United States.*[54]

This amendment permitted the member banks to secure from the Federal Reserve banks direct advances of not more than fifteen days maturity on their own notes, which were backed by eligible paper or Government securities. This arrangement made Government bonds more attractive as bank investments. Under the National Banking Act United States bonds were security merely for bank note currency, but under the amendment of 1916 they could be employed as collateral for Federal Reserve notes and used as the basis of bank deposit currency.[55] The amendment was not intended to be a major change in the spirit of the act or to supersede its basic principle that Federal Reserve credit was to be extended upon security of commercial paper,[56] although it did open the way to a new and even more significant integration of the public debt into the machinery of the money market.[57]

CONCLUSION

As a result of the Independent Treasury System the Treasury had become so powerful as a central banking institution that public

[52] U.S., Treasury Dept., *Annual Report of the Secretary, 1915*, p. 12.
[53] 39 Stat. 752.
[54] U.S., Treasury Dept., *Annual Report of the Secretary, 1916*, p. 568.
[55] Willis and Steiner, *Federal Reserve Banking Practice*, p. 174.
[56] *Federal Reserve Bulletin*, July, 1916, p. 323.
[57] Brown, "The Government and the Money Market," in Beckhart, ed., *The New York Money Market*, Vol. IV, p. 228.

opinion demanded the creation of a central bank free from Government intervention. The result was the establishment of the Federal Reserve banks, which took over most of the central banking powers previously held by the Treasury and also were given additional techniques. The Federal Reserve System was a compromise resulting from the historical struggle between the need for a central banking agency and unwillingness to grant so much power to any organization.

CHAPTER VII

Central Banking Activities of the Treasury during the First World War
1917–1919

THE FEDERAL RESERVE ACT was planned to free the commercial banks from the influence of the Treasury. But the Government, by marshaling and directing all forces in the country toward the one aim of winning the war, naturally assumed the dominant position in the money market. The Federal Reserve System has never regained the position of leadership to which it is entitled under the Act of December 23, 1913.

THE TREASURY AND THE FOREIGN EXCHANGE MARKET DURING THE WAR

Intervention on the part of the Treasury characterized the foreign exchange market during the war period. By September, 1916, the pound sterling had dropped to about $4.51.[1] The rapidly increasing volume of food stuffs and war materials purchased in this country by England contributed toward the lowering of the price of pounds sterling in New York and raised the price of dollars in London. To counteract further declines in the sterling rate of exchange the British authorities endeavored to build up dollar balances in New York. For that purpose gold was shipped to the United States, American securities were sold, and Americans in turn were induced to buy British securities. But all these methods were inadequate for a steady support of the rate of sterling exchange. Wide fluctuations could be prevented only by pegging the pound rate. This the British did in January, 1916, and they succeeded in maintaining the pegged rate of exchange at about $4.74.[2] In this task, however, they needed and

[1] *Federal Reserve Bulletin,* December, 1916, p. 729; Jaeger, *Stabilization of the Foreign Exchange,* p. 22.
[2] See Table VII.

TABLE VII

EXCHANGE RATES ON LEADING FOREIGN MONEY CENTERS
QUOTED IN NEW YORK CITY IN JANUARY DURING
THE YEARS 1914–1916 [a]

	1914		1915		1916	
	Low	*High*	*Low*	*High*	*Low*	*High*
London						
60-day bankers' bills: dollars	4.82	4.84	4.81	4.84	4.70	4.74
Sight drafts: dollars	4.86	4.87	4.83	4.85	4.74	4.78
Paris: francs	520.63	518.13	520.00	516.75	588.00	583.00
Berlin: dollars	94.69	95.00	86.63	88.38	73.00	76.75
Petrograd: dollars	51.50	51.75	42.38	43.50	29.32	30.00
Milan: lire	523.13	519.38	542.00	532.50	677.50	655.00
Amsterdam: dollars	40.13	40.31	40.06	40.50	42.50	45.88
Copenhagen: dollars	26.68	26.88	24.69	25.00	27.25	27.90
Zurich: francs	521.88	518.75	529.50	522.00	526.00	513.00

[a] Par rates—London, $4.8665; Paris, Milan, Zurich 518 francs per $100; Berlin $95.20 per 400 marks; Petrograd $51.50 per 100 rubles; Amsterdam $40.20 per 100 florins; Copenhagen $26.80 per 100 kroner. Figures compiled from *Federal Reserve Bulletin*, December, 1916, p. 727.

succeeded in getting assistance from the United States Treasury.[3] United States Treasury action supporting the efforts of the allied and associated powers became vigorous after our entry into the War.

By the Liberty Loan Acts of 1917 and 1918 [4] the Treasury was empowered to establish credits in favor of the Allies, and Congress appropriated $10,000,000,000 for this purpose.[5] The rising inter-allied debt meant the increasing indebtedness of England and other nations to the United States Treasury and of the United States Treasury in turn to the American public. The domestic debt in-

[3] "The financial history of the six months, from the end of the summer of 1916 up to the entry of the United States into the war, in April 1917, remains to be written. Very few persons, outside the half dozen officials of the British Treasury, who lived in daily contact with the immense anxieties of impossible financial requirements of those days can fully realize what steadfastness and courage were needed, and how entirely hopeless the task would soon have become without the assistance of the United States Treasury." Keynes, *Economic Consequences of the Peace*, p. 273, quoted in Brown, "The Government and the Money Market," in Beckhart, ed., *The New York Money Market*, Vol. IV, p. 235.

[4] April 24, 1917 (40 Stat. 35); September 24, 1917 (40 Stat. 288); April 4, 1918 (40 Stat. 502); July 9, 1918 (40 Stat. 844). See U.S., Treasury Dept., *Annual Report of the Secretary, 1917*, p. 17; U.S., Treasury Dept., *Annual Report of the Secretary, 1918*, p. 36.

[5] U.S., Treasury Dept., *Annual Report of the Secretary, 1917*, p. 17.

creased, the Treasury made large funds available to the Allies, and the Allies used the money to make purchases in America. To coordinate the demands of the Allies on the American Treasury, the Treasury established soon after America entered the war an Interallied Council on War Purchases, which eliminated unnecessary Treasury sales of sterling exchanges.[6]

Among the currencies of the belligerent nations, dollar exchange depreciated the least. Accordingly dollar exchange was at a premium in the allied countries and at a discount in the neutral areas. The neutrals sold dollar exchange to the Allies or used it to buy gold.[7] Gold shipments from New York depleted the gold stock available for Federal Reserve Bank reserves.[8] This gold drain was threaten-

TABLE VIII

RESERVES OF THE FEDERAL RESERVE BANK IN NEW YORK
FROM MARCH 30–JUNE 22, 1917
(In thousands of dollars)

Date	Total Reserves	Gold Coin and Certificates in Vault	Gold Settlement Fund	Gold Redemption Fund	Legal Tender Notes, Silver, etc.
March 30	237,626[a]	219,109	16,151	250	2,116
April 5–6	249,906	209,993	26,443	250	13,220
April 13	232,408	189,519	27,692	250	14,947
April 20	221,220	180,192	21,992	250	18,786
April 27	254,960[b]	155,072	75,767	250	23,871
May 4	244,149	183,376	27,345	250	33,178
May 11	279,314	178,416	71,493	250	29,155
May 18	248,103	189,625	37,809	250	20,419
May 25	293,957	168,255	95,376	250	30,076
June 1	210,447[c]	142,192	37,971	250	30,034
June 8	223,297	173,235	17,920	250	31,892
June 15	263,254	202,014	41,153	1,453	18,634
June 22	545,754[d]	330,989	38,748	5,202	28,397

[a] *Federal Reserve Bulletin*, May, 1917, p. 416.
[b] *Federal Reserve Bulletin*, June, 1917, p. 491.
[c] *Federal Reserve Bulletin*, July, 1917, p. 570.
[d] This figure includes: gold with foreign agencies, $18,738; gold with Federal Reserve Agent, $123,680.

[6] U.S., Treasury Dept., *Annual Report of the Secretary, 1920*, p. 70.
[7] U.S., Treasury Dept., *Annual Report of the Secretary, 1917*, p. 27.
[8] Brown, "The Government and the Money Market," in Beckhart, ed., *The New York Money Market*, Vol. IV, p. 240; see also Table VIII, above.

ing the expansion of bank credit, which was needed for the conduct of the war and would be made possible by the gold then in the Federal Reserve banks. To meet the situation specie redemption of paper currency to foreign holders was suspended by the imposition of an embargo on gold exports. Under the Espionage Act of June 15, 1917, the President was given the power to prohibit by proclamation the export of any article from the United States (40 Stat. 217). By the proclamation on September 7, 1917, exports of gold coin, bullion, and currency were so prohibited.[9] As regulated by the Presidential decree, permission to export gold had to be secured from the Federal Reserve Board, subject to the approval of the Secretary of the Treasury.[10] This arrangement made Treasury actions and policies completely overshadow the influence of Federal Reserve banks. The Treasury was now acting as a central bank in controlling the amount of gold to be shipped abroad.

Nevertheless, the exports of gold to neutral countries permitted by the Treasury continued,[11] and it was deemed necessary to control the foreign exchange rates absolutely, lest the enemy secure aid through dealings in neutral exchanges. Again acting under the au-

TABLE IX

UNITED STATES EXPORTS OF GOLD TO COUNTRIES BY MONTHS DURING 1917[a]

Country	January	February	March	April
France	$ 32,182	...	...	...
Spain	4,444,463	$ 3,616,827	$ 4,266,566	$ 4,400,300
England	10,828	...	...	...
Canada	1,842,377	91,866	1,611,434	142,592
Cuba	1,500,500	2,364,300	4,183,950	3,550,000
Other West Indies	6,000	51,000	54,000	5,000
All other North America	317,887	415,720	712,920	1,227,167
South America	10,259,995	10,949,240	3,512,994	1,378,051
China	...	...	...	...
British India	...	...	16,000	...
Hongkong	155,355	124,350	73,370	61,485
Japan	2,047,061	4,442,012	3,468,367	6,198,595
All other countries	103,750	12,744	20,000	2,000
Total	$20,719,898	$22,068,059	$17,919,601	$16,965,210

[9] U.S., Treasury Dept., *Annual Report of the Secretary, 1917*, p. 138.
[10] *Ibid.*, p. 137.   [11] See Table IX.

TABLE IX (CONTINUED)

Country	May	June	July	August
France	...	...	...	$ 15,841
Spain	$21,010,802	$15,983,400	$20,327,950	14,815,700
England	...	...	...	...
Canada	646,836	2,538,626	184,547	1,925,231
Cuba	1,260,900	1,300,020	850,305	400,311
Other West Indies	75,000	...	...	...
All other North America	1,254,824	1,533,903	578,867	696,584
South America	2,094,762	3,946,000	6,770,472	4,325,897
China	...	...	...	...
British India	300,000	2,700,000	3,307,306	3,300,532
Hongkong	64,545	51,925	462,090	64,850
Japan	30,356,250	38,413,250	36,561,320	20,481,346
All other countries	633,500	697,144	9,500	23,014
Total	$57,697,419	$67,164,268	$69,052,357	$46,049,306

Country	September	October	November	December
France	$ 32,701	$ 65	...	...
Spain	10,471,392	2,729,479	...	...
England	...	...	...	...
Canada	1,158,386	166,187	$ 167,080	$1,207,552
Mexico	820,687	1,056,752	2,691,045	2,430,578
Cuba	...	...	...	...
Other West Indies	...	...	...	...
South America				
Argentina	...	...	...	...
Chile	...	...	3,644,591	881,916
Peru	1,005,370	3,928,372	...	15,090
Uruguay	...	...	...	...
Venezuela	...	...	...	...
China	...	...	...	...
British India	2,936,748	2,450,000	...	...
Hongkong	47,840	...	...	...
Japan	13,499,525	...	...	...
All other countries	1,359,747	823,219	498,860	3,000
Total	$31,332,396	$11,151,074	$7,223,160	$4,538,136

[a] Figures appear on p. 5 of each U.S., Bureau of Foreign and Domestic Commerce, *Monthly Summary of Foreign Commerce of the United States,* January–December, 1917.

thority of the Espionage Act, of June 15, 1917 (40 Stat. 217), and the Trading with the Enemy Act of, October 6, 1917 (40 Stat. 411), the President, by the executive order of October 12, 1917, vested in the Secretary of the Treasury the power to regulate or entirely to prohibit any transaction in foreign exchange.[12]

Since the Secretary of the Treasury had inadequate facilities for handling all foreign exchange transactions, on November 23, 1917, he assigned the mechanical duties involved in foreign exchange control to the Federal Reserve Board as his agent. The President, by executive order on January 26, 1918, confirmed this transfer of duties to the Federal Reserve Board.[13] Here we have an early example of the trend in central banking in the United States to concentrate the power and authority in the Secretary of the Treasury and make the Federal Reserve System an efficient tool available to the Secretary in the performance of central banking functions.[14] Under the terms of the order of January 26, 1918, no person could engage in any foreign exchange transaction without obtaining specific approval from the Federal Reserve Board, in order that no transactions should take place which were "in the judgment of the Board incompatible with the best interests of the United States." [15]

THE TREASURY AND THE STABILIZATION OF FOREIGN EXCHANGES

In spite of all these measures the dollar remained at a discount in various neutral countries throughout the period of American belligerency,[16] and credit arrangements with neutral countries became necessary. In September, 1918, Secretary McAdoo made a series of special credit arrangements with neutral countries to provide a supply of neutral exchanges. These countries included Switzerland, Argentina, and other South American countries.[17] Still the Secretary of the Treasury felt his responsibilities were greater than his powers, and in a letter to Mr. Kitchen, chairman of the Ways and Means Committee of the House, dated September 5, 1918, Mr. McAdoo

---

[12] U.S., Treasury Dept., *Annual Report of the Secretary, 1918*, p. 40.   [13] *Ibid.*

[14] "The Federal Reserve System had been accepted by the Treasury Department as practically an unavoidable war auxiliary. It was a useful tool in the furtherance of the great work—the winning of the war." Willis, *Federal Reserve System*, p. 1201. In another national emergency in 1933, the Secretary of the Treasury again assumed control of the foreign exchanges by executive decree on March 10, 1933 (*Federal Reserve Bulletin*, March, 1933, p. 119). The authority was vested in the President by the Act of March 9, 1933 (48 Stat. 1) which amends the Act of October 6, 1917 (40 Stat 411).

[15] U.S., Federal Reserve Board, *Annual Report, 1918*, p. 46.

[16] *Federal Reserve Bulletin*, October, 1918, p. 941.   [17] *Ibid.*, pp. 941–942.

asked for legislation giving him the freedom of action which is possessed by finance ministers of European countries in stabilizing foreign exchange rates.[18]

In accordance with these wishes the Act to Supplement the Second Liberty Bond Act, approved on September 24, 1918, gave to the Secretary of the Treasury the power of stabilizing foreign exchange rates.[19]

That the Secretary of the Treasury may, during the war and for two years after its termination make arrangements in or with foreign countries to *stabilize the foreign exchange* and to *obtain* foreign currencies and credits in such currencies for the purpose of stabilizing or rectifying the foreign exchange and he may *designate depositories* in foreign countries with which may be deposited as he may determine all or any part of the avails of any foreign credits of foreign currencies.[20]

The power of stabilizing foreign exchanges and building up resources abroad for this purpose may well be considered as within the province of a central bank.[21]

[18] "In the negotiations which I have had and am having with or in foreign countries in the effort to stabilize foreign exchange, I find myself seriously hampered because I am without the freedom of action which is possessed by the finance ministers of European countries. I urge upon you, the incorporation in the law of the necessary authority to give greater flexibility to the operations of the Treasury in this respect." U.S., Treasury Dept., *Annual Report of the Secretary, 1918*, p. 16.

[19] "The central bank is conceived of as having the power to determine, when the country is on the specie standard, the conditions under which specie shall be exported and imported, and when off the specie standard, as having the power to determine the conditions under which foreigners may gain access to the paper currency created at home." Willis, *Theory and Practice of Central Banking*, p. 307.

[20] U.S., Treasury Dept., *Annual Report of the Secretary, 1918*, p. 176; 40 Stat. 965.

[21] However, this fact had not prevented earlier secretaries of the Treasury from attempting to control foreign exchange rates, notably Secretary Shaw (see p. 105). The most far-reaching and ambitious undertaking along these lines occurred in 1933 and 1934, when, as will be shown in Chapter IX, gold prices and foreign-exchange rates were artificially raised and a huge stabilization fund was placed at the disposal of the Secretary of the Treasury. This fund was created under Section 10 of the Gold Reserve Act of January 30, 1934, 48 Stat. 337. U.S., Treasury Dept., *Annual Report of the Secretary, 1934*, p. 192; see below p. 191. On September 25, 1936, the Secretary of the Treasury even entered into a sweeping tripartite exchange agreement with the Bank of England and the Banque de France. The operation of the tripartite agreement was to be implemented by the stabilization funds of the three nations. Through these funds it was proposed to provide a substitute for the automatic adjustments of the former gold standard (Crawford, *Monetary Management under the New Deal*, p. 277). On September 25, 1936, an announcement by Mr. Morgenthau indicated that the Treasury had entered the Tripartite agreement, because it was motivated by the desire to eliminate fluctuations in exchange rates and thereby protect the general business situation in the United States (*Federal Reserve Bulletin*, October, 1936, p. 759).

THE TREASURY AND THE CURRENCY DURING THE WAR

Treasury action in connection with the volume and the backing of currency in circulation was perhaps less spectacular at that time, but in the long run it was of greater importance than the effects made to stabilize foreign exchange rates. Changes in the structure of the currency system were not merely temporary; to a large extent they have continued. This is the more noteworthy when it is remembered that one of the declared purposes of the Federal Reserve Act was to separate our currency and the money market from the sphere of influence of the Treasury.

The first drastic change in our currency system caused by the war situation occurred on June 21, 1917.[22] The process of issuing notes was simplified by permission to issue them against gold alone or gold and eligible paper as security—the 40 percent gold reserve could now be counted as a part of the required 100 percent reserve against Federal Reserve notes.[23] The effective gold holdings of the Federal Reserve banks were augmented, and their credit-granting powers were increased.[24] When issued against gold, the Federal Reserve note virtually functions as a gold certificate. When issued against 60 percent commercial paper or only 40 percent of gold, it partakes more of the character of bank credit currency.

In addition, the amendment permitted the discounting of fifteen-day collateral notes of member banks secured by eligible commercial paper or by the bonds and notes of the United States Government. These notes could be used as security for Federal Reserve notes.[25] This is in striking contrast to the original regulations of the Federal Reserve Act, which restricted eligibility for rediscounting to self-liquidating commercial paper carrying an endorsement of the member bank (in effect making it double-name paper: customer and member bank). During the War and afterward the greater part of the discounted eligible paper was secured by Government bonds.[26]

[22] 40 Stat. 232.

[23] U.S., Treasury Dept., *Annual Report of the Secretary, 1917*, p. 22.

[24] U.S., Federal Reserve Board, *Annual Report, 1917*, pp. 11-12.

[25] U.S., Treasury Dept., *Annual Report of the Secretary, 1917*, p. 23; U.S., Board of Governors of the Federal Reserve System, *Digest of Rulings*, 1938, p. 584.

[26] For annual figures (1914-1940) showing investments of all member banks see

By these various means the Government helped commercial banks to extend large amounts of credit without endangering the adequacy of their reserves. The Federal Reserve banks were enabled to increase the amount of notes they could issue for each dollar of gold held.

In order to permit greater credit expansion, attempts were made in 1917 to concentrate the country's gold stock in the hands of the Federal Reserve System. It was reasoned that the concentration of gold would swell the base on which bank notes and bank deposit credit were to be built and so the war could be financed without resorting to the issue of unsecured Government paper money.[27] The gold reserves were built up partly by the gold embargo of 1917 under the Trading with the Enemy Act,[28] and by the policy instituted by the Federal Reserve banks of receiving gold certificates and of paying out Federal Reserve notes (Act of June 21, 1917; 40 Stat. 232). This latter provision had the effect of increasing both the gold reserve and the note liabilities of the Federal Reserve bank in equal amounts without changing the amount of currency in circulation. During the second half of the year 1917 about $700,000,000 in gold certificates was drawn into the Federal Reserve System by this means, and the increase of Federal Reserve notes in circulation was approximately the same.[29]

THE TREASURY AND THE PUBLIC DEBT DURING THE WAR

The tremendous need for funds in World War I, leading to a large increase in the public debt, was the main reason for the domination of the money market by the Treasury. Receipts from the sale of few

---

U.S., Federal Reserve Board, *Annual Report, 1933,* Table 78, p. 171; U.S., Board of Governors of the Federal Reserve System, *Annual Report, 1937,* Table 52, p. 112; *Federal Reserve Bulletin,* May, 1941, Table on p. 428.

[27] U.S., Federal Reserve Board, *Annual Report, 1917,* pp. 10–11.

[28] Act of October 6, 1917 (40 Stat. 411).

[29] Brown, "The Government and the Money Market," in Beckhart, ed., *The New York Money Market,* Vol. IV, p. 255.

Federal Reserve Notes in Circulation

December 30, 1917	$1,223,744,000
June 30, 1917	506,756,000
Increase	716,988,000

Source: U.S., Federal Reserve Board, *Annual Report, 1927,* p. 82.

large bond issues to the general public were heavily concentrated in relatively short periods and on few dates. On the other hand, expenditures continued in a steady, although increasing volume. The time of receipt and the time of disbursement of war funds by the Government failed to coincide. To even out the resulting dislocations, plans were devised to make Government receipts from revenue and loans more regular by selling tax-anticipation warrants and providing installment-purchase plans for Government bonds. Furthermore, at times unusually large Government accumulations were transferred from the Government balances of the Federal Reserve banks to the member banks.[30]

One method of smoothing out the highly irregular character of the Government's war-time receipts consisted in the sale of short-time certificates of indebtedness in anticipation of the tax and loan revenue. This method was first used on March 27, 1917, when $50,-000,000 of certificates of indebtedness were sold to the Federal Reserve banks in anticipation of corporation and individual income taxes due in June, 1917.[31] It was also used to smooth out the extreme variations in Government receipts which arose from the immense popular loans floated during the war.[32]

In order to insure a regular flow of funds in and out of the Treasury, use was made of the installment plan in paying for the popular loans and the income taxes. The first of these was adopted with the First Liberty Loan (40 Stat. 35); but the second was not used until the Revenue Act of February 24, 1919 (40 Stat. 1057). The main credit for avoiding major disturbances of the money market, however, should be given to the creation of a special depository system,[33] which is fully explained on the next few pages. The Treasury, in spite of the predominance of war considerations, fully realized its obligations as a central bank to prevent dislocations in the credit structure and the money market.

[30] U.S., Treasury Dept., *Annual Report of the Secretary, 1918*, p. 20.

[31] The authority to borrow in this way was contained in the Revenue Act of March 3, 1917 (39 Stat. 1000), which extended the already existing but limited powers to issue certificates of indebtedness vested in the Treasury by the Payne Aldrich Tariff Act of August 5, 1909 (36 Stat. 11).

[32] U.S., Treasury Dept., *Annual Report of the Secretary, 1918*, p. 20.

[33] *Ibid.*, p. 79.

SPECIAL DEPOSITORY SYSTEM

It was the intention of the Glass Bill, the first draft of the Federal Reserve Act, to concentrate all Government funds in the Federal Reserve banks.[34] However, to meet the needs of the war, the old system of special depositories had to be continued, and the policy of employing as depositories only Federal Reserve banks never became operative. When the first popular appeal for funds was instituted, under the Act of April 24, 1917 (40 Stat. 35), provision was made for an enlarged and special depository system. Banks could qualify as depositories of the Treasury by depositing specially designated securities with the Secretary of the Treasury.[35] The number of these special depositories grew throughout the war period.[36]

To prevent payments for Government bonds from producing money market dislocations, the Treasury, in Circular No. 79, laid down new conditions of payment for subscriptions to Liberty Loans by the special depository banks. The circular, issued May 16, 1917, introduced the idea of payment by credit on the books of the bank.

The Secretary of the Treasury has determined that banks and trust companies having payments to make on account of subscriptions for bonds, may make payment upon such subscriptions by credit on their books to the ac-

---

[34] Willis, *Federal Reserve System*, p. 513; U.S., Congress, House Committee on Banking and Currency, *Changes in Banking and Currency System of the United States*, House of Representatives, Report No. 69, 63d Cong., 1st Sess., p. 29.

[35] Treasury Circulars 79, 81, 82, 92 are quoted in U.S., Treasury Dept., *Annual Report of the Secretary, 1917*, pp. 83, 124, 133.

[36] Number of Special Depositories:

Date (as of June 30)	Number of Depositories
1912	929
1913	685
1914	625
1915	643
1916	608
1917	2,624
1918	7,169
1919	645
1920	19

Figures for 1912 and 1913 are from U.S., Treasury Dept., *Annual Report of the Secretary, 1913*, p. 210; figures for 1914 and 1915 are from U.S., Treasury Dept., *Annual Report of the Secretary, 1915*, p. 309; figures for 1916 and 1917 are from U.S., Treasury Dept., *Annual Report of the Secretary, 1917*, p. 366; figures for 1918 are from U.S., Treasury Dept., *Annual Report of the Secretary, 1918*, p. 556; figures for 1919 are from U.S., Treasury Dept., *Annual Report of the Secretary, 1919*, p. 723; figures for 1920 are from U.S., Treasury Dept., *Annual Report of the Secretary, 1920*, p. 871.

count of the Treasury of the United States. The amounts so credited will be withdrawn from time to time when and as required.[37]

This principle proved to be one of the most important elements in the entire relationship between the Government and the banks during the war. It made possible huge fiscal operations with little strain on the market.

Circular No. 81, issued May 30, 1917, further developed the new procedure; specified the method by which banks might become depositories; listed the securities acceptable as collateral for Government deposits, and laid down the procedure for making deposits by credit.

Each bank will be required to open and maintain for the account of the Treasury of the United States a separate account to be known as the "Liberty Loan deposit account." Such banks must then notify the Treasury of the United States and the Federal Reserve Bank of the district of the amount standing to the credit of the Treasury on its books in the Liberty Loan deposit account.[38]

Some slight changes were made in the lists of securities acceptable as collateral for Government deposits in Circulars No. 82 and 92.[39] By concrete examples we shall show how the provisions in these circulars worked:

1. A customer wished to borrow in order to buy Liberty bonds and discounted his note with the prospective bonds as collateral. The customer's account was temporarily credited, but the balance was immediately transferred to the Government account. No additional reserve was necessary against this Government deposit.

2. In the case of cash subscriptions the Treasury deposited the funds received with the Federal Reserve banks, which were directed by the Treasury to redeposit these amounts immediately with the depositary bank. Again the commercial bank found itself with Government deposits against which it did not need any reserve.

Methods 1 and 2 facilitated the sale of Liberty bonds, at the risk of credit inflation, but without disturbing the money market. Reserve requirements were lowered by eliminating the reserve against Government deposits. This was done by Section 7 of the First Liberty Loan Act, which expressly exempted Government deposits.[40]

---

[37] U.S., Treasury Dept., *Annual Report of the Secretary, 1917*, p. 131.
[38] *Ibid.*, pp. 127–128.   [39] *Ibid.*, p. 133.   [40] 40 Stat. 35.

This policy is reminiscent of Secretary Shaw's tactics and has the effect of lowering the total reserve required.[41]

It was necessary to prepare for all stages of the flow of funds from the subscribing public to the Treasury and back again to the public. For when creditors of the Government deposited their Government checks in banks, bank deposits previously created in favor of the Government, which had needed no reserve, were now transformed into bank deposits which did require reserves. To back up the new deposits, new bank reserves were needed. For that purpose the Government had instituted its gold policy.[42]

TREASURY INFLUENCES ON INTEREST RATES DURING THE WAR

Rates on Government Securities

As was to be expected, it was the policy of the Treasury during the war to keep the rate of interest on its borrowings as low as possible. How low a rate could be fixed for any particular bond issue depended upon the general investment market. When offering Liberty bonds to the general public, the appeal was primarily made on the basis of patriotism, not on the basis of extraordinary investment value, although the investment rating of the bonds was the highest, the interest rate fairly attractive, and certain tax-exemption feaures were granted.[43] The coupon rates are indicated in Table X. It was not until January 2, 1920, that the general investment market and the high prevailing interest rates forced the Treasury to pay

[41] Section 7 of the First Liberty Loan Act, April 24, 1917 (40 Stat. 35), is somewhat similar to Section 14 of the Act of May 30, 1908 (35 Stat. 546), which states that no reserve need be held against deposits of public money in national banks. Section 14 was reënacted in Section 27 of the Federal Reserve Act (38 Stat. 274). See also pp. 106, 120, 224.

[42] The imposition of the gold embargo (President's Proclamation of September 7, 1917) was part of the general policy of building up and concentrating a huge gold supply in the Federal Reserve banks and increasing the effectiveness of that supply as a basis for credit extensions. The amendment to Federal Reserve Act of June 21, 1917, dealing with Federal Reserve note issue, contributed to this end (40 Stat. 232). The act permitted gold deposited by the Federal Reserve banks with the Federal Reserve agents to be conceived not only as a deposit for the redemption of notes but also as backing for the notes. Also the act permitted member banks to convert Government bonds held by them into Federal Reserve notes. Finally gold was concentrated in the Federal Reserve banks by exchange of gold certificates for Federal Reserve notes. See below, pp. 153, 157.

[43] U.S., Treasury Dept., *Annual Report of the Secretary, 1919*, pp. 97, 98.

TABLE X

COUPON RATES OF LIBERTY LOANS, 1917–1919

Date	Name	Rate	Statute
April 24, 1917	First Liberty Loan	3½	40 Stat. 35
Sept. 24, 1917	Second Liberty Loan	4	40 Stat. 288
April 4, 1918	Third Liberty Loan	4¼	40 Stat. 502
July 9, 1918	Fourth Liberty Loan	4¼	40 Stat. 844
March 3, 1919	First Victory Loan	4¾	40 Stat. 1309

6 percent on its borrowings.[44] Ever since the first Government loans, the rate at which the Treasury borrowed and the yield on Government bonds have been the lowest rates in the investment market to which all other rates were adjusted.[45] This situation shows that it is possible for the Treasury to exert a strong influence on the general bond price level and on the money market.

To keep the cost of the war down, the Federal Reserve System helped the Treasury sell its securities advantageously by allowing a preferential rate on advances secured by Liberty bonds.[46] In these operations the Federal Reserve System functioned merely as an efficient tool of the Treasury. The Federal Reserve banks continued discounting ninety-day paper secured by Government obligations at preferential rates until July 1, 1921.[47] By exacting preferential treatment the Treasury influenced the credit policies of the Federal Reserve System and the reserve position of commercial banks.

Time and Demand Deposit Interest Rates

Heavy Treasury borrowing normally produced a shortage of investment funds for other purposes and rising interest rates. The

[44] Up to January 2, 1920, neither the loan certificates of the transition period following the Victory Liberty Loan nor the tax certificates sold in anticipation of 1920 income and excess profits taxes bore higher than 4½ percent interest. On that date a series of tax certificates were sold bearing 4¾ percent, followed by a series of other issues bearing rates rising progressively from 4¾ percent on the loan certificates of April 1, 1920, to 6 percent on the tax certificates of June 15, 1920. See U.S., Treasury Dept., *Annual Report of the Secretary, 1920*, pp. 303, 306.

[45] "The Treasury . . . felt that to raise the rate of interest to 4½ percent (Third Liberty Loan) would mean a corresponding increase in the cost of war and force still higher rates on future issues of industrial and other securities, as well as further to depress the price of existing long term bonds." See U.S., Treasury Dept., *Annual Report of the Secretary, 1918*, p. 6; see also p. 182, below.

[46] U.S., Federal Reserve Board, *Annual Report, 1917*, p. 256.

[47] *Federal Reserve Bulletin*, July, 1921, p. 885.

Treasury took special steps to prevent interest rates from going too high, and was at least partially successful in these endeavors. Due to favorable investment opportunities for bank funds in 1918 there was keen competition among banks for additional deposits, and the interest rates they offered to pay on deposits rose. This development disturbed the Treasury policy of financing the war at the lowest possible interest rates. Accordingly, at the instigation of the Treasury the New York Clearing House, at its conference of October 1, 1918, fixed a maximum rate of 3 percent on demand deposits and of 3½ percent on time deposits.[48] These rates were regarded as high enough to attract depositors and low enough to permit Treasury financing at low interest rates.

THE TREASURY AND CAPITAL FUNDS DURING THE WAR

The Treasury felt it was necessary for the successful prosecution of the war to exercise control not only over short-term credit but also over long-term or capital funds. Private borrowers could not be allowed to defeat Government aims by competing for long-term funds. For that reason, Secretary McAdoo wanted a central body to pass on new capital issues throughout the country. Securities were not to be issued whose rates were too high or whose purposes were non-essential for winning the war. The sale of such securities was regarded as incompatible with the public interest. Consequently the Secretary of the Treasury asked the Federal Reserve Board to undertake this work in every Federal Reserve district, the Treasury supplying the initiative, and the Federal Reserve banks doing the work. A central committee and subcommittees in every Federal Reserve district were formed,[49] which depended largely on moral persuasion for effective results.

Under the War Finance Act of April 5, 1918, the informal central committees became the formal Capital Issues Committee,[50] but they were granted the same limited powers. The subcommittees examined and checked every request for capital credit, with the result that few potential borrowers presented their demands unless certain of acceptance. The criteria for acceptance were: whether the funds were

[48] U.S., Federal Reserve Board, *Annual Report, 1918*, p. 337.
[49] Harding, *Formative Period of the Federal Reserve System*, p. 117.
[50] U.S., Treasury Dept., *Annual Report of the Secretary, 1918*, p. 61.

necessary for public health or welfare or a direct or indirect contribution toward winning the war.[51]

The work of the Capital Issues Committee did not touch some of the most difficult problems in connection with financing of industry during the war. Commercial banks were investing in Government securities rather than keeping their funds in the call-money market.[52] In this way they were helping the Government and securing paper eligible as security with the Federal Reserve banks. Discounts of such paper were even made at preferential rates, making the transaction doubly attractive. But savings banks had no access to Federal Reserve credit. When they found that many of their customers were withdrawing deposits, the savings banks feared that they would have to sell their Government securities at a loss. There was still another problem. Businessmen without well-established connections needed funds not only for short-term purposes but also for new plant structures. To tackle these problems of the savings banks and businessmen the War Finance Act set up the War Finance Corporation. The stock of the corporation was subscribed by the Treasury, and the chairman of the board was the Secretary of the Treasury. The other board members were chosen by the President.[53]

The corporation could make loans to any bank, banker, or trust company having outstanding loans to business needed in the war and/or which bought the obligations of such business. The corporation could also advance its funds for one year to savings banks which were aiding in the prosecution of the war. Finally, in exceptional cases loans were authorized to businessmen directly, if funds were not available to them through the regular banking channels. Most of the advances were made to the latter group.[54]

By the War Finance Act discounting was extended to include paper not considered eligible in the original Federal Reserve Act. The War Finance Corporation, wholly owned by the United States Treasury, had funds on deposit with the Federal Reserve banks and represented another example of the steadily increasing interrelationship between the Federal Reserve System and the Treasury.[55]

---

[51] Section 7; 40 Stat. 506.   [52] See p. 157n.
[53] Section 2; 40 Stat. 506; Kilborne, "The War Finance Corporation," *American Economic Review*, Vol. XV (December, 1925), pp. 810–820.
[54] U.S., Treasury Dept., *Annual Report of the Secretary, 1918*, pp. 245–248.
[55] Willis, *The Theory and Practice of Central Banking*, p. 38.

THE TREASURY AND ITS SHORT-TERM SECURITIES DURING THE WAR

The Treasury found that in addition to keeping the general interest rates low and giving certain tax-exemption features to its securities, it had to use moral pressure in order to distribute widely its short-term securities. A quota system was worked out,[56] and every bank was requested by the Secretary of the Treasury in a telegram sent February 6, 1918, to take an amount of Treasury certificates of indebtedness for payments on the next issue of Liberty bonds equal to 1 percent of the banks' gross resources.[57] The banks coöperated, and the system was successful. After the Treasury abandoned this quota system,[58] on August 25, 1919, it announced a policy of retiring all outstanding certificates of indebtedness. This step left only the tax-anticipation certificates outstanding as the Government's floating debt.[59] These tax-anticipation certificates matured on various income-tax dates. After the last certificates of indebtedness were refunded, on February 16, 1920,[60] the floating debt of $2,935,949,500 consisted exclusively of these tax-anticipation certificates, and the amounts of the maturities in no instance exceeded the estimated amount of income and profits taxes payable on the maturity date.[61] The method of spreading Government receipts by anticipation certificates formed a permanent link between the Treasury and the banks and is being used to the present day.

THE TREASURY AS THE CHIEF DEBTOR OF THE FEDERAL RESERVE MEMBER BANKS

The banks helped the Treasury to float its long-term debt by absorbing part of the interest-bearing debt. Under the leadership of Mr. Strong, Governor of the Federal Reserve Bank of New York, a Liberty Loan Committee was formed, with subcommittees on distribution, publicity, receipt of and payment for subscriptions to Liberty bonds. The member banks aided further by making advances to subscribers at low rates, arranging partial payments for small purchasers, by safekeeping the bonds of subscribers, and fi-

[56] U.S., Treasury Dept., *Annual Report of the Secretary, 1918*, p. 20.
[57] *Ibid.*, p. 20.
[58] U.S., Treasury Dept., *Annual Report of the Secretary, 1919*, p. 9.
[59] *Ibid.*, p. 18.   [60] *Ibid.*
[61] U.S., Treasury Dept., *Annual Report of the Secretary, 1920*, p. 12.

nally by subscribing themselves.[62] The Liberty Loan Committee came to have such importance that the Secretary of the Treasury turned this voluntary organization into a Government agency, the Government Loan Organization, paid by the Treasury, but supervised by the Governor of the Federal Reserve Bank of New York.[63]

In order, to keep the small purchaser interested in Government securities, a "borrow and buy" campaign was launched; [64] but it was soon obvious that most Government obligations were drifting into the hands of large institutional investors, for example, commercial banks, trust companies, savings banks, and insurance companies.[65] By June 30, 1918, the investments of the member banks of the Federal Reserve System in United States Securities reached a total of $2,500,000,000, as compared with $1,100,000,000 at the close of the preceding fiscal year, while the Federal interest-bearing debt had increased in the interval from $2,800,000,000 to $12,000,-000,000.[66] Until 1919 both the Federal interest-bearing debt and the member banks' investments in Government securities rose steadily. In 1920 the Treasury engaged in large refunding activities [67] and began its progressive withdrawal from the domestic credit market.[68] During the twenties the burdens placed upon the Treasury were light, and revenues were collected on a sufficiently high level to allow a steady reduction in the public debt.[69]

With interest rates in the general market rising from 1916 to 1921, all bonds with relatively low coupon rates tended to sell at a discount. This included the Liberty bonds, in spite of strong propaganda in their favor and their tax-exemption features.[70] Secretary McAdoo decided to support the Government bond market in earlier issues rather than to raise the interest rate on new issues. The War

[62] U.S., Federal Reserve Board, *Annual Report, 1917*, pp. 279–280.
[63] U.S., Federal Reserve Board, *Annual Report, 1918*, p. 365.
[64] U.S., Federal Reserve Board, *Annual Report, 1917*, p. 287.
[65] Brown, "The Government and the Money Market," in Beckhart, ed., *The New York Money Market*, Vol. IV, p. 373.
[66] See Table XI.
[67] U.S., Treasury Dept., *Annual Report of the Secretary, 1920*, p. 315.
[68] "The year has been characterized by the progressive relative withdrawal of the Treasury from the domestic credit market and from a position of dominant influence. By the beginning of the fall this withdrawal had reached the point where the influence of Treasury borrowing was comparatively limited." U.S., Treasury Dept., *Annual Report of the Secretary, 1920*, p. 6.
[69] U.S., Treasury Dept., *Annual Report of the Secretary, 1925*, p. 45; pp. 179–180.
[70] *Commercial and Financial Chronicle*, Vol. CIV, June 23, 1917, p. 2502.

TABLE XI

RELATION BETWEEN INVESTMENTS OF FEDERAL RESERVE
MEMBER BANKS IN GOVERNMENT SECURITIES AND THE
TOTAL INTEREST-BEARING FEDERAL DEBT, 1916-1941

(In millions of dollars)

End of Fiscal Year	Federal Reserve Member Bank Investments	Total Interest-Bearing Federal Debt	Percentage
1916	$ 703 [a]	$ 972 [c]	72.3
1917	1,065	2,713	89.3
1918	2,465	11,986	20.6
1919	3,803	25,234	15.0
1920	2,811	24,061	11.7
1921	2,561	23,737	10.7
1922	3,205	22,711	14.1
1923	2,835	22,008	17.4
1924	3,575	20,982	17.0
1925	3,780	20,211	18.7
1926	3,745	19,384	19.3
1927	3,796	18,251	20.8
1928	4,225	17,318	24.4
1929	4,155	16,639	25.0
1930	4,061	15,922	25.5
1931	5,343	16,520	32.3
1932	5,628	19,161	29.4
1933	6,887	22,158	31.1
1934	9,413 [b]	26,480	28.1
1935	11,430	27,645	24.2
1936	13,672	32,756	24.0
1937	12,689	35,803	28.2
1938	12,343 [d]	36,479	29.5
1939	13,777	39,891	29.0
1940	14,722	42,380	28.8
1941	18,078 [e]	48,405	26.8

[a] Table No. 78, U.S., Federal Reserve Board, Annual Report, 1933, p. 172.
[b] Table No. 52, U.S., Board of Governors of the Federal Reserve System, *Annual Report, 1937*, p. 112.
[c] Table No. 39, U.S., Treasury Dept., *Annual Report of the Secretary, 1941*, p. 591.
[d] *Federal Reserve Bulletin*, May, 1941, p. 428.
[e] *Federal Reserve Bulletin*, December, 1942, p. 1214.

Finance Corporation was authorized under the Act of April 5, 1918, to purchase Government bonds on a large scale,[71] and the Treasury reimbursed it out of funds allotted by Congress under the third

[71] 40 Stat. 506.

Liberty Loan Act, April 4, 1918, wherein a 5 percent bond purchase fund had been established.[72] But the upward trend of interest rates counteracted all these measures. Bonds of the second Liberty Loan issue (and later also of the third and fourth issues) continued to sell at a discount.[73] Only the first Liberty Loan bonds, which were entirely tax-exempt, did not sell at a discount. Exemption from surtax was a far more valuable privilege than exemption from normal income tax. Surtax rates kept on mounting, due to the rising need for revenue, and the first Liberty Loan bonds reflected in their price the value of their unique special tax-exemption. Since the second and third issues were exempt only from normal income tax, the Secretary decided to make this exemption more valuable and thereby the bonds more attractive. Accordingly he recommended an increase in normal income-tax rates to support the market of the second Liberty Loan bonds, which were exempt only from normal income tax.[74] His recommendation was enacted on September 24, 1918, in the supplement to the second Liberty Loan Act.[75] The increase in normal income-tax rates did help the Second Liberty Loan bonds, but even then their market price did not go to par.[76] The War Finance Corporation had been authorized to support only the third Liberty Loan bond issue.[77] The obvious effect of supporting one bond issue is to make the market prices of all other bond issues adjust themselves to this leading issue.[78] After the flotation of the Victory Loan bonds, with higher coupon rates, the Government abandoned the support of the Government bond market, so far carried on by the War Finance Corporation.[79]

[72] U.S., Treasury Dept., *Annual Report of the Secretary, 1918*, p. 82; 40 Stat. 502.

[73] U.S., Treasury Dept., *Annual Report of the Secretary, 1918*, p. 6.

[74] U.S., Treasury Dept., *Annual Report of the Secretary*, 1917, p. 4; U.S., Treasury Dept., *Annual Report of the Secretary, 1918*, p. 6.

[75] The Victory Liberty Loan Act (March 3, 1919) further developed the policy by providing more tax-exemption features. See 40 Stat. 1309; U.S., Treasury Dept., *Annual Report of the Secretary, 1919*, p. 97, contains a summary of the tax-exemption provisions on various Liberty Loans (40 Stat. 965).

[76] U.S., Treasury Dept., *Annual Report of the Secretary, 1918*, p. 6.

[77] Section 15, Act of April 5, 1918 (40 Stat. 506).

[78] Willis, *Theory and Practice of Central Banking*, pp. 39–40.

[79] In a public statement issued April 18, 1920, Mr. Houston (War Finance Corporation) announced that purchases for the bond purchase fund would close on July 1, 1920, when the new sinking fund (provided in the Victory Liberty Loan Act) went into effect. The Treasury would no longer borrow to buy its own bonds in the market, thus increasing its floating debt in order to reduce its funded debt. *Federal Reserve Bulletin*, May, 1920, p. 445.

SUMMARY

Major upheavals in this world leave their mark on the entire economic structure of the countries involved. It was only to be expected that the Federal Reserve System should emerge from World War I changed in outlook and methods. What these changes were is succinctly stated by Professor Willis, as follows:

From the entry of the United States into the World War in 1917, down to the present moment, the history of the Federal Reserve System has been one of encroachment by the national government upon the functions of banking and gradual determination by that government to use the Reserve banks as its instrumentalities for the political control of credit.[80]

[80] Willis, *The Theory and Practice of Central Banking*, p. 91.

CHAPTER VIII

Treasury Central Banking Activities during the Period of the Twenties

AGRICULTURAL EMERGENCY OF 1920–1921

THE PERIOD of the twenties was marked by a decline of Treasury activity in the money market and the rise of the Federal Reserve System as the central banking force. After the armistice, when millions of men returned to productive activities and conditions in Europe began to be more normal, forces were set in operation which resulted in financial and industrial dislocations typical of periods following great struggles.[1] The Nation emerged from the war in an apparently strong economic position. It had large liabilities, but it had also enormous resources. The momentum of great commercial activity carried the country through the winter of 1919. Wages and prices continued high. The high cost of living did not prevent extravagant spending. The expansion of credit, which was marked during the war, did not end with the armistice.[2] Credit extensions to commerce and agriculture were encouraged by a decline in Government borrowing and a very substantial reduction in the investments of member banks in Government securities.[3]

Toward the end of February, 1920, however, purchasing began to be hesitant and the volume of business diminished. By June the general price level began to fall. The downward course in prices was rapid and drastic.[4] Unemployment had developed, and the undue credit expansion of the last five years was being contracted.[5]

When this point had been reached, an additional problem presented itself to the Treasury and the Nation, the task of marketing a record crop. Europe's demand for food and raw materials was lessened,

[1] U.S., Treasury Dept., *Annual Report of the Secretary, 1920*, p. 1.
[2] *Ibid.*, p. 2.
[3] The figures for the years 1920–1921 can be obtained by reference to Table XI, see p. 168, above.
[4] See Table XII.
[5] U.S., Treasury Dept., *Annual Report of the Secretary, 1920*, p. 2.

TABLE XII

GROUP INDEX NUMBERS OF ALL COMMODITIES FROM JANUARY, 1913, TO DECEMEER, 1922, IN BUREAU OF LABOR STATISTICS—REVISED SERIES[a]

Month	1913	1914	1915	1916	1917	1918	1919	1920	1921	1922
January	100	98	98	113	153	184	199	233	170	138
February	100	99	99	115	157	186	193	232	160	141
March	100	98	99	119	162	187	196	234	155	142
April	100	98	99	121	173	190	199	245	148	143
May	99	97	100	122	183	190	202	247	145	148
June	99	97	99	123	185	191	203	243	142	150
July	100	97	100	123	188	196	212	241	141	155
August	100	101	100	126	189	200	216	231	142	155
September	102	102	100	130	187	204	216	226	141	153
October	101	97	102	136	183	202	211	211	142	154
November	100	97	104	146	183	203	217	196	141	156
December	99	97	108	149	182	202	223	179	140	156

[a] Figures from January, 1913, to July, 1922, are taken from *Federal Reserve Bulletin,* September, 1922, pp. 1092–1093. Figures from August, 1922, to December, 1922, are taken from *Federal Reserve Bulletin,* January, 1923, p. 83.

partly because of her own larger self-sufficiency, which had arisen from the return of millions of her people to productive efforts, partly because of the lack of purchasing power abroad, and partly because of the restoration of more normal conditions in marine transportation and the consequent reappearance of the agricultural products of distant countries in the markets of the world.[6]

The banks and the Treasury were called upon to finance the marketing of the crops in a gradual and orderly fashion and also to facilitate with holding commodities from the market for an indefinite period so that at least a predetermined minimum price might be realized. The problem was not easy. The crop-moving season found the banks still badly shaken, having many frozen assets left over from the collapse of the price level.[7]

The first impulse of many banks in agricultural regions was to turn to the Treasury as the only agency able to give the needed assistance. This disposition on the part of the banks—well developed before the war—was reinforced during hostilities by various instances when the Government supported the banks in order to achieve the successful prosecution of the war.[8] Producers whose products could

6 *Ibid.,* p. 3.   7 *Ibid.*   8 *Ibid.,* p. 4.

be marketed only at prices that were catastrophically low insisted that the Treasury intervene. They asked that the Treasury deposit money in certain sections to encourage large crop loans or that the activities of the War Finance Corporation be resumed.[9] "The Treasury had no money to lend and no money to deposit except for government purposes." The Secretary of the Treasury was not in the banking business and should not be.[10] Furthermore, even the War Finance Corporation was merely a war agency, created to help win the war. It was clearly desirable that war agencies should cease to function as quickly as possible. The War Finance Corporation had been permitted on March 3, 1919, to continue only one of its functions—the stimulation of exports by making advances to American exporters and such American banking institutions as needed assistance in the financing of exports.[11] But even these activities had been suspended in a statement issued by the Secretary of the Treasury on May 10, 1920.[12] At the request of the Secretary, Congress, on January 4, 1921, adopted a joint resolution directing him to revive activities of the corporation with a view of assisting in the financing of the exportation of agricultural and other products.[13] It was the work of this corporation under the direction of the Treasury Department which accomplished a great deal toward softening the blow to agriculture involved in the collapse of the war-inflated price level.[14] The

[9] *Ibid.*   [10] *Ibid.*

[11] Victory Liberty Loan Act—an act to amend Liberty Bond Acts and the War Finance Corporation Act. 40 Stat. 1309.

[12] U.S., Treasury Dept., *Annual Report of the Secretary, 1920*, p. 149.

[13] U.S., Treasury Dept., *Annual Report of the Secretary, 1921*, p. 49; 41 Stat. 1084.

[14] "The benefit which came through the loans made by the War Finance Corporation cannot be measured by these loans alone. The renewed confidence which swept through the country was most helpful. Money became easier to borrow; a more liberal policy on farm loans was generally adopted. The wholesale sacrificing of grain and live stock was checked. The hope of farmers was renewed. It is not pleasant to think of what would have happened to agriculture if this emergency money had not been made available.

"The value of the service rendered by Congress in recreating and enlarging the powers of the War Finance Corporation serves to illustrate the importance of taking the affirmative rather than the negative view in time of difficulty. Many good people were disposed to accept the disastrous break in farm prices as inevitable—they thought nothing could be done; that government action could not relieve the situation. These good people were of the same sort as those pious folks in days gone by who looked upon death in the family from tuberculosis or typhoid fever as a visitation of the wrath of God, and not as a thing for which they were responsible and which they might have avoided by giving attention to the laws of health and sanitation." Secretary Wallace of the Department of Agriculture on "What Has Been Done to Meet Agricultural Depression," *Commercial and Financial Chronicle*, Vol. CXV (November 11, 1922), pp. 2115–2117.

effects of the revival in agriculture were felt in other industries.[15]

Notwithstanding the aid which the Treasury had given to relieve the financial situation of the agricultural community, it was the firm belief of Mr. Mellon, then Secretary of the Treasury, that the Treasury Department should be primarily the fiscal agent of the Government, not the Nation's central bank.[16] Accordingly, in the nineteentwenties the Treasury tried to withdraw from many fields connected with central banking.

THE TREASURY AND INTER-ALLIED DEBTS

With the end of hostilities the need for a financial supreme command, the Treasury, to subordinate all policies and activities to the one aim of winning the war had ceased. Accordingly, Treasury influence as a central bank diminished, and the discretionary policy shaping powers of the Federal Reserve System was strengthened. The passing of the emergency was no reason, however, to expect a reversal in the long-term trend toward Treasury dominance in the field of central banking. The Treasury's former function was merely held in abeyance.

In the field of foreign exchange control and foreign lending the Treasury confined itself largely to liquidating the inheritance of the war. After the armistice Treasury funds were no longer used to support British and other allied exchanges,[17] and on June 9, 1919, the President approved the recommendation of the Treasury that the embargo on the export of gold and currency and the control over the exchange market be terminated.[18]

The end of the war, furthermore, found the Treasury holding large foreign investments in the form of unfunded Government loans. It was a long time before the complications and well-nigh insurmountable difficulties arising out of attempts to collect the huge intergovernmental debts were recognized. In the meantime the desire to get

---

[15] U.S., Treasury Dept., *Annual Report of the Secretary, 1922*, p. 1.

[16] "This attitude [of turning to the Treasury for 'full economic salvation'] so extremely manifested is unwholesome and menacing, and it is of the highest importance that individuals and communities return to a normal degree of self-help and self-reliance. We have demobilized money groups, but we have not demobilized those whose gaze is concentrated on the Treasury." U.S., Treasury Dept., *Annual Report of the Secretary, 1920*, p. 4.

[17] *Ibid.*, pp. 340–348.

[18] U.S., Treasury Dept., *Annual Report of the Secretary, 1919*, p. 15.

these intergovernmental advances funded at an early date controlled Government policy. The State Department was consulted before any bankers made loans to any foreign government or corporation. This custom was started in May, 1921, to prevent loans to countries which had not funded their indebtedness to the United States, or which were to use the proceeds for militaristic purposes.[19] The record does not show that the State Department objected to many requests for permission to float foreign loans.[20]

THE TREASURY AND PUBLIC DEPOSITS

During the war period additional Government depositories had been created for purposes connected with belligerent activities. With the resumption of peaceful relations the necessity for some depositories ceased to exist. Furthermore, since the Federal Reserve banks and their branches were utilized as depositories and fiscal agents of the Government, it had gradually developed that the greater part of the Government's disbursements were made through the Federal Reserve banks. The practice of permitting the larger part of the revenues of the Government to be deposited with national banks delayed to a considerable extent the receipt of those revenues at the Federal Reserve banks and branches for disbursement.

During the fiscal year 1920 the Treasury undertook a concerted effort to reduce its balances carried with national bank depositories, both for the purpose of cashing checks and as a basis for handling receipts, to the minimum amounts necessary for the transaction of essential Government business. To that end it announced in Circular Number 176, dated December 31, 1919, definite regulations concerning Government deposits of public money. Cash receipts only could be deposited in national bank depositories. The operation of this regulation made possible reductions in balances in depositories which

[19] Statement issued by the State Department on March 3, 1922, quoted in the *Federal Reserve Bulletin*, March, 1922, p. 282.

[20] "The Department of State never approves a loan but rather states whether it has any objection to it. Banks are under no legal obligation to follow the department's wishes in case a loan does not meet with its approval, and there is no obligation on the part of the bankers, tacit, or otherwise to seek the opinion of the department. The practice of asking the opinion of the department, began in 1921 after consultations between President Harding and the bankers in which they expressed a willingness to seek the opinion of the department." Mr. Coolidge's views in the Senate, June 16, 1930, 71st Cong. 2d Sess., U.S., Congress, *Congressional Record*, Vol. LXXII, Part 10, p. 10875.

had heretofore received revenues, in fact, their total elimination.[21]

By 1920 the subtreasuries were no longer needed by the Treasury in connection with the fiscal operations of the Government for the collection and disbursement of the public moneys, because the Federal Reserve banks were already performing many of the functions and duties previously performed by the sub-treasuries.[22] Believing that the work of the sub-treasuries could be performed more efficiently and economically by the Federal Reserve banks, the Secretary of the Treasury, on April 18, 1919, designated a committee to report on the advisability of discontinuing the sub-treasuries and transferring their duties and functions to the mints or assay offices or Federal Reserve banks. The committee submitted a report to the Secretary of the Treasury in the form of a tentative draft of a bill to provide for the discontinuance of the sub-treasuries and the transfer of their duties and functions. The Secretary of the Treasury made these recommendations to Congress. An Act was passed May 29, 1920 (41 Stat. 654), authorizing the Secretary of the Treasury to discontinue the sub-treasuries and transfer their duties to the Federal Reserve banks.[23]

THE TREASURY AND THE CURRENCY IN THE TWENTIES

The Treasury retained its responsibility as holder of the great trust funds (Act of March 14, 1900; 31 Stat. 45). Furthermore, the Treasury could still influence the currency through silver purchases under the Pittman Act.[24] In the case of gold, the continuation of the provision by the Treasury for a convenient paper representative of gold which was acceptable to the people as hand-to-hand currency made possible the substitution of gold for Federal Reserve notes and vice

---

[21] U.S., Treasury Dept., *Annual Report of the Secretary, 1920*, pp. 172–173; see also p. 160, above.

[22] See p. 137, above.

[23] U.S., Treasury Dept., *Annual Report of the Secretary, 1920*, pp. 167–171.

[24] The Pittman Act authorized the "Secretary of the Treasury from time to time to retire silver certificates and as such silver certificates are retired to melt or break up and sell as bullion the silver dollars represented by such certificates up to the limit of 350,000,000 standard silver dollars." Furthermore, the act required the replacement of this silver by the purchase of domestic bullion at $1 an ounce by the Treasury. Act of April 23, 1918, quoted in U.S., Treasury Dept., *Annual Report of the Secretary, 1918*, p. 176; 40 Stat. 535.

versa in hand-to-hand circulation. It made possible that exchange of Federal Reserve notes for gold certificates at the beginning of the war which facilitated war-time credit expansion.[25]

The main intent of the Federal Reserve Act was to supplement our existing currency system by an additional variety of currency which, based on commercial paper, would be elastic in volume and give elasticity to the grand total of currency in circulation. The inelastic National Bank notes were no longer needed, and their retirement could not cause a money stringency. Consequently the Treasury announced early on November 1, 1924, that it intended to redeem all bonds bearing the circulation privilege.[26] But the national banks protested. The bonds were not yet callable, and they sold above par; consequently open-market purchases became too expensive, and the scheme was abandoned.[27] The Government bonds bearing the circulation privilege remained outstanding until they were called on March 11, 1935, for redemption on July 1 and August 1, 1935.[28]

In many ways during the twenties the Treasury continued to be directly or indirectly connected with the currency of the country. The various types of currency then in circulation were:

Gold coins.—They were available for circulation until the order of the Secretary of the Treasury of December 28, 1933, as amended and supplemented on January 11 and 15, 1934. All gold coin domestically owned (with minor exceptions) was required to be delivered for the account of the Treasurer of the United States, and under the Gold Reserve Act of January 30, 1934 (48 Stat. 337), withdrawn from circulation and formed into bars. Gold coin ($287,000,-000) shown on Treasury records as being then outstanding was dropped from the monthly circulation statement as of January 31, 1934.[29]

Gold certificates.—The Treasury held the gold represented by these certificates under the Act of March 3, 1863 (12 Stat. 709); the

---

[25] Act of June 21, 1917 (40 Stat. 232); see also p. 158, above.

[26] U.S., Treasury Dept., *Annual Report of the Secretary, 1924*, p. 31.

[27] Brown, "The Government and the Money Market," in Beckhard, ed., *The New York Money Market*, Vol. IV, p. 346.

[28] U.S., Treasury Dept., *Annual Report of the Secretary, 1935*, pp. 22, 206; see also pp. 146–147, above.

[29] U.S., Treasury Dept., *Annual Report of the Secretary, 1939*, p. 506.

Act of July 12, 1882 (22 Stat. 162); the Act of March 14, 1900 (31 Stat. 45).[30] Many of them were put back into circulation after 1919 [31] and remained there until 1933.[32]

Silver dollars.—These were minted early in the history of the United States.[33] Most parts of the country disliked silver dollars by reason of their size and weight; they circulated primarily in the Far West.

Silver certificates.—The Treasury held the silver represented by these certificates for redemption.[34] These certificates were and are outstanding in large quantities.

[30] Gold certificates were first issued under authority of Section 5 of the Act of March 3, 1862 (12 Stat. 709) which authorized the Secretary of the Treasury to receive deposits of gold coin and gold bullion in sums of not less than $20 and to issue certificates therefore. The first certificates issued under this act were on November 15, 1865, and the last on or about January 1, 1879, when the practice was discontinued by order of the Secretary of the Treasury in order to prevent the holders of United States notes from presenting such notes for redemption in gold and redepositing the gold in exchange for gold certificates. Gold certificates were not issued again until the passage of Section 12 of the Act of July 12, 1882 (22 Stat. 162) which substantially reënacted the provisions of the prior act, with the additional provision that the Secretary of the Treasury shall suspend the issue of gold certificates whenever the amount of gold coin and gold bullion, reserve for the redemption of United States notes, falls below $100,000,000. There is no limit to the amount of such certificates that may be issued except as controlled by the amount of gold coin and gold bullion owned by the Government. The law provides that of the gold held against gold certificates an amount equal to at least one-third of such certificates outstanding must be in the form of gold coin. They are legal tender in payment of all debts and dues, public and private. U.S., Treasury Dept., *Annual Report of the Secretary, 1928,* pp. 597–598. For discussion of the Act of March 14, 1900 (31 Stat. 45), see pp. 97–100, above.

[31] Under the Act of June 21, 1917 (40 Stat. 232), the Federal Reserve banks had followed the policy of receiving gold certificates and paying out Federal Reserve notes in order to build up the gold reserves to help in the financing of the War. See p. 158, above. "Since the beginning of the War it has been the policy of the Treasury to conserve gold and discourage its circulation. It is just as important as ever that gold, which is the foundation of our reserves and the backbone of all credit transactions, should be concentrated in the Federal Reserve banks as reserves. The circulation of gold coin and gold certificates tends to dissipate the reserves. Persons requesting gold are invited to accept other currency instead, but gold has not been and will not be refused to persons who, after giving consideration to the Treasury's policy, demand it and are entitled to receive it by reason of the presentation and surrender of gold obligations." U.S., Treasury Dept., *Annual Report of the Secretary, 1920,* pp. 181–182. Gold certificates of the United States payable to bearer on demand shall be legal tender in payment of all debts, dues, public and private. Act of December 24, 1919 (41 Stat. 370).

[32] See Appendix VII below and Gold Reserve Act of January 30, 1934 (48 Stat. 337).

[33] Act of April 2, 1792 (1 Stat. 246); Act of June 18, 1837 (5 Stat. 136).

[34] Act of February 28, 1878 (20 Stat. 25); Act of April 23, 1918 (40 Stat. 335); Act of May 12, 1933 (48 Stat. 31); Act of June 19, 1934 (48 Stat. 1178).

United States notes—Ever since the Act of May 31, 1878 (20 Stat. 87), $346,681,016 have been outstanding. The Treasury holds the $150,000,000 gold reserves against them required by the Act of March 14, 1900 (31 Stat. 45).

Treasury notes of 1890.—The bulk of these notes issued under the Act of July 14, 1890 (26 Stat. 289), has long been withdrawn from circulation. The notes still outstanding are largely in the hands of collectors. They are also backed by the $150,000,000 gold reserve in the Treasury under the Act of March 14, 1900 (31 Stat. 45).

Federal Reserve notes.—These notes are the most important type of paper currency in circulation. Federal Reserve agents hold the gold and commercial paper which are the reserves against the notes under the Act of December 23, 1913 (38 Stat. 265). After the Act of February 27, 1932 (47 Stat. 56) Government obligations may be used instead of commercial paper as collateral.[35]

Federal Reserve Bank notes.—Government bonds were the collateral under the Act of December 23, 1913 (38 Stat. 265). Except during times of emergency, these bank notes have not circulated.

National Bank notes.—Government bonds were employed as collateral under the Act of June 3, 1864 (13 Stat. 99). These notes were outstanding in large amounts until 1935. Since then their volume has steadily declined.[36]

Minor coins.—These coins are a form of credit money "printed" upon metal. The metals used are bronze, copper, nickel and silver. The coins have less value as bullion than as coins and they are fractional parts of the dollar. Appendix VII contains figures on minor coins from 1900 only, since satisfactory data were not available for earlier years and the stock was small.

THE TREASURY AND THE PUBLIC DEBT IN THE TWENTIES

Secretary Mellon, who held the Treasury post in the period of the twenties, adopted as his major policy the encouragement of business by a slow, but gradual and steady, reduction of wartime taxes, by a sound Treasury position and by a persistent reduction in the Gov-

[35] For further discussion of the extensions of the Act of February 27, 1932, see pp. 145–146, 191–193.

[36] See pp. 146–147, 193; see Appendix VII, below.

ernment debt.[37] All these steps in turn achieved low interest rates on the remaining Government debt, which again facilitated tax reduction and bond redemption.[38]

If not regulated so as to coincide in time and amount, the receipts and disbursements of the Treasury, always have disturbing effects on the reserves of commercial banks. During the war period a huge debt had been built up by expenditures which were incurred daily, and devices had to be found to spread the revenue, whether derived from rapidly mounting borrowing or rising taxes, evenly in time and amount.[39] After the war a period of debt reduction began, and a similar problem arose in connection with offsetting quarterly tax receipts by quarterly net debt reductions. In a solution of this problem the first step was to refund the war debt so that all Government obligations matured on the quarterly tax-payment dates. These maturities were then arranged as nearly as possible in amounts that could be met from taxes. The periodic debt reduction and the lowering of the interest burden were facilitated under the Mellon administration by introducing on June 15, 1921 the three-year Treasury note [40] and the Treasury bill [41] on November 26, 1929. In the fall of 1922 the Treasury began also to refund long-term bond issues by exchanging Liberty bonds and Victory bonds for Treasury notes and long-term Treasury bonds [42] at substantially lower interest rates.

The initiative in the issue of Government securities rested entirely with the Treasury Department as to both amounts and terms of issue. The extent to which the Treasury consulted with Federal Reserve officials and bankers before issuing such securities was and still is a matter of discretion of the Secretary of the Treasury. One of the difficult tasks of the Treasury always has been to judge how the market would receive new bonds in order to obtain an interest rate as low as possible, but high enough to make possible a complete sale of the new issue. In the decade of the twenties the Treasury adjusted its

[37] U.S., Treasury Dept., *Annual Report of the Secretary, 1921,* p. 1.

[38] "The Redemption Act of November 23, 1921 (42 Stat. 227), made a substantial reduction in the tax burden and has provided for the repeal or reduction of several of the most vexatious and burdensome taxes. It has refunded about $700,000,000 of short dated debt into later maturities and has reduced the Victory notes outstanding to about $3,600,000,000 and the Treasury certificates to about $2,300,000,000." U.S., Treasury Dept., *Annual Report of the Secretary, 1921,* p. 2.

[39] See p. 159 above, on certificates of indebtedness in anticipation of income taxes.

[40] U.S., Treasury Dept., *Annual Report of the Secretary, 1921,* p. 4.

[41] U.S., Treasury Dept., *Annual Report of the Secretary, 1929,* pp. 38–42.

[42] U.S., Treasury Dept., *Annual Report of the Secretary, 1922,* pp. 3–5.

rates to the market situation. The Federal Reserve banks merely acted as the agent handling the details connected with Government bond issues. They informed member banks of the amount, character, terms, and so forth of the new bonds, Treasury notes, certificates of indebtedness, and Treasury bills; they took subscriptions, issued certificates, arranged for conversion, and so forth.[43]

The operations of the War Finance Corporation in buying Liberty bonds and Victory notes actively in the market for sale later to the 5 percent bond-purchase fund under the Act of April 5, 1918 (40 Stat. 506) continued until April 18, 1920.[44] Prices of outstanding Liberty bonds and Victory notes showed a gradual downward tendency. In a public statement issued April 18, 1920, Mr. Houston announced that purchases for the bond-purchase fund would close on July 1, 1920, when the next sinking fund went into effect (Act of March 3, 1919; 40 Stat. 1309). The discount on war bonds gradually disappeared, until by July, 1922, the bonds were at par.[45] In each subsequent year ·the computed rate of interest on the Government debt declined.[46]

TABLE XIII

COMPUTED RATE OF INTEREST ON THE INTEREST-BEARING DEBT, 1916–1941[a]

End of Fiscal Year June 30	Percentage	End of June 30	Percentage
1916	2.376	1929	3.946
1917	3.120	1930	3.807
1918	3.910	1931	3.566
1919	4.178	1932	3.505
1920	4.225	1933	3.350
1921	4.339	1934	3.181
1922	4.240	1935	2.716
1923	4.214	1936	2.559
1924	4.180	1937	2.582
1925	4.105	1938	2.589
1926	4.093	1939	2.600
1927	3.960	1940	2.583
1928	3.877	1941	2.518

[a] U.S., Treasury Dept., *Annual Report of the Secretary, 1942*, p. 577, Table 55.

[43] Treasury Department Circular No. 418, November 22, 1929, quoted in U.S., Treasury Dept., *Annual Report of the Secretary, 1930*, p. 283.
[44] U.S., War Finance Corporation, *Annual Report, 1920*, p. 6.
[45] U.S., Treasury Dept., *Annual Report of the Secretary, 1922*, pp. 458–459.
[46] See Table XIII.

In the 1925 report the Secretary of the Treasury expressly stated that the Government aimed to sell its securities at the lowest possible interest rate and at a yield consistent with general credit conditions.[47] This view is based on the belief that general credit conditions which determine the price of Government bonds cannot be changed to suit the Treasury. During the twenties the Treasury supported its own bonds by buying them on a large scale for its debt-reduction program. The long-continued debt-reduction program (based on a large surplus in the Treasury) first influenced the demand for and consequently the price of Government bonds and lastly the price of bonds in general. In addition, the Sinking Fund was used to buy up bonds that were below par and even above par, for the provision in the Sinking Fund requires that the average cost shall not be above par.[48] Also, the Treasury bought securities for special trust funds and thus diminished their available supply on the market.[49] In short, the Treasury was the most important single buyer in the bond market, and its major policies, supported by adequate means and continued persistently, did influence the major trends of general credit conditions.

United States Government securities have always been in demand by banks, because they were needed as collateral for Government deposits against which no reserves were necessary, and because they provide excellent means of access to the Federal Reserve bank credit.[50]

[47] U.S., Treasury Dept., *Annual Report of the Secretary, 1925,* p. 40.

[48] Act of March 3, 1919 (40 Stat. 1309); the use of the War Finance Corporation created under the War Finance Act of April 5, 1918 (40 Stat. 506), to support Liberty bonds was an expedient which was clearly limited to the war period, and though used during the second half of 1919 to support the Victory notes, it was superseded by an entirely new arrangement provided for in the Victory Liberty Loan Act (40 Stat. 1300). This was the provision for a cumulative sinking fund of $2\frac{1}{2}$ percent calculated to retire the whole interest-bearing public debt, exclusive of the principal amount of the loans to foreign governments, in twenty-five years. The fund was extended to apply to loans issued after July 1, 1920, under the amendment of March 2, 1923 (42 Stat. 1427). Bonds and notes purchased, redeemed, or paid out of the sinking fund shall be canceled and retired and shall not be reissued. Additional appropriations to the sinking fund were made in the Acts of May 29, 1928 (45 Stat. 987), January 30, 1934 (48 Stat. 344), July 21, 1932 (47 Stat. 716), March 7, 1933 (47 Stat. 1492), March 15, 1934 (48 Stat. 428). The provisions of the Victory Liberty Loan Act in setting up this sinking fund were of immense money market importance. The fund was destined to be not only an extremely important factor in the day-to-day operations of the Government bond market but also a major factor in the rapid reduction of the public debt.

[49] U.S., Treasury Dept., *Annual Report of the Secretary, 1927,* p. 39.

[50] See p. 157 for discussion of the Act of September 7, 1916 (39 Stat. 752), of the Act of June 21, 1917 (40 Stat. 232), pp. 157, 179, 191–193; for the Act of February 27, 1932 (47 Stat. 56); p. 224 for the Act of August 23, 1935 (49 Stat. 703).

Table XI shows the increase in Federal Reserve member-bank investments of Government securities. United States Government securities have been in active demand by corporations because of their marketability and acceptability as collateral for borrowing purposes. Furthermore, they have certain tax-exemption features. Until 1941 the interest on Government bonds was wholly tax-exempt for corporations.[51] As a result the demand for Government securities has been high. This factor helped the Treasury throughout the period of the twenties in the refunding of the debt at lower interest rates.

Again, banks were in the market for Government bonds because by pledging them as collateral commercial banks would qualify as special Treasury depositories.[52] Such transactions were doubly attractive, since banks could pay for newly issued Government bonds by merely crediting the Government account on their books. They did not need to pay out funds to the Reserve banks unless called upon to do so by the Treasury, which happened infrequently. In the meantime they could sell the Government obligations, or if they kept them as an investment, the commercial banks gained the difference between the yield on the bonds and the low interest paid to the Treasury on its credit balance.[53]

The practice of discounting at the Federal Reserve banks the fifteen-day notes of member banks secured by a pledge of Government securities was granted in the amendments to the Federal Reserve Act [54] and formed one of the strongest links between the Treasury and the banks. The banks became the largest single creditor of the Government. Consequently the price and interest rates of Government securities were of the utmost importance to the banking system because of their effect on the banks' portfolios and on prices of other securities in the market.

While in the twenties the Government could follow its traditional

[51] Revenue Act of June 25, 1940 (54 Stat. 516).

[52] U.S., Treasury Dept., *Annual Report of the Secretary, 1929*, p. 40.

[53] *Ibid.*, p. 41; prior to 1908 interest had never been required on Government deposits. After the Act of May 30, 1908, interest at the rate of 1 percent per annum was collected from National banks (35 Stat. 546). On April 30, 1913, the Secretary announced that beginning June 1, 1913, all Government depositories would be required to pay interest at the rate of 2 percent per annum on Government funds. U.S., Treasury Dept., *Annual Report of the Secretary, 1913*, p. 5; Federal Reserve banks were designated by the Treasury Government depositories as of June 1, 1916, and were exempt from interest charges on public deposits. U.S., Treasury Dept., *Annual Report of the Secretary, 1916*, pp. 6, 7.

[54] Act of September 7, 1916 (39 Stat. 752); June 21, 1917 (40 Stat. 232).

policy of paying back its debt as speedily as possible, the severe and long depression which began in 1929 forced the Government to intervene more actively in the economic life of the Nation. An increase in the public debt could not be avoided.

CONCLUSION

In previous chapters we have shown that before 1929 various secretaries of the Treasury sought to control, and even partially succeeded in controlling and directing the credit system of the Nation. When the United States entered World War I the Treasury, under the plea that it was necessary for national defense, directed and controlled the credit system of the Nation. During the ten years following the armistice the Treasury continued, though to a lesser extent, to oversee and to direct the policies of the Federal Reserve System in order to expedite the Treasury's fiscal programs. These continual practices plus the emergency actions taken during the Panic of 1929 and the Depression of 1933 finally led to the conclusion that the leadership of the banking field actually belonged to the Treasury. Effective monetary management presupposes a centralization of authority in a single agency. Credit control is a part of general economic planning, and the Treasury is more closely connected with the administration of the general program than any other agency including the Federal Reserve System.

CHAPTER IX

Treasury Central Banking from 1929 to 1941 with Special Reference to the Gold Policies

AT ANY ONE TIME the type of relationship of the Government to economic life is primarily determined by the ideas prevalent in the minds of those persons who are in a position to give their views wide circulation. For a century and a half the people of the United States have been under the influence of an economic ideology, of which a rather extreme type of individualism and the right of private action were central parts.

The depressions of the thirties had a profound effect on these ideas. The distress brought about by the widespread unemployment during this period formed the basis for public acceptance and even for public demand for a considerable extension of governmental activities designed to relieve suffering and provide safeguards against the deepening of the depression. The ideas of relief, of the revival of business activity, of the prevention of further depressions, and of economic and social reform were all inextricably combined in the programs undertaken, as were all the problems of integrating these new activities in the system of private enterprise and of financing and administering them. The shifting of emphasis from relief to recovery and from recovery to reform was unavoidable in the process.

THE TREASURY AND THE DEPRESSION OF 1929

In spite of all the study given to the subject of business cycles, there is still no agreement on the precise nature of the impulses that periodically cause the upturns and downturns in economic activity. It has been asserted that the depression of 1929 originated from monetary, and from nonmonetary causes; that it was the result of underconsumption, and overinvestment; and that it was caused by psychological considerations. Data covering the era are so abundant that they furnish evidence for almost any theory. Most explanations agree that the prosperity of the twenties concealed maladjustments arising from the war and perpetuated throughout the twenties.

To supply the war needs of our country and of the European allies required a tremendous expansion of agriculture and industry in the United States, and the postwar decade saw no reversal of this trend. In the years after the war foreign markets continued to absorb this torrent of American goods.[1] But eventually exports have to be paid

TABLE XIV

IMPORTS AND EXPORTS OF MERCHANDISE,
CALENDAR YEARS 1914 TO 1930[a]

Year	Imports of Merchandise	Exports of Merchandise	Excess of Exports over Imports
1914	$1,789,276,001	$3,113,624,050	$1,324,348,049
1915	1,778,596,695	3,554,670,847	1,776,074,157
1916	2,391,635,335	5,482,641,101	3,091,005,766
1917	2,952,465,955	6,226,255,654	3,273,789,699
1918	3,031,304,721	6,149,241,951	3,117,935,230
1919	3,904,364,932	7,920,425,990	4,016,061,058
1920	5,278,481,490	8,228,061,307	2,949,534,817
1921	2,509,147,570	4,485,031,356	1,975,833,786
1922	3,112,746,833	3,831,777,469	719,030,636
1923	3,792,065,963	4,167,494,080	375,427,117
1924	3,609,962,579	4,590,983,845	981,021,266
1925	4,226,589,263	4,909,847,511	683,258,248
1926	4,430,888,000	4,808,660,000	377,772,000
1927	4,184,720,000	4,865,375,000	680,633,000
1928	4,091,444,000	5,128,356,000	1,036,912,000
1929	4,399,361,000	5,240,995,000	841,634,000
1930	3,060,908,000	3,843,181,000	782,273,000

[a] U.S., Treasury Dept., *Annual Report of the Secretary, 1931*, p. 868.

for by goods imported or services rendered. The United States did not make such payments easy. On the contrary, the building of the American merchant marine reduced the shipping services that Europeans had customarily supplied to the United States, and the high tariff policy of the Fordney-McCumber Act of Sept. 21, 1922 (42 Stat. 858), and of the Hawley-Smoot Act of June 17, 1930 (46 Stat. 590) seriously interfered with attempts of foreign countries to pay for American exports by shipping goods to the United States.[2] Until

[1] See Table XIV.   [2] See Table XV.

TABLE XV

DUTIABLE GOODS AND TOTAL IMPORTS
1914–1930[a]

	Year Ending	Ratio of Dutiable Goods to Total Imports	RATIO OF DUTIES TO VALUE OF	
			Dutiable Imports	Total Imports
June 30	1914	39.55	37.60	14.88
	1915	37.34	33.43	12.49
	1916	31.35	30.67	9.62
	1917	30.54	27.18	8.31
	1918	26.09	24.11	6.30
December 31	1918 (6 mos.)	20.86	24.39	5.09
	1919	29.16	21.27	6.20
	1920	38.92	16.40	6.38
	1921	38.82	29.55	11.44
	1922	38.57	38.07	14.68
	1923	41.98	36.17	15.18
	1924	40.75	36.53	14.89
	1925	35.14	37.61	13.21
	1926	34.03	39.34	13.39
	1927	35.62	38.76	13.81
	1928	34.31	38.76	13.30
	1929	33.62	40.11	13.55
	1930	33.17	44.71	14.83

[a] U.S., Treasury Dept., *Annual Report of the Secretary, 1932*, p. 382.

1929 the inconsistency between a creditor position, on the one hand, and high tariffs, on the other, were concealed by large loans abroad. These only postponed the day of final payment, for as soon as the United States ceased to make these foreign loans, the volume of American foreign trade declined drastically, with unsettling consequences to American agriculture and industry.[3]

[3] "World War Debt Postponement," an excerpt from the message of the President to the Congress on our foreigen affairs, December 10, 1931.

"The world-wide depression has affected the countries of Europe more severely than our own. Some of these countries are feeling to a serious extent the drain of this depression on national economy. The fabric of intergovernmental debts, supportable in normal times, weighs heavily in the midst of the depression.

"From a variety of causes arising out of the depression, such as the fall in the price of foreign commodities and the lack of confidence in economic and political stability abroad, there is an abnormal movement of gold to the United States which is lower-

In addition to the international complications, the domestic scene showed serious maladjustments. A reasonable balance between actual consumption and productive capacity was not maintained. One factor in this phenomenon was the increased industrial expansion of the twenties, which was not accompanied by a sufficient lowering of prices

TABLE XVI

BUSINESS INDICES OF INDUSTRIAL PRODUCTION, FREIGHT CAR LOADINGS, COMMODITY PRICES, FACTORY EMPLOYMENT, FACTORY PAY ROLLS, 1919–1941[a]

Year	Industrial Production Base is average of years 1935–1939 = 100	Freight Car Loadings Base is average of years 1935–1939 = 100	Commodity Prices Base is year 1926 = 100	Factory Employment Base is average of years 1923–1925 = 100	Factory Pay Roll
1919	72	120	139	107	98
1920	75	129	154	108	117
1921	58	110	98	82	76
1922	73	121	97	91	81
1923	88	142	101	104	103
1924	82	139	98	96	96
1925	91	146	104	100	101
1926	96	152	100	102	104
1927	95	147	95	100	102
1928	99	148	97	100	104
1929	110	152	95	106	110
1930	91	131	86	92	89
1931	75	105	73	78	68
1932	58	78	65	66	47
1933	69	82	66	73	50
1934	75	89	75	86	65
1935	87	92	80	91	74
1936	103	107	81	99	86
1937	113	111	86	109	103
1938	88	89	79	91	78
1939	108	101	77	100	91
1940	123	109	79	108	105
1941	156	130	87	129	149

[a] *Federal Reserve Bulletin*, December, 1942, p. 1231.

ing the credit stability of many foreign countries. These and the other difficulties abroad diminish buying power for our exports and in a measure are the causes of our continued unemployment and continued lower prices to our farmers." U.S., Treasury Dept., *Annual Report of the Secretary, 1932*, p. 286.

to consumers.[4] As a result the economies of increased production were reflected primarily in an increase of profits. The large profits led to the employment of credit to finance speculation in securities. The collapse of the speculative boom marked the beginning of the great depression. Many economists declared that this overexpansion of credit could have been avoided.[5] Some economists have censured the banking policy for lack of discrimination in extending credit for legitimate business purposes and for speculative excesses as well.[6] Other theorists have asserted that if a greater fall in prices or an increase in wages had placed larger purchasing power in the hands of the consumer economic developments would have been sounder.[7]

The depression cut deeply into the lives of the people. Prices were lowered to dispose of inventories. Replacement demand dried up, industrial activity shrank, profit expectations seriously diminished. Cost cutting in manufacturing to meet the lower prices became necessary, and variable costs, notably labor costs, were cut severely.[8] Rents fell, railroads became bankrupt, and finally banks became disorganized.

In 1929, and for a year or two thereafter, many believed that the depression was a transitory phenomenon. The Government made only minor attempts to stem the decline in business activity. Income taxes were further reduced.[9] Protective tariffs were further increased, a step in the wrong direction.[10] The Federal Reserve System sought to encourage borrowing by following a cheap-money policy by a lower rediscount rate [11] and the purchase of Government securities.[12] Add-

[4] See Table XVI.

[5] Crawford, *Monetary Management under the New Deal,* p. 6.

[6] Willis, *The Theory and Practice of Central Banking,* p. 136.

[7] Kirkland, *A History of American Economic Life,* p. 705.

[8] U.S., Treasury Dept., *Annual Report of the Secretary,* 1931, p. 6; see above, Table XVI.

[9] Act of December 16, 1929, 46 Stat. 47.

[10] Act of June 17, 1930, 46 Stat. 590.

[11] Beginning with the reduction in the discount rate at the New York bank from 6 percent to 5 percent on November 1, 1929, there were successive reductions at all reserve banks. U.S., Treasury Dept., *Annual Report of the Secretary, 1930,* p. 21.

[12] The Glass-Steagall Act, of February 27, 1932 (47 Stat. 56), liberalized certain features of the Federal Reserve Act and rendered the resources of the system more readily available. The act for a period of one year gave the Federal Reserve banks authority to use the United States Government securities as collateral for Federal Reserve Notes. The reserve banks purchased a large volume of United States Government securities. See below, pp. 157, 167 for further discussion of this act. U.S., Treasury Dept., *Annual Report of the Secretary, 1932,* p. 5; see also Table XI, above.

ing to the funds available for lending, lowering interest rates, and strengthening bank reserves are effective in stimulating borrowing and business activity only when a shortage of funds has been the cause of the economic dislocations. Since this was clearly not the case in 1929 or thereafter, the various steps taken by the Government and the Federal Reserve System increased member bank reserves, but not economic activity.[13]

By 1931 the half-hearted attempts at remedying our business problems during the preceding year had clearly proved insufficient. The world-wide crumbling of the financial structure, beginning with the refusal of the permission for a customs union between Germany and Austria and the resulting collapse of the Austrian Credit Anstalt, in May, 1931, compelled action. President Hoover recognized the impossibility of large intergovernment payments among various countries under the then prevailing conditions, and on July 6, 1931, he announced that all international creditor governments except Yugoslavia had accepted his offer of June 20, 1931, to postpone for a year all payments of interest and principal on reparations and other intergovernment debts.[14] Hoover's policy of an international moratorium did not meet with much popular approval, nor did it prevent the further collapse of European currencies.[15]

At home the continued disintegration of business forced our Government into further action. By 1931 the depression was undermining the solvency of even our strongest corporations, specifically, railroads and banks.[16] Their credit standing had deteriorated to such an extent that they could no longer borrow directly in the investment market. If they were to be saved from bankruptcy, an agency with superior credit standing would have to guarantee their debts or raise funds on its own credit standing and relend the proceeds to corporations in distress. The solution recommended by the Treasury Department and finally enacted into law on January 22, 1923, provided for the Reconstruction Finance Corporation (47 Stat. 5). It

[13] U.S., Treasury Dept., *Annual Report of the Secretary, 1932*, p. 5; see also Table XVIII and pp. 222–223, below.

[14] U.S., Treasury Dept., *Annual Report of the Secretary, 1931*, p. 83.

[15] U.S., Treasury Dept., *Annual Report of the Secretary, 1932*, p. 3.

[16] "During the past 3 years the problems facing our entire banking system have been accentuated owing to the strain occasioned by the credit crisis which has accompanied a world wide depression." U.S., Treasury Dept., *Annual Report of the Secretary, 1932*, p. 30.

was modeled upon a device of war years, the War Finance Corporation.[17]

The corporation was originally authorized to issue and have outstanding at any one time its notes, bonds, or other obligations, guaranteed by the United States, in an amount not to exceed $500,000,-000. The Secretary of the Treasury was authorized to purchase, at his discretion, any obligations of the corporation, and the law provided that the purchase and sales of such obligations by the Treasury should be treated as public-debt transactions of the United States.[18] The funds made available to the corporation were to be loaned to farmers through the Department of Agriculture and directly to railroads, banks, and other financial institutions. The Treasury, in turn, was to borrow either on its own short- or long-term obligations from individuals, corporations, or banks in order to purchase the securities of the Reconstruction Finance Corporation. Thus, in essence the Government began to finance industry and commerce, extending credit and assuming the risks.

Created as a type of banking institution, the Reconstruction Finance Corporation followed the example of the bigger commercial and investment-banking firms of its time and confined its activities to the financing of large corporations, the top of the economic pyramid. The idea was that the funds supplied to the large business organizations would filter through the entire economic structure and finally reach the laborers, for whom additional jobs would be provided.[19]

The seepage worked too slowly; therefore, on July 21, 1932, the act was broadened (47 Stat. 709). The Reconstruction Finance Corporation was authorized to borrow an additional $1,800,000,000 and to make loans to states and municipalities "to be used in furnishing relief and relief work to needy and distressed people."

Another remedial measure adopted by the United States Government was the act of February 27, 1932, known as the "Glass-Steagall

---

[17] The War Finance Corporation was created by the Act of April 5, 1918 (40 Stat. 506), as an instrumentality to supply essential credits to the war industries of the country. The scheme of the act was that the corporation should extend financial assistance to those industries primarily, indirectly through the banks of the country and only in "exceptional cases" directly to the war industries themselves. U.S., Treasury Dept., *Annual Report of the Secretary, 1918*, pp. 56, 245–254; for fuller discussion of this corporation see pp. 164–165, above.

[18] U.S., Treasury Dept., *Annual Report of the Secretary, 1932*, pp. 69-70.

[19] U.S., Treasury Dept., *Annual Report of the Secretary, 1933*, p. 13.

Act" (47 Stat. 56). It was designed to allow exceptional advances by the Federal Reserve banks to member banks. The act amended Section 10 (b) of the Federal Reserve Act by allowing the Federal Reserve bank, in exceptional and exigent circumstances, to make advances to individual member banks having a capital not exceeding $5,000,000 and lacking sufficient eligible and acceptable assets to enable them to obtain adequate credit accommodations from the Federal Reserve banks by the customary methods. The act also amended Section 16 of the Federal Reserve Act so as to authorize the Federal Reserve Board to permit the use of direct obligations of the United States as collateral security for Federal Reserve notes when it was deemed in the public interest.[20] The latter provision was to remain in effect only until March 3, 1933, but it was extended for another year before President Hoover went out of office, on February 3, 1933 (47 Stat. 795); it was subsequently continued for a third year, and authority was given to the President to extend it for two additional years by the Act of March 6, 1934 (48 Stat. 398). Under that authority President Roosevelt extended it to March 3, 1937. An Act of March 1, 1937 (50 Stat. 23) extended it to June 30, 1939, on which date it was extended to June 30, 1941 (53 Stat. 991). On June 30, 1941, the act was extended to June 30, 1943 (55 Stat. 395). The most recent extension was made despite the fact that gold certificates were being used as collateral security in an amount greater than all Federal Reserve notes outstanding.[21] This amendment to the Federal Reserve Act further linked the Treasury to the currency of the country.

In order to satisfy to a greater extent the demand for an expansion of the currency the Borah-Glass National Bank Note Expansion Amendment to the Home Loan Bank Act was passed on July 22, 1932 (47 Stat. 725). The amendment authorized national banks (which are under the jurisdiction of the Treasury Department) to issue national bank notes on the basis of all Government bonds carrying an interest rate of 3⅜ percent or less, the circulation privilege having previously been restricted to the 2 percent consols and Panama Canal bonds. This emergency authority was granted for three years. Un-

---

[20] U.S., Federal Reserve Board, *Annual Report, 1933*, p. 36; U.S., Treasury Dept., *Annual Report of the Secretary, 1933*, p. 25.

[21] U.S., Treasury Dept., *Annual Report of the Secretary, 1941*, p. 356; for another aspect of the Glass-Steagall Amendment to the Federal Reserve Act see p. 146n.

der the terms of the law the total amount of national bank notes that could be issued was in excess of $900,000,000.[22]

Federal Reserve authorities looked upon the measure with disfavor. It was their contention that there had been no shortage of currency and that the new national bank notes would tend to replace other forms of currency in circulation, particularly Federal Reserve notes. To this extent it was held that the expansion of national bank notes would tend to interfere with the control which might be exercised by the Federal Reserve System over credit and to increase the Treasury's control.[23]

The Federal Reserve authorities did not believe that there would be any real demand for the new national bank notes, although it was recognized that banks might be inclined to make use of the authority because of the extra profits. The national banks issuing notes secured by 2 percent bonds were realizing an annual profit of about ½ of 1 percent. The margin of profit was increased when it became possible to use bonds bearing 3⅜ percent.[24]

The experience under the Borah-Glass Amendment confirmed the opinion of those who had been skeptical about any great benefit resulting. Even after as much as two years had elapsed, the increase in national bank notes outstanding totaled less than $200,000,000.[25] A few months before the amendment expired, in July, 1935, the Treasury commenced the retirement of all national bank notes.[26]

ROOSEVELT FURTHERS IDEA OF GOVERNMENT INTERVENTION

The thirties seemed to demand experimentation, especially on the part of the Government. Beginning in 1933, Roosevelt responded with what has been termed the "New Deal." The philosophy of the New Deal involved a much closer supervision and coördination of all branches of business activity through Government agencies. These governmental policies at times appeared to favor special-interest groups unduly—notably the laborers and the farmers. Evidence of

---

[22] U.S., Treasury Dept., *Annual Report of the Secretary, 1932*, p. 32.

[23] *Federal Reserve Bulletin*, August, 1932, pp. 475–476.

[24] *Ibid.*   [25] See Appendix VII, below.

[26] On March 11, 1935, the Treasury called for redemption on July 1 and August 1 of all Government bonds bearing 2 percent interest and having the circulation privilege. U.S., Treasury Dept., *Annual Report of the Secretary, 1935*, pp. 204–206.

this partisanship may be seen in the following enactments: National Industrial Recovery Act, June 16, 1933 (48 Stat. 195), Agricultural Adjustment Act, May 12, 1933 (48 Stat. 31), National Labor Relations Act, July 5, 1935 (49 Stat. 449), and Fair Labor Standards Act, June 25, 1938 (52 Stat. 1060) which was a substitute for the labor provision of the National Industrial Recovery Act. Also there was evident distrust of big business, particularly of public utilities, evidenced by the Tennessee Valley Authority Act, May 18, 1933 (48 Stat. 58) and the Public Utility Holding Company Act, August 26, 1935 (49 Stat. 803). The New Deal philosophers stressed the needs of the moment, which included fighting the depression and enacting reform policies even if these steps involved throwing overboard traditional procedures. The "New Dealers" were not entirely consistent in their actions and displayed a fair amount of opportunism. For example, they switched to nationalism rather than international coöperation during the course of the London Conference of 1933.[27]

In conformity with the whole philosophy of the New Deal, which included credit control as a part of general economic planning, execution of the monetary policies designed to bring about "sound economic" conditions were entrusted to the Treasury rather than to the Federal Reserve System, partly because it is more closely connected with the administration. Also the New Deal monetary measures planned to achieve the regulation of the supply of currency and credit, not through the traditional machinery provided by the Federal Reserve System, but by newly devised Treasury policies.

Through these policies the Treasury went even more deeply into the field of central banking than heretofore. The regulation of the currency is considered one of the most important functions of a central bank. Traditionally a central bank is expected to regulate the internal credit supply so that the currency may be maintained at par with its gold value in the domestic and foreign exchange market. When disequilibrium occurs between the domestic and the world price level, the former is to be adjusted to meet the latter.[28] The Roosevelt administration's attitude has been to reverse the process by giving precedence to the domestic price level. Many of the monetary meas-

[27] See below, pp. 200–201 for discussion of the World Monetary and Economic Conference held during the summer of 1933.
[28] Willis, *The Theory and Practice of Central Banking*, p. 400.

ures were designed for internal price stability and gave the Treasury powers which constituted it the real central bank.

TREASURY GOLD POLICIES AND THE CURRENCY

On March 6, 1933, President Roosevelt signed a proclamation under authority of the Trading-with-the-Enemy Act (40 Stat. 411) which vested the Executive for wartime or other emergency purposes with power to regulate or prohibit transactions in foreign exchange or gold and silver and also to prevent the hoarding of silver and gold coin, gold bullion, and paper currency.[29] In his proclamation the President declared a four-day bank holiday, an embargo on the withdrawal or transfer for export or domestic use of gold or silver. During the holiday banks were not to pay out any coin, bullion, or currency or to transact any other banking business whatsoever, except as might be permitted by the Secretary of the Treasury. On March 7 the Secretary of the Treasury issued a regulation that member banks should deliver to Federal Reserve banks in exchange for other forms of coin or currency all gold and gold certificates held by them.[30] The same order prohibited the Reserve banks from paying any gold or gold certificates to member banks. On March 9, 1933, the Emergency Banking Act was passed (48 Stat. 1) which gave the executive branch of the Government power to open banks which had been ascertained to be in sound condition and to reorganize others. Reopening of the banks was handled by the Federal Reserve System, but under the supervision of the Secretary of the Treasury. The act confirmed the President's emergency powers to control foreign-exchange transactions, gold and currency movements, and banking transactions.

The act amended Section 11 of the Federal Reserve Act and gave authority to the Secretary of the Treasury to call in all gold held by individuals and corporations.

Under Title IV it was made possible to issue bond-secured and asset-secured currency through the Federal Reserve banks entirely distinct from the gold-secured Federal Reserve notes. Title IV amended the Federal Reserve Act to permit the issuance by Federal Reserve banks of Federal Reserve bank notes which could be secured by direct obligations of the United States Government up to 100 percent of their value, or by any notes, drafts and bills acquired by

[29] *Federal Reserve Bulletin*, March, 1933, p. 113. [30] *Ibid.*, p. 125.

the Federal Reserve banks up to 90 percent of their value. It was not required that any reserves should be held against these notes.

The law was more liberal concerning the conditions under which Federal Reserve banks were authorized in unusual circumstances to make loans to member banks on collateral otherwise considered ineligible. Authority was also given to the Reserve banks to make advances to individuals, partnerships, and corporations on notes secured by Government obligations.

Under these emergency provisions it was made possible for any member bank to meet all demands for currency, provided it had sound assets and regardless of the technical eligibility of these assets under the Federal Reserve Act.

On March 10 the President issued an order which prohibited the exportation of gold coin, gold bullion, or gold certificates except under license issued by the Secretary of the Treasury.[31] Furthermore, no banking institution could pay out gold coin, gold bullion, or gold certificates, except as authorized by the Secretary of the Treasury, or engage in any transaction in foreign exchange, except for reasonable trading and other personal requirements, for fulfillment of contrasts entered into prior to March 6, 1933.

In the opinion of Leo Pasvolsky of the Brookings Institution, the Executive Order of March 10 constituted the formal suspension of the gold standard by the United States.[32] Mr. Pasvolsky pointed out that the order did not result in any substantial depreciation of the dollar in foreign exchanges or in more than slight fluctuations in the dollar exchange rate. While the United States currency was no longer redeemable in gold and free exports were prohibited, it was still possible to obtain gold under license for purposes of international transactions. While foreign exchange transactions were placed under regulation, enough latitude was permitted to allow normal international settlements to continue as usual.

President Roosevelt, on April 5, 1933, issued an order forbidding the hoarding of gold.[33] All persons were required to deliver on or before May 1 to any Federal Reserve bank, branch, agency, or mem-

---

[31] *Federal Reserve Bulletin*, March, 1933, p. 119.

[32] Pasvolsky, *Current Monetary Issues*, p. 40; Professors Warren and Pearson, in *Prices*, take the position that the gold standard was suspended internally by the proclamation of March 6, which stopped payments in gold.

[33] *Federal Reserve Bulletin*, April, 1933, pp. 213–214.

ber bank, all gold coin, gold bullion, and gold certificates owned by them or coming into their ownership on or before April 28. Member banks were to deliver all gold received to the Federal Reserve bank of their district.

Finally, on April 20 the President issued an order which completely abandoned the gold standard.[34] To some extent the April 20 order was a reiteration of the one of March 10 placing an embargo on gold exports except under license. The order also authorized control by license of transactions in foreign exchange and transfers of credit and currency to foreign countries.[35]

In Mr. Roosevelt's book *On Our Way* he explains his motives for the April 20 order. He says that while early in April the stocks of gold appeared adequate to meet the demands for currency and credit, there was some fear that there might be a sudden and uncontrollable flight of gold abroad. It was then that he decided with Secretary Woodin "to prevent the export of any more gold."[36]

In his press conference on April 19[37] the President referred to an article by Walter Lippmann[38] as presenting the best explanation of the reasons for his action. The Lippmann article, which had appeared the previous day, urged Congress to defend the internal price level of the country rather than the external value of the currency. Mr. Lippmann said, "No nation has been able to do both. No nation has been able to maintain the value of its currency in terms of gold and also to stabilize the domestic purchasing power of its currency. A choice has had to be made between keeping up prices at home and of keeping up the gold value of the currency abroad."

The Thomas Inflation Amendment

Abandonment of the gold standard and approval of the Thomas Inflation Amendment formed parts of a program by which the President hoped to raise the price level. The Thomas Inflation Amendment

[34] *Federal Reserve Bulletin*, May, 1933, p. 266.

[35] Executive orders modifying the system of control of foreign exchange were issued on August 28, 1933 (U.S., Treasury Dept., *Annual Report of the Secretary, 1934*, p. 203), and January 15, 1934 (*ibid.*, p. 204). These orders granted blanket licenses for all transactions in foreign exchange, transfers of credit and exports of currency other than gold certificates, including silver coins.

[36] Roosevelt, *On Our Way*, p. 59.

[37] Roosevelt, *Public Papers and Addresses*, Vol. II, p. 140.

[38] Lippmann, article in New York *Herald Tribune*, April 18, 1933, p. 15, col. 1.

formed Title III of the Agricultural Adjustment Act of May 12, 1933 (48 Stat. 31). The amendment bore the name of Senator Elmer Thomas, Oklahoma Democrat, a most persistent inflationist and advocate of managed money.

The Thomas Amendment provided for an expansion of Federal Reserve credit, issuance of greenbacks, changes in the monetary standard, and acceptance of silver in payment for foreign debts, and conferred legal-tender power on all forms of currency.[39]

The President was authorized to direct the Secretary of the Treasury to enter into an agreement with the Federal Reserve Board for expansion of the currency and credit through ordinary open-market operations or through purchase by the Federal Reserve banks of Treasury bills or other United States Government obligations up to three billion dollars in addition to those they might then hold.

If the Secretary of the Treasury could not secure the assent of the Federal Reserve authorities to these measures, or if the operations were inadequate, the President might direct the Secretary of the Treasury to issue United States notes or greenbacks up to three billion dollars. This currency would be used to meet maturing Federal obligations and to purchase Government obligations. The Secretary of the Treasury was to retire and cancel annually 4 percent of the greenbacks thus issued.

Provision was made that "such notes and all other coins and currencies heretofore or hereafter coined or issued by or under the authority of the United States shall be legal tender for all debts public and private." Subsequently, in the resolution abrogating the gold clause, approved June 5, 1933, the language was made more specific.[40]

Section 43 of the amendment authorized the President to reduce the weight of the gold dollar up to 50 percent. The President was given the power to fix the weight of the silver dollar at a definite ratio with relation to the gold dollar, both nine-tenths fine, "at such amounts as he finds necessary from his investigation to stabilize domestic prices or to protect the foreign commerce against the adverse effect of depreciated foreign currencies." The President was to provide for the unlimited coinage of gold and silver at the ratio so fixed.

Section 46 of the Thomas Amendment gave the Federal Reserve

[39] *Federal Reserve Bulletin,* June, 1933, pp. 336–337; Thomas Amendment is quoted.
[40] *Ibid.,* p. 338; see below, p. 199.

Board, upon the affirmative vote of not less than five of its members and with the approval of the President, power to declare that an emergency existed by reason of credit expansion and to increase or decrease reserve balances required to be maintained against either demand or time deposits during such emergency.[41]

The powers granted the President and the Secretary of the Treasury in the Thomas Amendment were far-reaching, but as it turned out, they did not take undue advantage of the authority granted them. They never used the power to issue United States notes or greenbacks. The authority to devalue the dollar was not used until the provision was reënacted in amended form in the Gold Purchase Act of January 30, 1934 (48 Stat. 337).

Abrogation of the Gold Clause

The aim of the new monetary policy was, not the maintenance of the gold standard, but of a "desired general price level." The abrogation of the gold clause was the next important step in the development of this policy. A joint resolution providing that all debts, public and private, should be satisfied by payment in legal-tender money and eliminating the gold clause from Government obligations was signed by the President on June 5, 1933.[42]

The first section of the resolution declared that every obligation, past or future, whether with or without a gold clause, "shall be discharged upon payment, dollar for dollar, in any coin or currency which at the time of payment is legal tender for public and private debts." The second section was the amendment to the clause of the Thomas Inflation Amendment, making all coins and currencies of the United States legal tender for all debts, public and private, public charges, taxes, duties, and dues.

Inasmuch as the resolution was retroactive, it raised a question of bad faith on the part of the Government in the repudiation of its obligations to pay outstanding securities in gold.[43] Except for the

[41] If the authorization to increase the reserve percentage required of member banks against their deposit liabilities had been used immediately, excess reserves would have been diminished and the possibilities of a credit inflation reduced. These powers were not used until the Act of August 23, 1935 (49 Stat. 703); see below, pp. 218–222.

[42] *Federal Reserve Bulletin*, June, 1933, p. 338; Public Resolution No. 10, 73d Cong., 1st Sess. Quoted in 48 Stat. 112.

[43] The use of the gold clause in contracts was adopted by the Federal Government in 1910. The act of February 4, 1910, provided that "any bonds and certificates of

Treasury bills, virtually the entire public debt of the Government, which, at the time of the abrogation of the gold clause stood at about $22,000,000,000, was by contract payable in gold.[44]

The adoption of the policy was a natural accompaniment to other steps taken by the Government. The suspension of the gold standard (April 20, 1933, Executive Order) had made it impossible to pay in gold coin.

The adoption of the resolution was regarded by the Secretary of the Treasury as strengthening its drive against hoarding and as tending to eliminate uncertainties in business. The placing of the old gold clause and new legal-tender obligations on the same footing with respect to payment was considered highly desirable.[45]

A World Monetary and Economic Conference had been summoned to meet at London on June 12, 1933, to consider means of restoring international trade and international currency stability. President Roosevelt was chiefly responsible for fixing the date June 12, 1933, for the convening of the conference.[46] Some of the leading nations would have preferred further delay. They were given to understand that the President was ready to join in a program of international coöperation. In the beginning it appeared that Mr. Roosevelt was very anxious that this conference should succeed, especially in establishing the international gold standard.[47] However, it soon became obvious that attempts to solve international problems were bound to conflict with domestic recovery. President Roosevelt concentrated on domestic recovery and felt that raising domestic prices and a free hand in controlling the value of the dollar in for-

---

indebtedness of the United States, hereafter issued, should be payable, principal and interest, in United States gold coin of the present standard of value" (36 Stat. 192). This policy was reiterated in the Second Liberty Bond Act, under which wartime as well as post-war obligations have been issued (40 Stat. 288). There was no specific requirement for the payment in gold in the case of Treasury bills, which had been issued under an Act of June 17, 1929 (46 Stat. 19).

[44] U.S., Treasury Dept., *Annual Report of the Secretary, 1934,* p. 7.

[45] Statement of Secretary Woodin on May 26, 1933, upon the introduction of the resolution to Congress quoted in the *Federal Reserve Bulletin,* June, 1933, p. 333.

[46] The New York *Times,* March 17, 1933, p. 11, col. 4, reported that President Roosevelt in conversation with the British, French, and German ambassadors urged the fixing of the earliest possible date for the World Conference.

[47] President Roosevelt had issued the following statement as early as May 6, 1933: "We are in agreement that a fixed measure of exchange values must be reëstablished in the world, and we believe that this measure must be gold." Quoted in Pasvolsky, *Current Monetary Issues,* Appendix B, Part III, p. 156.

eign trade were of prime importance in achieving his aim. Therefore, on July 3, 1933, he dispatched a wireless message to the conference: "The sound internal economic system of a nation is a greater factor in its well being than the price of its currency in changing terms of the currencies of other nations." [48] The President's statement indicated that the administration intended to focus more attention on domestic affairs than on international economic relations. This marked the turning point in the shaping of Mr. Roosevelt's monetary policies. The President definitely committed himself against the restoration of an inflexible international gold standard and in favor of a management of the currency which would give preference to domestic considerations. The President's repudiation of a proposed agreement for an international stabilization of currencies was the cause of the collapse of the conference. The shattering of plans for international stabilization meant that other nations had no alternative but to perfect systems of currency management. While the development of currency systems managed by the Treasury on a nationalistic basis might have been checked at the time of the London Conference in 1933, monetary events in the succeeding years, devaluation of the dollar and the stabilization fund, made such action increasingly difficult.[49]

Banking Act of June 16, 1933

While the framers of the Banking Act of 1933 (Senator Glass and Representative Steagall) did not have in mind the linking of powers over banking with economic planning, except as a defense against adverse conditions, the provisions of the law paved the way for the subsequent extension of authority to facilitate monetary management.[50]

The Act helped to make possible easy money conditions. Section 7 prohibited the payment of interest upon demand deposits by member banks of the Federal Reserve System and gave the board authority to limit the rates of interest paid on time and savings deposits. Sec-

[48] The New York *Times*, July 4, 1933, p. 1, col. 8; the President's views were in harmony with those of John Maynard Keynes, British economist, whose theories were out of harmony with policies of his own government (Fisher, *Stable Money*, p. 358). Mr. Keynes contended that the attainment of internal price stability through a managed currency system was preferable to external price stability though a gold standard (Keynes, *Essays in Persuasion*, pp. 244–270).

[49] Crawford, *Monetary Management under the New Deal*, pp. 50–66.

[50] *Ibid.*, p. 116.

tion 12A gave a statutory basis to an existing open-market committee which consisted of one representative of each of the twelve Federal Reserve banks.

The Federal Reserve Board was authorized to prescribe regulations for the conduct of open-market operations, and its members were privileged to sit with the committee. The board continued to be without authority to initiate open-market operations.

With respect to relations with foreign central banks, which were to become important in the stabilization of foreign exchange, the board was given complete control.

The numerous restrictions and control devices set up in the act for the purpose of preventing the improper use of banking funds in speculation helped to pave the way for currency management. The various provisions in Sections 20 and 21 relating to bank loans were intended to (1) control and limit brokers' loans, (2) to restrain the diversion of bank funds to an undue degree into direct loans upon securities, and (3) to prevent speculative market loans by corporations engaged in industrial or business enterprises.

Provisions in Sections 22 and 24 for the divorcement of security affiliates from banks, the regulations of group banking, and a strengthening of the capital structure of banks tended to increase the Government's power, although it did not in all instances promote the flexibility of control desirable for monetary management.

The Federal Reserve Board, which at the time of the passage of the act was not dominated by "New Dealers," expressed sympathy with its purpose to strengthen the supervision of the Government over general credit conditions, but thought that restrictions upon the character of loans and investments might impede business recovery.[51]

The Banking Act of 1933 did not give as much power to the President and the Secretary of the Treasury over monetary problems as had other important laws enacted during the Roosevelt Administration. However, it was this act which directed Roosevelt advisers toward a further revision of banking laws to facilitate monetary management.[52]

[51] *Federal Reserve Bulletin,* April, 1932, pp. 206–225; for Banking Act of 1933, see *Federal Reserve Bulletin,* May, 1933, pp. 385, 401.
[52] Crawford, *Monetary Management under the New Deal,* p. 118.

Gold Purchase Plan

One of the methods devised for monetary control was the Gold Purchase Plan. On April 20, 1933, the United States had definitely abandoned the gold standard. Professor Warren, one of the President's favorite advisers, attributed the steady rise in commodity prices to that phenomenon.[53] The next step in the monetary program

TABLE XVII

WHOLESALE COMMODITY PRICE INDICES FOR
THE YEAR 1933[a]

Base Year is 1926 = 100

Month	Index	Month	Index
January	61.0	July	68.9
February	59.8	August	69.5
March	60.2	September	70.8
April	60.4	October	71.2
May	62.7	November	71.1
June	65.0	December	70.8

[a] *Federal Reserve Bulletin*, February, 1934, p. 138.

was to maintain the advance in prices.[54] Professor Warren advocated further depreciation of the dollar and further stimulation of commodity prices by the manipulation of the price of gold.

The President announced his new plan in a radio speech on October 22, 1933.[55] He believed international stability should be sacrificed for measures designed to bring about stability of the domestic price level. This was a reiteration of the statement in his message to the London Conference in July.[56] In his opinion, the dollar was altogether too greatly influenced by the accidents of international trade, by the internal policies of other nations, and by political disturbance in other continents. Therefore the United States should take firmly in its own hands the control of the gold value of the dollar in order to prevent dollar disturbances from causing a deviation from the ultimate goal, which was the continued recovery of commodity prices.

[53] Dr. George F. Warren, professor of farm management at the Agricultural College of Cornell University, had for many years studied money and prices with special relation to agriculture. See below, pp. 204–205 for discussion of the Warren theories.

[54] See Table XVII, above.   [55] Roosevelt, *On Our Way*, p. 174.

[56] See above, pp. 200–201.

As an affective means to this end he established a Government market for gold in the United States. The President authorized the Reconstruction Finance Corporation,[57] under the Executive order of October 25, 1933,[58] to buy gold newly mined in the United States at prices to be determined by consultation with the Secretary of the Treasury and the President. Whenever necessary the corporation shall buy or sell gold in world markets.

The President indicated in the radio speech of October 22 that this policy was to be used not merely to offset a temporary fall in prices but also as a move toward a managed currency.[59]

The Reconstruction Finance Corporation paid for the gold with its own notes. The authority of the corporation to buy gold was questioned, and consequently the Treasury took over the purchase of gold on January 15, 1934.[60] On January 1, 1934, Mr. Morgenthau, former governor of the Farm Credit Administration, had been appointed Secretary of the Treasury, and he was sympathetic to the Warren theories.

Under the old gold standard the seller of gold received in payment gold coin or gold certificates which soon found their way into bank reserves. Under the 1933 plan Reconstruction Finance Corporation notes (later Treasury notes) were issued to obtain money to buy gold. Thus the Treasury was sterilizing gold just as if it had raised commercial bank reserve requirements, which is a central banking power. Undoubtedly, the purpose of the gold purchase policy was inflationary, but the method of purchase prevented the rise in the gold stock from increasing member bank reserves.

Warren Theories

The gold purchase policy was based upon the Warren theory that the supply of and demand for gold were the most important considerations in the movement of commodity prices.[61] Professor Warren contended that prices were not dependent exclusively on the supply and demand for a particular commodity, but that four variables were to

[57] See above, p. 191, for discussion of the activities of this corporation.
[58] *Federal Reserve Bulletin,* November, 1933, p. 674; U.S., Federal Reserve Board, *Annual Report, 1933,* p. 327.
[59] Roosevelt, *On Our Way,* p. 174.
[60] U.S., Treasury Dept., *Annual Report of the Secretary, 1934,* p. 27.
[61] The Warren theories are elaborated by Warren and Pearson in *Prices.*

be considered, not two. A high price might be due to a short supply of the commodity or to a high demand for it, or it might be due to a large supply of the commodity used as money or to a low demand for it, or it might be due to some combination of these variables.[62] The fact that payment might be made by check or paper currency did not alter the importance of gold, for gold was the basis of the credit and monetary structure and the unit in which the value of currency was expressed.

According to that theory, price was the ratio between two values— the value of the commodity and the value of gold. Consequently, "if gold stocks increased more rapidly than other things, prices rose. If they increased less rapidly, prices fell." [63]

Professor Warren subscribed to the theory of Professor Gustav Cassel, of Sweden, that monetary gold stocks should increase by approximately the same amount as the production of commodities in order to maintain a stable price level.[64] Professor Warren contended that world gold production since 1915 had not increased fast enough to maintain a stable price level with a normal increase in business and normal demand for gold. The great rise in prices was due to the fact that most of the gold-using countries had ceased to use gold. When the world began to bid frantically for gold, after its return to the gold standard following World War I, the value of gold rose and commodity prices collapsed.[65]

The depression, according to Professor Warren, "was not a business cycle, was not due to extravagant living, unsound business practices, overproduction, increased efficiency or lack of confidence. Instead it was due to a high demand for gold following a period of low demand for gold." [66] On the basis of these ideas Professor Warren contended that the proper step was to devalue the dollar by reducing its gold equivalent, which process had the effect of increasing in terms of dollars the monetary gold stocks exercising a dominant influence upon commodity prices.[67]

Without a readjustment of the relationship between currency and

[62] Warren and Pearson, *Prices*, p. 112.   [63] *Ibid.*, p. 81.

[64] Cassel, *The Theory of Social Economy*, p. 442; Cassel has shown that for the period 1850–1910 "The main cause of the secular variations of the general price level lies in the changes of the relative gold supply." He indicates that the gold supply must increase about 3 percent annually to maintain stable prices; Warren and Pearson, *Prices*, pp. 82, 96.

[65] *Ibid.*, p. 90.   [66] *Ibid.*, p. 125.   [67] *Ibid.*, p. 171.

gold, steadily declining prices were inevitable.[68] Furthermore, Professor Warren maintained that a country off the gold standard might have any price level it desired by manipulating the gold value of its currency.[69] His contention was that an increase of 75 percent in the price of gold would eventually insure a return to the 1926 price level and that an increase of 100 percent would result in a price level somewhat higher than in 1926.[70]

A 75 percent increase would have meant a price of $36.17 per ounce, while an increase of 100 percent would have meant $41.34 per ounce.[71] A 75 percent increase in the price of gold would be equivalent to a 43 percent reduction in the gold content of the dollar which under the old law contained 23.22 grains of gold.[72] A 100 percent increase would be equivalent to a 50 percent reduction in the gold content, the limit possible under the authority granted originally to President Roosevelt in the Thomas Amendment and incorporated subsequently in the Gold Reserve Act of 1934 (48 Stat. 337).

Gold Reserve Act of 1934

After ten months of experimentation the Administration, in January, 1934, advocated the adoption of a quasi-gold standard under conditions intended to facilitate management of the currency. Authorization for the new monetary system was contained in the Gold Reserve Act, which was signed by the President on January 30, 1934. The act gave the President many powers; among them was the power to change the gold content of the dollar and the power to influence foreign exchange through a stabilization fund.[73]

Section 2 vested title to all monetary gold stocks in the Treasury. It transferred all gold held by the Federal Reserve banks to the Treasury in exchange for gold certificates. The Federal Reserve banks were authorized to maintain reserves of gold certificates instead of gold against Federal Reserve notes.

Section 5 stated that no gold should thereafter be coined, that no

[68] *Ibid.*, p. 176.   [69] *Ibid.*, p. 110.   [70] *Ibid.*, p. 174.   [71] *Ibid.*

[72] Under the old law 23.22 grains of gold were valued at $20.67. With a 75 percent increase in the price of the gold, the value is $36.17 ($20.67 × 1.75). Gold valued at $36.17 should contain under the old law 40.635 grains (23.22 × 1.75). Gold valued at $36.17 and containing only 23.22 grains resulted in a 43 percent devaluation of the dollar, because the dollar contained only 57 percent (23.22 ÷ 40.635) of the grains which it should have.

[73] U.S., Treasury Dept., *Annual Report of the Secretary, 1934*, pp. 189–194, wherein the Gold Reserve Act is quoted.

gold should be paid out or delivered by the United States, and that all coin then in circulation should be withdrawn and formed into bars. It was made possible to release gold bars to pay foreign balances and for industrial, professional, and artistic uses.

Section 7 provided that in the event of a reduction in the weight of the gold dollar the resulting increase in the value of gold should be taken into the Treasury as a miscellaneous receipt. In the event of a subsequent increase in the weight of the gold, the resulting decrease in gold reserves for United States notes, Treasury notes, and gold certificates would be compensated by transfers of gold bullion from the general fund.

Section 9 authorized the Secretary of the Treasury to purchase gold in any amount at home or abroad at such rates and upon such terms and conditions as he deemed most advantageous to the public interest, all such gold to be included as an asset in the general fund of the Treasury. The Secretary of the Treasury was permitted to sell gold in any amount at home or abroad, but sales from the reserves or security for currency were to be made only to the extent necessary to maintain the currency at a parity with the gold dollar.

Section 10 set up a Stabilization Fund with $2,000,000,000 out of the gold profit accruing from the devaluation of the dollar. Through this fund authority was given to the Secretary of the Treasury "to deal in gold and foreign exchange and other instruments of credit and securities" as a means of stabilizing the exchange value of the dollar. Purchase of Government securities by the fund, as well as of gold, silver, and foreign exchange, was provided.

Section 12 provided a 60 percent upper limit for the devaluation of the dollar.

Section 19c, added at the request of the Treasury, granted authority to issue gold certificates against any unobligated gold held by the Treasury. By this provision it was possible to convert all free gold in the Treasury, including the gold profit, into currency by the simple process of depositing gold certificates with Federal Reserve banks. The Treasury might spend the gold by drawing checks on the accounts in the Federal Reserve banks created from the gold certificates. The checks, when deposited in member banks, would contribute to their reserves. Such action made possible a pyramiding of reserves and increased the dangers from excess reserves.

The act was criticized by Professor E. W. Kemmerer, of Princeton

University, Dr. Benjamin M. Anderson, Jr., then economist of the Chase National Bank, of New York, and the late Professor H. P. Willis, of Columbia University among others.[74] They were particularly concerned over the vesting of powers in the Secretary of the Treasury in connection with the operation of the Stabilization Fund. The use of this fund would have effects similar to open-market operations of Federal Reserve banks and might tend to nullify Federal Reserve credit-control policies. Furthermore, open-market operations have long been considered the province of a central bank rather than of the Government Treasury. Expenditures from the fund would add to excess reserves of member banks, thereby creating an instrument of inflation.

It was the work of such men as Senator Carter Glass which resulted in the placing of time limits upon the use of the Stabilization Fund and upon the exercise of the President's authority to change the gold content of the dollar. In both cases it was provided that the authority should continue for two years, and permission was granted to the President to extend the powers for one additional year.[75]

In the President's message to Congress on January 15, 1934, he gave a comprehensive explanation of some of the provisions incorporated in the Gold Reserve Act.[76] Experience has shown, he said, that the free circulation of gold coins was unnecessary, led to hoarding, and tended to a possible weakening of national financial structures in times of emergency. The transfer of gold was essential only for the payment of international trade balances. Therefore it was wise to vest title to and possession of all monetary gold in the Government and keep it in bullion rather than in coin. He also proposed the setting up of the $2,000,000,000 fund out of the gold profit accruing from the devalua-

[74] U.S., Congress, Senate, Committee on Banking and Currency, 73d Cong., 2d Sess., *Hearings on the Gold Reserve Act*, p. 232.

[75] Section 10c, 48 Stat. 337. On January 10, 1936, shortly before the expiration of a two-year period following the enactment of the Gold Reserve Act, President Roosevelt, by proclamation, extended for a third year the two sections which were not permanent law (U.S., Treasury Dept., *Annual Report of the Secretary, 1936*, p. 269). By this action the Stabilization Fund and the President's authority to change the gold content of the dollar were continued to January 30, 1937. On January 23, 1937 (50 Stat. 4), a law was passed extending the Stabilization Fund and the President's authority to change the gold content of the dollar until June 30, 1939. On July 6, 1939 (53 Stat. 998), a similar law was passed to be effective until June 30, 1941. On the latter date, the law was extended until June 30, 1943 (55 Stat. 395).

[76] U.S., Congress, *Congressional Record*, 73d Cong., 2d Sess., p. 643.

tion of the dollar, the fund to be handled by the Secretary of the Treasury to promote stability in foreign exchange rates. He asserted that under the Thomas Inflation Amendment (48 Stat. 31) he was authorized to reduce the gold content of the dollar by a maximum of 50 percent: careful study had led him to believe, he indicated, that any revaluation at more than 60 percent would not be in the public interest.

Devaluation of the Dollar

Devaluation promptly followed the enactment of the Gold Reserve Act. On January 31, 1934, the President signed a formal proclamation, under which the new dollar contained 13.71 grains of gold, nine-tenths fine, instead of 23.22.[77] The reduction amounted to 59.06 percent.[78] The proclamation asserted that the new weight of the gold dollar, as fixed therein, was necessary "in order to stabilize domestic prices and to protect the foreign commerce against the adverse effect of depreciated foreign currencies." On January 30, 1934, the Secretary of the Treasury announced that beginning February 1, 1934, all gold tendered to the Government would be bought by the Treasury at $35 an ounce, which was equivalent to a 59.06 percent devaluation of the dollar.[79] The $35 announced price represented an increase of about 69 percent from the former century-old price of $20.67.

By the act of devaluation there accrued to the Treasury a profit representing the difference between the value of all monetary gold stocks of the United States at the former price of $20.67 and the new price of $35 an ounce. The daily statement of the Treasury of January 31, 1934, showed gold assets, including gold deposited by the Federal Reserve banks in connection with the issuance of gold certificates, to an amount of $4,034,867,780.67. On February 1, 1934, the daily statement showed gold assets amounting to $7,018,263,925.70. Under miscellaneous receipts in the general fund of the Treasury was a new item "increment resulting from a reduction in the weight of the gold dollar" amounting to $2,805,516,060.87.

[77] U.S., Treasury Dept., *Annual Report of the Secretary, 1934,* p. 28.
[78] This was the first substantial change since the Act of June 28, 1834 (4 Stat. 699), which set the price of gold at $20.67. Congress, on April 2, 1792 (1 Stat. 246), set the price of gold at $19.39 per ounce.
[79] *Federal Reserve Bulletin,* February, 1934, p. 69.

Of the amount of the profits credited to the Stabilization Fund only $200,000,000 has been used.[80] The process by which the gold was used included the issuance of gold certificates against it, their deposit with a Federal Reserve bank, and the drawing of checks against the account thus created.

THE TREASURY AND FOREIGN EXCHANGE

Capital Movements before Stabilization Funds

Stabilization funds are merely new agencies for performing the old task of offsetting international capital movements. Credit tends to expand in the country receiving gold and to contract in the one losing the metal thereby affecting prices and interest rates in such a way as to stop the movement. As the years passed, central banks discovered more refined techniques to reduce gold movements, such as changing the bank rate and open-market operations.

Gold imports are usually attracted by high interest rates and low prices. In 1933 and especially after 1933 short-term funds were no longer primarily influenced by bank rates and price levels, but rather by political and economic considerations. Necessarily, therefore, they ceased to correct dislocations in the money market of price structure. On the contrary, these movements of funds tended to call attention to the lack of confidence in the political and economic situation of the gold-exporting country and thereby increased the export of gold.[81]

Stabilization Fund

Under Section 10 of the Gold Reserve Act (48 Stat. 337) Congress authorized the use of $2,000,000,000, of gold profit from devaluation of the dollar in a fund to stabilize the exchange value of the dollar and to provide resources for further gold dealings. The fund was to be operated by the United States Treasury.[82] Since the fund was com-

---

[80] U.S., Treasury Dept., *Daily Statement of the United States Treasury*, April 27, 1934.

[81] Gayer, *Monetary Policy and Economic Stabilization*, p. 28.

[82] Theorists of the type of Professor Willis saw the danger that the Federal Reserve System might cease to be a central bank in its own right and recommended that the Federal Reserve Open Market Committee conduct the stabilization operations. Furthermore, he pointed out that "currency stabilization" is a function of a central bank, not the Treasury Department. See U.S., Congress, Senate, Committee on Banking and Currency, 73d Cong., 2d Sess., *Hearings on the Gold Reserve Act of 1934*, p. 232.

prised of gold, it could be used to offset capital outflow, but not capital inflow. The latter would continue as long as the Treasury, as part of its regular activities, was buying all gold offered at $35 an ounce.[83]

Stabilization funds may consist of and will eventually consist of gold, foreign exchange, domestic currency, or any combination of these. The British fund, known as the Exchange Equalization Account, was established in April, 1932, seven months after Great Britain abandoned the gold standard, September 21, 1931.[84] Its purpose was to prevent excessive fluctuations in foreign exchanges. Instead of gold, with which the American fund started, the account was supplied with Treasury bills which could be sold for sterling with which to buy foreign exchange or gold. This device had the merit of making it possible to keep gold which had been accumulated by the account from influencing internal credit conditions. In effect gold held by the account was sterilized, but it could be shifted to the Bank of England when desired. From this standpoint, the British plan has been regarded as having an advantage over the American scheme, under which the use of gold has meant an increase in reserves of the banking system. If central banks had a sufficiently large portfolio of securities, this result could also be achieved by open-market operations, long considered a central banking function.

It was soon discovered that a fund which consists exclusively of gold, such as the American fund at its inception, can offset a tendency to overvalue our currency by being used to buy gold and sell dollars abroad. Since it did not have dollars, it was necessary to deposit gold certificates issued against its gold holdings with the Federal Reserve banks and thereby create a dollar balance available in any form of currency. But adding gold certificates to the holdings of the Federal Reserve banks increases their funds available as reserve for credit extensions. The Stabilization Fund thus goes beyond its sphere of international currency relations and makes a domestic credit inflation possible.[85] The fund can insulate the internal credit system against internal influences as long as its working balance lasts. In the American fund the amount of gold available is limited, but the amount to which domestic currency may be issued is unlimited, since Govern-

---

[83] Beckhart and Hyslop, *The Gold Problem*, p. 21.
[84] Waight, *The History and Mechanism of the Exchange Equalization Account*, p. 8.
[85] Crump, "Development of Exchange Funds," *Lloyds Bank, Ltd., Monthly Review*, (January, 1937), Vol. VIII p. 8.

ment obligations may take the place of the required gold and commercial paper collateral for Federal Reserve notes for three years.[86]

In reality the purpose of the American fund was, not to iron out short-term fluctuations and to offset capital movements, but rather to make and keep effective the desired degree of dollar depreciation and to give the Government manipulatory powers over the foreign exchanges. The fund, as established by the Gold Reserve Act, could not fulfill any of these objectives without influencing the internal credit base. Exchange stability could not be secured as long as the fund had no dollars to sell in foreign markets. To secure dollars, it had to deposit its gold with the Federal Reserve banks, thus adding to the gold reserves of the Federal Reserve banks. Expansion of these reserves by $2,000,000,000, the balance in the Stabilization Fund, was possible. If the whole amount had been deposited, the result would have been similar to gold imports.

The use of the Stabilization Fund was first officially mentioned on February 11, 1935, when the Secretary of the Treasury disclosed that its operations had served to maintain stability of the dollar.[87] Detailed information as to operations of the fund was made public officially for the first time early in 1939. While the fund had been in existence for five years, little was known of its status until Secretary Morgenthau appeared before the House Committee on February 28, March 3, and March 7, and before the Senate Committee on March 2, 1939, in connection with legislation for the extension of the President's monetary powers.[88] Secretary Morgenthau made public at that time balance sheets of the fund as of June 30 and December 31, 1938, together with information as to earnings, investments, and adminis-

[86] The Glass-Steagall Act of February 27, 1932 (47 Stat. 56); the Act of February 3, 1933 (47 Stat. 795), extended these provisions as did the Act of March 6, 1934 (48 Stat. 398). The Presidential Proclamation of February 14, 1935, extended the period for two years. The Act of March 1, 1937 (50 Stat. 23), set the terminal date at June 30, 1939. The Act of June 30, 1939 (53 Stat. 991), provided for a two-year extension, as did the Act of June 30, 1941 (55 Stat. 395). See pp. 145–146, 191–193. U.S., Treasury Dept., *Annual Report of the Secretary, 1941,* p. 356.

[87] U.S., Treasury Dept., *Annual Report of the Secretary, 1935,* p. 265.

[88] U.S., Congress, House, Committee on Coinage, Weights and Measures, 76th Cong., 1st Sess., *Hearings on the Act of July 6, 1939,* February 28 to March 23, 1939, and U.S., Congress, Senate, Committee on Banking and Currency, *Hearings on the Act of July 6, 1939,* March 2 to March 18, 1939.

trative expenses. He announced that he would make public similar statements each quarter of the year. Since Congress, on July 6, 1939 (53 Stat. 998), enacted a law extending the President's power to devalue the dollar and the Stabilization Fund until June 30, 1941, and on the latter date, Congress again extended the provisions until June 30, 1943 (55 Stat. 395) Congress must have been satisfied that the Stabilization Fund helped to promote stability of exchange in the absence of an automatic international gold standard. The only change in the existing law applying to the Stabilization Fund was the requirement that the annual audit for the information of the President be made available to Congress. (Section 2 of the Act of July 6, 1939; 53 Stat. 998).

Mr. Morganthau said,

The purpose of the Fund is to stabilize the exchange value of the dollar. In carrying out this purpose, the Fund undertakes a variety of operations. Sometimes, it is called upon to prevent violent fluctuations in exchange rates induced by political developments which cause flights of capital from one country to another.

In speaking of the Czechoslovakian crisis he said,

If there had been no Stabilization Fund, the dollar exchange would have fluctuated so violently as to disrupt our trade. International chaos might have ensued. . . .

The Stabilization Fund is, under present conditions, a potent instrument for the protection of our stake in world trade and of every American producer who competes in the American market with foreign producers. The only persons in the United States who can possibly be injured by the operation of the Stabilization Fund are speculators in foreign exchange. Whereas the business man needs stability in exchange, the speculator thrives on exchange fluctuations. Any business man who has had to deal in foreign currency knows that the dollar is the most stable and the soundest currency in the world today. The Stabilization Fund has been an important and essential instrument in maintaining that stability.[89]

While the law creating the Stabilization Fund permits the purchase of Government securities without restriction (Gold Reserve Act Section 10b; 48 Stat. 337), it was denied by Secretary Morgenthau that this had been done at any time for the purpose of supporting the

---

[89] U.S., Congress, House, Committee on Coinage, Weights and Measures, 76th Cong., 1st Sess., *Hearings on the Act of July 6, 1939*, p. 3.

market. Treasury bonds were bought to provide earnings for the fund.[90]

Again in a statement before the Senate Committee on Banking and Currency on June 13, 1941, in support of a bill to extend the powers of the Stabilization Fund, the Secretary declared that the fund had proved its value during years of unparalleled crises and stated that "we are going forward into times of even greater peril. We are in the midst of many systems of currency and exchange controls. Some are operated with no friendly intent toward the United States. Our Stabilization Fund is a potent weapon of defense in our international economic relations. . . . Economic warfare as well as military warfare, is being waged on all sides of us. There is no certainty that even with peace, these aggressive economic instruments will be abandoned by other countries. Nobody can say what kind of international economy will emerge from this war. But it would surely be unwise, if we chose this time to let speculators and foreign governments determine the exchange value of the dollar." [91]

Opposition to the continuance of the Stabilization Fund and of the President's authority to change the value of the dollar was strongly in evidence during the hearings held in connection with the Act of July 6, 1939. The witnesses on behalf of the Economists' National Committee on Monetary Policy were not agreed on the merits of the Stabilization Fund, one of them contending that it was unnecessary and might properly be abolished.[92]

Even if Mr. Morgenthau's viewpoint is accepted, namely, that the Stabilization Fund should be continued because it helps maintain stability in the exchange value of the currency, which is a central banking function, it follows that control over the Stabilization Fund belongs in the hands of the Federal Reserve System, not in the Treasury Department. However, the Fund has been and probably will remain under the control of the Treasury Department because of the

---

[90] U.S., Congress, Senate, Committee on Banking and Currency, 76th Cong., 1st Sess., *Hearings on the Act of July 6, 1939*, p. 32.

[91] U.S., Treasury Dept., *Annual Report of the Secretary, 1941*, p. 53.

[92] Testimony of Professor Walter E. Spahr, New York University, *ibid.*, pp. 60–89; Professor Frederick A. Bradford, Lehigh University, before the House Committee, on Coinage, Weights and Measures, 76th Cong., 1st Sess., *Hearings on the Act of July 6, 1939*, pp. 97–121; and Professor B. H. Beckhart, Columbia University, before the House Committee, *ibid.*, pp. 124–157. Professor Beckhart favored the abolition of the Stabilization Fund and the use of the gold as a reserve for United States notes and silver certificates.

present-day movement for greater governmental intervention in economic affairs.

Tripartite Agreement

On May 13, 1935, Secretary Morgenthau extended an informal invitation to foreign nations to join in a movement for stabilization of currencies.[93] This policy appears to be inconsistent with the Government's position established during the London Conference in 1933. However, in a statement issued on September 25, 1936, announcing a tripartite agreement by the United States, Great Britain, and France concerning the stabilization of currencies, Mr. Morgenthau reserved the right to give precedence to domestic considerations over international stability.[94] This attitude was in accord with that established during the London Conference, but it indicated that the United States was more ready to believe that international stability would be beneficial to the internal economy of the United States.

The text of the Secretary of the Treasury's invitation states,

The Government of the United States must, of course, in its policy toward international monetary relations, take into full account the requirements of internal prosperity, as corresponding considerations will be taken into account by the governments of France and Great Britain; it welcomes this opportunity to reaffirm its purpose to continue the policy which it has pursued in the course of recent years, one constant object of which is to maintain the greatest possible equilibrium in the system of international exchange and to avoid to the utmost extent the creation of any disturbance of that system by American monetary action.[95]

The tripartite agreement remained in operation until the outbreak of the World War II, although no break occurred in relations bebetween the United States and the other parties to the agreement concerning control of exchange and gold transactions.

Operations connected with the control of foreign exchange and gold transactions belong to the field of central banking. The Federal Reserve System, not the Treasury Department, was the proper agency for supervision of the activities under the Tripartite Agreement.

[93] Radio Address of May 13, 1935, quoted in U.S., Congress, *Congressional Record*, 76th Cong., 1st Sess., pp. 7447–7449.
[94] *Federal Reserve Bulletin*, October, 1936, p. 759.   [95] *Ibid.*

GOLD CONCENTRATION IN THE UNITED STATES

About the time of the passage of the Gold Reserve Act of January 30, 1934,[96] attention of the Treasury was intensively directed to the monetary effects derived from the concentration of gold in the United States. The immediate monetary effects included the rise in excess reserves,[97] the increase in commercial bank deposits, declining rates of interest, and the change in the composition of bank portfolios. The future monetary problems included the possibility of further credit expansion, the threat of inflation, and change in the form of the gold standard.[98]

It should not be inferred from the selection of the Gold Reserve Act that the increase in the price of gold was mainly responsible for the increases in gold holdings. Although it played a role of great importance, there were other factors of some significance. Other factors contributing to the increase in the gold stock included imports (gold from mines, from reserves of central banks and governments, from private hoards, and from the return of scrap and coins abroad) and domestic production, gold acquired under the gold-buying program of 1933,[99] and purchase of domestic scrap gold.[100]

The flow of gold to the United States was caused by the devaluation of the dollar, the development of political tensions and fears, and the needs of rearmament. The devaluation of the gold dollar and the establishment of a fixed price for gold [101] were the first factors which stimulated gold importation. Devaluation tended to encourage the export trade of the United States. It induced Europeans to repay American indebtedness, and it led to a repatriation of American capital.[102] The establishment of a fixed price at which the Government would buy gold eliminated the element of risk which the placement of funds here might involve.

The second factor which gave rise to a demand for dollars or to a flow of gold to this country was the influence of internal political crises

---

[96] This Act (48 Stat. 337) which reduced the gold content of the dollar and raised the price of gold amended Title III of the Act of May 12, 1933 (48 Stat. 31) ; see above, p. 206.

[97] See below, pp. 222–223 and also Table XII, above.

[98] Beckhart and Hyslop, *The Gold Problem*, p. 22.   [99] See above, pp. 203–204.

[100] Beckhart and Hyslop, *The Gold Problem*, p. 13.

[101] Presidential Proclamation on January 31, 1934. See above, p. 209.

[102] Beckhart and Hyslop, *The Gold Problem*, p. 22.

and the increasing fear of war in various European countries. French parliamentary crises, Italian activities in Northern Africa, Germany's reoccupation of the Rhineland, absorption of Austria and invasion of Czechoslovakia increased the flow of gold. The Munich "settlement" of September, 1938, augmented the gold movement.

The final factor which explains the increased concentration of gold in the United States is the great European demand for American products to be used for armament purposes and private consumption. At about the time of the American depression of 1937 the American demand for foreign goods fell. These circumstances resulted in a favorable balance of trade and increased the flow of gold to the United States.[103]

The immediate monetary problem caused by the concentration of gold was the increase in member bank total and excess reserves and in member bank demand deposits. This initial increase in demand deposits is termed "primary expansion." If the excess reserves themselves are used as the basis for credit expansion, the accompanying increase in demand deposits is termed "secondary." The latter can be eliminated by legislative and administrative action relative to excess reserves. Excess reserves are a legal concept and could be eliminated overnight by appropriate legal action. Some action along these lines was taken by the passage of the Banking Act of August 23, 1935 (49 Stat. 703), which is discussed below.

The increase in the reserves of member banks has led to declining interest rates or an easy-money policy.[104] Declining interest rates have forced important changes in the character of bank portfolios. Banks have been compelled to seek new uses for their funds. This has included not only purchases of Government obligations [105] but also the extension of capital loans to industry and the granting of consumer credit loans to individuals. The Treasury was particularly pleased with the results of the easy-money policy, namely, the low cost of floating securities. At the same time, individuals dependent upon income from securities and bonds whose yields have declined find it difficult to maintain their standard of living.[106]

[103] *Ibid.*
[104] Crump, "Development of Exchange Funds," *Lloyds Bank, Ltd., Monthly Review,* Vol. VIII (January, 1937), p. 7.
[105] See Table XI, above.
[106] Beckhart and Hyslop, *The Gold Problem,* p. 16; see also above, Table XIII.

By 1935 the volume of excess reserves was alarming, because it afforded a base for an inflationary credit expansion unexampled in the history of the country. Discouraging in its implications was the fact that the traditional controls available to our monetary authorities were woefully inadequate.[107] Fortunately, under the Banking Act of 1935 a major instrument was given to the Board of Governors in the form of new powers over reserve requirements. Section 207 amended Section 19, paragraph 6, of the Federal Reserve Act (38 Stat. 265) and extended the Thomas Amendment (48 Stat. 31) by a provision giving the Board of Governors of the Federal Reserve System the power to increase reserve requirements to be maintained against time and demand deposits by all member banks up to twice their existing level "in order to prevent injurious credit expansion." [108] The act gave no power to decrease reserve requirements below the percentages set by the June 21, 1917, amendment to the Federal Reserve Act (40 Stat. 232). The power given to the Board of Governors to raise member bank requirements in order to strengthen credit conditions was used on August 15, 1936, for the first time.[109] The statutory limit for increasing reserve percentages was reached November 1, 1941.[110]

The Banking Act of 1935

The administration was pleased with the easy-money conditions which prevailed around 1935. The Treasury was particularly anxious to continue the *status quo,* and in order to insure the interests of the Treasury, Secretary Morgenthau favored a Federal monetary authority or a Government-owned central bank.[111] The Secretary of the Treasury was an advocate of monetary management and was a sponsor of the Banking Act of 1935.[112] It is difficult to understand why Secretary Morgenthau advocated a Government-owned central bank. He already enjoyed as many powers as the head of any foreign

---

[107] Beckhart and Hyslop, *The Gold Problem,* p. 16.

[108] Section 207, 49 Stat. 703; Banking Act of August 23, 1935, quoted in *Federal Reserve Bulletin,* September, 1935, pp. 612–614.

[109] U.S., Board of Governors of the Federal Reserve System, *Annual Report, 1938,* p. 60; see below, p. 196.

[110] See below, p. 231.

[111] "I happen to belong to that school that thinks that the government should own the stock of the Federal Reserve System . . ." Secretary Morgenthau's statement in U.S., Senate, Committee on Banking and Currency, 74th Cong., 1st Sess., *Hearings on the Banking Act of 1935,* p. 507.

[112] For statement of Secretary Morgenthau see *ibid.*

central bank,[113] and under the Thomas Inflation Amendment (48 Stat. 31), the Gold Reserve Act (48 Stat. 337), and various monetary laws enacted in 1933 and 1934 [114] the Secretary of the Treasury, subject to the approval of the President, was the most important official in the scheme of monetary management, while the Governors of the Federal Reserve System occupied a subordinate role. This state of affairs is still true.

The Banking Act of 1935, when finally passed, did not contain any provision for a Government-owned central bank, but it did provide for a "centralized authority over and fixed responsibility for monetary management." [115] That the act did not go as far along the lines of establishing a Federal monetary authority as the Secretary of the Treasury would have liked was perhaps due to the criticisms directed against the bill during the Senate hearings by such well-known authorities as Winthrop W. Aldrich, chairman of the Chase National Bank of New York; Benjamin M. Anderson, Jr., the economist for that bank; Professor Edwin W. Kemmerer, of Princeton University, and the late Professor Henry P. Willis, of Columbia University.[116]

Mr. W. W. Aldrich said:

The bill would grant powers more extensive than are granted to any foreign central bank.[117]

Mr. B. M. Anderson said:

The new theory behind this bill is that it is the business of the Federal Reserve System to try to keep the volume of demand deposits, and money in circulation at such a level as will keep commodity prices, the volume of business on a fixed level, ignoring this more fundamental thing of the quality of credit and the duty of tightening up to stop unsound tendencies.[118]

Professor E. W. Kemmerer said:

The bill provides for an increased governmental and political control of our banking and credit system.[119]

Professor H. P. Willis said:

The great objection to this bill is not that it is going to change immediately very drastically what is actually being done at the present time. . . . The

---

[113] See statement of W. W. Aldrich in *ibid.*, p. 389.   [114] See pp. 197–199, 206–209.
[115] Statement of Governor Marriner S. Eccles, the New York *Times*, August 24, 1935, p. 19, col. 8.
[116] U.S., Senate, Committee on Banking and Currency, 74th Cong., 1st Sess., *Hearings on the Banking Act of 1935*, p. 389.
[117] *Ibid.*   [118] *Ibid.*, p. 437.   [119] *Ibid.*, p. 330.

harm in it is that it seems to consolidate the bad tendencies in existing legislation, and practically renders them permanent, and treats them as the fruit
of valuable experience during the emergency of the past two or three years,
and thus seemingly looks forward to their remaining on the statute books
indefinitely.[120]

Senator Glass, chairman of the subcommittee which held the hearings was able to obtain substantial modifications of the administration
bill. Senator Glass was a sponsor of the original Federal Reserve Act
of 1913, which followed the principles that a central bank should be
free from political domination and that it should be privately
owned.[121]

Section 201 of Title II of the Banking Act of 1935 changed the
organization of the Federal Reserve banks. It provided for a president
and vice-president of each, appointed by the directors for terms of five
years, subject to the approval of the Board of Governors of the Federal Reserve System.

Section 203 abolished the old Federal Reserve Board and created in
its place, effective February 1, 1936, a Board of Governors of the
Federal Reserve System. Except that terms were adjusted at the beginning so that not more than one would expire in any two-year period,
the seven members appointed by the President would serve for fourteen years and be ineligible for reappointment. Salaries were raised
to $15,000. The President was authorized to select a chairman and
vice-chairman from the members for four-year terms.

The President was authorized to appoint not more than one member from any Federal Reserve district and to have "due regard to a
fair representation of the financial, agricultural, industrial and commercial interests, and geographical divisions of the country." Members might be removed by the President "for cause."

Elimination of the Secretary of the Treasury and Comptroller of
the Currency as ex officio members was designed to keep the board
free from undue influence with respect to the Treasury's fiscal needs.
While the President and political agencies were not assured of complete control of the board, nevertheless it was made fairly certain that
henceforth the Federal Reserve System would be recognized as an
agency responsive to the program of the Government. Abolishment
of the old board and giving President Roosevelt an opportunity to

[120] *Ibid.*, p. 855.
[121] See above, p. 148; Crawford, *Monetary Management under the New Deal*, p. 119.

appoint all the members of the new body assured him of control so long as he remains in office.[122]

An important factor tending to promote centralized planning was the increased power given to the Board of Governors. Previously, even if the Federal Reserve Board was disposed to follow the wishes of the President, it was possible for a Federal Reserve Bank to display independence.[123] Under the Banking Act of 1935 the board was given greater power over open-market operations, rediscount rates, reserves, and management of the Reserve banks.

Section 205 created a Federal Open Market Committee, consisting of the seven members of the Board of Governors and five representatives of the Federal Reserve banks. Open-market operations by the Reserve banks were required to conform to policies established by the committee. Such operations should be conducted "with a view to accommodating commerce and business and with regard to their bearing upon the general credit situation of the country." The Board of Governors was instructed to incorporate in its annual reports a record of all official actions on open-market policies both by the board itself and by the open-market committee.

Section 206 strengthened the control of the Board of Governors over rediscount rates of the Reserve banks by a requirement that the banks must submit rates to the board for its approval every fourteen days, or oftener if deemed necessary by the board.

Section 207 gave the board new powers over reserve requirements,[124] and Section 208 include authorization for advances by Reserve banks to member banks on demand or time notes with maturities of not more than four months, a liberalization of real estate loans by national banks.

Although the administration by no means got everything it desired in the new law, one of its spokesmen, Mr. Eccles, expressed satisfaction. He said:

Considering the objectives and purposes of the legislation as originally proposed and as finally enacted, I am very well satisfied with the outcome. . . . In my judgment, the banking act marks an important advance in the development of the country's banking system and the

---

[122] *Ibid.*, p. 133.

[123] The Federal Reserve Board was vested only with supervisory authority. The power to initiate policies was lodged for the most part in the twelve Federal Reserve banks. Section 4, Federal Reserve Act, 38 Stat. 265.

[124] See above, p. 218.

adaptation of monetary administration to present day conditions and national needs . . . [125]

Gold Imports and Increased Reserve Requirements

In the second half of 1935 the gold imports continued and excess reserves continued to rise.[126] The amount of gold certificates obtained

TABLE XVIII

FEDERAL RESERVE MEMBER BANK RESERVE BALANCES, EXCESS RESERVES, AND GOLD STOCK, 1917–1941[a]

MEMBER BANK RESERVE BALANCES (In millions of dollars)			
Calendar Year	Total	Excess	Gold Stock
1917	1,447	78	2,868
1918	1,636	51	2,873
1919	1,890	68	2,707
1920	1,743	..	2,639
1921	1,753	99	2,373
1922	1,919	..	3,642
1923	1,898	14	3,957
1924	2,220	59	4,212
1925	2,212	−44	4,112
1926	2,194	−56	4,205
1927	2,487	63	4,092
1928	2,389	−41	3,854
1929	2,355	−73	3,997
1930	2,471	96	4,306
1931	1,961	−33	4,173
1932	2,509	576	4,226
1933	2,729	859	4,036
1934	4,096	1,814	8,238
1935	5,587	2,844	10,125
1936	6,606	1,984	11,258
1937	7,027	1,202	12,760
1938	8,724	3,205	14,512
1939	11,653	5,209	17,644
1940	14,026	6,615	21,995
1941	12,450	3,085	22,737

[a] Figures through 1937 taken from Table No. 5, U.S., Board of Governors of the Federal Reserve System, *Annual Report, 1937,* pp. 47–48. Figures for 1938–1941 taken from Table 15, U.S., Board of Governors of the Federal Reserve System, *Annual Report, 1941,* p. 48.

[125] Statement of Governor Marriner S. Eccles, New York *Times,* August 25, 1935, p. 19, col. 8.

[126] See Table XVIII.

for this gold by the Federal Reserve banks increased and was available to these Federal Reserve banks as reserve for a possible credit expansion. Wholesale commodity prices rose from 66 to 86 in the years 1933 to 1937.[127] The Treasury was satisfied with these de-

TABLE XIX

GOLD IMPORTS INTO THE UNITED STATES AND THE
WHOLESALE COMMODITY PRICES FOR THE
YEARS 1919–1941

Year	Gold Imports into the United States In thousands of dollars	Wholesale Commodity Prices Base year is 1926 = 100
1919	76,534[a]	139[b]
1920	417,068	154
1921	691,248[c]	98
1922	275,170	97
1923	322,716	101
1924	319,721	98
1925	128,273	104
1926	213,504	100
1927	207,535	95
1928	168,897	97
1929	291,649	95
1930	396,054	86
1931	612,119	73
1932	363,315	65
1933	193,197	66
1934	1,131,944 [d]	75
1935	1,739,019	80
1936	1,116,584	81
1937	1,585,503	86
1938	1,973,569	79
1939	3,574,151	77
1940	4,744,472	79
1941	982,378	87

[a] U.S., Treasury Dept., *Annual Report of the Secretary, 1931*, p. 868, contain figures for 1919 and 1920.

[b] Figures are taken from *Federal Reserve Bulletin*, December, 1942, p. 1231.

[c] Figures from 1921 to 1933 are taken from Table No. 32, U.S., Board of Governors of the Federal Reserve System, *Annual Report, 1937*, p. 82.

[d] Figures represent custom valuations which, with some exceptions, are at rate of $20.67 a fine ounce through January, 1934, and $35 a fine ounce thereafter. Figures for 1934 to 1941 are taken from *Federal Reserve Bulletin*, December, 1942, p. 1253.

[127] See Table XIX.

velopments, since the main aim of the Treasury all along was to raise domestic prices and stimulate business by an easy money policy. The Federal Advisory Council, chosen by the banks of the twelve districts and composed of bankers not entirely in accord with the expansionist policy of the administration, did not agree with the Treasury in these matters.[128] It feared an uncontrolled inflation because the funds which poured in did not represent to any large extent payment for trade balances, but rather resulted from a flight of capital.[129]

The methods at the disposal of the Federal Reserve System were hardly sufficient to meet the problem. Raising discount rates and open-market operations were ruled out as directly at cross purposes with the Treasury. The Board of Governors, itself, under the influence of Chairman Eccles, wished to continue the easy-money policy of the administration, although it finally became convinced of the danger of inflation and yielded to the suggestion of the Federal Advisory Council to scale down excess reserves. Also, Winthrop W. Aldrich and Benjamin M. Anderson, Jr., made statements urging action for the purpose of absorbing a considerable part of excess reserves.[130] The reduction of excess reserves without tightening the money market unduly was possible, since reserves were far above the legal requirements.[131] Therefore the Board of Governors raised the reserve requirements of member banks several times.[132]

Section 324 of the Banking Act of 1935 was also of assistance in reducing excess reserves. It amended section 19 of the Federal Reserve Act (38 Stat. 274) by "providing that member banks shall be required to maintain the same reserves against deposits of public money by the United States as they are required to maintain against other deposits." [133] This was a reversal of an old policy embodied in Section 7 of the First Liberty Bond Act of April 24, 1917 (40 Stat. 35), which stipulated that member banks were not required to keep reserves

[128] *Federal Reserve Bulletin*, January, 1936, pp. 5–6.
[129] Beckhart and Hyslop *The Gold Problem*, p. 24; see above, p. 216.
[130] Mr. Aldrich's statement appeared in the New York *Times*, September 12, 1935, p. 39, col. 8; Mr. Anderson's statement appeared in the New York *Times*, October 31, 1935, p. 32, col. 1.
[131] U.S., Board of Governors of the Federal Reserve System, *Annual Report, 1936*, p. 217.
[132] See Table XX.
[133] U.S., Board of Governors of the Federal Reserve System, *Digest of Rulings*, p. 195; 49 Stat. 703; see pp. 106, 161, above.

TABLE XX

FEDERAL RESERVE MEMBER BANK
PERCENTAGE RESERVE REQUIREMENTS, 1917–1941[a]

Classes of Deposits and banks	June 21, 1917–Aug. 15, 1936	Aug. 16, 1936–Feb. 28, 1937	Mar. 1, 1937–Apr. 30, 1937	May 1, 1937–Apr. 15, 1938	Apr. 16, 1938–Oct. 31, 1941	Nov. 1, 1941 and thereafter
On net demand deposits						
Central-reserve city	13	19.50	22.50	26	22.75	26
Reserve city	10	15	17.50	20	17.50	20
Country	7	10.50	12.25	14	12	14
On time deposits						
All member banks	3	4.50	5.25	6	5	6

a Figures for first 5 columns taken from U.S. Board of Governors of the Federal Reserve System, *Annual Report, 1939*, p. 52; figures for last column taken from *Federal Reserve Bulletin*, November, 1941, p. 1145.

against deposits of public money.[134] Section 324 of the Banking Act of 1935 helped in a small measure to counteract the effects of gold imports.[135]

Gold Sterilization and Reserves

The inflow of gold which had caused the Federal Reserve Board to raise percentage reserve requirements on August 15, 1936, led also to Treasury action.[136] A plan was worked out whereby the Treasury could continue to buy gold without a further swelling of excess reserves. On December 22, 1936, the policy was announced.[137] The Treasury continued to buy all newly mined gold at $35 an ounce, paying for it with the proceeds of sales of Government obligations rather than by the issuance of gold certificates. Although gold imports would continue to increase the total volume of member bank deposit liabilities, they would not increase member bank reserve balances. The fact that total reserve balances of member banks remained the same at a time when their deposit liabilities were increasing would mean a re-

[134] See above, p. 161. Somewhat earlier Secretary Shaw ruled that no reserves need be kept against Government deposits (see above, p. 119). Section 14 of the Act of May 30, 1908 (35 Stat. 546) stated that no reserves need be held against deposits of public money in national banks (see above, p. 129). Section 14 of the Act of May 30, 1908, was reënacted in Section 27 of the Federal Reserve Act.

[135] For further discussion of the Banking Act of 1935 see above, pp. 218–222.

[136] Statement made by Mr. Morgenthau in the New York *Times,* December 22, 1936, p. 1, col. 6.

[137] U.S., Treasury Dept., *Annual Report of the Secretary, 1937,* p. 262, Exhibit 32.

duction in the volume of excess reserves and consequently a tendency toward higher rates of interest.[138]

The metal, as acquired by the Treasury, would be set aside in an "inactive account." The gold did not pass into the reserve base in the form of gold certificates, and in this sense the measure was anti-inflationary. Even without further increases, excess reserves were large and could finance a very substantial increase in industrial activity if additional demands for credit should develop. Even though in the twenties excess reserves were low, yet when fully utilized, credit expansion was great. In the thirties, although excess reserves were large, there was no important demand for credit from business sources.[139]

By the sterilization program the Treasury hoped to counteract the tendency of gold imports further to increase excess reserves at a time when prices and business activity were rising. This brake on inflationary developments early in 1937 was so effective that not only was the rapid rise of prices and business activity checked, but, whether for this or other reasons, the depression of 1937 ensued. To prevent the decline from gathering momentum, the Federal Open Market Committee,[140] recommended to the Treasury that it "release approximately $300,000,000 of gold from the Treasury's inactive account." The board made the request because it desired to carry out its usual policy "to facilitate the financing of and orderly marketing of crops and of autumn trade." On September 12, 1937, the Treasury agreed and placed the funds at the disposal of the Federal Reserve banks, increasing their reserves.[141] The board said this action was in line with its "easy credit conditions" policy. The deposit of $300,000,000 in gold was a reversion to the old method used when the Secretary of the Treasury deposited funds to help move crops.[142] The Treasury sterilized further accumulations of new gold until February 14, 1938, when announcement was made that, retroactive to January 1, only

---

[138] Beckhart and Hyslop, *The Gold Problem*, p. 45.

[139] See above, Table XVIII and also p. 223.

[140] It was created under the Banking Act of June 16, 1933 (48 Stat. 162). See above, pp. 201–202. It is further defined in Section 295 of the Act of August 23, 1935, as an amendment to Section 12A of the Federal Reserve Act. U.S., Board of Governors of the Federal Reserve System, *Digest of Rulings,* p. 378.

[141] U.S., Board of Governors of the Federal Reserve System, *Annual Report, 1937,* p. 218.

[142] See above, pp. 101, 144*n.*

additions to the gold stock in excess of $100,000,000 per quarter would be placed in the inactive account. This curtailment of the sterilization program was for the purpose of relaxing credit conditions.[143]

By making use of sterilized gold in the manner indicated, reserves of member banks increased permanently, whereas if open-market purchases had been used, the reserves could be reduced later by open-market sales of securities. Furthermore, the inactive account should have been used only in the event of withdrawal of foreign funds against which the gold serves as a reserve. It was established to counteract capital movements, not to regulate internal credit conditions.

Desterilization of Gold and the Depression of 1937

As the depression of 1937–1938 deepened, the wisdom of the gold sterilization program was questioned. Was the new depression provoked by the deflationary effects of the raised reserve requirements and of the establishment of an inactive gold account? Such queries seem to imply that monetary forces alone were of paramount importance in bringing about the depression. The causes are partly to be found in increases in cost and price; for example, labor and materials,[144] the sudden stoppage of large Government disbursements of the pump-priming variety, and the changed outlook of business. At no time was business starved for credit or funds. Excess reserves were never below $700,000,000 even after the sterilization program went into effect. The cheap-money policy prevailed, although without material effect on business.

Nevertheless, there were still advocates of a "very-easy-money" policy and of an increase in the quantity of money as remedies of the renewed depression. They advocated the release of the inactive gold fund, the abandonment of the sterilization program, the purchase of securities by Federal Reserve banks, and the reduction of percentages required in member bank reserve.[145] In addition, the decline in Government bond prices in the early months of 1937 disturbed the Treasury. Sterilization leads to a reduction in excess reserves. Consequently

---

[143] *Federal Reserve Bulletin,* March, 1938, p. 181.
[144] Beckhart, *Sterilization of Gold,* p. 19.
[145] *Federal Reserve Bulletin,* October, 1937, p. 965.

there is a tendency for interest rates to rise. To take advantage of the increased rate of interest, holders of Government bonds might sell them and seek new uses for their funds.[146] This might result in a general decline in the price of outstanding bonds. Consequently the market for new Government bond issues would be poor, and higher interest rates would have to be offered to secure additional funds or refund maturing issues. To counteract the decline in bond prices, the Federal Reserve banks purchased $96,000,000 of bonds during April, 1937.[147] The Federal Reserve banks were also selling their short-term Treasury notes and bills, not needing support in favor of long-term Treasury bonds, most affected by the declining market. Such action, of course, had no effect on reserves. During the winter of 1937–1938 the acute phase of the depression passed, and by April, 1938, the Federal Reserve banks reversed their policy and sold securities to keep bond prices down.[148] It is unfortunate that the banks' earning assets are tied up in Government obligations, but this condition will exist as long as the Treasury demands that general interest rates be low to aid its fiscal problems.[149] In furthering the Treasury's fiscal program, the Federal Reserve System has become subservient to the Treasury.

In the spring of 1938 the Government was anxious to continue the movement toward recovery, to keep interest rates low, to increase appropriations for public works. This type of program entailed the complete abolition of the sterilization policy. Consequently President Roosevelt, in his message to Congress on April 14, 1938, stated that action would be taken to make bank resources more readily available for credit.[150] The Secretary of the Treasury, on April 14, 1938, announced that the gold in the Treasury's inactive account, about $1,400,000,000, would be released to the Federal Reserve banks for reserve purposes and member bank reserve requirements against deposits would be reduced.[151] Bank balances obtained by depositing gold certificates in Federal Reserve banks would be used to retire Treasury bills and meet current deficits. In accordance with the policy

---

[146] Beckhart and Hyslop, *The Gold Problem*, p. 15.
[147] *Federal Reserve Bulletin*, April, 1937, p. 283.
[148] *Federal Reserve Bulletin*, February, 1938, p. 134.
[149] Beckhart, *Sterilization of Gold*, p. 26.
[150] U.S., Congress, *Congressional Record*, 75th Cong., 3d Sess., p. 5382.
[151] *Federal Reserve Bulletin*, May, 1938, pp. 343–344.

of creating monetary ease, the Board of Governors on April 16, 1938, reduced member bank reserve percentages.[152]

As anticipated, some of the results of desterilization were a sharp rise in bond prices and in excess reserves.[153] Good borrowers were just as few as ever, interest rates declined and idle funds looked to the bond market for investment. Bond prices rose sharply and the easy-money policy once more prevailed.

Summary of the Sterilization of Gold

An important instrument for the control of the monetary mechanism, such as the gold sterilization, was managed by the Treasury rather than by the Federal Reserve System, the legally constituted central bank. Under the sterilization program gold imports were not to result in overexpansion of the reserves of commercial banks to avoid an outright inflation, which would inevitably have led to a new crash. Under the desterilization program gold imports were to affect the credit base, the reserves of commercial banks.

The sterilization program which was in effect from December 22, 1926, to April 14, 1938, gave the Treasury greater control over gold imports and the reserves of member banks than that possessed by the Federal Reserve System. Even though the sterilization program has been abandoned, the stabilization fund, which is managed by the Treasury, can exert as strong an influence on the money market, interest rates, and the credit structure as the gold sterilization and desterilization program.

Inability of the Federal Reserve System to match forces with the Treasury is frankly conceded by its officials. The assertion that the power of the Treasury to influence the volume of reserves "outweighs" that of the Federal Reserve System was made in the annual report of the Board of Governors of the Federal Reserve System for 1938 [154] and also in a statement transmitted by the board to the chairmen of the Committees on Banking and Currency of the Senate and House on April 8, 1939.[155] The Treasury derives much of its present

---

[152] U.S., Board of Governors of the Federal Reserve System, *Annual Report, 1938,* p. 60; see also Table XX above.

[153] See Table XVIII.

[154] U.S., Board of Governors of the Federal Reserve System, *Annual Report, 1938,* p. 21.

[155] *Federal Reserve Bulletin,* May, 1939, pp. 363–364.

power in the monetary field from the gold-purchase program [156] which in turn has helped create the gold problem. Whether Treasury control in the monetary field will be diminished depends to a large extent on the solution to the gold problem which has been considerably intensified by the outbreak of World War II.

POSITION OF THE TREASURY UNDER PROPOSED SOLUTIONS TO THE GOLD PROBLEM

Prior to 1941 considerable thought was given to the possibility of removing the dangers caused by excessive gold holdings. One group of proposals centered in the reduction of the volume and/or the monetary value of gold imports. The solutions included placing an embargo on gold imports, reducing the price of gold, placing sliding tariff duties on gold imports, while paying compensatory bounties on gold exports, and reintroducing the sterilization program.

The Secretary of the Treasury, with authority from the President, could have stopped further gold purchases. Such action was thought to be undesirable, for it was feared that the results of discontinuing gold buying might initiate a deflationary cycle.[157] The buying of gold by the Treasury places purchasing power in the hands of the sellers; if the funds are used by domestic producers, they contribute somewhat to employment. It would have been difficult for the Government to face the charge that it was deliberately contributing to unemployment. Another strong objection to any modification of the gold policy prior to 1941, when the problem was acute, was that it would have seriously interfered with our aid to Britain and the allies in the present war. A gold embargo would have tended to disrupt "the normal channels of international trade." The dollar would have risen in the international exchange markets. This would have harmed our export trade and the ability of Britain and her allies to purchase in the American market.

Under Section 9 of the Gold Reserve Act (48 Stat. 337) the Secretary of the Treasury can pay any price that he may desire for gold. If the price should be reduced, the monetary value of the present gold stock and the volume of future gold imports would be decreased. The

[156] Gold Reserve Act of 1934 (48 Stat. 337).
[157] Cadman, "Prospecting for a Gold Solution," *Banking*, Vol. XXXIII (July, 1940), pp. 27–28.

reduction in price would not affect the existing volume of excess reserves. The arguments advanced against the imposition of a gold embargo held, to a large extent, with respect to the proposal that the price of gold be reduced.

Another proposal for reducing the volume and value of future gold imports is that the Treasury should impose sliding tariff duties upon gold imports and should give compensatory gold bounties on gold exports.[158] The plan partakes of all the disadvantages of a reduction in the price of gold and confers dangerously great discretionary powers upon the Treasury Department.

The final proposal in this particular group of plans for insulating the credit structure from gold movements, is sterilization. This method was operative in the United States from December 22, 1936, to April 14, 1938, and gave the Treasury Department great monetary power.[159] Under sterilization the Treasury pays for gold by the sale of Government obligations rather than by the issuance of gold certificates. Although gold imports increase deposit liabilities, they do not increase the total reserves of member banks. The result is a reduction in excess reserves and a tendency toward higher rates of interest. Sterilization, of course, involves an increase in the national debt.[160]

A second group of proposed solutions to the gold problem included those which endeavored to reduce the credit-supporting power of gold. These suggestions included giving additional powers to the Board of Governors of the Federal Reserve System to raise the reserve requirements of member banks, requiring 100 percent reserves against certain categories of deposits, and relating credit expansion to capital-deposit ratios. This group of proposals has the merit of placing control over the credit mechanism where it belongs, in the hands of the central bank. However, before any of these methods could be adopted, the Treasury Department must be consulted and its consent would have to be obtained.

The raising of the reserve requirements of member banks is obviously the most direct way to bring about a reduction in the credit-supporting power of reserves. This method was employed on August 15, 1936, March 1, 1937, May 1, 1937, and November 1, 1941.[161] The

---

[158] Jack, "The Gold Problem," *The Canadian Banker*, April, 1940, pp. 280–287; Beckhart and Hyslop, *The Gold Problem*, p. 45.

[159] See above, p. 225.   [160] Beckhart and Hyslop, *The Gold Problem*, p. 46.

[161] See Table XX, above.

increase in reserve percentages, effective November 1, 1941, brought the reserve requirements of member banks back to the statutory limit set by Section 207, Banking Act of 1935 (49 Stat. 703). A further increase in reserve requirements would require Congressional enactment. If the increases were drastic, they would probably disturb the Government bond market, in view of the fact that adjustments in the reserve position of commercial banks take place through changes in holdings of Government obligations. It might be wise to stipulate, if additional powers were granted, that the amount of the increase in member bank reserve requirements should be no greater than that required to bring excess reserves within the scope of control of the existing volume of the open-market portfolio of the Federal Reserve banks.

Another proposal which could be administered by the Board of Governors of the Federal Reserve System and would reduce excess reserves is the requirement that member banks shall maintain a 100 percent reserve against various categories of deposits; for example, foreign deposits, bankers' balances, and future additions to deposit liabilities. Requiring a 100 percent reserve against future increases in deposit liabilities would limit deposit expansion to a one to one ratio to future gold imports. Secondary expansion on the basis of these imports could not take place. This plan possesses merit in that it limits the effect of the gold inflow. Its introduction would require Congressional enactment and could be applied to member banks only. This would discriminate against some elements in the banking system. The suggestion that member banks be required to maintain a 100 percent reserve against bankers' balances and/or foreign deposits would weigh disproportionately on the banks which possessed such deposits. Furthermore, when foreign deposits are spent and bankers' balances withdrawn, these accounts either become private deposits or serve as a basis for private deposits. Reserve requirements would then be reduced.

In the 1940 session of Congress a bill was introduced into the Senate designed to render it impossible for the present volume of member bank excess reserves to serve as the basis of multiple credit expansion by requiring the maintenance of a definite ratio between deposit liabilities and bank capital funds. According to the provisions of the bill, the Board of Governors of the Federal Reserve System may "from time to time, fix the ratio between capital surplus, and undivided profits and deposit liabilities at not less than six nor more than twelve times the aforesaid capital surplus and undivided profits." [162] Deposits are permitted to exceed the ratio, but the excess must be covered by a 100 percent reserve. Inasmuch as the capital funds of banks are not likely to increase greatly in the near future, the adoption of this proposal would mean that as soon as the ratio set was exceeded, future increases in deposit liabilities would have to be covered by a 100 percent deposit account with the Federal Reserve banks.[163] It would seem preferable to advocate simply that all future increases in deposit liabilities be covered by a 100 percent reserve.

A further suggestion, designed to limit credit expansion, is the proposal that member banks hold Government obligations to the extent of 25 percent of their demand deposits. All deposits in excess of this ratio must be secured by a 100 percent reserve with the Federal Reserve banks. The fact that banks had to hold Government obligations as reserve against deposits would give the Treasury a secure market for all future issues of its obligations. By changes in reserve requirements, the Treasury could force the commercial banks to take additional quantities of Government bonds and might do so in view of the financial needs of the future. The banks would become more deeply involved in Federal finances. Theoretically commercial bank credit expansion should be related to holdings of commercial and business paper, not to holdings of the Federal debt.

Another suggestion designed to reduce the base for credit expansion is gold coin redemption. Those who want gold would be able to obtain it and total member bank reserves would decline by an amount equivalent to the extent to which gold could be obtained and actually hoarded. The effect of such a policy would be too small to warrant consideration, since it could not achieve a substantial reduction in reserves. However, it would establish the domestic gold standard on a firm basis. The values of gold and paper money could not differ, interchangeable as they would be.[164] The gold coin redemption plan would probably be administered by the Treasury, which had been performing this duty in the past.[165]

[162] Senate Bill 3867—76th Cong., 3d Sess., U.S., Congress, *Congressional Record*, p. 5061.

[163] U.S., Federal Deposit Insurance Corporation, *Annual Report, 1939*, pp. 12–13.

[164] Beckhart and Hyslop, *The Gold Problem*, p. 56.

[165] Act of March 14, 1900 (31 Stat. 45) ; see above, p. 98.

The proposals cited above did not constitute fundamentally a solution of the gold problem. They simply coped with the immediate problems raised by gold concentration. The basic solution must await a return to peace and freedom in international trade. Whether this can be achieved in the near future is questionable; and how dominant a position the Treasury will occupy in the monetary field will depend upon the type of economic and political organization which emerges in Western Europe following the termination of the present war.

Should the British Empire and its allies be victorious, for several reasons it is reasonable to expect that the peace settlement would endeavor to restore some form of the international gold standard. First, Great Britain has a strong interest in the restoration of some measure of freedom of trade; freedom of trade and the operation of the gold standard supplement each other.[166] Secondly, South Africa, Canada, and Australia have a strong interest in gold production. The prosperity of the gold mining industry depends largely upon the use of that metal as a monetary base. Thirdly, the desire to propitiate the United States, whose help will be necessary for the rehabilitation of Europe, will lead to a favorable consideration of America's desire to make full use of her gold stocks.

After peace has been restored, it seems unlikely that revived international trade alone, will serve to redistribute the gold stock concentrated in the United States except over a long period of time; that is, after the reconstruction loans to Europe have ceased and after Europe has serviced her debts to the United States by means of goods rather than by means of gold.[167] During that long period the United States Treasury, as guardian of the Nation's gold stocks, would be performing many central banking functions.[168]

However, restoration of the international gold standard in the form in which it prevailed from the close of the Franco-Prussian War to the opening of World War I might result in increasing the powers of the central bank, the Federal Reserve System, and decreasing the influence of the Treasury over monetary affairs. But the return of that type of international gold standard is unlikely, because it implies major changes in the Nation's tariff policies, in the regula-

---

[166] Beckhart and Hyslop, *The Gold Problem*, p. 58.
[167] *The Statist*, Vol. CXXXV (February 23, 1940), p. 201.
[168] Act of March 14, 1900 (31 Stat. 45). See above, pp. 98–100.

tion and control of industry, and in the public finances. The present trend indicates greater Government control. Consequently, continued monetary management under Treasury control appears more probable than the revival of the gold standard.

In the event of a stalemate the restoration of the freedom of trade and an international gold standard is unlikely. It would be a period of rapid rearmament. Economic life would be subordinated to military needs. To the Treasury would be delegated the task of monetary management.

In the improbable event of a Nazi success the future of the international gold standard would have depended upon the extent of the German victory—that is, whether or not Germany would have gained control of the South African mines (which seemed at least possible at one time)—and also upon the unpredictable plans of the German rulers. If the German Government should have seized the South African mines, doubtless she would have liked to use the gold for exchange purposes with the United States. However, if the statements made by Walther Funk, Reich Economic Minister, to the effect that the new Nazi Europe would have no use for gold either for banking or international trade, were a preview of things to come, the future of an international gold standard appeared gloomy.[169] Under the latter circumstances it would have seemed wiser for America to have stopped buying gold from overseas.

The cessation of gold purchases from overseas would raise the value of our gold holdings in terms of domestic purchasing power. Member bank total and excess reserves would be smaller, and the possibility of gold inflation would be lessened. America need not stop purchasing domestically produced gold, for this action would have distastrous effects upon our industry, which has grown to rely on Government support. If along with the domestic gold purchase program, gold coin redemption were reintroduced, the purchasing power of gold could not differ from that of paper money or of bank deposits. This program would aid the stabilization of the currency—which is a central banking function. Yet, gold coin redemption and domestic gold purchases would probably be administered by the Treasury, as they have been in the past.[170]

[169] Beckhart and Hyslop, *The Gold Problem,* p. 59.
[170] See above, pp. 202–203.

From the foregoing comments it appears that the gold problem is international and cannot be adequately solved until the present war is ended. The gold problem is related to world economics and to American and other ideologies as to what constitutes good economic procedure. The best that can be done during this war is to continue the present policy of purchasing gold at $35 an ounce, because it gives financial assistance to Britain and its allies. It seems that whatever program is finally evolved for the settlement of the gold problem, it will probably be administered by the Treasury rather than by the Federal Reserve System.

SUMMARY

The years from 1929 to 1941, inclusive, marks a period in which the Treasury was recognized as the real central bank. Although leadership in the banking field rightfully belonged to the Federal Reserve System, no sooner had the Federal Reserve Act become effective than the economic crisis arising from World War I diverted the policies of the system and subjected it to the Treasury's one aim of winning the war. The postwar reaction, which brought falling prices and a depression in 1920, forced the Federal Reserve System to help the Treasury bring about recovery. In the later twenties the Treasury directed the policies of the Federal Reserve System in order to expedite the refunding program. While there were many factors contributing to the Panic of 1929 and the prolonged depression thereafter, the extreme hardships caused by falling prices made it natural that defects in the banking and monetary structure should receive attention as the Government sought remedies. The Government favored the leveling of peaks and troughs of the business cycles by monetary action. This implied the development of a managed currency system accompanied by a strengthening of the Treasury's control over the Federal Reserve System.[171]

During the past decade, the monetary laws of the United States have been largely rewritten, and the banking laws have been revised. Throughout the process of revision the Government has had as its goal a currency and banking system subject to Treasury management. The additional central banking authority given to the Treasury took shape under laws relating to currency, credit, gold, and silver. At the

[171] Crawford, *Monetary Management under the New Deal*, p. 8.

same time, the privileges enjoyed by the Treasury rendered the powers of the Federal Reserve System inadequate to meet the problems of credit control. One of these baffling problems centered in the continued flow of an enormous quantity of unwanted gold to the United States. Solutions immediately suggested for this problem were many and varied. They included placing an embargo on gold imports, reducing the price of gold, placing sliding tariff duties on gold imports, while paying compensatory bounties on gold exports, and reintroducing the sterilization program. Any of these methods, if introduced, would have been administered by the Treasury Department. On the other hand, another group of solutions were advocated which could have been administered by the Federal Reserve System, but which would have required consultation with the Treasury Department. These solutions included giving additional powers to the Board of Governors of the Federal Reserve System to increase member bank reserve requirements, requiring 100 percent reserves against certain categories of deposits and relating credit expansion to capital-deposit ratios.

The final solution of the gold problem must await the peace treaty of the present war. Whatever economy emerges from the war, even if it be extreme individualism or extreme state control (totalitarianism), the Treasury is likely to play a dominant role in the monetary and banking fields. The outbreak of World War II has increased the monetary management powers of the Treasury, because all forces must be subordinated to the aims of victory.

CHAPTER X

Treasury Central Banking from 1929 to 1941 with Special Reference to the Silver Policies

THE SILVER PROGRAM was undertaken at the request of the powerful silver interests predominating in the western mining states. Representatives of these states succeeded in obtaining the support of inflationists, quantity theorists, debtors, and farmers. Large purchases of silver and a corresponding increase in the circulation of silver certificates, it was asserted, would bring about an increase in the price of both silver and other commodities, an expansion of the metal base of our money, and an increase of money in circulation. Finally, it was maintained that an increase in the value of silver would increase the purchasing power of the silver standard countries in the Far East and materially increase our exports to these countries. These reasons, combined with political logrolling, proved strong enough to secure the various silver enactments passed between May, 1933, and June, 1934.

THE BACKGROUND FOR SILVER LEGISLATION

For many years the West and the South have sought economic relief in currency expansion and easy credit terms. The Bland Allison Act of February 28, 1878 (20 Stat. 25), and the Sherman Silver Purchase Act of July 14, 1890 (26 Stat. 289), bear out this theory. Both acts were passed by a combination of silver interests and agricultural debtors.[1]

One of the advocates of the silver interests was Senator Pittman. His name had been attached to the wartime Pittman Act of April 23, 1918 (40 Stat. 535), under which American silver dollars, which were melted at the urgent request of Great Britain to meet emergency needs of India, were replaced after the war by the purchase of silver at $1

[1] See above, pp. 73–75.

an ounce.[2] In the postwar years Senator Pittman offered various silver bills which failed to make headway in Congress. During the period of the twenties the Treasury Department rejected one silver bill after another on the ground that there was no need of further silver in the monetary system and that the purpose of the various schemes was to obtain a Government subsidy for the silver producing industry.[3]

On April 22, 1930, Senator Pittman was appointed to the Senate Foreign Relations Committee.[4] On April 29 a subcommittee was created under Resolution No. 256 to investigate and report upon the depression of United States trade and commerce with China.[5] The subcommittee reported on February 11, 1931, and maintaining that the decrease in exports of the United States to China was due to the fall in the price of silver. It was further contended that the people of China could not afford to buy American products because of the low exchange value of their money in terms of American money.[6] One of the resolutions introduced by Senator Pittman in the Senate on February 11, 1931, on the basis of the subcommittee's recommendations requested the President to call an international conference on silver. The Senate adopted the resolution on February 20, 1931.[7] After finding that Great Britain and other interested governments were not favorably inclined toward the idea, President Hoover refused to call a conference.[8]

On February 8, 1932, a resolution was introduced by Mr. Somers authorizing the House Committee on Coinage, Weights and Measures to conduct an investigation of the cause and effect of the depressed value of silver.[9] Mr. Somers related in the House on February 25, 1932, that the subcommittee favored the adoption of a resolution requesting the President to call a conference of all nations "interested

[2] U.S., Treasury Dept., *Annual Report of the Secretary, 1918*, pp. 41–42; U.S., Treasury Dept., *Annual Report of the Secretary, 1925*, p. 371.

[3] Crawford, *Monetary Management under the New Deal*, p. 63.

[4] U.S., Congress, *Congressional Record*, 71st Cong., 1st Sess., p. 246.

[5] U.S., Congress, *Congressional Record*, 71st Cong., 2d Sess., p. 7930; Bratter, "The Silver Episode," *Journal of Political Economy*, Vol. XLVI (October, 1938), p. 612.

[6] Senate Report No. 1716, U.S., Congress, *Congressional Record*, 71st Cong., 1st Sess., p. 5493.

[7] Senate Resolution 442, U.S., Congress, *Congressional Record*, 71st Cong., 3d Sess., p. 4557.

[8] Bratter, "The Silver Episode," *Journal of Political Economy*, Vol. XLVI (October, 1938), p. 613.

[9] House Resolution 72, U.S., Congress, *Congressional Record*, 72d Cong., 1st Sess., p. 3536; also see Bratter, *The Silver Market*, p. 80; see also Table XXI, below.

TABLE XXI

PRICE OF SILVER ADJUSTED TO REFLECT CHANGES IN THE PURCHASING POWER OF THE GOLD DOLLAR, 1901–1931

Year	Index Number of Whole Commodity Prices in the U.S. Base year is 1926 = 100 [a]	Prices of Silver in N.Y. in Cents per Fine Ounce [b]	Adjusted Prices of Silver in Cents per Fine Ounce [c]
1901	55.3	59.7	107.9
1902	58.9	52.8	89.6
1903	59.6	54.2	91.0
1904	59.7	57.8	96.8
1905	60.1	61.0	101.5
1906	61.8	67.4	109.0
1907	65.2	66.0	101.2
1908	62.9	53.5	85.0
1909	67.6	52.2	77.2
1910	70.4	54.2	77.0
1911	64.9	54.0	83.2
1912	69.1	62.0	89.7
1913	69.8	61.2	87.7
1914	68.1	56.3	82.7
1915	69.5	51.1	73.5
1916	85.5	67.2	78.6
1917	117.5	84.0	71.5
1918	131.3	98.4	74.9
1919	138.6	112.1	80.9
1920	154.4	101.9	66.0
1921	97.6	63.1	64.7
1922	96.7	67.9	70.2
1923	100.6	65.2	64.8
1924	98.1	67.1	68.4
1925	103.5	69.4	67.1
1926	100.0	62.4	62.4
1927	95.4	56.7	59.4
1928	97.7	58.5	59.9
1929	96.5	53.3	55.2
1930	86.3	38.5	44.4
1931	71.1	28.7	40.0

[a] Index numbers of the Bureau of Labor Statistics of the United States Department of Labor.

[b] U.S., Director of the Mint, *Annual Report, 1931*, pp. 125–126.

[c] Ratio of Column 2 to Column 1.

in the restoration of the commodity price level through the stabilization of the international exchange by restoring the equilibrium in
the metallic basis of the money systems or otherwise." [10] On June 17,
1932, the House adopted a resolution approving and encouraging efforts being made toward the holding of an international economic
conference "for the purpose of considering methods for the improvement of general economic and monetary conditions." [11] President
Hoover accepted the invitation of the Lausanne Conference (which
terminated its session on July 9, 1932) to a world financial and economic conference.[12] Preliminary work took place, even though the
President disapproved of most of the proposals which were advanced
in connection with silver.[13] The administration's resistance to silver
perceptibly weakened as the election approached.

To gain the support of the silver states in the election campaign of
1932, both parties made concessions to silver by advocating international conferences to discuss the role of the metal.[14]

During the banking crisis of 1933, when "scrip" was issued and
barter used, the agitation for silver monetization returned. The West-
erners feared "a scarcity of money." The silver mine owners were
anxious to create a demand for the metal because of the declining
price. The fall in price (from $1.339 an ounce in December, 1920, to
$.246 in December, 1932) was due to falling demand and increased
production here and abroad. The latter was in part the result of the

[10] U.S., Congress, *Congressional Record*, 72d Cong., 1st Sess., p. 4739.

[11] House Resolution 247, U.S., Congress, *Congressional Record*, 72d Cong., 1st Sess.,
p. 13317.

[12] For text of resolutions of the Lausanne Conference see *International Conciliation*,
No. 282, September, 1932.

[13] Bratter, "The Silver Episode," *Journal of Political Economy*, Vol. XLVI
(October, 1938), p 629.

[14] Mr. Roosevelt, in his Salt Lake City address, said: "And one of the greatest of
questions of international relationship, is that of money, of gold and of silver! I am
glad to take official notice of the fact that the administration in Washington has at last
come to recognize the existence of silver. To move in the direction of consideration of
that question is in accord with the Democratic platform which says: 'We favor a sound
currency to be preserved at all hazards and an international monetary conference called
on the invitation of our government to consider the rehabilitation of silver and related
questions!" Roosevelt, *Public Papers and Addresses*, Vol. I, pp. 712–713. Republican
Platform: "We favor the participation by the United States in an international conference to consider matters relating to monetary questions, including the position of
silver, exchange problems and commodity prices, and possible coöperative action concerning them." Quoted in Bratter, "The Silver Episode," *Journal of Political Economy*,
Vol. XLVI (October, 1938), p. 631.

strong demand for copper, zinc, and lead in the production of which silver was obtained as a by-product.[15] The depression decreased the demand for silver, and countries like India and China seemed anxious to dispose of their stock.

Inflationists, such as Wheeler, Pittman, Dies, and Feisinger, repeated the assertion that the low price of silver was hurting trade with silver producing countries and that the high price of gold was leading to a panic, contraction, and the lack of money. They urged the United States Government to create a demand for silver by purchasing and remonetizing it. Furthermore, they argued that the high price of silver would enable the Orient to increase its imports. They neglected the fact that the low price of silver made the Orient an excellent place for purchases.

Because of increasing agitation for inflation of the currency to raise the price level during the session of Congress in the spring of 1933, impetus was given to a number of bills dealing with silver. These ranged from measures proposing purchase of moderate quantities of silver at the market price to unlimited free coinage of silver at a ratio with gold of 16:1.[16] Finally in May, 1933, the silver agitators succeeded in convincing Congress of the need for silver legislation.

SILVER REGULATIONS UNDER THE THOMAS AMENDMENT TO THE AGRICULTURAL ADJUSTMENT ACT, MAY 12, 1933

Under Section 44 of the Act of May 12, 1933 (48 Stat. 31), the President was authorized to fix the weight of the silver dollar at a definite ratio with relation to the gold dollar, both nine-tenths fine, "at such amounts as he finds necessary from his investigation to stabilize domestic prices or to protect the foreign commerce against the adverse effect of depreciated foreign currencies." The President was further authorized to provide for the unlimited coinage of gold and silver at the ratio so fixed.[17] It was made the duty of the Secretary of the Treasury to maintain this ratio. Section 45 of this amendment provided for the acceptance by the Treasury of silver at 50 cents an

[15] Kemmerer, *Kemmerer on Money*, p. 118.

[16] Crawford, *Monetary Management under the New Deal*, p. 65; Bratter, "The Silver Episode," *Journal of Political Economy*, Vol. XLVI (October, 1938), p. 647.

[17] The entire amendment is quoted in U.S., Federal Reserve Board, *Annual Report, 1933*, pp. 267–268.

ounce in payment of debts due from any foreign government. The total value of the silver so accepted was not to exceed $200,000,000.[18] The Treasury never received more than 10 percent of the allotted amount due to the defaults in intergovernmental payments which began at about that time.[19]

SILVER RESOLUTIONS AT THE LONDON ECONOMIC CONFERENCE

The advocates of silver legislation were not satisfied with mere authorizations and a potential increase of the currency through the Thomas Amendment and sought further solace at the World Economic Conference, which sat in London from June 12 to July 27, 1933. Senator Pittman was one of the United States delegates. When Senator Pittman was selected by President Roosevelt as a member of the American delegation to the London Conference, it was obvious that an effort was to be made to do something, for ostensibly the choice of Senator Pittman was due to his connection with the silver issue. It was taken for granted that the Senator would devote himself to the silver interests. These assumptions proved to be correct. At the conference, on June 19, 1933, he advocated an agreement between silver consuming and silver producing nations in an attempt to mitigate fluctuations in the price of silver.[20] The silver consuming nations— India, China, and Spain—agreed not to "dump" silver on world markets; each country agreed it would not dispose of more than an allotted amount of silver for the next four years.[21] The producing countries—Australia, Canada, Mexico, Peru, and the United States —agreed to absorb 35,000,000 ounces annually for four years. Under the terms of the agreement the United States was to take a minimum of 70 percent of the 35,000,000 ounces of silver produced annually, or approximately 24,500,000 ounces.[22] Its allotted amount, therefore, constituted a large share of the entire silver production. The pact was of enormous importance to the domestic silver industry in the United States, inasmuch as it furnished a basis for the subsequent purchase of all newly mined domestic silver by the Treasury at a price con-

[18] 48 Stat. 31.
[19] U.S., Treasury Dept., *Annual Report of the Secretary, 1933,* p. 27.
[20] For text of Pittman Resolution see Pasvolsky, *Current Monetary Issues,* Appendix C, Part II, p. 159
[21] *Ibid.*   [22] See Table XXII.

TABLE XXII

SCHEDULE OF REQUIRED ANNUAL SILVER PURCHASES
UNDER THE ALLOTMENT AGREEMENT OF THE
LONDON ECONOMIC CONFERENCE, 1933[a]

| Country | ALLOTMENT | | Production Percent of World Total |
	Ounces	Percent	
U.S.A.	24,421,410	69.78	23.0
Mexico	7,159,108	20.45	41.4
Canada	1,671,802	4.78	9.2
Peru	1,095,325	3.13	7.9
Australia	652,355	1.86	3.6
Total	35,000,000	100.00	85.1

[a] Bratter, "The Silver Episode," *Journal of Political Economy*, Vol. XLVI (October, 1938), p. 643.

siderably above the market. Provisions of the agreement applying to countries other than the United States did not represent any material concessions on their part. The major burden of the obligation rested upon the United States.[23]

The results favorable to the cause of silver were due to the persistence of Senator Pittman and to the fact that Great Britain, France, and other important nations were indifferent to the silver pact, but were willing to allow the resolution to go through on the assumption that the United States Government wanted it.[24]

The contribution of the London silver pact to the development of a currency system managed by the Treasury was fairly substantial. The prime motive of the sponsors of the rehabilitation of silver as a monetary metal was to advance the interests of the producing industry. Nevertheless, the broadening of the metallic base of the monetary system, the power given to the Treasury to issue silver certificates, and the substantial increase in the amount of currency based on silver, and the consequent increase in excess banking reserves must be recognized as factors bearing on currency management. These developments had their roots in the London pact.

[23] Leavens, *Silver Money*, pp. 250–251.
[24] Bratter, "The Silver Episode," *Journal of Political Economy*, Vol. XLVI (October, 1938), p. 635.

THE PRESIDENT'S PROCLAMATION, DECEMBER 21, 1933, REGARDING SILVER

In the latter part of 1933 new experiments in currency management by the Treasury were launched in the form of purchases of silver. The silver program, inaugurated late in December, was put forward as part of the movement for higher commodity prices, although the sponsors were obviously most interested in its subsidy features. The silver agreement of the London Economic Conference was ratified for the United States by the presidential proclamation on December 21, 1933.[25] The preamble of the Proclamation was evidence of the part which the silver purchase program was intended to play in currency management. The purpose was

. . . to assist in increasing and stabilizing domestic prices, to augment the purchasing power of peoples in silver using countries, to protect our foreign commerce against the adverse effect of depreciated foreign currencies, and to carry out the understanding between the sixty-six governments that adopted the resolution.

With the issuance of the order there commenced a steady absorption of silver into the nation's currency structure. The ratification proclamation provided for the purchase of all American mined silver, not merely 24,421,410 ounces. The order also provided for free coinage of silver at the ratio in weight and fineness of the silver dollar to the gold dollar. This meant the 16:1 ratio represented by the old dollar of 23.22 grains of pure gold and 371.25 grains of pure silver. The proclamation limited the free coinage to newly mined domestic silver, and it provided that one-half the bullion brought to the mint should be retained by the Treasury as seigniorage.

Since the monetary value of the pure silver contained in a standard silver dollar is $1.2929, the retention of one-half the silver as seigniorage meant that the producer received $.6464 an ounce. The proclamation provided that one-half the silver should be coined into standard silver dollars, which were to be delivered to the owner of the silver in payment. The other half of the silver was to be retained as bullion by the Treasury and was not to be disposed of prior to December 31, 1937, except for coinage.

Subsequently, Section 12 of the Gold Reserve Act of January 30,

[25] *Federal Reserve Bulletin*, January, 1934, p. 8.

1934 (48 Stat. 337) [26] provided that silver certificates, instead of silver dollars, might be issued in payment of silver. The same section made it possible for the Treasury to issue currency against all unobligated silver, which included that held as seigniorage. Section 12 gave the Treasury authority to prescribe different terms and conditions and to make seigniorage charges for the coinage of silver of foreign production different from that of domestic production. It gave authority to the President to reduce the weight of the standard silver dollar in proportion to the extent to which he reduces the weight of the gold dollar.[27]

The silver purchases initiated under the proclamation served as a prelude to the much broader program subsequently adopted in the Silver Purchase Act (48 Stat. 1178).

SILVER PURCHASE ACT OF 1934

As has been previously stated, the major support for a greater use of silver in the monetary system came from those anxious to obtain assistance for the domestic silver producing industry and the western area dependent upon the metal. The arguments for silver legislation stressed possible favorable effects upon economic conditions through a broader metallic monetary base and issuance of a greater volume of currency. The silver advocates believed that their program would contribute to an advance in commodity prices.[28]

In the spring of 1934 the enthusiasts for the white metal renewed their efforts toward legislation which would increase the price of silver. Bills to increase the price of silver were introduced in the House by Representatives Feisinger and Dies, but the President did not appear to be satisfied with them.[29] On May 22 he sent a message to Congress incorporating recommendations for silver purchase legisla-

[26] The clauses devoted to silver in the Gold Reserve Act were passed as amendments which were sponsored by Senator Pittman. See Bratter, "The Silver Episode," *Journal of Political Economy*, Vol. XLVI (October, 1938), p. 807.

[27] U.S., Treasury Dept., *Annual Report of the Secretary, 1934*, p. 193.

[28] Dies and Pittman asserted that silver or silver certificates would increase the supply of currency in circulation and thus raise prices. Also, the widening of the metallic base for our currency would stabilize prices, if they were based on two metals, instead of one. See *Commercial and Financial Chronicle*, Vol. CXXXVIII (April 4, 1934), p. 2506.

[29] House of Representatives, Bill No. 1597; House of Representatives, Bill No. 7581; U.S., Congress, *Congressional Record*, 73d Cong., 2d Sess., pp. 249, 1795; Bratter, "The Silver Episode," *Journal of Political Economy*, Vol. XLVI (October, 1938), p. 817.

tion along the lines of a compromise agreed to in conferences with the Congressional leaders.[30] Senator Pittman introduced on the same day Senate Bill No. 3658, which had been prepared by the Treasury Department under the instruction and supervision of the President. This bill became the Silver Purchase Act on June 19, 1934, (48 Stat. 1178).

Section 2 of the Silver Purchase Act declared it to be the policy of the United States that the proportion of silver to gold in monetary stocks should be increased, with the ultimate objective of having and maintaining one-fourth of the total metallic monetary stocks in silver.

The Secretary of the Treasury was authorized and directed in Section 3 to purchase silver at home or abroad with any direct obligations, coin, or currency or with any funds in the Treasury not otherwise appropriated at such rates, times, and upon such terms and conditions as he might deem reasonable and most advantageous to the public interest.

Section 3 provided that no purchase of silver should be made at a price in excess of the monetary value and, further, that no purchase of silver situated in the continental United States on May 1, 1934, should be made at a price in excess of fifty cents an ounce.

Under Section 4 the Secretary of the Treasury might sell silver if the market price exceeded the monetary value or if silver in the metallic stock increased above the 25 percent ratio.

Section 5 governed the issuance of silver certificates. The Treasury was required to issue silver certificates up to the cost value of the silver acquired under the act. Such certificates should be placed in actual circulation. The Secretary of the Treasury was to maintain as security for all silver certificates an amount of silver bullion and standard silver dollars of a monetary value equal to the face amount of the certificates. All silver certificates of the United States were declared full legal tender and redeemable on demand in standard silver dollars.

Section 6 insured ample power to the Treasury to regulate silver trading in the United States. The Secretary of the Treasury was given authority to investigate, regulate, or prevent by means of licenses or otherwise the acquisition, importation, exportation, or transportation of silver. The penalty for violation of any provision was fixed

[30] U.S., Congress, *Congressional Record*, 73d Cong., 2d Sess., p. 9209.

at a maximum of $10,000 fine, imprisonment for not more than ten years, or both.

Provisions for nationalization (the taking over by the Government) of silver appeared in Section 7. Whenever the Treasurer so desired, he was given the authority to require the delivery to the United States mints of any or all silver, by whomever owned or possessed. Such silver was to be taken in at not less than the fair value as determined by the market price over a reasonable period. The silver so acquired would be coined into standard silver dollars or otherwise added to the monetary stocks of the Nation. The payment for the silver nationalized was to be in standard silver dollars or any other coin equal to the monetary value of the silver less seigniorage.

Section 8 contained the details governing the 50 percent tax on silver trading profits. This tax was intended to apply only to speculative transactions. Its purpose was "to limit undue profits by persons who buy silver in competition with the government for the purpose of selling it later at a higher price, directly or indirectly to the government."

Section 10 defined the monetary value of silver as "a value calculated on the basis of $1 for an amount of silver or gold equal to the amount at the time contained in the standard silver dollar and the gold dollar, respectively." This meant $1.29 an ounce so long as the silver dollar remained at its old weight.

The Silver Purchase Act did not alter the status of silver under the century-old law of January 18, 1837 (5 Stat. 136). The weight of the standard silver dollar, nine-tenths fine, was 371.25 grains (.9 of 412.5 grains, which was gross weight). Prior to devaluation of the gold dollar [31] the ratio of the 371.25 grains of fine silver in a silver dollar to the 23.22 grains of fine gold (.9 of 25.8 grains, which was gross weight) [32] in a gold dollar was approximately 16:1. With gold worth $20.67 an ounce, the monetary value of the silver contained in a silver dollar was one-sixteenth of the gold price, or approximately $1.29.

With the reduction of fine gold in the dollar to 13.71 grains, under the devaluation proclamation of January 31, 1934, the ratio between

[31] President's Proclamation January 31, 1934; see above, p. 209.
[32] Act of June 28, 1834 (4 Stat. 700); see above, p. 209.

the weights of the silver dollar and the gold dollar became 29:1. Since there was no change made in the weight of the silver dollar, the monetary value of the silver remained $1.29 an ounce. The $1.29 value is one-twenty-seventh of the gold price of $35 an ounce. If the President were to reduce the silver content of the standard silver dollar [33] to correspond with the reduction in the gold content of the dollar, the result would be a monetary value for silver of $2.19 an ounce.[34] If the silver dollar were devalued by the full amount authorized by law, the monetary value of silver could be increased to $2.58.[35] The Treasury would be in a position to convert the profit into currency if any increase were made in the value of silver. The power to increase the currency has been recognized as a central banking function.

At the time of the passage of the Silver Purchase Act, the Treasury decided to issue silver certificates up to the monetary value of $1.29 per ounce against all free silver held by the the Treasury up to June 14, 1934.[36] This policy affected 62,000,000 ounces of silver, which made possible the issuance of about $80,000,000 of silver certificates. This was an inflationary move and typical of the Treasury's power to increase the currency. Fortunately Section 5 of the Silver Purchase Act (48 Stat. 1178) permitted the Treasury to issue silver certificates only to a face value equal to the cost of newly purchased silver. Issuing silver certificates at cost price was less inflationary than issuing them at monetary value. Nevertheless, the possibilities for inflation were great under the Silver Purchase Act (48 Stat. 1178), especially if the Treasury should attempt to maintain one-fourth of the monetary value of the total stocks in silver. Still greater possibilities for inflation existed under the terms of the Gold Reserve Act (48 Stat. 337). Under Section 12 of the Act of January 30, 1934, the Secretary of the Treasury might convert any unobligated silver into currency at its monetary value, which meant that the Secretary of the Treasury could issue silver certificates for a much larger value than the cost of

[33] The President had this authority under Section 12 of the Gold Reserve Act, January 30, 1934 (48 Stat. 337).

[34] $\dfrac{\$20.67}{\$35.00} = \dfrac{\$1.29}{\$2.19}$ or $1.29 = 59.06$ per cent of $2.19.

[35] A 100 percent increase in the old price of silver, which is the equivalent of a 50 percent devaluation of the silver dollar, the maximum allowed under Section 12 of the Gold Reserve Act (48 Stat. 337).

[36] U.S., Treasury Dept., *Annual Report of the Secretary, 1934*, p. 210.

domestic and foreign silver. Section 12 further increased inflationary possibilities by giving the President power to change the monetary value of silver to correspond with that of gold.

In conformity with the Silver Purchase Act, the Secretary of the Treasury, on June 28, 1934, issued an order forbidding the export of silver except under license.[37] The reason for this order was that speculative interests were contemplating the exportation of silver with the hope of receiving a higher price for domestic silver than the 50 percent limitation imposed in Section 3 of the Silver Purchase Act (48 Stat. 1178).

On August 9, 1934, the President issued an order for the nationalization of all domestic silver stocks. The owners of silver were to receive standard silver dollars, silver certificates, or other currency of the United States equal to the monetary value of the silver ounce, $1.29, less $61\frac{8}{25}$ percent for seigniorage, brassage, and coinage. This meant a payment of approximately 50 cents an ounce, a price which the Treasury considered fair on the basis of the market value over a "reasonable" period. The method of setting the price was determined in Section 7 of the Silver Purchase Act (48 Stat. 1178). The nationalization order remained in effect until April 28, 1938. Various orders of the Secretary of the Treasury regarding silver were revoked at that time, including the order of June 28, 1934.[38]

TREASURY OPERATIONS UNDER THE SILVER PURCHASE PROGRAM

There was much opposition from the silver interests to the nationalization of silver at 50.01 cents an ounce.[39] In order to appease them, the Treasury decided it was expedient to purchase more silver, and the market price of silver rose. To keep pace with the rise in market price, the President proclaimed the domestic price on April 10, 1935, at 71.11 cents an ounce; [40] on April 24 it was set at 77.57 cents.[41] The world price of silver kept rising, and on April 26, 1935,

---

[37] *Ibid.*, pp. 210–212.

[38] U.S. Treasury Dept., *Annual Report of the Secretary, 1938*, p. 266.

[39] Monetary value of one ounce $1.2929

Less $61\frac{8}{25}$ percent for seigniorage and other mint charges   .7928

Silver certificate issued $ .5001

[40] U.S., Treasury Dept., *Annual Report of the Secretary, 1935*, p. 260; the order reduced the seigniorage charge to 45 percent.

[41] *Ibid.*, p. 261; the order reduced the seigniorage charge to 40 percent.

it was 81.31 cents. When the Treasury failed to raise the domestic price, the world price started to sag. There was reason to believe that the Treasury failed to raise the price because the Secretary of the Treasury was convinced that higher prices for silver would cause deflation and depression in China, the largest silver using country.[42]

China abandoned the silver standard in December, 1935, and her holdings of silver became available for sale. By February, 1936, the world price of silver had dropped to 45.06 cents an ounce, and the Treasury adopted that figure for foreign silver.[43] In June, 1934, the time of the passage of the Silver Purchase Act (48 Stat. 1178) the world price of silver had been 45.125 cents an ounce. The London Agreement regarding silver, which was ratified by the United States in the Presidential Proclamation of December 21, 1933, expired on December 31, 1937.[44] On December 30, 1937, the Treasury announced that domestic producers of silver would receive 64.64 cents an ounce instead of 77.57 cents.[45] On March 29, 1938, the Treasury reduced its buying price for foreign silver to 43.06 cents,[46] the lowest price since the spring of 1934. On December 31, 1938, the Treasury issued an order continuing the price of 64.64 cents for domestic silver until June 30, 1939,[47] when the President's authority to establish bimetallism under the Thomas Inflation Amendment was to expire (Section 43 of the Agricultural Adjustment Act, May 12, 1933; 48 Stat. 31). Commencing in July, 1939, the Treasury has maintained a price of 35 cents an ounce for foreign silver, which is little more than half the price for domestic silver.

[42] Secretary Morgenthau, in testimony before a subcommittee of a House Committee on Appropriation on December 16, 1936, said that the Treasury had allowed the market price of silver to drop to its natural level because of his belief that it was "not in the public interest" to buy foreign silver at a higher price. He said, the price dropped "until it found its natural level, which seemed to be around 45¢; and at around 45¢, the world price more or less maintains itself, buying as we do." See U.S., Congress, House, Subcommittee of Committee on Appropriations, 75th Cong., 3d Sess., *Hearings on Treasury Department Appropriation Bill for 1939*, p. 34.

[43] U.S., Treasury Dept., *Annual Report of the Secretary, 1936*, p. 166.

[44] See above, pp. 200–201.

[45] U.S., Treasury Dept., *Annual Report of the Secretary, 1938*, p. 264; under this order dated December 30, 1937, a 50 percent seigniorage charge was restored. The order of April 24, 1935, had set a 40 percent seigniorage charge (U.S., Treasury Dept., *Annual Report of the Secretary, 1935*, p. 261).

[46] U.S., Treasury Dept., *Annual Report of the Secretary, 1938*, p. 185.

[47] U.S., Treasury Dept., *Annual Report of the Secretary, 1939*, p. 282.

THE SILVER PURCHASE ACT OF 1939

In the years following the enactment in 1934 of the Silver Purchase Act (48 Stat. 1178), various proposals to amend the law kept the subject intermittently before Congress. Senator Thomas proposed, on March 23, 1935, a bill providing for the issuance of silver certificates to the full monetary value of the silver acquired by the Treasury, not merely to the extent of the cost, and providing that silver certificates should be kept actively in circulation.[48] The Treasury opposed this bill.[49] Representative White of Idaho introduced on January 5, 1937, a bill for the free coinage of silver at a ratio of 16 to 1 based on the new value of gold.[50] Senator Pittman, on January 19, 1939, introduced a bill for the purchase of domestic newly mined silver at the full monetary value of $1.29 an ounce, but restricting foreign silver at prices within the discretion of the Secretary of the Treasury.[51] On April 10, 1939, Representative White introduced a resolution authorizing the President to call an international conference of nations for the purpose of entering into an agreement for an unlimited coinage and full legal tender of both gold and silver at a fixed ratio.[52] These measures were not given serious consideration.

The silver bloc achieved one of its greatest victories when Congress provided for the purchase of all domestic silver mined after July 1, 1939, at a price of 71.11 cents an ounce. The new law, approved by the President on July 6, 1939, made a seigniorage charge of 45 percent on silver brought to the mints.[53] While the price was not as high as the silver group would have liked, it represented an increase over the existing price of 64.64 cents an ounce.[54] The world price at the

[48] U.S., Congress, *Congressional Record*, 74th Cong., 1st Sess., p. 4362.

[49] *Ibid.*, p. 4349.

[50] House Resolution 113, U.S., Congress, *Congressional Record*, 75th Cong., 1st Sess., p. 26.

[51] Senate Resolution 800, U.S., Cong., *Congressional Record*, 76th Cong., 1st Sess., p. 471.

[52] House Resolution 262, U.S., Congress, *Congressional Record*, 76th Cong., 1st Sess., p. 4055.

[53] Section 4b (53 Stat. 998):

Monetary value	$1.2929
Less-45 % seigniorage	.5818
Payment to owner	$ .7111

[54] Presidential Order of December 30, 1937, U.S., Treasury Dept., *Annual Report of the Secretary, 1938*, p. 264; Presidential Order of December 31, 1938, U.S., Treasury Dept., *Annual Report of the Secretary, 1939*, pp. 282–283.

time of the passage of the Act of July 6, 1939 (53 Stat. 998), had dropped below 40 cents.

Senator Pittman frankly stated that the purpose of the Silver Purchase Act of 1939 was to provide a subsidy for the domestic silver industry.[55] No mention was made of the objectives of the silver purchase program; namely, "to assist in increasing and stabilizing domestic prices, to augment the purchasing power of peoples in silver using countries, and to protect our foreign commerce against the adverse effect of depreciated foreign currencies." Such statements had been made in the Presidential Proclamation of December 21, 1933.[56]

THE TREASURY, SILVER, AND RESERVES

It was asserted that since silver certificates would be issued at cost price, not at the monetary value of the purchased silver, there would be no serious increase in the amount of currency in circulation or risk of inflation. This opinion was not only based on the belief that more money cannot be kept in circulation than is needed considering all such factors as business conditions, general confidence, and hoarding. It was supported by the fact that the new issues of silver certificates coincided with the gradual withdrawal of national bank notes from circulation due to the calling of the bonds carrying the note-issuing privilege.[57] The increase in circulation of silver certificates (1933–1940) was about $1,220,963,000 and was offset by the decrease in circulation of about $754,459,000 of national bank notes and $103,472,000 of federal reserve bank notes.[58] While no actual inflation resulted from the silver purchase policy, it must be remembered that a possibility for inflation was created and still exists.

The following arithmetic problem, based on Dr. Johnson's book, might illustrate the points: [59] Suppose the Treasury were to buy 1,000 ounces of silver at 71.11 cents an ounce, it will thereupon put $711.10 worth of silver valued at $1.2929 an ounce, or about 550

[55] U.S., Congress, *Congressional Record*, 76th Cong., 1st Sess., pp. 8562–8563.

[56] *Federal Reserve Bulletin*, January, 1934, p. 8; see above, pp. 245–246.

[57] On March 11, 1935, the Treasury announced that it would retire on July 1, $600,000,000 of 2 percent consols of 1930, and on August 1, $75,000,000 Panama Canal bonds of 1916–1936 and 1918–1938. U.S., Treasury Dept., *Annual Report of the Secretary, 1935*, p. 22; see also above, pp. 146, 177–179, and Appendix VII, below.

[58] U.S., Treasury Dept., *Annual Report of the Secretary, 1940*, p. 810.

[59] Johnson, *The Treasury and Monetary Policy, 1933–1938*, p. 194.

ounces, into "Silver in General Fund" and will add $319.99 to "seigniorage" (the difference between $711.10 and the cost of the 550 ounces); the residue, 450 ounces will be valued at cost and the resulting $319.99 added to "silver bullion" (cost value). The revalued silver will remain in "Silver in General Fund" until the Treasury actually deposits $711.10 of silver certificates with the Federal Reserve banks, thus increasing its working balance and eventually member bank reserves.

Silver in general fund: 550 ounces $\times$ 1.2929 = $711.10
Seigniorage: 550 ounces $\times$ .5818 = 319.99
Silver bullion (cost):   450 ounces $\times$ .7111 = 319.99

Now it becomes immediately evident that by permitting silver to accumulate in "Silver in General Fund" or by withdrawing such silver the Treasury can significantly influence movements in member bank reserves; that item measures the lag between the purchase of silver and the issuance of certificates against the revalued portion. Of course, if the increase or decrease in that item represents merely a corresponding reduction or rise in the Treasury balances at the Federal Reserve banks, the effects of changes in that item are temporarily offset. In practice the Federal Reserve banks draw on the "Silver in General Fund" whenever they can dispose of the silver certificates. The effect on member bank reserves has been relatively insignificant and has therefore been ignored because of the huge expansion of reserves from other causes.[60]

Of vastly more importance, however, is the item "silver bullion" (cost value) which the Treasury holds in reserve; it measures the power of expansion by issuing silver certificates at monetary value ($1.29). Senator Thomas and other silverites realized that this possibility for inflation existed and urged the issuance of silver certificates against unobligated bullion. They maintained that in general a higher price level and recovery could be achieved by expanding the currency.[61] However, the Treasury had stated that it had no intention of using the unobligated bullion.[62] Yet it cannot be supposed that the bullion will remain unused forever. At some time in the near future, perhaps by easy stages or in time of war or depression, the bullion

---

[60] *Ibid.*
[61] U.S., Congress, *Congressional Record*, 74th Cong., 1st Sess., pp. 11918–11921.
[62] U.S., Treasury Dept., *Annual Report of the Secretary, 1935*, pp. 264–265.

is likely to be drawn upon, and the potential expansion of member bank reserves is likely to be realized.[63] Still another way to inflate the currency is implicit in the President's power to reduce the weight of the silver dollar to the same extent to which he reduces the weight of the gold dollar.[64] The President has not devalued the silver dollar, but if he did so the profits from devalution could be used.

FUTURE OF THE SILVER PURCHASE POLICY OF THE TREASURY

The truth is that the leadership in the United States Treasury is now convinced of the expense and folly of the silver purchase program. Secretary Morgenthau announced that "he would raise no objection to the abandonment of the American silver purchase program." [65] It is not surprising that after eight years the silver purchase program should have lost the sympathy of the Roosevelt administration. Its monetary significance was lost many years ago. It is no consolation to know that it helped reflation, since today the Federal Reserve System still has excess reserves. Far from "rehabilitating" silver as a monetary metal in the eyes of governments and peoples everywhere, the silver purchase policy drove the metal out of circulation from the few countries that still adhered to this standard. On the other hand, the program has afforded an opportunity to foreign holders to unload their silver on the United States Treasury in exchange for gold at extremely favorable prices; and, of course, domestic producers have profited by subsidy prices. As long as the United States Treasury continues to pay a subsidized price for domestic silver, abandonment of the purchase of foreign silver would raise no great resentment.

Discussion about the suspension of silver purchases culminated in the passage of a Senate bill, May 9, 1940, repealing the Silver Purchase Acts and directing the sale of surplus silver.[66] Fear that the purchase of silver might cease has resulted in the fall of the price of silver.[67] Subsequent adjustment of the world price of silver must

---

[63] Johnson, *The Treasury and Monetary Policy, 1933–1938*, p. 195.

[64] Section 12 of the Gold Reserve Act (48 Stat. 337).

[65] The Economist (London) Vol. CXLI (August 16, 1941), p. 206.

[66] Senate Resolution 785 sponsored by Senator Townsend, U.S., Congress, *Congressional Record*, 76 Cong., 3d Sess., p. 8950.

[67] The price in May, 1940, was 35 cents an ounce which figure the Treasury maintained since July, 1939. The average for the fiscal year 1939 was 42.9 cents. U.S., Treasury Dept., *Annual Report of the Secretary, 1939*, p. 174.

depend on the policy of the United States Treasury, which as the holder of the world's largest stock of the metal, will, whether it likes it or not, be the arbiter of the metal's fate. If it refuses to buy, there may be an appreciable slump in the price. If it attempts to sell, the word "slump" would be quite inadequate to describe the movement in the quotation.

However, American silver holdings are now so large that they cannot possibly be liquidated in the measurable future. A mere suspension of further purchases would present the silver markets with the formidable task of attempting to absorb current production, now running at a high level due to the war demand for lead and zinc. Such a move would be an especially severe blow to Mexico, and it is possible in this case that some exception from the suspension of further purchases might be made in return for a suitable *quid pro quo* on the oil question.

Whether the cessation of the silver purchase program of the Treasury will be achieved is still unknown. But under the present policy the Treasury, like a central bank, is in a position to influence the currency and the reserves of the commercial banks of the country. The Treasury can issue silver certificates against the "silver bullion" held in reserve.[68] The Treasury is still operating under the instructions of Section 2 of the Silver Purchase Act (48 Stat. 1178) to accumulate silver until the 3:1 ratio is attained. Meanwhile the continued

TABLE XXIII

MONETARY STOCKS OF GOLD AND SILVER, 1934–1941[a]

Date	Gold ($35 per fine ounce)	Silver ($1.29 per fine ounce)	Ratio of Silver to Gold and Silver in Monetary Stocks
June 30, 1934	$ 7,856,200,000	$ 898,200,000	10.3
June 30, 1935	9,115,600,000	1,463,100,000	13.8
June 30, 1936	10,608,400,000	2,249,500,000	17.5
June 30, 1937	12,318,300,000	2,542,100,000	17.2
June 30, 1938	12,963,000,000	3,066,400,000	19.1
June 30, 1939	16,110,000,000	3,605,200,000	18.3
June 30, 1940	19,963,100,000	3,935,400,000	16.5
June 30, 1941	22,624,198,000	4,148,700,000	15.5

[a] U.S., Treasury Dept., *Bulletin*, May 1943, p. 76.

[68] Section 12, Gold Reserve Act (48 Stat. 337).

inrush of gold has emphasized the huge amounts of silver which would have to be acquired to realize the desired 25 percent goal.[69] Finally, if the President should devalue the silver dollar,[70] the Treasury would realize a profit from devaluation and member bank reserves would be correspondingly increased by the expenditure of the profit.

[69] See Table XXIII.   [70] Section 12, Gold Reserve Act (48 Stat. 337).

CHAPTER XI

Conclusion and Future of Treasury Central Banking

THE FINAL STATUS of the Treasury as the real central bank of the United States, in fact, if not in theory, was attained, not by any sudden or dramatic change, but by a long-continued and persistent enhancement of Treasury powers. Even in the earliest days of the republic the Treasury exercised monetary as well as fiscal functions. In fact, as is shown in Chapter II, the first intimation of the exercise of central banking functions by the Treasury of the United States may be regarded as dating from the very organization of the Treasury Department. At that time the legislators did not intend to endow the Treasury with the powers of a central bank. They were opposed to the concept of centralized government, and the very idea of a central bank was distasteful to them. But by delegating to the Treasury the safekeeping and disbursing of public funds, Congress inevitably provided the Treasury with a means for influencing the reserves of commercial banks. By the simple device of depositing Treasury funds the Treasury could raise the reserves of commercial banks and increase their power to extend credit. The withdrawal of funds, if on a large enough scale, would result in a substantial decrease of reserves and would diminish their ability to extend credit.[1] More specifically, if the Treasury desired to aid a bank which could not meet the cash demands of its creditors, the Treasury could strengthen the distressed bank by depositing funds with it.[2] But even if the United States Treasury had no desires to influence the money market, it has from the beginning been a deciding factor in the banking field, because it has always been in the unique position of being the largest receiver and disburser of funds.

Originally reluctant to act as a central bank, the Treasury has at times left the details of central banking operations to other institu-

---

[1] See above, pp. 3-9.   [2] See above, pp. 18-24.

tions. The first example of such delegation was the case of the first Bank of the United States. This bank was expected to deal in a limited amount of the public debt (open-market operations), to conserve the specie stock of the nation, to subject the commercial banks of the country to the obligation of the redemption of their notes, to insist upon bank note currency of uniform value, free from the danger of local depreciation, and to secure satisfactory conditions of clearance and transfer among the banks.[3] Thus early in our financial history the Bank of the United States shared what we now consider to be central banking functions with the Treasury Department, and neither the public nor Congress were fully aware of the implication that such powers constituted a modest beginning of central banking on the part of these Government agencies. But the trend had set in. For awhile there seemed to be no further increase in central banking activities by the Treasury.

During the period between the first Bank of the United States and the second Bank of the United States the Treasury continued its original functions and exercised the same influence as heretofore. Thereafter the second Bank of the United States was again given the duties and responsibilities previously exercised by the first Bank of the United States. But even during the life of the second Bank of the United States the Treasury, in its fiscal operations, continued to wield monetary powers, while the Federal bank did much of the work of the Treasury without equaling its influence. After the abolition of the second bank the power of the Treasury was greatly increased. The Treasury became more dominant in the monetary sphere during the era of state banking, when no national bank existed and chaotic conditions in banking prevailed.[4] Treasury activities exceeded anything seen before when the Treasury tried to mitigate the effects of the Panic of 1837.

Due partly to politics and partly to the public's ignorance of banking needs, a third Federal bank was not chartered. Thus, the possibility of a rival central banking institution was eliminated, and the Treasury was left in possession of the field. In 1840 the Independent Treasury System was created for the express purpose of severing the connection between the banks of the country and the Government. In its original form this system lasted only a few months,

---

[3] See above, pp. 16–27. [4] See above, pp. 30–31.

but it was revived some six years later, and it continued in operation for many decades. However, the legislators kept the Independent Treasury in its dominant position, resembling that of a central banking agency, by continuing its former fiscal functions. After 1846 the Treasury was to keep the public funds safe in its own vaults. It was to accept only specie payments and make disbursements in specie. This requirement gave to the country a foundation for sound currency and to the Treasury a position as its monetary guardian.

In the actual operation of the Independent Treasury System the Treasury, while carrying on its normal fiscal duties, also went far into the field of monetary control. Various secretaries of the Treasury saw that the United States needed a central banking agency with the power of coördinating the monetary processes with the rest of the activities in the economic order. Guided by these secretaries, the Treasury often intentionally filled the gap created by the absence of a special central bank. It extended relief to banks in times of difficulty (Panic of 1857), influenced prices of goods and securities, issued paper money, and regulated the supply of credit through various fiscal devices.[5]

With the establishment of the National Banking System the trend toward a concentration of the central banking activities in the Treasury seemed to be temporarily interrupted. But it soon reasserted itself. The National Banking System was established in 1864 to help the Treasury finance the Civil War by creating a market for Government bonds. At first glance this step would seem to deprive the Treasury of some central banking influence. The national banks were made Government depositories of all funds received in payment of Government obligations and for receipts from internal revenue the national banks also maintained a uniform bank-note currency by issuing notes based upon Government bonds, which in turn were backed by Government credit. The National Banking Act provided for definite reserve requirements against deposit liabilities, but no agency existed within the National Banking System which offered rediscounting facilities. It is true that the Treasury did not possess the discount power, but through various fiscal devices, it could and did alter the quantity and percentage requirements of commercial bank reserves;[6] and control over the reserves of banks is the core of central banking

---

[5] See above, pp. 52–57, 60.   [6] See above, pp. 68–70, 75–76, 78–83.

power. The Treasury employed fiscal devices in attempting to restore normal business conditions during the Panic of 1873, the
monetary stringency of 1890, the Panic of 1893, and the Panic of
1907. In fact the Treasury under Secretary Shaw (1901–1907) went
so far as to anticipate and avoid the regular autumnal stringency
caused by the annual marketing of the crops.[7] Throughout this period
the influence of the Treasury upon the banking system became more
certain and effective.

By the first decade of the twentieth century the Independent Treasury was clearly recognized as the central banking agency, and fear was
expressed, both by some secretaries of the Treasury and by the public,
that the combination of fiscal and central banking power in the hands
of the Treasury was unwise.[8] The objection was not against central
banking as such. The banking community had become accustomed
to reliance upon a central banking agency, the Treasury, for aid in
normal times and particularly in times of crisis. Now the banking
community agitated for a separate central bank. This bank was to
be free from governmental influence and to have specific powers over
the monetary system, including the rediscounting function. As a result, an apparently independent central banking system, the Federal
Reserve System, was evolved, which was intended by the legislators
to replace the Treasury as the policy-making agency of the money
and banking system.[9]

This hope was not realized. Unusual circumstances following the
establishment of the Federal Reserve System worked against its assumption of a role of leadership in the money market. In World War I
the Treasury assumed the guardianship of the money market, and
the Federal Reserve System became subordinate to the Treasury.[10]
At the close of the first World War it was again hoped that the Federal Reserve System would assume a more independent position and
establish itself as the true central bank of the United States, and
this period of the twenties is marked by at least some decline in
Treasury influence in the monetary field.[11] This reversal of the trend
toward greater central banking control by the Treasury, however,
was short-lived, as all similar periods in Treasury history had been.

[7] See above, pp. 104–110.   [8] See above, p. 131.   [9] See above, pp. 132–133.
[10] See chap. vii for description of the war period.
[11] See chap. viii, which covers the events of the nineteen-twenties.

Because of the Government's desire to bring about recovery, it introduced a system of managed currency in the 1930's. This situation meant doom to the ideal of an independent central banking system, and its subordination to a government-controlled currency and credit system. The legislators gave to a more directly responsible Government agency, the United States Treasury, various central banking powers more potent for the meeting of financial emergencies than any ever possessed by the Federal Reserve System. The Federal Reserve System still continues its discounting and open-market operations, but these traditional activities have been correlated to Government policies and are overshadowed by the gold policies of the Treasury, by the latent powers of the stabilization fund,[12] and by the silver policies of the Treasury.[13]

The early years of the nineteen forties again enhanced the position of the Treasury. The United States is now an active participant in World War II. Once again all energies are directed to the great aim of winning a war. Again the leadership of the Treasury in the monetary field is unquestioned. This phenomenon is in accordance with the past procedure established in earlier American banking history, wherein the Treasury always assumed the powers normally intrusted to a central bank or central banking system whenever a great emergency arose which, it was thought, required the mobilization under one command of all resources including the monetary and banking system.

The immediate future is not likely to reverse this trend. As long as the war and its inevitable aftermath last, there seems to be little possibility that the Treasury will withdraw from its extraordinary activities and dominance in the field of monetary policy. If we add to these special war activities the normal fiscal functions of the Treasury, greatly expanded as they are by the high level of Government expenditures, it seems evident that the war economy plus the apparent need for continued governmental action after the war indicate that in the predictable future monetary control will probably not be vested in the hands of an independent central bank, but will remain entwined with fiscal policies and be a part thereof. This linking of monetary and fiscal powers is merely another manifestation of the seemingly irresistible trend toward greater centralized control of our economy through increased governmental activity.

[12] See chap. ix, which describes the activities of the gold policies.
[13] See chap. x, which treats the silver program.

Appendixes

APPENDIX I

Secretaries of the Treasury and the Presidents under Whom They Served [a]

Presidents	Secretaries of the Treasury	Term of Service From	To
Washington	Alexander Hamilton, N.Y.	Sept. 11, 1789	Jan. 31, 1795
	Oliver Wolcott, Conn.	Feb. 3, 1795	Mar. 3, 1797
Adams, J.	Oliver Wolcott, Conn.	Mar. 4, 1797	Dec. 31, 1800
	Samuel Dexter, Mass.	Jan. 1, 1801	Mar. 3, 1801
Jefferson	Samuel Dexter, Mass.	Mar. 4, 1801	May 13, 1801
	Albert Gallatin, Pa.	May 14, 1801	Mar. 3, 1809
Madison	Albert Gallatin, Pa.	Mar. 4, 1809	Apr. 17, 1813
	George W. Campbell, Tenn.	Feb. 9, 1814	Oct. 5, 1814
	Alexander J. Dallas, Pa.	Oct. 6, 1814	Oct. 21, 1816
	William H. Crawford, Ga.	Oct. 22, 1816	Mar. 3, 1817
Monroe	William H. Crawford, Ga.	Mar. 4, 1817	Mar. 6, 1825
Adams, J. Q.	Richard Rush, Pa.	Mar. 7, 1825	Mar. 5, 1829
Jackson	Samuel D. Ingham, Pa.	Mar. 6, 1829	June 20, 1831
	Louis McLane, Dela.	Aug. 8, 1831	May 28, 1833
	William J. Duane, Pa.	May 29, 1833	Sept. 22, 1833
	Roger B. Taney, Md.	Sept. 23, 1833	June 25, 1834
	Levi Woodbury, N.H.	July 1, 1834	Mar. 3, 1837
Van Buren	Levi Woodbury, N.H.	Mar. 4, 1837	Mar. 3, 1841
Harrison	Thomas Ewing, Ohio	Mar. 6, 1841	Apr. 4, 1841
Tyler	Thomas Ewing, Ohio	Apr. 5, 1841	Sept. 11, 1841
	Walter Forward, Pa.	Sept. 13, 1841	Mar. 1, 1843
	John C. Spencer, N.Y.	Mar. 8, 1843	May 2, 1844
	George M. Bibb, Ky.	July 4, 1844	Mar. 4, 1845
Polk	George M. Bibb, Ky.	Mar. 5, 1845	Mar. 7, 1845
	Robert J. Walker, Miss.	Mar. 8, 1845	Mar. 5, 1849
Taylor	William M. Meredith, Pa.	Mar. 8, 1849	July 9, 1850
Fillmore	William M. Meredith, Pa.	July 10, 1850	July 22, 1850
	Thomas Corwin, Ohio	July 23, 1850	Mar. 6, 1853
Pierce	James Guthrie, Ky.	Mar. 7, 1853	Mar. 6, 1857
Buchanan	Howell Cobb, Ga.	Mar. 7, 1857	Dec. 8, 1860
	Philip F. Thomas, Md.	Dec. 12, 1860	Jan. 14, 1861
	John A. Dix, N.Y.	Jan. 15, 1861	Mar. 6, 1861
Lincoln	Salmon P. Chase, Ohio	Mar. 7, 1861	June 30, 1864
	William P. Fessenden, Me.	July 5, 1864	Mar. 3, 1865
	Hugh McCullough, Ind.	Mar. 9, 1865	Apr. 15, 1865
Johnson	Hugh McCullough, Ind.	Apr. 16, 1865	Mar. 3, 1869
Grant	George S. Boutwell, Mass.	Mar. 12, 1869	Mar. 16, 1873
	William A. Richardson, Mass.	Mar. 17, 1873	June 3, 1874

[a] U.S., Treasury Dept., *Annual Report of the Secretary, 1932*, pp. xxvii–xxi; U.S., Treasury Dept., *Annual Report of the Secretary, 1933*, p. xiii.

Presidents	Secretaries of the Treasury	Term of Service	
		From	To
	Benjamin H. Bristow, Ky.	June 4, 1874	June 20, 1876
	Lot M. Morrill, Me.	July 7, 1876	Mar. 3, 1877
Hayes	Lot M. Morrill, Me.	Mar. 4, 1877	Mar. 9, 1877
	John Sherman, Ohio	Mar. 10, 1877	Mar. 3, 1881
Garfield	William Windom, Minn.	Mar. 8, 1881	Sept. 19, 1881
Arthur	William Windom, Minn.	Sept. 20, 1881	Nov. 13, 1881
	Charles J. Folger, N.Y.	Nov. 14, 1881	Sept. 4, 1884
	Walter A. Gresham, Ind.	Sept. 25, 1884	Oct. 30, 1884
	Hugh McCullough, Ind.	Oct. 31, 1884	Mar. 3, 1885
Cleveland	Hugh McCullough, Ind.	Mar. 4, 1885	Mar. 7, 1885
	Daniel Manning, N.Y.	Mar. 8, 1885	Mar. 31, 1887
	Charles S. Fairchild, N.Y.	Apr. 1, 1887	Mar. 3, 1889
Harrison, B.	Charles S. Fairchild, N.Y.	Mar. 4, 1889	Mar. 6, 1889
	William Windom, Minn.	Mar. 7, 1889	Jan. 29, 1891
	Charles Foster, Ohio	Feb. 23, 1891	Mar. 3, 1893
Cleveland	Charles Foster, Ohio	Mar. 4, 1893	Mar. 6, 1893
	John G. Carlisle, Ky.	Mar. 7, 1893	Mar. 3, 1897
McKinley	John G. Carlisle, Ky.	Mar. 4, 1897	Mar. 5, 1897
	Lyman G. Gage, Ill.	Mar. 6, 1897	Sept. 14, 1901
Roosevelt, T.	Lyman G. Gage, Ill.	Sept. 15, 1901	Jan. 31, 1902
	L. M. Shaw, Iowa	Feb. 1, 1902	Mar. 3, 1907
	George B. Cortelyou, N.Y.	Mar. 4, 1907	Mar. 7, 1909
Taft	Franklin MacVeagh, Ill.	Mar. 8, 1909	Mar. 5, 1913
Wilson	W. G. McAdoo, N.Y.	Mar. 6, 1913	Dec. 15, 1918
	Carter Glass, Va.	Dec. 16, 1918	Feb. 1, 1920
	David F. Houston, Mo.	Feb. 2, 1920	Mar. 3, 1921
Harding	Andrew W. Mellon, Pa.	Mar. 4, 1921	Aug. 2, 1923
Coolidge	Andrew W. Mellon, Pa.	Aug. 3, 1923	Mar. 3, 1929
Hoover	Andrew W. Mellon, Pa.	Mar. 4, 1929	Feb. 12, 1932
	Ogden L. Mills, N.Y.	Feb. 13, 1932	Mar. 3, 1933
Roosevelt, F. D.	William M. Woodin, N.Y.	Mar. 4, 1933	Dec. 31, 1933
	Henry Morgenthau, Jr., N.Y.	Jan. 1, 1934	To date

United States Treasury Balances in Treasury Vauls and in Depository Banks [a]

BALANCE IN THE TREASURY

Dates	In Treasury Offices	In Depository Banks	Total	Number of Depository Banks
1789—December 31	...	$ 28,239.61	$ 28,239.61	3
1790—March 31	...	60,613,14	60,613.14	3
1790—June 30	...	155,320.23	155,320.23	3
1790—September 30	...	349,670.23	349,670.23	3
1790—December 31	...	570,023.80	570,023.80	3
1791—June 30	$10,490.54	571,699.00	582,189.54	3
1791—September 30	...	679,579.99	679,579.99	4
1791—December 31	...	973,905.75	973,905.75	6
1792—March 31	...	751,377.34	751,377.34	6
1792—June 30	...	623,133.61	623,133.61	9
1792—September 30	...	420,914.51	420,914.51	9
1792—December 31	232.14	783,212.37	783,444.51	8
1793—March 31	...	1,035,973.09	1,035,973.09	8
1793—June 30	...	561,435.33	561,435.33	8
1793—December 31	...	753,661.69	753,661.69	8
1794—December 31	...	1,151,924.17	1,151,924.17	8
1795—December 31	...	516,442.61	516,442.61	8
1796—December 31	...	888,995.42	888,995.42	8
1797—December 31	...	1,021,899.04	1,021,899.04	8
1798—December 31	...	617,451.43	617,451.43	8
1799—December 31	...	2,161,867.77	2,161,867.77	8
1800—December 31	...	2,623,311.99	2,623,311.99	8
1801—December 31	...	3,295,391.00	3,295,391.00	8
1802—December 31	...	5,020,697.64	5,020,697.64	8
1803—December 31	...	4,825,611.60	4,825,611.60	14
1804—December 31	...	4,037,005.26	4,037,005.26	16
1805—December 31	...	3,999,388.99	3,999,388,99	15
1806—December 31	...	4,538,123.80	4,538,123,80	15
1807—December 31	...	9,643,850.07	9,643,850.07	15
1808—December 31	...	9,941,809.96	9,941,809.96	15
1809—December 31	...	3,848,056.78	3,848,056.78	15
1810—December 31	...	2,672,296.57	2,672,296.57	15
1811—December 31	...	3,502,305.80	3,502,305.80	15

[a] U.S., Treasury Dept., *Annual Report of the Secretary, 1918,* pp. 620–622. The figures relative to Appendix II since 1918 are not now available for preparing the table since that date. Division of Research, Treasury Department, Washington, D.C. A statement to this effect was made by Miss Marion Banister, Assistant Treasurer, in a letter to the author dated May 27, 1941.

Dates	In Treasury Offices	In Depository Banks	* Total	Number of Depository Banks
1812—December 31	...	$ 3,862,217.41	$ 3,862,217.41	15
1813—December 31	...	5,196,542.00	5,196,542.00	15
1814—December 31	...	1,727,848.63	1,727,848.63	15
1815—December 31	...	13,106,592.88	13,106,592.88	15
1816—December 31	...	22,033,519.19	22,033,519.19	94
1817—December 31	...	14,989,465.48	14,989,465.48	94
1818—December 31	...	1,478,526.74	1,478,526.74	29
1819—December 31	...	2,079,992.38	2,079,992.38	29
1820—December 31	...	1,198,461.21	1,198,461.21	29
1821—December 31	...	1,681,592.24	1,681,592.24	29
1822—December 31	...	4,193,690.68	4,193,690.68	58
1823—December 31	...	9,431,333.20	9,431,333.20	55
1824—December 31	...	1,887,799.80	1,887,799.80	58
1825—December 31	...	5,296,306.74	5,296,306.74	60
1826—December 31	...	6,342,289.48	6,342,289.48	56
1827—December 31	...	6,649,604.31	6,649,604.31	56
1828—December 31	...	5,965,974.27	5,965,974.27	59
1829—December 31	...	4,362,770.76	4,362,770.76	40
1830—December 31	...	4,761,409.34	4,761,409.34	40
1831—December 31	...	3,053,513.24	3,053,513.24	50
1832—December 31	...	911,863.16	911,863.16	41
1833—December 31	...	10,658,283.61	10,658,283.61	62
1834—December 31	...	7,861,093.60	7,861,093.60	24
1835—December 31	...	25,729,315.72	25,729,315.72	44
1836—December 31	$ 700,000.00	45,056,833.54	45,756,833.54	91
1837—December 31	1,025,610.63	5,779,343.01	6,804,953.64	54
1838—December 31	1,268,827.62	5,364,887.61	6,633,715.23	43
1839—December 31	691,097.04	3,992,319.44	4,683,416.48	27
1840—December 31	1,414,029.62	290,532.18	1,704,561.80	11
1841—December 31	205,330.74	170,361.73	375,692.47	19
1842—December 31	380,199.04	1,699,709.09	2,079,908.13	26
1843—June 30	669,889.11	10,525,267.10	11,195,156.21	30
1844—June 30	390,199.04	8,222,651.19	8,612,850.23	34
1845—June 30	725,199.04	7,385,450.82	8,110,649.86	43
1846—June 30	768,000.00	8,915,869.83	9,683,869.83	49
1847—June 30	5,446,382.16	...	5,446,382.16	49
1848—June 30	758,332.15	...	758,332.15	
1849—June 30	3,208,822.43	...	3,208,822.43	
1850—June 30	7,431,022.72	...	7,431,022.72	
1851—June 30	12,142,193.97	...	12,142,193.97	
1852—June 30	15,097,880.36	...	15,097,880.36	
1853—June 30	22,286,462.49	...	22,286,462.49	
1854—June 30	20,300,636.61	...	20,300,636.61	
1855—June 30	19,529,841.06	...	19,529,841.06	
1856—June 30	20,304,844.78	...	20,304,844.78	
1857—June 30	18,218,770.40	...	18,218,770.40	
1858—June 30	6,698,157.91	...	6,698,157.91	
1859—June 30	4,685,625.04	...	4,685,625.04	
1860—June 30	3,931,287.72	...	3,931,287.72	
1861—June 30	2,005,285.24	...	2,005,285.24	
1862—June 30	18,265,984.84	...	18,265,984.84	

Dates	In Treasury Offices	In Depository Banks	Total	Number of Depository Banks
1863—June 30	$ 8,395,443.73	...	$ 8,395,443.73	
1864—June 30	72,022,019.71	$ 39,980,756.39	112,002,776.10	204
1865—June 30	2,374,744.10	24,066,186.19	26,440,930.29	330
1866—June 30	78,352,599.12	34,124,171.54	112,476,770.66	382
1867—June 30	135,270,243.53	25,904,930.78	161,175,174.31	385
1868—June 30	92,353,732.90	22,779,797.62	115,133,529.82	370
1869—June 30	117,944,915.43	8,597,927.34	126,542,842.77	276
1870—June 30	105,279,800.67	8,206,180.34	113,485,981.01	148
1871—June 30	84,819,993.41	6,919,745.59	91,739,739.00	159
1872—June 30	61,935,763.46	12,501,595.08	74,437,358.54	163
1873—June 30	52,528,793.53	7,233,551.11	59,762,346.64	158
1874—June 30	64,723,630.48	7,435,966.69	72,159,597.17	154
1875—June 30	51,712,042.19	11,562,679.52	63,274,721.71	145
1876—June 30	51,427,414.23	7,520,194.76	58,947,608.99	143
1877—June 30	84,394,007.01	7,299,999.28	91,694,006.29	145
1878—June 30	130,570,578.15	46,928,268.56	177,498,846.71	124
1879—June 30	159,020,734.90	208,033,840.24	367,054,575.14	127
1880—June 30	160,528,170.50	7,771,233.90	168,299,404.40	131
1881—June 30	173,974,146.61	8,704,830.83	182,678,977.44	130
1882—June 30	152,941,618.24	9,381,712.90	162,323,331.14	134
1883—June 30	151,579,255.91	9,803,381.79	161,382,637.70	140
1884—June 30	154,557,552.96	10,488,827.63	165,046,380.59	135
1885—June 30	171,851,780.21	10,770,579.96	182,622,360.17	132
1886—June 30	218,277,107.25	13,822,070.80	232,099,178.05	160
1887—June 30	188,625,383.03	18,975,315.41	207,600,698.44	200
1888—June 30	189,395,440.65	54,698,728.36	244,094,169.01	290
1889—June 30	167,646,333.23	43,090,750.53	210,737,083.76	270
1890—June 30	164,061,481.40	26,779,703.32	190,841,184.72	205
1891—June 30	135,448,137.33	21,399,689.16	156,847,826.49	185
1892—June 30	118,728,662.52	10,450,130.01	129,178,792.53	159
1893—June 30	114,862,278.94	9,962,526.00	124,824,804.94	160
1894—June 30	108,462,220.55	10,423,767.61	118,885,988.16	155
1895—June 30	185,369,687.37	10,978,505.80	196,348,193.17	160
1896—June 30	258,221,832.65	11,415,474.42	269,637,307.07	160
1897—June 30	232,304,043.90	12,162,158.05	244,466,201.95	168
1898—June 30	175,438,942.32	33,843,700.81	209,282,643.13	172
1899—June 30	214,193,189.26	70,295,326.94	284,488,516.20	357
1900—June 30	214,206,233.65	92,621,371.72	306,827,605.37	442
1901—June 30	234,964,115.04	93,442,683.09	328,406,798.13	448
1902—June 30	245,045,797.03	117,141,564.13	362,187,361.16	577
1903—June 30	248,685,097.53	140,001,016.70	388,686,114.23	713
1904—June 30	217,591,929.57	104,459,638.45	322,051,568.02	842
1905—June 30	230,674,025.59	64,803,466.30	295,477,491.89	837
1906—June 30	249,958,296.77	80,731,058.05	330,689,354.82	928
1907—June 30	255,257,493.51	166,803,951.96	422,061,445.47	1255
1908—June 30	247,479,310.94	147,692,036.79	395,171,347.73	1436
1909—June 30	215,947,902.41	60,427,525.69	276,375,428.10	1414
1910—June 30	216,263,086.09	40,631,589.58	256,894,675.67	1380
1911—June 30	254,128,166.75	36,048,759.38	290,176,926.13	1362
1912—June 30	279,239,692.85	37,912,786.14	317,152,478,99	1353
1913—June 30	246,214,851.64	69,746,133.15	315,960,984.79	1535

Dates	In Treasury Offices	In Depository Banks	Total	Number of Depository Banks
1914—June 30	$234,941,577.40	$ 76,671,038.13	$ 311,612,615.53	1584
1915—June 30	178,481,503.73	78,665,638.68	257,147,142.41	1491
1916—June 30	184,524,331.24	146,946,109.97	331,470,441.21	1381
1917—June 30	152,979,025.63	967,247,123.48	1,120,226,149.11	3402
1918—June 30	152,979,025.63	623,774,518.85	776,753,544.48	7962

APPENDIX III

Receipts and Expenditures for the Fiscal Years 1789–1941 [a]

Year	Total Ordinary Receipts	Total Expenditures Chargeable against Ordinary Receipts	Surplus (+) or Deficit (−) of Ordinary Receipts over Expenditures Chargeable against Ordinary Receipts
1789–91 December 31	$4,418,931	$4,269,027	+$149,886
1792 December 31	3,669,960	5,079,532	−1,409,572
1793 December 31	4,652,923	4,482,313	+170,610
1794 December 31	5,431,905	6,990,839	−1,558,934
1795 December 31	6,114,534	7,539,809	−1,425,275
1796 December 31	8,377,530	5,726,986	+2,650,544
1797 December 31	8,688,781	6,133,634	+2,555,147
1798 December 31	7,900,496	7,676,504	+223,992
1799 December 31	7,546,813	9,666,455	−2,119,642
1800 December 31	10,848,749	10,786,075	+62,674
1801 December 31	12,935,331	9,394,582	+3,540,749
1802 December 31	14,995,794	7,862,118	+7,133,676
1803 December 31	11,064,098	7,851,653	+3,212,445
1804 December 31	11,826,307	8,719,442	+3,106,865
1805 December 31	13,560,693	10,506,234	+3,054,459
1806 December 31	15,559,931	9,803,617	+5,756,314
1807 December 31	16,398,019	8,354,151	+8,043,868
1808 December 31	17,060,662	9,932,492	+7,128,170
1809 December 31	7,773,473	10,280,748	−2,507,275
1810 December 31	9,384,215	8,156,510	+1,227,705
1811 December 31	14,423,529	8,058,337	+6,365,192
1812 December 31	9,801,133	20,280,771	−10,479,638
1813 December 31	14,340,410	31,681,852	−17,341,442
1814 December 31	11,181,625	34,720,926	−23,539,301
1815 December 31	15,729,024	32,708,139	−16,979,115
1816 December 31	47,677,671	30,586,691	+17,090,980
1817 December 31	33,099,050	21,843,820	+11,255,230
1818 December 31	21,585,171	19,825,121	+1,760,050

[a] U.S., Treasury Dept., *Annual Report of the Secretary, 1941*, pp. 412–417.

Year	Total Ordinary Receipts	Total Expenditures Chargeable against Ordinary Receipts	Surplus (+) or Deficit (—) of Ordinary Receipts over Expenditures Chargeable against Ordinary Receipts
1819 December 31	$24,603,375	$21,463,810	+$3,139,565
1820 December 31	17,880,670	18,260,627	—379,957
1821 December 31	14,573,380	15,810,753	+1,237,373
1822 December 31	20,232,428	15,000,220	+5,232,208
1823 December 31	20,540,666	14,706,840	+5,833,826
1824 December 31	19,381,213	20,326,708	—945,495
1825 December 31	21,840,858	15,857,229	+5,983,629
1826 December 31	25,260,434	17,035,797	+8,224,637
1827 December 31	22,966,364	16,139,168	+6,827,196
1828 December 31	24,763,630	16,394,843	+8,368,787
1829 December 31	24,827,627	15,203,333	+9,624,294
1830 December 31	24,844,116	15,143,066	+9,701,050
1831 December 31	28,526,821	15,247,651	+13,279,170
1832 December 31	31,865,561	17,288,950	+14,576,611
1833 December 31	33,948,427	23,017,552	+10,930,875
1834 December 31	21,791,936	18,627,569	+3,164,367
1835 December 31	35,430,087	17,572,813	+17,857,274
1836 December 31	50,826,796	30,868,164	+19,958,632
1837 December 31	24,954,153	37,243,496	—12,289,343
1838 December 31	26,302,562	33,865,059	—7,562,497
1839 December 31	31,482,749	26,899,128	+4,583,621
1840 December 31	19,480,115	24,317,579	—4,837,464
1841 December 31	16,860,160	26,565,873	—9,705,713
1842 December 31	19,976,198	25,205,761	—5,229,563
1843 January 1– June 30	8,302,702	11,858,075	—3,555,373
1844 June 30	29,321,374	22,337,571	+6,983,803
1845 June 30	29,970,106	22,937,408	+7,032,698
1846 June 30	29,699,967	27,766,925	+1,933,042
1847 June 30	26,495,769	57,281,412	—30,785,643
1848 June 30	35,735,779	45,377,226	—9,641,447
1849 June 30	31,208,143	45,051,657	—13,843,514
1850 June 30	43,603,439	39,543,492	+4,059,947
1851 June 30	52,559,304	47,709,017	+4,850,287
1852 June 30	49,846,816	44,194,919	+5,651,897
1853 June 30	61,587,054	48,184,111	+13,402,943
1854 June 30	73,800,341	58,044,862	+15,755,479
1855 June 30	65,350,575	59,742,668	+5,607,907
1856 June 30	74,056,699	69,571,026	+4,485,673

Year	Total Ordinary Receipts	Total Expenditures Chargeable against Ordinary Receipts	Surplus (+) or Deficit (—) of Ordinary Receipts over Expenditures Chargeable against Ordinary Receipts
1857 June 30	$ 68,965,313	$ 67,795,708	+$1,169,605
1858 June 30	46,655,366	74,185,270	—27,529,904
1859 June 30	53,486,465	69,070,977	—15,584,512
1860 June 30	56,064,608	63,130,598	—7,065,990
1861 June 30	41,509,931	66,546,645	—25,036,714
1862 June 30	51,987,456	474,761,819	—422,774,363
1863 June 30	112,163,790	714,740,725	—602,043,434
1864 June 30	264,626,771	865,322,642	—600,695,871
1865 June 30	333,714,605	1,297,555,224	—963,840,619
1866 June 30	558,032,620	520,809,417	+37,223,203
1867 June 30	490,634,010	357,542,675	+133,091,335
1868 June 30	405,638,083	377,340,285	+28,297,798
1869 June 30	370,943,747	322,865,278	+48,078,469
1870 June 30	411,255,477	309,653,561	+101,601,916
1871 June 30	383,325,945	292,177,188	+91,146,757
1872 June 30	374,106,868	277,517,963	+96,588,905
1873 June 30	333,738,205	290,345,245	+43,392,960
1874 June 30	304,978,756	302,633,873	+$2,344,883
1875 June 30	288,000,051	274,623,393	+13,376,658
1876 June 30	294,095,865	265,101,085	+28,994,780
1877 June 30	281,406,419	241,334,475	+40,071,944
1878 June 30	257,763,879	236,964,327	+20,799,522
1879 June 30	273,827,185	266,947,884	+6,879,301
1880 June 30	333,526,611	267,642,958	+65,883,653
1881 June 30	360,782,293	260,712,888	+100,069,405
1882 June 30	403,525,250	257,981,440	+145,543,810
1883 June 30	398,287,582	265,408,138	+132,879,444
1884 June 30	348,519,870	244,126,244	+104,393,626
1885 June 30	323,690,706	260,226,935	+63,463,771
1886 June 30	336,439,726	242,483,139	+93,956,587
1887 June 30	371,403,277	267,932,181	+103,471,096
1888 June 30	379,266,075	267,924,801	+111,341,274
1889 June 30	387,050,059	299,288,978	+87,761,081
1890 June 30	403,080,984	318,040,711	+85,040,273
1891 June 30	392,612,447	365,773,904	+26,838,543
1892 June 30	354,937,784	345,023,331	+9,914,453
1893 June 30	385,819,629	383,477,953	+2,341,676
1894 June 30	306,355,316	367,525,281	—61,169,965
1895 June 30	324,729,419	356,195,298	—31,465,879

Year	Total Ordinary Receipts	Total Expenditures Chargeable against Ordinary Receipts	Surplus (+) or Deficit (—) of Ordinary Receipts over Expenditures Chargeable against Ordinary Receipts
1896 June 30	$338,142,447	$352,179,446	—$14,036,999
1897 June 30	347,721,705	365,774,159	—18,052,454
1898 June 30	405,321,335	443,368,583	—38,047,248
1899 June 30	515,960,621	605,072,179	—89,111,558
1900 June 30	567,240,852	520,860,847	+46,380,005
1901 June 30	587,685,338	524,616,925	+63,068,413
1902 June 30	562,478,233	485,234,249	+77,243,984
1903 June 30	561,880,722	517,006,127	+44,874,595
1904 June 30	541,087,085	583,659,900	—42,572,815
1905 June 30	544,274,685	567,278,914	—23,004,229
1906 June 30	594,984,446	570,202,278	+24,782,168
1907 June 30	665,860,386	579,128,842	+86,731,544
1908 June 30	601,861,907	659,196,320	—57,334,413
1909 June 30	604,320,498	693,743,885	—89,423,387
1910 June 30	675,511,715	693,617,065	—18,105,350
1911 June 30	701,832,911	691,201,512	+10,631,399
1912 June 30	692,609,204	689,881,334	+2,727,870
1913 June 30	724,111,230	724,511,963	—400,733
1914 June 30	734,673,167	735,081,431	—408,264
1915 June 30	697,910,827	760,586,802	—62,675,975
1916 June 30	782,534,548	734,056,202	+48,478,346
1917 June 30	1,124,324,795	1,977,681,751	—853,356,956
1918 June 30	3,664,582,865	12,697,836,705	—9,933,253,840
1919 June 30	5,152,257,136	18,522,894,705	—13,370,637,569
1920 June 30	6,694,565,389	6,482,090,191	+212,475,198
1921 June 30	5,624,932,961	5,538,209,190	+86,723,772
1922 June 30	4,109,104,151	3,795,302,500	+313,801,651
1923 June 30	4,007,135,481	3,697,478,020	+309,657,461
1924 June 30	4,012,044,702	3,506,677,715	+505,366,987
1925 June 30	3,780,148,685	3,529,643,446	+250,505,239
1926 June 30	3,962,755,690	3,584,987,874	+377,767,816
1927 June 30	4,129,394,441	3,493,584,519	+635,809,921
1928 June 30	4,042,348,156	3,643,519,875	+398,828,281
1929 June 30	4,033,250,225	3,848,463,190	+184,787,035
1930 June 30	4,177,941,702	3,994,152,487	+183,789,215
1931 June 30	3,189,638,632	4,091,597,712	—901,959,080
1932 June 30	2,005,725,437	4,947,776,888	—2,942,051,451
1933 June 30	2,079,696,742	4,325,149,722	—2,245,452,980
1934 June 30	3,115,554,050	6,370,947,347	—3,255,393,297

Year	Total Ordinary Receipts	Total Expenditures Chargeable against Ordinary Receipts	Surplus (+) or Deficit (—) of Ordinary Receipts over Expenditures Chargeable against Ordinary Receipts
1935 June 30	$3,800,467,202	$7,583,433,562	—$3,782,966,360
1936 June 30	4,115,956,615	9,068,885,572	—4,952,928,957
1937 June 30	5,028,840,237	8,281,379,956	—3,252,539,719
1938 June 30	5,854,661,227	7,304,287,108	—1,449,625,881
1939 June 30	5,164,823,626	8,765,338,031	—3,600,514,405
1940 June 30	5,387,124,670	9,127,373,806	—3,740,249,136
1941 June 30	7,607,211,852	12,774,890,324	—5,167,678,472

APPENDIX IV

Customs Receipts [a] 1789–1941

Year		Amount	Year		Amount	Year		Amount
1789–91	Dec. 31	$4,399,473	1841	Dec. 31	$14,487,217	1891	June 30	$219,522,205
1792	Dec. 31	3,443,071	1842	Dec. 31	18,187,909	1892	June 30	177,452,964
1793	Dec. 31	4,255,307	1843	June 30	7,046,844	1893	June 30	203,355,017
1794	Dec. 31	4,801,065	1844	June 30	26,183,571	1894	June 30	131,818,531
1795	Dec. 31	5,588,461	1845	June 30	27,528,113	1895	June 30	152,158,617
1796	Dec. 31	6,567,988	1846	June 30	26,712,668	1896	June 30	160,021,752
1797	Dec. 31	7,549,650	1847	June 30	23,747,865	1897	June 30	176,554,127
1798	Dec. 31	7,106,062	1848	June 30	31,757,071	1898	June 30	149,575,062
1799	Dec. 31	6,610,449	1849	June 30	28,346,739	1899	June 30	206,128,482
1800	Dec. 31	9,080,933	1850	June 30	39,668,686	1900	June 30	233,164,871
1801	Dec. 31	10,750,779	1851	June 30	49,017,568	1901	June 30	238,585,456
1802	Dec. 31	12,438,236	1852	June 30	47,339,327	1902	June 30	254,444,708
1803	Dec. 31	10,479,418	1853	June 30	58,931,866	1903	June 30	284,479,582
1804	Dec. 31	11,098,565	1854	June 30	64,224,190	1904	June 30	261,274,565
1805	Dec. 31	12,936,487	1855	June 30	58,025,794	1905	June 30	261,798,857
1806	Dec. 31	14,667,698	1856	June 30	64,022,863	1906	June 30	300,251,878
1807	Dec. 31	15,845,522	1857	June 30	63,875,905	1907	June 30	332,233,363
1808	Dec. 31	16,363,551	1858	June 30	41,789,621	1908	June 30	286,113,130
1809	Dec. 31	7,296,021	1859	June 30	49,565,824	1909	June 30	300,711,934
1810	Dec. 31	8,583,309	1860	June 30	53,187,512	1910	June 30	333,683,445
1811	Dec. 31	13,313,223	1861	June 30	39,582,126	1911	June 30	314,497,071
1812	Dec. 31	8,958,778	1862	June 30	49,056,398	1912	June 30	311,321,672
1813	Dec. 31	13,224,623	1863	June 30	69,059,642	1913	June 30	318,891,396
1814	Dec. 31	5,998,772	1864	June 30	102,316,153	1914	June 30	292,320,014

Year	Date	Amount	Year	Date	Amount	Year	Date	Amount
1815	Dec. 31	7,282,942	1865	June 30	84,928,261	1915	June 30	209,786,672
1816	Dec. 31	36,306,875	1866	June 30	179,046,652	1916	June 30	213,185,846
1817	Dec. 31	26,283,348	1867	June 30	176,417,811	1917	June 30	225,962,393
1818	Dec. 31	17,176,385	1868	June 30	164,464,600	1918	June 30	179,998,385
1819	Dec. 31	20,283,609	1869	June 30	180,048,427	1919	June 30	184,457,867
1820	Dec. 31	15,005,612	1870	June 30	194,538,374	1920	June 30	322,902,650
1821	Dec. 31	13,004,447	1871	June 30	206,270,408	1921	June 30	308,564,391
1822	Dec. 31	17,589,762	1872	June 30	216,370,287	1922	June 30	365,443,387
1823	Dec. 31	19,088,433	1873	June 30	188,089,523	1923	June 30	561,928,867
1824	Dec. 31	17,878,326	1874	June 30	163,103,834	1924	June 30	545,637,504
1825	Dec. 31	20,098,713	1875	June 30	157,167,722	1925	June 30	547,561,226
1826	Dec. 31	23,341,332	1876	June 30	148,071,985	1926	June 30	579,430,093
1827	Dec. 31	19,712,283	1877	June 30	130,956,493	1927	June 30	605,499,983
1828	Dec. 31	23,205,524	1878	June 30	130,170,680	1928	June 30	568,986,188
1829	Dec. 31	22,681,966	1879	June 30	137,250,048	1929	June 30	602,262,786
1830	Dec. 31	21,922,391	1880	June 30	186,522,064	1930	June 30	587,000,903
1831	Dec. 31	24,224,442	1881	June 30	198,159,676	1931	June 30	378,354,005
1832	Dec. 31	28,465,237	1882	June 30	220,410,730	1932	June 30	327,754,969 b
1833	Dec. 31	29,032,509	1883	June 30	214,706,497	1933	June 30	250,750,251
1834	Dec. 31	16,214,957	1884	June 30	195,067,490	1934	June 30	313,434,302
1835	Dec. 31	19,391,311	1885	June 30	181,471,939	1935	June 30	343,335,054
1836	Dec. 31	23,409,941	1886	June 30	192,905,023	1936	June 30	386,811,954
1837	Dec. 31	11,169,290	1887	June 30	217,286,893	1937	June 30	486,356,599
1838	Dec. 31	16,158,800	1888	June 30	219,091,174	1938	June 30	359,187,249
1839	Dec. 31	23,137,925	1889	June 30	223,832,742	1939	June 30	318,837,311
1840	Dec. 31	13,499,502	1890	June 30	229,668,585	1940	June 30	348,590,636
						1941	June 30	391,870,013

a U.S., Treasury Dept., *Annual Report of the Secretary, 1941*, pp. 414-416.
b Beginning with the fiscal year 1932, tonnage tax has been covered into the Treasury as miscellaneous receipts.

APPENDIX V

Public Debt, Interest Paid on Public Debt, Public Debt Retired
1789–1941

Year	Amount of Public Debt [a]	Interest on the Public Debt [b]	Total Public Debt Retirements Chargeable against Public Debt Receipts and Surplus Revenue [c]
Dec. 30, 1791	$77,227,924	$2,349,437	$2,938,512
1792	80,358,634	3,201,629	4,062,038
1793	78,427,404	2,772,242	3,047,263
1794	80,747,587	3,490,293	2,311,286
1795	83,762,172	3,189,151	2,985,260
1796	82,064,479	3,195,055	2,640,792
1797	79,228,529	3,300,043	2,492,379
1798	78,408,669	3,053,281	937,013
1799	82,976,294	3,186,288	1,410,589
1800	83,976,294	3,374,705	1,203,665
1801	80,712,632	4,412,913	2,878,794
1802	77,054,686	4,125,039	5,413,966
1803	86,427,120	3,848,828	3,407,331
1804	82,312,150	4,266,583	3,905,205
1805	75,723,270	4,148,999	3,220,891
1806	69,218,398	3,723,408	5,266,477
1807	65,196,317	3,369,578	2,938,142
1808	57,023,192	3,428,153	6,832,092
1809	53,173,217	2,866,075	3,586,479
1810	48,005,587	2,845,428	5,163,477
1811	45,209,737	2,465,733	5,543,471

[a] Figures from 1791 to 1857 were taken from the U.S., Treasury Dept., *Annual Report of the Secretary, 1900*, p. xcix. Figures from 1858 to 1941 were taken from the U.S., Treasury Dept., *Annual Report of the Secretary, 1941*, pp. 417, 550–551.

[b] *Annual Report of the Secretary, 1940*, pp. 646, 647, 648, 649.

[c] Figures from 1791 to 1931 were taken from the U.S., Treasury Dept., *Annual Report of the Secretary, 1931*, p. 457. Figures from 1932 to 1941 were computed by the Assistant Commissioner of Accounts, of the Treasury Dept., for the author.

Year	Amount of Public Debt	Interest on the Public Debt	Total Public Debt Retirements Chargeable against Public Debt Receipts and Surplus Revenue
Dec. 30, 1812	$55,962,827	$2,451,273	$1,998,350
1813	81,487,846	3,599,455	7,505,668
1814	99,833,660	4,593,239	3,307,305
1815	127,334,933	5,754,469	6,874,354
1816	123,491,965	7,213,259	17,657,804
1817	103,466,633	6,389,210	19,041,826
1818	95,529,648	6,016,447	15,279,755
1819	91,015,566	5,163,538	2,540,388
1820	89,987,427	5,126,097	3,502,397
1821	93,546,676	5,087,274	3,279,822
1822	90,875,877	5,172,578	2,676,371
1823	90,269,777	4,922,685	607,332
1824	83,788,432	4,996,562	11,571,832
1825	81,054,059	4,366,769	7,728,576
1826	73,987,357	3,973,481	7,067,602
1827	67,475,043	3,486,072	6,517,597
1828	58,421,413	3,098,801	9,064,637
1829	48,565,406	2,542,843	9,841,025
1830	39,123,191	1,913,533	9,442,215
1831	24,322,235	1,383,583	14,790,795
1832	7,001,698	772,562	17,067,748
1833	4,760,082	303,797	1,239,747
1834	33,733	202,153	5,974,412
1835	37,513	57,863	328
1836	336,957	. . .	. . .
1837	3,308,124	. . .	21,823
1838	10,434,221	14,997	5,590,724
1839	3,575,343	399,834	10,718,154
1840	5,250,875	174,598	3,912,016
1841	13,594,480	284,978	5,315,712
1842	20,201,226	773,550	7,801,990
June 30, 1843	32,742,922	523,595	338,013
1844	23,461,652	1,833,867	11,158,451
1845	15,925,303	1,040,932	7,536,349
1846	15,550,202	842,723	375,100
1847	38,826,534	1,119,215	5,596,068
1848	47,044,862	2,390,825	13,038,373
1849	63,061,858	3,565,578	12,804,829
1850	63,452,773	3,782,331	3,655,035

Year	Amount of Public Debt	Interest on the Public Debt	Total Public Debt Retirements Chargeable against Public Debt Receipts and Surplus Revenue
June 30, 1851	$68,304,796	$3,696,721	$ 654,951
1852	66,199,341	4,000,298	2,151,754
1853	59,804,661	3,665,833	6,412,574
1854	42,243,765	3,071,017	17,574,145
1855	35,588,499	2,314,375	6,656,066
1856	31,974,081	1,953,822	3,614,619
1857	28,701,375	1,678,265	3,276,606
1858	44,913,424	1,567,056	7,505,251
1859	58,498,381	2,638,464	14,702,543
1860	64,843,831	3,177,315	14,431,350
1861	90,582,417	4,000,174	18,142,900
1862	524,177,955	13,190,325	96,096,922
1863	1,119,773,681	24,729,847	181,086,635
1864	1,815,830,814	53,685,422	384,793,665
1865	2,677,929,012	77,397,712	591,785,660
1866	2,755,763,929	133,067,742	514,094,370
1867	2,650,168,223	143,781,592	558,279,011
1868	2,583,446,456	140,424,046	583,783,439
1869	2,545,110,590	130,694,243	115,460,526
1870	2,436,453,269	129,235,498	117,775,308
1871	2,322,052,141	125,576,566	178,630,961
1872	2,209,990,838	117,357,840	257,708,218
1873	2,151,210,345	104,750,688	65,063,994
1874	2,159,932,730	107,119,815	137,445,005
1875	2,156,276,649	103,093,545	125,450,502
1876	2,130,845,778	100,243,271	162,077,302
1877	2,107,759,903	97,124,512	176,290,280
1878	2,159,418,315	102,500,875	156,007,870
1879	2,298,912,643	105,327,949	487,938,927
1880	2,090,908,872	95,757,575	286,836,853
1881	2,019,285,728	82,508,741	98,455,380
1882	1,856,915,644	71,077,207	183,313,863
1883	1,721,958,918	59,160,131	461,983,037
1884	1,625,307,444	54,578,379	128,124,025
1885	1,578,551,169	51,386,256	74,504,860
1886	1,555,659,550	50,580,146	74,141,431
1887	1,465,485,294	47,741,577	165,327,657
1888	1,384,631,656	44,715,007	125,026,170
1889	1,249,470,511	41,001,484	167,674,910

Year	Amount of Public Debt	Interest on the Public Debt	Total Public Debt Retirements Chargeable against Public Debt Receipts and Surplus Revenue
June 30, 1890	$1,122,396,584	$36,099,284	$138,297,689
1891	1,005,806,561	37,547,135	126,332,084
1892	968,218,841	23,378,116	40,580,808
1893	961,431,766	27,264,392	9,747,555
1894	1,016,897,817	27,841,406	11,185,983
1895	1,096,913,120	30,978,030	15,562,919
1896	1,222,729,350	35,385,029	18,517,253
1897	1,226,793,713	37,791,110	22,470,858
1898	1,232,743,063	37,585,056	45,932,522
1899	1,436,700,704	39,896,925	31,271,639
1900	1,263,416,913	40,160,333	40,699,851
1901	1,221,572,245	32,342,979	54,749,237
1902	1,178,031,357	29,108,045	76,309,193
1903	1,159,405,913	28,556,349	42,880,919
1904	1,136,259,016	24,646,490	49,559,702
1905	1,132,357,095	24,590,944	26,462,599
1906	1,142,522,970	24,308,576	24,968,847
1907	1,147,178,193	24,481,158	55,827,298
1908	1,177,690,403	21,426,138	73,891,907
1909	1,148,315,372	21,803,836	104,996,770
1910	1,146,939,969	21,342,979	33,049,696
1911	1,153,984,937	21,311,334	35,223,336
1912	1,193,838,505	22,616,300	28,648,328
1913	1,193,047,745	22,899,108	24,191,611
1914	1,188,235,400	22,863,957	26,961,327
1915	1,191,264,068	22,902,897	17,253,491
1916	1,225,145,568	22,900,869	24,668,914
1917	2,975,618,585	24,742,702	677,544,783
1918	12,243,628,719	189,743,277	7,806,879,075
1919	25,482,034,419	619,215,569	15,837,566,010
1920	24,297,918,412	1,020,251,622	17,036,444,272
1921	23,976,250,608	999,144,731	8,759,212,164
1922	22,964,079,190	991,000,759	6,607,836,513
1923	22,349,687,758	1,055,923,690	7,561,162,070
1924	21,251,120,427	940,602,913	2,847,802,415
1925	20,516,272,174	881,806,662	3,420,773,791
1926	19,643,183,079	831,937,700	3,394,070,467
1927	18,510,174,266	787,019,578	5,798,528,112
1928	17,604,290,563	731,764,476	7,220,978,399

Year	Amount of Public Debt	Interest on the Public Debt	Total Public Debt Retirements Chargeable against Public Debt Receipts and Surplus Revenue
June 30, 1929	$16,931,197,748	$678,330,400	$5,317,830,844
1930	16,185,308,299	659,347,613	3,914,976,016
1931	16,801,485,143	611,559,704	5,516,858,677
1932	19,487,009,766	599,276,631	6,536,071,584
1933	22,538,672,164	689,364,106	6,183,815,625
1934	27,053,085,988	756,617,127	8,708,648,497
1935	28,701,167,092	820,926,353	10,904,152,952
1936	33,545,384,622	749,396,802	8,873,168,693
1937	36,427,091,021	866,384,331	6,606,313,719
1938	37,167,487,451	926,280,714	8,815,338,536
1939	40,445,417,318	940,539,764	9,750,609,992
1940	42,971,043,956	1,040,935,697	10,508,671,945
1941	48,978,919,410	1,110,692,812	11,788,219,407

APPENDIX VI

Number of Colonial and State Banks from 1774 to 1872 [a]

Year	Number of Banks	Year	Number of Banks	Year	Number of Banks
1774	...	1816	246	1844	696
1784	3	1817	...	1845	707
1790	4	1818	27	1846	707
1791	6	1819	...	1847	715
1792	16	1820	307	1848	751
1793	17	1821	28	1849	782
1794	17	1822	33	1850	824
1795	23	1823	34	1851	879
1796	24	1824	37	1852	...
1797	25	1825	41	1853	750
1798	25	1826	55	1854	1,208
1799	26	1827	60	1855	1,307
1800	28	1828	108	1856	1,398
1801	31	1829	329	1857	1,416
1802	32	1830	329	1858	1,422
1803	36	1831	91	1859	1,476
1804	59	1832	172	1860	1,562
1805	75	1833	175	1861	1,601
1806	15	1834	506	1862	1,492
1807	16	1835	704	1863	1,466
1808	16	1836	713	1864	1,089
1809	29	1837	788	1865	349
1810	28	1838	829	1866	297
1811	88	1839	840	1867	272
1812	29	1840	901	1868	247
1813	...	1841	784	1869	259
1814	...	1842	692	1870	325
1815	208	1843	691	1871	452
				1872	566

[a] U.S., Comptroller of the Currency. *Annual Report, 1916,* Table 95, pp. 913, 914.

Money in Circulation, by Kinds, at the End of Each Fiscal Year, 1800–1940 [a]

(In thousands of dollars)

June 30	Estimated Bank Notes Outstanding	Estimated Specie in United States	Total Money in Circulation
1800	$10,500	$16,000	$26,500
1810	28,000	27,000	55,000
1820	44,800	22,300	67,100
1830	61,000	26,344	87,344
1831	77,000	26,045	103,045
1832	91,500	25,897	117,397
1833	91,500	28,638	120,138
1834	94,840	29,296	124,136
1835	103,692	42,108	145,800
1836	140,301	60,000	200,301
1837	149,186	68,000	217,186
1838	116,139	82,500	198,639
1839	135,171	84,533	219,704
1840	106,969	79,336	186,305
1841	107,290	79,013	186,303
1842	83,734	79,770	163,504
1843	58,564	88,550	147,114
1844	75,168	92,142	167,310
1845	89,609	88,341	177,950
1846	105,552	88,874	193,426
1847	105,520	118,299	223,819
1848	128,506	103,899	232,405
1849	114,743	117,815	232,558
1850	131,367	147,395	278,762
1851	155,165	175,089	330,254
1852	171,673	189,368	361,041
1853	188,181	214,057	402,238

[a] Figures from 1800 to 1859 were compiled from U.S., Treasury Dept., *"Information Respecting U.S. Bonds, Paper Currency and Coin, Production of Precious Metals, etc.,*" pp. 45–46. Figures from 1860 to 1912 were taken from U.S., Treasury Dept., *Annual Report of the Secretary, 1928*, pp. 554–555. Figures from 1913 to 1941 were taken from U.S., Treasury Dept., *Annual Report of the Secretary, 1941*, p. 627.

June 30	Estimated Bank Notes Outstanding	Estimated Specie in United States	Total Money in Circulation
1854	$204,689	$220,862	$425,551
1855	186,952	231,068	418,020
1856	195,748	230,099	425,847
1857	214,779	242,288	457,067
1858	155,208	253,602	408,810
1859	193,307	245,661	438,968

June 30	Gold Coin	Gold Certificates	Standard Silver Dollars	Silver Certificates	Treasury Notes of 1890	Subsidiary Silver
1860	$207,305	...	...	...	$207,102	$21,000
1861	266,400	...	...	...	202,006	16,000
1862	283,000	...	...	...	183,792	13,000
1863	260,000	...	...	...	238,677	11,000
1864	184,346	...	...	...	179,158	9,375
1865	148,557	...	...	...	142,920	8,713
1866	109,705	$10,505	...	...	19,996	8,241
1867	72,882	18,678	...	...	4,484	7,082
1868	63,758	17,643	...	...	3,164	6,520
1869	62,129	29,956	...	...	2,559	5,695
1870	81,183	32,085	...	...	2,223	8,978
1871	72,391	17,790	...	...	1,968	12,022
1872	76,575	26,412	...	...	1,701	12,064
1873	62,718	34,251	...	...	1,399	13,679
1874	78,948	18,015	...	...	1,162	14,940
1875	64,446	17,549	...	...	964	22,141
1876	74,839	24,175	...	...	1,047	26,055
1877	78,111	32,298	...	...	909	42,885
1878	84,740	24,898	$ 1,209	$ 7	806	58,918
1879	110,505	15,280	8,036	414	...	61,347
1880	225,696	7,964	20,111	5,790	...	48,512
1881	315,313	5,760	29,342	39,111	...	46,839
1882	358,251	5,029	32,404	54,506	...	46,380
1883	344,653	59,807	35,651	72,621	...	46,474
1884	340,624	71,147	40,690	96,427	...	45,661
1885	341,668	126,730	39,087	101,531	...	43,703
1886	358,220	76,044	552,669	88,116	...	46,174
1887	376,541	91,225	55,549	142,118	...	48,584
1888	391,114	121,095	45,527	200,760	...	50,362
1889	376,482	117,130	5,457	257,156	...	51,447
1890	374,259	130,831	56,279	297,556	*Treasury Notes of 1890*	54,033
1891	407,319	120,063	58,826	307,236	40,349	58,219
1892	408,569	141,094	56,817	326,693	98,259	63,294
1893	408,536	92,642	56,930	326,824	140,856	65,470
1894	495,977	66,340	52,565	326,991	134,681	58,511
1895	479,638	48,381	51,986	319,623	115,943	60,350
1896	454,905	42,198	52,117	330,657	95,045	60,204
1897	517,590	37,285	51,940	357,849	83,470	59,616
1898	657,950	35,812	58,483	390,127	98,306	64,057
1899	679,738	32,656	61,481	402,137	92,562	69,066

June 30	Minor Coin	United States Notes	Fractional Currency	Other United States Currency	National Bank Notes	Total Money in Circulation
1860	...	...	...	...	...	$ 435,407
1861	...	...	...	...	...	484,406
1862	...	$ 72,866	...	$53,040	...	605,698
1863	...	312,481	$15,884	93,230	...	931,274
1864	...	415,116	19,133	169,252	$31,235	1,007,615
1865	...	378,917	21,729	236,567	146,138	1,083,541
1866	...	327,792	24,687	162,739	276,013	939,678
1867	...	319,438	26,306	123,727	286,764	859,360
1868	...	328,572	28,999	28,859	294,369	771,884
1869	...	314,767	30,442	3,343	291,750	740,641
1870	...	324,963	34,379	2,507	288,648	774,966
1871	...	343,069	34,446	1,064	311,406	794,156
1872	...	346,169	36,403	849	329,037	829,209
1873	...	348,464	38,076	701	338,962	838,252
1874	...	371,421	38,234	620	340,266	863,606
1875	...	349,686	37,905	551	340,547	833,789
1876	...	331,447	32,939	500	316,121	807,124
1877	...	337,899	20,242	456	301,289	814,090
1878	...	320,906	16,368	428	311,724	820,004
1879	...	301,644	...	...	321,405	818,632
1880	...	327,895	...	...	337,415	973,382
1881	...	328,127	...	...	349,746	1,114,238
1882	...	325,255	...	...	352,465	1,174,290
1883	...	323,242	...	...	347,856	1,230,306
1884	...	318,687	...	...	330,690	1,243,926
1885	...	331,219	...	...	308,631	1,292,569
1886	...	323,813	...	...	307,665	1,252,701
1887	...	326,667	...	...	276,855	1,317,539
1888	...	308,000	...	...	245,313	1,372,171
1889	...	316,439	...	...	207,221	1,380,362
1890	...	334,689	...	...	181,605	1,429,251
1891	...	343,207	...	...	162,221	1,497,441
1892	...	339,400	...	...	167,222	1,601,347
1893	...	330,774	...	...	174,670	1,596,701
1894	...	325,525	...	...	200,220	1,660,809
1895	...	319,094	...	...	206,953	1,601,968
1896	...	256,140	...	...	215,168	1,506,435
1897	...	306,915	...	...	226,318	1,640,983
1898	...	310,134	...	...	222,991	1,837,860
1899	...	328,627	...	...	237,805	1,904,072

June 30	Gold Coin	Gold Certificates	Standard Silver Dollars	Silver Certificates	Treasury Notes of 1890	Subsidiary Silver
1900	$610,806	$200,733	$65,889	$408,466	$75,304	$76,161
1901	629,791	247,036	66,921	429,644	47,525	79,235
1902	632,394	306,399	68,747	446,558	29,803	85,721
1903	617,261	377,259	72,391	454,733	19,077	92,727
1904	645,818	465,655	71,314	461,139	12,902	95,528
1905	651,064	485,211	73,584	454,865	9,272	101,438
1906	668,655	516,562	77,001	471,520	7,337	111,630
1907	561,697	600,072	81,710	470,211	5,976	121,777
1908	613,245	782,977	76,329	465,279	4,964	124,178
1909	599,338	815,005	71,988	477,717	4,203	132,332
1910	590,878	802,754	72,433	478,597	3,663	135,584
1911	589,296	930,368	72,446	453,544	3,237	138,422
1912	610,724	943,436	70,340	469,224	2,916	145,034
1913	608,401	1,003,998	72,127	469,129	2,657	154,458
1914	611,545	1,026,149	70,300	478,602	2,428	159,966
1915	587,537	821,869	64,499	463,147	2,245	159,043
1916	624,939	1,050,266	66,234	476,279	2,098	171,178
1917	666,545	1,082,926	71,754	468,365	1,970	193,745
1918	537,230	511,190	77,201	370,349	1,851	216,492
1919	474,875	327,552	79,041	163,445	1,745	229,316
1920	474,822	259,007	76,749	97,606	1,656	248,863
1921	447,272	200,582	65,883	158,843	1,576	235,295
1922	415,937	173,342	57,973	265,335	1,510	229,310
1923	404,181	386,456	57,262	364,258	1,460	247,307
1924	393,330	801,381	54,015	364,414	1,423	252,995
1925	402,297	1,004,823	54,289	382,780	1,387	262,009
1926	391,703	1,057,371	51,577	377,741	1,356	270,072
1927	384,957	1,007,075	48,717	375,798	1,327	275,605
1928	377,028	1,019,149	46,222	384,577	1,304	278,175
1929	368,488	934,994	43,684	387,073	1,283	284,226
1930	357,236	994,841	38,629	386,915	1,260	281,231
1931	363,020	996,510	34,326	377,149	1,240	273,147
1932	452,763	715,683	30,115	352,605	1,222	256,220
1933	320,939	265,487	27,995	360,699	1,186	256,865
1934	(a)	149,740	30,013	401,456	1,189	280,400
1935	(a)	117,167	32,308	701,474	1,182	295,773
1936	(a)	100,771	35,029	954,592	1,177	316,476
1937	(a)	88,116	38,046	1,078,071	1,172	340,827
1938	(a)	78,500	39,446	1,230,156	1,169	341,942
1939	(a)	71,930	42,407	1,453,573	1,166	361,209
1940	(a)	66,793	46,020	1,581,662	1,163	384,187
1941	(a)	62,872	52,992	1,713,508	1,161	433,485

June 30	Minor Coin	United States Notes	Fractional Currency	Other United States Currency	National Bank Notes	Total Money in Circulation
1900	$26,080	$317,677	...	...	$300,115	$2,081,231
1901	27,890	330,045	...	...	345,111	2,203,198
1902	29,724	334,292	...	...	345,477	2,279,114
1903	32,040	334,249	...	...	399,997	2,399,732
1904	33,763	333,759	...	...	433,028	2,552,906
1905	35,458	332,421	...	...	480,029	2,623,340
1906	38,043	335,940	...	...	548,001	2,774,690
1907	40,907	342,270	...	...	589,242	2,813,863
1908	41,139	339,396	...	...	631,649	3,079,155
1909	42,585	340,118	...	...	665,539	3,148,826
			Federal Reserve Notes	*Federal Reserve Bank Notes*		
1910	46,328	334,778	...	...	683,660	3,148,684
1911	49,049	338,989	...	...	687,701	3,263,051
1912	50,707	337,697	...	...	705,142	3,335,220
1913	54,954	337,215	...	...	715,754	3,418,692
1914	57,419	337,846	...	...	715,180	3,459,434
1915	58,516	309,796	$ 70,810	...	782,120	3,319,582
1916	62,998	328,227	149,152	$ 1,683	716,204	3,649,258
1917	68,411	311,595	506,756	3,702	690,635	4,066,404
1918	74,958	291,859	1,698,190	10,970	691,407	4,481,697
1919	81,780	274,119	2,450,278	155,014	639,472	4,876,638
1920	90,958	278,144	3,064,742	185,431	689,608	5,467,589
1921	91,409	259,170	2,599,598	129,942	721,421	4,910,992
1922	89,157	292,343	2,138,715	71,868	727,681	4,463,172
1923	93,897	302,749	2,234,660	19,969	711,076	4,823,275
1924	96,952	297,790	1,843,106	10,066	733,835	4,849,307
1925	100,307	282,578	1,636,108	6,921	681,709	4,815,208
1926	104,194	294,916	1,679,407	5,453	651,477	4,885,266
1927	108,132	292,205	1,702,843	4,606	650,057	4,851,321
1928	111,061	298,438	1,626,433	4,029	650,212	4,796,626
1929	115,210	262,188	1,692,721	3,616	652,812	4,746,297
1930	117,436	288,389	1,402,066	3,206	650,779	4,521,988
1931	117,393	299,427	1,708,429	2,929	648,363	4,821,933
1932	113,619	289,076	2,780,229	2,746	700,894	5,695,171
1933	112,532	268,809	3,060,793	125,845	919,614	5,720,764
1934	119,142	279,608	3,068,404	141,645	901,872	5,373,470
1935	125,125	285,417	3,222,913	81,470	704,263	5,567,093
1936	134,691	278,190	4,002,216	51,954	366,105	6,241,200
1937	144,107	281,459	4,168,780	37,616	268,862	6,447,056
1938	145,625	262,155	4,114,338	30,118	217,441	6,460,891
1939	154,869	265,962	4,483,552	25,593	186,480	7,046,743
1940	168,977	247,887	5,163,284	22,373	165,155	7,847,501
1941	193,963	299,415	6,684,209	20,268	150,460	9,612,432

Index Numbers of Wholesale Commodity Prices—United States—Foreign Countries 1840–1920 [a]

Year	Index No.	Year	Index No.	Year	Index No.
1840	116.8	1867	172.2	1894	102.1
1841	115.8	1868	160.5	1895	94.6
1842	107.8	1869	153.5	1896	80.1
1843	101.5	1870	142.3	1897	84.1
1844	101.9	1871	136.0	1898	92.3
1845	102.8	1872	138.8	1899	93.4
1846	106.4	1873	137.5	1900	99.4
1847	106.5	1874	133.0	1901	101.7
1848	101.4	1875	127.6	1902	116.3
1849	98.7	1876	118.2	1903	107.5
1850	102.3	1877	110.9	1904	108.7
1851	105.9	1878	101.3	1905	110.7
1852	102.7	1879	96.6	1906	114.4
1853	109.1	1880	106.9	1907	117.9
1854	112.9	1881	105.7	1908	125.8
1855	113.1	1882	108.5	1909	133.9
1856	113.2	1883	106.0	1910	137.2
1857	112.5	1884	99.4	1911	131.1
1858	101.8	1885	93.0	1912	143.3
1859	100.2	1886	91.9	1913	140.8
1860	100	1887	92.6	1914	146.1
1861	100.6	1888	94.2	1915	148.1
1862	117.8	1889	94.2	1916	175.7
1863	148.6	1890	109.3	1917	261.8
1864	190.5	1891	119.5	1918	287.1
1865	216.8	1892	108.6	1919	295.6
1866	191.0	1893	116.1	1920	282.8

[a] "Index Numbers of Wholesale Commodity Prices," compiled by the *Annalist* and published in *Index Numbers of Wholesale Prices in the United States and Foreign Countries,* by W. C. Mitchell, U.S. Bureau of Labor Statistics, Bulletin No. 284, October, 1921, pp. 158–161.

Figures from 1840 to 1889 were computed on the assumption that the base was the year 1860; figures from 1890 to 1920 were computed on the assumption that the base was the average for the years 1890–1899.

Bibliography

GOVERNMENT PUBLICATIONS

The publications in this list are published by the Government Printing Office, Washington, D.C., unless otherwise indicated.

Miscellaneous

U.S. Commerce Department. Bureau of Foreign and Domestic Commerce. Monthly Summary of Foreign Commerce of the United States, 1914–1940.

U.S. Congress. American State Papers . . . selected and edited under the authority of Congress. Finance Vols. I–IV. Washington, D.C., Gales and Seaton, 1832–1861.

—— Annals of Congress; Debates and Proceedings in the Congress of the United States 1st to 18th Congress, First Session; March 3, 1789–May 27, 1824. Washington, Gales and Seaton, 1834–1856. 42 vols.

—— Register of Debates in Congress . . . 18th Congress, Second Session to 25th Congress, First Session. Washington, Gales and Seaton, 1825–1837. 14 vols.

—— Congressional Globe . . . 23d Congress to the 42d Congress. December 12, 1833–March 3, 1873. Washington, Globe Office, 1834–1873. 46 vols.

—— Congressional Record . . . 43d Congress, March 4, 1873–date.

—— House. Committee on Appropriations. Treasury Department Appropriation Bill for 1939. Hearings before the Subcommittee. 75th Congress, 3d Session, 1938.

—— Committee on Banking and Currency. Changes in Banking and Currency System of the United States; Report to Accompany H.R. 7837, 1913. House Report 69, 63d Congress, 1st Session.

—— Committee on Coinage, Weights and Measures. Extension of Stabilization Fund and Powers, etc. Act of July 6, 1939, Hearing, 76th Congress, 1st Session on H.R. 3325. February 28–March 23, 1939.

—— Senate. Committee on Banking and Currency. Banking Act of 1935. Hearings before Subcommittee, 74th Congress, 1st Session on S. 1715 and H.R. 7617 . . . April 19–June 3, 1935.

—— Committee on Banking and Currency. Devaluation of Dollar and Stabilization Fund. Act of July 6, 1939. Hearings, 76th Congress, 1st Session, March 2, to May 18, 1939.

—— Committee on Banking and Currency. Gold Reserve Act of 1934. Hearings, 73d Congress, 2d Session on S. 2366 . . . January 19–23, 1934.

U.S. Congress. Committee on Foreign Relations. Commercial Relations with China, Report to Accompany Senate Resolution 442. Senate Report 1716, 71st Congress, 3d Session.

U.S. Federal Deposit Insurance Corporation. Annual Report. 1934–date.

U.S. Federal Reserve Board. Annual Report. 1914–1935.

U.S. Board of Governors of the Federal Reserve System. Annual Report. 1936–date.

—— Federal Reserve Bulletin. 1914–date.

—— The Federal Reserve System; Its Purposes and Functions. 1939.

—— Digest of Rulings, 1914–October 1, 1937. 1938.

—— Circulars and press releases. 1934–date.

U.S. President. Executive Orders and Proclamations of the President.

—— Messages, press releases and speeches of the President.

U.S. Reconstruction Finance Corporation. Quarterly Report. February 2, 1932–1940.

U.S. Treasury Department. Annual Reports of the Secretary on the State of the Finances. 1790–1941.

The title varies as follows: Report on the Finances, Report on the State of the Finances, Report of the Secretary on the Finances, Report of the Secretary on the State of the Finances; the word "Annual" appears in the title for the first time in 1870.

The footnotes refer to the following publications: Reports of the Secretary, 1790–1848, 7 volumes. Washington, D.C. Blair and Rives, 1837–1849; Report of the Secretary, 1849–1869; and Annual Report of the Secretary, 1870–date.

—— Bulletin. 1939–1941.

—— Bureau of the Mint. Annual Report of the Director of the Mint. 1874–date.

—— Comptroller of the Currency. Annual Report. 1863–1941.

—— Circulars and press releases.

—— Daily Statement of the United States Treasury. 1895–1941.

—— Information respecting United States Bonds, Paper Currency and Coin, Production of Precious Metals . . . Rev. July 1, 1915.

—— Response of the Secretary of the Treasury to Senate Resolution Number 33 . . . Calling for Certain Information in Regard to Treasury Operations, 1908. Senate Document 208, 60th Congress, 1st Session.

—— Transactions with Certain National Banks; Letter from the Secretary of the Treasury . . . 1900. House Document 264, 56th Congress, 1st Session.

U.S. War Finance Corporation. Annual Report. 1918–1929.

Laws, Statutes, etc.

PUBLIC BILLS AND RESOLUTIONS INTRODUCED IN CONGRESS

House Bill 1597; 73d Congress, 2d Session

House Bill 7581; 73d Congress, 2d Session

House Resolution 72; 72d Congress, 1st Session

House Resolution 247; 72d Congress, 1st Session
House Resolution 113; 75th Congress, 1st Session
House Resolution 262; 76th Congress, 1st Session
Senate Bill 3867; 76th Congress, 3d Session
Senate Resolution 442; 71st Congress, 3d Session
Senate Resolution 800; 76th Congress, 1st Session
Senate Resolution 785; 76th Congress, 3d Session

LAWS OF THE UNITED STATES RELATING TO MONEY,
BANKING AND CURRENCY FROM 1789 TO DATE

Laws	*Source*
Act of September 2, 1789	1 Statutes at Large 65
Act of August 12, 1790	1 Statutes at Large 186
Act of February 25, 1791	1 Statutes at Large 191
Act of April 2, 1792	1 Statutes at Large 246
Act of March 3, 1795	1 Statutes at Large 433
Act of June 30, 1812	2 Statutes at Large 766
Act of February 25, 1813	2 Statutes at Large 801
Act of March 4, 1814	3 Statutes at Large 100
Act of December 26, 1814	3 Statutes at Large 161
Act of February 24, 1815	3 Statutes at Large 213
Act of April 10, 1816	3 Statutes at Large 266
Act of March 3, 1817	3 Statutes at Large 379
Act of June 28, 1834	4 Statutes at Large 699
Act of June 23, 1836	5 Statutes at Large 52
Act of June 18, 1837	5 Statutes at Large 136
Act of October 12, 1837	5 Statutes at Large 201
Act of May 21, 1838	5 Statutes at Large 310
Act of March 2, 1839	5 Statutes at Large 323
Act of March 31, 1840	5 Statutes at Large 370
Act of July 4, 1840	5 Statutes at Large 385
Act of February 15, 1841	5 Statutes at Large 411
Act of August 13, 1841	5 Statutes at Large 439
Act of January 31, 1842	5 Statutes at Large 469
Act of August 31, 1842	5 Statutes at Large 581
Act of July 22, 1846	9 Statutes at Large 39
Act of August 6, 1846	9 Statutes at Large 59
Act of January 28, 1847	9 Statutes at Large 118
Act of March 3, 1849	9 Statutes at Large 369
Act of December 23, 1857	11 Statutes at Large 257
Act of June 14, 1858	11 Statutes at Large 365
Act of June 22, 1860	12 Statutes at Large 79
Act of March 2, 1861	12 Statutes at Large 178
Act of July 17, 1861	12 Statutes at Large 259

Laws	*Source*
Act of February 25, 1862	12 Statutes at Large 345
Act of July 11, 1862	12 Statutes at Large 532
Act of March 3, 1863	12 Statutes at Large 719
Act of June 3, 1864	13 Statutes at Large 99
Act of June 3, 1864	13 Statutes at Large 108
Act of June 3, 1864	13 Statutes at Large 113
Act of June 3, 1864	13 Statutes at Large 116
Act of April 12, 1866	14 Statutes at Large 31
Act of July 14, 1870	16 Statutes at Large 274
Act of February 12, 1873	17 Statutes at Large 424
Act of June 20, 1874	18 Statutes at Large 123
Act of January 14, 1875	18 Statutes at Large 296
Act of February 28, 1878	20 Statutes at Large 25
Act of May 31, 1878	20 Statutes at Large 87
Act of March 3, 1881	21 Statutes at Large 457
Act of July 12, 1882	22 Statutes at Large 162
Act of March 3, 1887	24 Statutes at Large 559
Act of July 14, 1890	26 Statutes at Large 289
Act of October 1, 1890	26 Statutes at Large 567
Act of November 1, 1893	28 Statutes at Large 4
Act of July 24, 1897	30 Statutes at Large 151
Act of June 13, 1898	30 Statutes at Large 466
Act of June 27, 1898	30 Statutes at Large 481
Act of March 14, 1900	31 Statutes at Large 45
Act of March 14, 1900	31 Statutes at Large 46
Act of March 14, 1900	31 Statutes at Large 47
Act of June 28, 1902	32 Statutes at Large 481
Act of March 4, 1907	34 Statutes at Large 1289
Act of March 4, 1907	34 Statutes at Large 1290
Act of May 30, 1908	35 Statutes at Large 546
Act of August 5, 1909	36 Statutes at Large 11
Act of February 10, 1910	36 Statutes at Large 192
Act of March 2, 1911	36 Statutes at Large 965
Act of August 22, 1911	37 Statutes at Large 30
Act of December 23, 1913	38 Statutes at Large 265
Act of August 4, 1914	38 Statutes at Large 682
Act of September 7, 1916	39 Statutes at Large 752
Act of March 3, 1917	39 Statutes at Large 1000
Act of April 24, 1917	40 Statutes at Large 35
Act of June 15, 1917	40 Statutes at Large 217
Act of June 21, 1917	40 Statutes at Large 232
Act of September 24, 1917	40 Statutes at Large 288
Act of October 6, 1917	40 Statutes at Large 411
Act of April 4, 1918	40 Statutes at Large 502

Laws	Source
Act of April 5, 1918	40 Statutes at Large 506
Act of April 23, 1918	40 Statutes at Large 535
Act of July 9, 1918	40 Statutes at Large 844
Act of September 24, 1918	40 Statutes at Large 965
Act of February 24, 1919	40 Statutes at Large 1057
Act of March 3, 1919	40 Statutes at Large 1309
Act of December 24, 1919	41 Statutes at Large 370
Act of May 29, 1920	41 Statutes at Large 654
Act of January 4, 1921	41 Statutes at Large 1084
Act of November 23, 1921	42 Statutes at Large 227
Act of March 2, 1923	42 Statutes at Large 1427
Act of May 29, 1928	45 Statutes at Large 987
Act of June 17, 1929	46 Statutes at Large 19
Act of December 16, 1929	46 Statutes at Large 47
Act of July 17, 1930	46 Statutes at Large 590
Act of February 27, 1932	47 Statutes at Large 56
Act of July 21, 1932	47 Statutes at Large 716
Act of February 3, 1933	47 Statutes at Large 795
Act of March 7, 1933	47 Statutes at Large 1492
Act of March 9, 1933	48 Statutes at Large 1
Act of May 12, 1933	48 Statutes at Large 31
Act of June 16, 1933	48 Statutes at Large 163
Act of January 30, 1934	48 Statutes at Large 337
Act of January 30, 1934	48 Statutes at Large 344
Act of March 6, 1934	48 Statutes at Large 398
Act of March 15, 1934	48 Statutes at Large 428
Act of June 19, 1934	48 Statutes at Large 1178
Act of August 23, 1935	49 Statutes at Large 703
Act of January 23, 1937	50 Statutes at Large 4
Act of March 1, 1937	50 Statutes at Large 23
Act of June 30, 1939	53 Statutes at Large 991
Act of July 6, 1939	53 Statutes at Large 998
Act of June 25, 1940	54 Statutes at Large 516
Act of June 30, 1941	55 Statutes at Large 395

BOOKS AND ARTICLES

Andrew, Abram Piatt, "Partial Responsibility of Secretaries Gage and Shaw for the Crisis of 1907," *Bankers Magazine,* Vol. LXXVI (April, 1908), pp. 493–499.

—— "The Treasury and the Banks under Secretary Shaw," *Quarterly Journal of Economics,* Vol. XXI (August, 1907), pp. 519–568.

Beard, Charles, and Mary Beard, *The Rise of American Civilization.* 2 vols. New York, Macmillan, 1937.

Beckhart, B. H., Qualitative Credit Control. Chicago, 1936. Association of Reserve City Bankers, Bulletin 10.

—— Sterilization of Gold. New York, Chase National Bank, 1938. Monograph of the Department of Financial and Business Research.

Beckhart, Benjamin Haggott, ed., *The New York Money Market*. 4 vols. New York, Columbia University Press, 1931–1932.

Beckhart, Benjamin Haggott, and E. M. Hyslop, the Gold Problem. New York, Chase National Bank, 1940. Monograph of the Department of Financial and Business Research.

Bratter, Herbert M., "The Silver Episode," *Journal of Political Economy*, Vol. XLVI (October–December, 1938), pp. 609–652, 802–837.

—— The Silver Market. Washington, D.C., Government Printing Office, 1932. U.S. Bureau of Foreign and Domestic Commerce, Trade Promotion Series, No. 139.

Brown, William Adams, Jr., "The Government and the Money Market," in B. H. Beckhart, ed., *The New York Money Market*, New York, Columbia University Press, 1932. Vol. IV, pp. 183–414.

Cadman, Paul F., "Prospecting for a Gold Solution," *Banking*, Vol. XXXIII (July, 1940), pp. 27–28.

Carey, Henry C., Financial Crises: Their Causes and Effects. Philadelphia, Baird, 1864.

Cassell, Gustav, The Theory of Social Economy; translated by Joseph McCabe. New York, Harcourt Brace, 1924; London, Unwin, 1923.

Catterall, Ralph C. H., The Second Bank of the United States. Chicago, The University of Chicago Press, 1903.

Chapman, John Martin, Fiscal Functions of the Federal Reserve Banks. New York, Ronald Press, 1923.

Clay, Henry, Life and Speeches; compiled and edited by Daniel Mallory. 2 vols. New York, Van Amringe and Bixby, 1844.

Commercial and Financial Chronicle, Vols. XLV–CXL.

Conant, C. A., History of Modern Banks of Issue. New York, Putnam's, 1927.

Crawford, Arthur Whipple, Monetary Management under the New Deal. Washington, D.C., American Council on Public Affairs, 1940.

Crawford, William, "Report on Currency," February 24, 1820, in U.S., Treasury Dept., *Reports of the Secretary*, Vol. II, pp. 481–525.

—— "Report on Loans from the Treasury to Individuals or Banking Institutions since March 3, 1789," (Feb. 28, 1823) in U.S., Congress, *American State Papers, Finance*, IV, 265–267. Also published as Senate Paper 40, 17th Congress, 2d Session, Washington, Gales and Seaton, 1823.

Crump, Norman, "Development of Exchange Funds," *Lloyds Bank, Ltd., Monthly Review*, Vol. VIII (January, 1937), pp. 3–13.

Dewey, Davis R., Financial History of the United States. 7th ed. New York, Longmans, 1920.

Dewey, Davis R., The Second Bank of the United States, Washington, Government Printing Office, 1910. U.S. Monetary Commission Publications, Vol. IV, Senate Document 571, 61st Congress, 2d Session.

Dunbar, Charles F., comp., Laws of the United States Relating to Currency, Finance and Banking. Boston, Ginn, 1897.

Dutton, George, The Present Crisis or the Currency; by "Bank Crash," Esq. Rochester, 1857.

Economist, The, London, August 16, 1941. Vol. CXLI.

Everett, Edward, Mount Vernon Papers. New York, Appleton, 1860.

Fisher, Irving, Stable Money. New York, Adelphi, 1934.

Gallatin, Albert, Consideration of the Currency and Banking System. Philadelphia, Casey and Lea, 1831.

—— "Report on Bank of the United States," January 23, 1811, in U.S., Congress, American State Papers, Finance, Vol. II, pp. 469–470.

—— Suggestions on the Banks and Currency of the Several United States. New York, Wiley and Putnam, 1841.

—— Writings. Vol. I, edited by Henry Adams. Philadelphia, Lippincott, 1879.

Gayer, Arthur D., Monetary Policy and Economic Stabilization. New York, Macmillan, 1937.

Gouge, William M., The Curse of Paper Money and Banking; a Short History of Paper Money and Banking in the United States. Philadelphia, Usteck, 1833.

Grosvenor, William Mason, American Securities. New York, Daily Commercial Bulletin, 1885.

Hamilton, Alexander, "Report on a National Bank," December 13, 1790, in U.S., Treasury Department, Reports of the Secretary of the Treasury, 1790, Vol. I, pp. 54–77; "Report on Public Credit," January 9, 1790, in U.S., Treasury Department, Reports of the Secretary of the Treasury, 1790, Vol. I, pp. 3–52; "Report on Public Credit," January 19, 1795, in U.S., Treasury Department, Reports of the Secretary of the Treasury, 1795, Vol. I, pp. 157–215.

Hamilton, Alexander, Work; edited by John C. Hamilton. 7 vols. New York, 1850–1851.

Harding, William Proctor Gould, Formative Period of the Federal Reserve System. New York, Houghton Mifflin, 1925.

Hardy, C. O., Control of Prices and Business by the Federal Reserve System. Chicago, Association of Reserve City Bankers, Commission on Banking Law and Practice, 1936. Bulletin 8.

Hepburn, A. Barton, History of Coinage and Currency in the United States and the Perennial Contest for Sound Money. New York, Macmillan, 1903.

Hoggson, Noble Foster, Epochs in American Banking. New York, John Day, 1929.

Holdsworth, J. T., First Bank of the United States. Washington, Government Printing Office, 1910. U.S. Monetary Commission Publications, Vol. IV; Senate Doc. 571, 61st Congress, 2d Session.

Hollander, Jacob Harry, War Borrowing. New York, Macmillan, 1919.

International Conciliation, Number 282, September, 1932.

Jack, L. B., "The Gold Problem," *The Canadian Banker*, Vol. XLVII (April, 1940), pp. 280–287.

Jaeger, Ruth M., Stabilization of the Foreign Exchange. New York, 1922. Columbia University PhD dissertation.

Johnson, Gove Griffith, Jr., The Treasury and Monetary Policy, 1933–1938. Cambridge, Harvard University Press, 1939.

Kemmerer, Edwin Walter, Kemmerer on Money. Philadelphia, Winston, 1934.

Keynes, J. M., Essays in Persuasion. New York, Harcourt Brace, 1932.

Kilborne, R. D., "The War Finance Corporation," *American Economic Review*, XV (December, 1925), 810–820.

Kinley, David, Independent Treasury of the United States. Washington Government Printing Office, 1910. U.S. National Monetary Commission Publications, Vol. VII; Senate Document 587, 61st Congress, 2d Session.

Kirkland, Edward C., A History of American Economic Life. New York, 1939.

Kisch, C. H., and W. A. Elkin, Central Banks. New York, Macmillan, 1928.

Leavens, Dickson H., Silver Money. Bloomington, Principia Press, Inc., 1939.

Lewis, Lawrence A., Bank of North America. Philadelphia, Lippincott, 1882.

Lippmann, Walter, article in New York *Herald Tribune*, (April 18, 1933), p. 15, col. 1.

Love, Robert Alonzo, Federal Financing. New York, Columbia University Press, 1937.

Miller, Harry E., Banking Theories in the United States before 1860. Cambridge, Harvard University Press, 1927.

Mitchell, Wesley Clair, Index Numbers of Wholesale Prices in the United States and Foreign Countries, Washington, Government Printing Office, 1921. U.S., Bureau of Labor Statistics, Bulletin No. 284, October, 1921.

Myers, Margaret G., The New York Money Market, in Beckhart, ed., *The New York Money Market*, Vol. I.

New York *Times*. July 4, 1933, p. 1, col. 8; March 17, 1933, p. 11, col. 4; August 25, 1937, p. 19, col. 8; September 12, 1937, p. 39, col. 8; October 31, 1937, p. 32, col. 1; December 22, 1936, p. 1, col. 6.

Pasvolsky, Leo, Current Monetary Issues. Washington, Brookings Institution, Washington.

Patton, Eugene G., "Secretary Shaw and Precedents as to Treasury Control over the Money Market," *Journal of Political Economy* (February, 1907), Vol. XV, pp. 65–87.

Phillips, John B., Methods of Keeping the Public Money of the United States. Ann Arbor, Inland Press, 1900.

Roosevelt, Franklin D., On Our Way. New York, Day, 1934.
—— Public Papers and Addresses. Vol. II. New York, Random House, 1938.
Schurz, Carl, Henry Clay. 2 vols. Boston, Houghton Mifflin, 1899. "American Statesmen Series," Vol. XX.
Shannon, Frederick A., America's Economic Growth. New York, Macmillan, 1940.
Sprague, O. M. W., "The Crisis of 1914 in the United States," American Economic Review, Vol. V (September, 1915), pp. 499–533.
—— History of Crises under the National Banking System. Washington, D.C., Government Printing Office, 1910. U.S. National Monetary Commission, Publications, Vol. V; Senate Document 538, 61st Congress, 2d Session.
Statist, The, London, Vol. CXXXV (February 23, 1940), No. 3235.
Sumner, W. C., History of American Currency; with Chapters on the English Bank Restriction and American Paper Money. New York, Holt, 1878.
Taney, R. B., "Removal of Public Deposits," December, 1833, in U.S., Treasury Department, Reports of the Secretary of the Treasury, Vol. III, pp. 337–376.
Turner, Robert C., Member Bank Borrowing, Columbus, Ohio, Ohio State University Press, 1939.
Vanderlip, F. A., "Lessons of Our War Loan," The Forum, Vol. XXVI (September, 1898), pp. 27–36.
Waight, Leonard, The History and Mechanism of the Exchange Equilization Account. Cambridge, England, Cambridge University Press, 1939.
Walley, Samuel H., The Financial Revulsion of 1857; an Address before the American Statistical Association on February 10, 1857, Boston, 1857.
Warren, George F., and Frank A. Pearson, Prices. New York, Wiley, 1933.
Webster, Daniel, Writings and Speeches. National edition. 18 vols. New York, Taylor, 1903. Vol. VIII.
Willis, Henry Parker, The Federal Reserve System. New York, Ronald Press, 1923.
—— The Theory and Practice of Central Banking. New York, Harper, 1936.
Willis, Henry Parker, and W. H. Steiner, Federal Reserve Banking Practice. New York, Appleton, 1926.
Woodbury, Levi, "On the Public Money," December 12, 1834, in U.S., Treasury Department, Reports of the Secretary of the Treasury, Vol. III, pp. 557–625.

Index